Nicolas Sendrier (Ed.)

Post-Quantum Cryptography

Third International Workshop, PQCrypto 2010
Darmstadt, Germany, May 25-28, 2010
Proceedings

Springer

Volume Editor

Nicolas Sendrier
Centre de Recherche INRIA Paris-Rocquencourt
Projet-team SECRET
B.P. 105, 78153 Le Chesnay Cedex, France
E-mail: Nicolas.Sendrier@inria.fr

Library of Congress Control Number: 2010926250

CR Subject Classification (1998): E.3, K.6.5, D.4.6, C.2, J.1, G.2.1

LNCS Sublibrary: SL 4 – Security and Cryptology

ISSN 0302-9743
ISBN-10 3-642-12928-5 Springer Berlin Heidelberg New York
ISBN-13 978-3-642-12928-5 Springer Berlin Heidelberg New York

springer.com

Printed in Germany

Typesetting: Camera-ready by author, data conversion by Scientific Publishing Services, Chennai, India
Printed on acid-free paper 06/3180

Lecture Notes in Computer Science 6061

Foreword

The recent development of quantum computing and quantum algorithmics has raised important questions in cryptography. With Shor's algorithm (Peter W. Shor, "Polynomial-Time Algorithms for Prime Factorization and Discrete Logarithms on a Quantum Computer", *SIAM J. Sci. Statist. Comput.* 41 (2): 303-332, 1999) the collapse of some of the most widely used techniques for securing digital communications has become a possibility. In consequence, the everlasting duty of the cryptographic research community to keep an eye on alternative techniques has become an urgent necessity. Post-quantum cryptography was born. Its primary concern is the study of public-key cryptosystems that remain secure in a world with quantum computers. Currently, four families of public-key cryptosystems seem to have this potential: code-based, hash-based, lattice-based and multivariate public-key cryptosystems. Other techniques may certainly join this rapidly growing research area. With the PQCrypto conference series, this emerging community has created a place to disseminate results, exchange new ideas and define the state of the art. In May of 2006, the First International Workshop on Post-Quantum Cryptography was held at the Katholieke Universiteit Leuven in Belgium with support from the European Network of Excellence ECRYPT. The Second International Workshop on Post-Quantum Cryptography, PQCrypto 2008, was held at the University of Cincinnati, USA, in October 2008.

The third event of this series, PQCrypto 2010, was organized in Darmstadt by the Center for Advanced Security Research Darmstadt (CASED) at the Technische Universität Darmstadt during May 25-28, 2010. The Program Committee received 32 proposals of contributed talks from which 16 were selected. Each paper was thoroughly examined by several independent experts from the Program Committee and additional external reviewers. The papers along with the reviews were then scrutinized by the Program Committee members during a discussion phase after which recommendations were given to all authors. Revised versions of the accepted contributions are published in these proceedings. We would like to thank the authors of all the papers for submitting their quality research work to the conference. Special thanks go to the Program Committee members and to the external reviewers for the time and energy they spent throughout the selection process to offer a conference and a volume of high scientific quality.

In addition to the contributed talks, we were fortunate to have three outstanding keynote lectures given by Oded Regev (Tel Aviv University, Israel), Renato Renner (ETHZ, Switzerland) and Gregory Neven (IBM Research Zurich, Switzerland).

Finally, a special thank goes to Matthieu Finiasz and Markus Rückert for organizing the very lively "recent result session," and, on behalf of the community, let me say that we are all indebted to Johannes Buchmann, Markus Rückert and CASED for organizing this meeting.

May 2010 Nicolas Sendrier

Organization

PQCrypto 2010 was organized by the Center for Advanced Security Research Darmstadt (CASED)

General Chairs

Johannes Buchmann	Technische Universität Darmstadt, Germany
Markus Rückert	Technische Universität Darmstadt, Germany

Program Chair

Nicolas Sendrier	INRIA, France

Program Committee

Daniel Augot	INRIA, France
Paulo Barreto	Universidade de São Paulo, Brazil
Dan Bernstein	University of Illinois at Chicago, USA
Gilles Brassard	Université de Montréal, Canada
Claude Crépeau	McGill University, Canada
Erik Dahmen	Technische Universität Darmstadt, Germany
Jintai Ding	University of Cincinnati, USA
Matthieu Finiasz	ENSTA, France
Philippe Gaborit	Université de Limoges, France
Gert-Martin Greuel	Universität Kaiserslautern, Germany
Tanja Lange	Technische Universiteit Eindhoven, The Netherlands
Pierre Loidreau	CELAR, France
Vadim Lyubashevsky	Tel Aviv University, Israel
Christof Paar	Ruhr-Universität Bochum, Germany
Chris Peikert	Georgia Tech, USA
Gerhard Schabhüser	BSI, Germany
Nicolas Sendrier	INRIA, France
Graeme Smith	IBM T.J. Watson Research Center, USA
Damien Stehlé	CNRS, France and University of Sydney/Macquarie University, Australia
Michael Szydlo	Akamai, USA
Shigeo Tsujii	Chuo University, Japan
Ralf-Philipp Weinmann	Université du Luxembourg, Luxembourg
Bo-Yin Yang	Academia Sinica, Taiwan

Additional Reviewers

John Baena
Stanislav Bulygin
Chen-Mou Cheng
Crystal Clough
Ryo Fujita
Tim Güneysu
Stefan Heyse
Cédric Lauradoux
Markus Rückert
Kohtaro Tadaki
Hamid Usef
Christopher Wolf
Chaoping Xing

PQCrypto Steering Committee

Dan Bernstein	University of Illinois at Chicago, USA
Johannes Buchmann	Technische Universität Darmstadt, Germany
Claude Crépeau	McGill University, Canada
Jintai Ding	University of Cincinnati, USA
Philippe Gaborit	Université de Limoges, France
Tanja Lange	Technische Universiteit Eindhoven, The Netherlands
Daniele Micciancio	University of California at San Diego, USA
Werner Schindler	BSI, Germany
Nicolas Sendrier	INRIA, France
Shigeo Tsujii	Chuo University, Japan
Bo-Yin Yang	Academia Sinica, Taiwan

Sponsors

The organizers thank the following companies and institutions for their generous financial support.

CASED, Darmstadt, Germany
CAST e.V., Darmstadt, Germany
cv cryptovision GmbH, Gelsenkirchen, Germany
Deutsche Bank AG, Frankfurt, Germany
Horst-Görtz-Stiftung, Neu-Anspach, Germany
IBM Deutschland GmbH, Ehningen, Germany
KOBIL Systems GmbH, Worms, Germany
Siemens AG, München, Germany
Software AG, Darmstadt, Germany

Table of Contents

Cryptanalysis of Multivariate Systems

Properties of the Discrete Differential with Cryptographic Applications 1
Daniel Smith-Tone

Growth of the Ideal Generated by a Quadratic Boolean Function 13
Jintai Ding, Timothy J. Hodges, and Victoria Kruglov

Mutant Zhuang-Zi Algorithm 28
Jintai Ding and Dieter S. Schmidt

Cryptanalysis of Two Quartic Encryption Schemes and One Improved MFE Scheme 41
Weiwei Cao, Xiuyun Nie, Lei Hu, Xiling Tang, and Jintai Ding

Cryptanalysis of Code-Based Systems

Cryptanalysis of the Niederreiter Public Key Scheme Based on GRS Subcodes 61
Christian Wieschebrink

Grover vs. McEliece 73
Daniel J. Bernstein

Information-Set Decoding for Linear Codes over $\mathbf{F}_q$ 81
Christiane Peters

A Timing Attack against the Secret Permutation in the McEliece PKC 95
Falko Strenzke

Practical Power Analysis Attacks on Software Implementations of McEliece 108
Stefan Heyse, Amir Moradi, and Christof Paar

Design of Encryption Schemes

Key Exchange and Encryption Schemes Based on Non-commutative Skew Polynomials 126
Delphine Boucher, Philippe Gaborit, Willi Geiselmann, Olivier Ruatta, and Felix Ulmer

Designing a Rank Metric Based McEliece Cryptosystem 142
Pierre Loidreau

Secure Variants of the Square Encryption Scheme 153
Crystal Lee Clough and Jintai Ding

Low-Reiter: Niederreiter Encryption Scheme for Embedded Microcontrollers 165
Stefan Heyse

Design of Signature Schemes

Strongly Unforgeable Signatures and Hierarchical Identity-Based Signatures from Lattices without Random Oracles 182
Markus Rückert

Proposal of a Signature Scheme Based on STS Trapdoor 201
Shigeo Tsujii, Masahito Gotaishi, Kohtaro Tadaki, and Ryo Fujita

Selecting Parameters for the Rainbow Signature Scheme 218
Albrecht Petzoldt, Stanislav Bulygin, and Johannes Buchmann

Author Index 241

Properties of the Discrete Differential with Cryptographic Applications

Daniel Smith-Tone

Department of Mathematics, Indiana University
smithdc@indiana.edu

Abstract. Recently, the C^{*-} signature scheme has been completely broken by Dubois et al. [1,2]. As a consequence, the security of SFLASH and other multivariate public key systems have been impaired. The attacks presented in [1,2] rely on a symmetry of the differential of the encryption mapping. In [3], Ding et al. experimentally justify the use projection as a method of avoiding the new attack, and some theoretical backing to this method is given in [4]. In this paper, we derive some properties of the discrete differential, extend the theoretical justification for the reparation in [3], and establish the exact context in which this attack is applicable.

Keywords: Matsumoto-Imai, multivariate public key cryptography, discrete, differential, SFLASH, symmetry, HFE.

1 Introduction

In recent years much focus in public key cryptography has shifted to multivariate systems. This change is due to several factors: the problem of solving a system of quadratic equations is hard; to date, no great reduction of the complexity of this problem has been found in the quantum model; there are very efficient implementations of multivariate systems; and finally, it is easy to parameterize many multivariate systems in such a way that vastly different schemes are derived with potentially vastly different resistances to specialized attacks.

One multivariate scheme which has recently been broken by Dubois et al. in [1,2] is the C^{*-} signature scheme. In particular, the attack breaks the SFLASH signature scheme and some variants of the scheme by using a special property of the differential of the encryption map to recover a full C^* public key, compatible with the C^{*-} public key, to which Patarin's attack in [5] may be applied.

More recently, Ding et al., see [3], have repaired the SFLASH scheme using projection, which also, ironically, has been called "fixing," see [6]. They were able to show strong experimental evidence that projection protects the scheme from the differential attack. In [4], Ding et al. present some theoretical evidence for this protection.

This paper is organized as follows. First, we review the C^*, HFE, C^{*-}, and SFLASH schemes. Next, we look at the new attack on C^{*-} of Dubois, et al. In the following section, we present some useful results on the differential of a field map and establish limits for the effectivity of the new attack in the more

N. Sendrier (Ed.): PQCrypto 2010, LNCS 6061, pp. 1–12, 2010.

general HFE setting. We then extend the theoretical analysis presented in [4] which suggests that projection avoids the new attack. Finally, we discuss the implications of these results.

2 C^*, HFE, and SFLASH

The SFLASH signature scheme can be considered a special case of the C^{*-} signature scheme which is derived from the Matsumoto-Imai cryptosystem, often called the C^* scheme, originally presented in [7]. Each of these schemes was designed to take advantage of the difficulty of solving a nonlinear system of equations over a finite field.

2.1 The C^* Scheme

The idea of the C^* scheme is to use affine maps to hide a "quadratic" monomial map. This can be accomplished by composing functions, each of which is easily invertible.

Choose a finite field $\mathbb{F}_q$ of even characteristic and a degree n extension k. The map $f : k \to k$ defined by $f(x) = x^{1+q^\theta}$ is a permutation polynomial for coprime values of n and θ. Choosing two $\mathbb{F}_q$-affine transformations, U and T, we can encrypt via the composition

$$P = T \circ f \circ U. \tag{1}$$

Note that the map $x \mapsto x^{q^\theta}$, a Frobenius map, is $\mathbb{F}_q$-linear since

$$(x+a)^{q^\theta} = (x+a)^{p^{k\theta}} = \sum_{i=0}^{p^{k\theta}} \binom{p^{k\theta}}{i} a^i x^{p^{k\theta}-i} = x^{q^\theta} + a^{q^\theta}, \tag{2}$$

where the last equality is due to the fact that $\binom{p^{k\theta}}{i} = 0$ for $0 < i < p^{k\theta}$ in a field of characteristic p, and the fact that $x \mapsto x^{q^\theta}$ is the identity map on $\mathbb{F}_q$. Therefore, we can represent f as $f(x) = x(L_\theta x)$, where $L_\theta x = x^{q^\theta}$ is the exponentiation expressed as an $\mathbb{F}_q$-linear transformation. For this reason we call f $\mathbb{F}_q$-quadratic or simply "quadratic." Encryption can thus be expressed as a system of n multivariate quadratic equations over $\mathbb{F}_q$. On the other hand, decryption is accomplished by inverting each of the above maps, circumventing the problem of solving a nonlinear system of equations:

$$P^{-1} = U^{-1} \circ f^{-1} \circ T^{-1}. \tag{3}$$

In [5], Patarin showed that C^* is insecure. His attack is based on a relation on the input and output of the monomial map. Given $v = f(u)$ we have the following:

$$v^{q^\theta} u = v u^{q^{2\theta}}. \tag{4}$$

By composing with the affine maps, T and U, we have $T^{-1}y = f(Ux)$ which we can express as the following bilinear relation on the plaintext, x, and ciphertext, y:

$$(T^{-1}y)^{q^\theta}(Ux) = (T^{-1}y)(Ux)^{q^\theta}. \tag{5}$$

Once such a bilinear relation between x and y is obtained by computing a large number of plaintext-ciphertext pairs, we have an efficient alternate means of decryption.

2.2 HFE

The HFE cryptosystem, introduced by Patarin [8] is a generalization of C^*. HFE still uses the setting of a finite field, $\mathbb{F}_q$, and an n-dimensional extension k over $\mathbb{F}_q$. There is one main difference. Specifically, the hidden mapping, f, is no longer necessarily a monomial; it can be a more general quadratic polynomial. While general HFE schemes have the desirable quality of being resistant to Patarin's attack on C^*, there are some problems as well.

It is difficult to find permutation polynomials which are not translations of monomial maps. Some conditions are known which guarantee that a polynomial is a permutation polynomial, such as those given in [9] and [10], but no criteria are known for the construction of general quadratic permutation polynomials. For this reason, the HFE scheme is implemented with an encryption map which is not, in general, bijective. This quality of the cryptosystem has the effect of making collisions possible and rendering decryption and signature generation much less efficient.

2.3 The C^{*-} Scheme

To prevent an attack exploiting the bilinear relation, (5), it was suggested in [11] to remove some of the coordinate equations. The resulting scheme, suitable for signatures, is commonly called the C^{*-} scheme.

Suppose we delete the last r equations in the public key of a C^* scheme. Let P_Π denote the projection of P onto the first $n-r$ coordinates. To sign, a user needs only compute a preimage of $y = P_\Pi(x)$ which is easily accomplished by padding y with r random coordinate values and using the decryption algorithm. Since $|\{x|P_\Pi(x) = y\}| = q^r$, it is apparent that allowing r to be too large renders the scheme inefficient in the sense that the size of the field must be quite large to maintain the improbability of collision detection. If r is too small, however, there are methods to reduce the C^{*-} scheme to a C^* scheme, as shown in [11].

The difficulty in removing r of the public equations lies in the fact that, although (4) is still valid, (5) can no longer be used. We don't know r of the coordinates of y, and therefore, we are missing terms in each equation we generate over $\mathbb{F}_q$. Alternatively, we may consider T to be an $r \times n$ matrix, since the new encryption mapping does not have access to r of the rows of T. As a consequence, it is impossible to deterministically compute coefficients involving T^{-1}.

2.4 SFLASH

SFLASH is a signature scheme based on the C^{*-} scheme. The choice of parameters which were considered secure by the New European Schemes for Signature, Integrity, and Encryption, NESSIE, consortium are $q = 2^7$, $[k : \mathbb{F}_q] = 37$, $\theta = 11$, and $r = 11$. This scheme was widely heralded for nearly ten years until more recently SFLASH and some possible variants were broken completely in [1,2].

3 The New Attacks on C^{*-} Schemes

Dubois et al. in [1] and [2] based the attacks on C^{*-} on a property of the bilinear differential, $Df(a, x) = f(a + x) - f(a) - f(x) + f(0)$, of the encryption map, f, which they called "multiplicative." The attacks utilize a linear symmetry of f which guarantees the existence of L and $\Lambda_{f,L}$, $\mathbb{F}_q$-linear maps, satisfying the following relation:

$$Df(La, x) + Df(a, Lx) = \Lambda_{f,L}Df(a, x). \tag{6}$$

In particular, the attacks focus on finding L which correspond to left multiplication by an element $\sigma \in k$. Therefore, we are interested in discovering properties of f guaranteeing the existence of the following *multiplicative symmetry* for all $\sigma \in k$:

$$Df(\sigma a, x) + Df(a, \sigma x) = p_f(\sigma)Df(a, x), \tag{7}$$

where $p_f : k \rightarrow k$ is a polynomial, which we call the *separation polynomial.*

Notice that if an $\mathbb{F}_q$-linear transformation is found which corresponds, when factored through the encryption, to a nontrivial multiplication, it is likely that new linearly independent relations on the output of the monomial function will be found. Specifically, we have the following:

$$DP_\Pi(N_\sigma a, x) + DP_\Pi(a, N_\sigma x) = \Pi \circ T \circ M_{p(\sigma)} \circ Df(Ua, Ux), \tag{8}$$

where $N_\sigma = U^{-1}M_\sigma U$ and M_τ is the matrix of multiplication by τ. In practice, equation (8) is used to find relations satisfied by these multiplication map conjugates. If enough new relations are derived in this manner to generate such a N_σ, it is likely that a new full rank C^* scheme may be constructed by gathering new linearly independent relations from the following mapping, where f specifically is multiplicative, as is the case for SFLASH,

$$\begin{aligned} P_\Pi \circ N_\sigma &= \Pi \circ T \circ f \circ U \circ N_\sigma \\ &= \Pi \circ T \circ f \circ M_\sigma \circ U \\ &= \Pi \circ T \circ M_{f(\sigma)} \circ f \circ U. \end{aligned} \tag{9}$$

At this point, Patarin's attack may be applied. If the system is not full rank, or close enough to full rank to apply another attack, the process of finding a nontrivial multiplication is repeated.

Dubois et al. use this method in [2] to break variants of SFLASH in which the θ parameter and the degree of the extension are not coprime. In [1] the same method is used to break SFLASH with the NESSIE parameters. Both of these attacks may be considered instances of the same attack since both use the multiplicative symmetry above. The only difference is that in the former the attack focuses specifically on finding multiplications by roots of the separation polynomial, whereas in the latter the focus is on finding multiplications by elements which are not roots of the separation polynomial.

The question was asked in [1] to what extent these methods involving the differential can be applied to the HFE^- scheme, i.e., to what extent can we use such a symmetry relation when the monomial function is replaced by a more general polynomial?

4 Multiplicative Symmetric Properties of the Differential

To answer the questions posed in [1], we form a classification of polynomial maps $f : k \to k$ having the multiplicative symmetry. We first need to establish some basic definitions and ground work. Here we establish the convention that, unless otherwise specified, the terms "linearity," "bilinearity," etc. refer to linearity over a base field.

Definition 1. *Given a field $\mathbb{F}$, a field extension k, and a multivariate function $f : k^m \to k$, the* discrete partial differential *of f with respect to x_i is the following function of $m+1$ variables:*

$$\begin{aligned} D_{x_i}f(x_1,\dots,x_{i-1},a,x_i,\dots,x_m) =& f(x_1,\dots,x_{i-1},a+x_i,x_{i+1},\dots,x_m) \\ &- f(x_1,\dots,x_{i-1},x_i,x_{i+1},\dots,x_m) \\ &- f(x_1,\dots,x_{i-1},a,x_{i+1},\dots,x_m) \\ &+ f(x_1,\dots,x_{i-1},0,x_{i+1},\dots,x_m). \end{aligned} \tag{10}$$

We should note that the discrete partial differential operator has the desired property of $\mathbb{F}$-linearity, i.e., $D_{x_i}(Mf + Ng) = MD_{x_i}f + ND_{x_i}g$ for $\mathbb{F}$-linear operators M and N. Using this property we are able to prove the following useful result about bilinear maps, the proof of which generalizes to the multilinear case.

Theorem 1. *Let k be an extension field of $\mathbb{F}$ and let $f = \sum_i g_i = \sum_i c_i x^{\alpha_i} y^{\beta_i}$ be a bivariate polynomial in its canonical representation. If f is k-bilinear, then then any monomial summand, g_i, of f is k-bilinear.*

Proof. Without loss of generality suppose by way of contradiction that g_0 is not bilinear; in particular, suppose that g_0 is not linear with respect to x. Since the discrete partial differential operator is $\mathbb{F}$-linear, we have the following identity:

$$D_x f = D_x \sum_i g_i = \sum_i D_x g_i. \tag{11}$$

Also, by the bilinearity of f, $D_x f = 0$. Therefore, applying the definition of D_x to the right side of (11), we have the following:

$$\begin{aligned} 0 = \sum_i D_x g_i &= \sum_i c_i y^{\beta_i} \left[(x+a)^{\alpha_i} - x^{\alpha_i} - a^{\alpha_i} \right] \\ &= \sum_i c_i y^{\beta_i} \sum_{j=1}^{\alpha_i - 1} \binom{\alpha_i}{j} a^j x^{\alpha_i - j}, \end{aligned} \tag{12}$$

for all $a, x, y \in k$, where, of course, the binomial coefficients are taken modulo the characteristic of k. Note that since the multidegree of each g_i is unique, the multidegree of each term in this expression is also unique. Let n be the maximum multidegree in this sum. The collection $\{a^r x^s y^t | r + s + t \leq n\}$, for nonnegative integral r, s, and t, is linearly independent in $k[a, x, y]$. This fact is easily verified: if

$$0 = \sum_{r+s+t \leq n} \lambda_{r,s,t} a^r x^s y^t \tag{13}$$

is in canonical form, the homomorphism evaluating a and x at 1 gives us,

$$0 = \sum_{r+s+t \leq n} \lambda_{r,s,t} y^t, \tag{14}$$

for all $y \in k$; hence, all $\lambda_{r,s,t} = 0$. Applying this linear independence to (12), we obtain:

$$0 = c_i \binom{\alpha_i}{j}, \tag{15}$$

for all i and all $0 < j < \alpha_i$. Since g_0 is not linear with respect to x, there is a j such that $\binom{\alpha_0}{j} \neq 0$. Consequently, by (15), $c_0 = 0$. This fact, however, implies that $g_0 = 0$, contradicting our assumption that g_0 is not bilinear. Thus every monomial summand, g_i, of f is bilinear.

The above result rigorously verifies the intuitional notion that there cannot be cancelation of nonlinear components of monomial functions via summation. Since we are interested in this property for the classification of polynomial functions based on attributes of the discrete differential, this theorem is useful for the following important corollary, which, again, is valid for arbitrary fields.

Corollary 1. *Let $f : k \to k$ be a polynomial, and let $g : k \to k$ be a monomial summand of f. If Df is bilinear, then Dg is bilinear.*

Proof. Given $f = \sum_i g_i$, by the linearity of the discrete differential operator, we have

$$Df = \sum_i Dg_i. \tag{16}$$

Note that, since each g_i has a unique degree, each term in the right side of (16) has a unique multidegree. Now by Theorem 1, since Df is bilinear, each monomial summand of Df is bilinear, and therefore, any sum of such summands is bilinear. Thus Dg_i is bilinear for all i.

Now we focus on the multiplicative symmetry and restrict to the finite field setting. Notice that the above corollary is as general as possible in this setting because finite fields have the distinguishing quality of being the only rings for which every function from the ring to itself is a polynomial. In the following results, k denotes a degree n extension of the finite field $\mathbb{F}_q$.

Lemma 1. *Let g be a monomial function with a nontrivial $\mathbb{F}_q$-bilinear differential. Then g has the multiplicative symmetry. Furthermore, two such monomial functions, g_1 and g_2, are quadratic, and share the same separation polynomial if and only if $g_1 = cg_2$ for some constant $c \in k$.*

Proof. Since g is a monomial function, $Dg(a,x) = c\sum_{i=1}^{k-1}\binom{k}{i}a^i x^{k-i}$. Dg is bilinear and thus, any monomial with nonzero coefficient in this sum must be linear in both a and x. Therefore $k = q^{\theta_1} + q^{\theta_2}$ for some $0 \leq \theta_1, \theta_2 \leq n$. Hence, $g(x) = cx^{q^{\theta_1}+q^{\theta_2}}$. As a consequence, we have $Dg(a,x) = ca^{q^{\theta_1}}x^{q^{\theta_2}} + ca^{q^{\theta_2}}x^{q^{\theta_1}}$. Letting $p(x) = x^{q^{\theta_1}} + x^{q^{\theta_2}}$, we obtain $Dg(\sigma a, x) + Dg(a, \sigma x) = p(\sigma)Dg(a,x)$. By the above construction of the separation polynomial, two quadratic monomial functions share the same separation polynomial if and only if they are constant multiples of each other.

The following theorem gives a classification of polynomial functions with the multiplicative symmetry.

Theorem 2. *A polynomial $f : k \to k$ with a bilinear differential has the multiplicative symmetry if and only if it has one quadratic monomial summand.*

Proof. ($\Leftarrow$) Suppose that f has exactly one quadratic monomial summand, g, and all other monomial summands are linear. Then $Df = Dg$. Thus f has the multiplicative symmetry with the same separation polynomial as that of g.

($\Rightarrow$) By Corollary 1, we know that all monomial summands of f have a bilinear differential. Suppose that f has r distinct quadratic monomial summands, g_m. We know $Df = \sum_{m=1}^{r} Dg_m$. Therefore,

$$Df(\sigma a, x) + Df(a, \sigma x) = p_f(\sigma)\sum_{m=1}^{r} Dg_m(a,x) \tag{17}$$

On the other hand,

$$\begin{aligned} Df(\sigma a, x) + Df(a, \sigma x) &= \sum_{m=1}^{r}(Dg_m(\sigma a, x) + Dg_m(a, \sigma x)) \\ &= \sum_{m=1}^{r} p_{g_m}(\sigma)Dg_m(a,x). \end{aligned} \tag{18}$$

Therefore, taking the difference of 17 and 18,

$$\sum_{m=1}^{r}(p_f - p_{g_m})(\sigma)Dg_m(a,x) = 0, \tag{19}$$

for all $\sigma, a, x \in k$. We know from Lemma 1 that $g_m(x) = c_m x^{q^{\theta_m}+q^{\tau_m}}$. We can, therefore, rewrite (19) as:

$$\sum_{m=1}^{r} c_m(p_f - p_{g_m})(\sigma)(a^{q^{\theta_m}} x^{q^{\tau_m}} + a^{q^{\tau_m}} x^{q^{\theta_m}}) = 0. \tag{20}$$

The collection $\{a^i x^j\}$ is linearly independent in $k[a, x]$, thus for any arbitrary fixed $\sigma \in k$, we obtain:

$$c_m(p_f - p_{g_m})(\sigma) = 0, \tag{21}$$

for all $1 \leq m \leq r$. Since $c_m \neq 0$ for each m, and σ is arbitrary, we have that $p_f = p_{g_m}$ for all m. Since the g_m are distinct, by Lemma 1, r is zero or one. Thus, f has at most one quadratic monomial summand.

Now we have an answer to the questions posed in [1]. Both of the attacks presented in [2,1] require the existence of a hidden field map with the multiplicative symmetry. In particular, the experiments in [1] suggest that for large field extensions the general linear and multiplicative symmetries of equations 6 and 7 are intertwined, i.e., f has a linear symmetry only if there is a nonsingular linear map, L, such that $f \circ L$ has the multiplicative symmetry. The above results show that the multiplicative symmetry is only present for field maps which differ from a C^* monomial by an affine map; thus, HFE is not, in general, susceptible to the multiplicative symmetry attack.

5 The Effect of Projection

In [3], Ding et al. proposed projection as a method of securing the C^{*-} scheme from the attack based on the multiplicative symmetry. Experimentally, it has been verified that the projection onto a codimension 1 or more affine space breaks the symmetry. In addition, Ding et al. in [4] prove that in the case of a codimension 1 projection, the multiplicative symmetry is destroyed. Some schemes, for example Square, see [12], can be considered to have an implicit projection onto a higher codimensional affine space. In light of the results of the previous section, we can give a more categorical explanation for the behavior of such systems under projection.

In the case of fixing m variables, projecting corresponds to the following mapping:

$$P(x) = T \circ f \circ M_{a_1,\ldots,a_m} \circ U, \tag{22}$$

where $M_{a_1,\ldots,a_m}$ is the linear transformation which acts as the identity on the first $n - m$ coordinates and replaces the last m coordinates with $a_i \cdot x$, where $a_i \in \mathbb{F}_q^n$ has last m coordinates zero.

Let us first consider the singularity of $M_{a_1,\ldots,a_m}$ to be subsumed by f. We prove that the composition of f with a general singular factor of $M_{a_1,\ldots,a_m}U$ cannot have the multiplicative symmetry over k.

Theorem 3. *Let M be an $\mathbb{F}_q$-affine transformation and let f be a C^* monomial map, $f(x) = x^{1+q^\theta}$. The composition $f \circ M$ has the multiplicative symmetry if and only if M is a translation of a linear monomial map, i.e. $Mx = cx^{q^i} + d$ for some $i < n$.*

Proof. If we write $Mx = \hat{M}x + d$, then $f(Mx) = ((\hat{M}x)^{q^\theta} + d^{q^\theta})(\hat{M}x + d)$. The quadratic part of this expression is independent of d, therefore it suffices to consider linear maps.

($\Leftarrow$) Suppose M is a linear monomial map, $Mx = c_M x^{q^i}$ for some $i < n$. Therefore, $f \circ M(x) = c_M^{q^\theta+1} x^{q^{\theta+i}+q^i}$, where, of course, the sum in the exponents of q is taken modulo n. As a consequence of Theorem 2, $f \circ M$ has the multiplicative symmetry.

($\Rightarrow$) Let $\hat{f} = f \circ M$. Since every $\mathbb{F}_q$-linear transformation, M, can be written $M = \sum_{i=0}^{n-1} c_i x^{q^i}$, we have the following:

$$\begin{aligned} \hat{f}(x) &= f \circ M(x) \\ &= f \circ \sum_{i=0}^{n-1} c_i x^{q^i} \\ &= (\sum_{i=0}^{n-1} c_i x^{q^i})^{1+q^\theta} \\ &= \sum_{i,j<n} c_i c_{j-\theta}^{q^\theta} x^{q^i+q^j} \\ &= \sum_{i=0}^{n-1} c_i c_{i-\theta}^{q^\theta} x^{2q^i} + \sum_{i<j<n} (c_i c_{j-\theta}^{q^\theta} + c_j c_{i-\theta}^{q^\theta}) x^{q^i+q^j}. \end{aligned} \tag{23}$$

Note that the right hand side expression is simplified because the equality $q^i + q^j = q^k + q^l$ implies either $(i, j) = (k, l)$ or $(i, j) = (l, k)$.

We have two distinct types of coefficients of $\hat{f}$. The first type, $c_i c_{i-\theta}^{q^\theta}$, corresponds to a product along a column in the following matrix, while the second type, $c_i c_{j-\theta}^{q^\theta} + c_j c_{i-\theta}^{q^\theta}$, which we will call minors for lack of a better term, corresponds to the sum of the products along the diagonals of the square submatrix formed from the ith and jth columns.

$$\begin{pmatrix} c_0 & c_1 & \cdots & c_{n-1} \\ c_{-\theta}^{q^\theta} & c_{1-\theta}^{q^\theta} & \cdots & c_{n-1-\theta}^{q^\theta} \end{pmatrix} \tag{24}$$

Suppose $\hat{f}$ has the multiplicative symmetry. By Theorem 2, the coefficient of at most one power of x in (23) is nonzero. Therefore, the coefficient matrix must have either one column with a nonzero product and no nonzero minors, no column with a nonzero product and exactly one nonzero minor, or no nonzero entries, in which case M is trivial.

In the first case, in which the one nonzero coefficient is of the form $c_i c_{i-\theta}^{q^\theta}$, suppose that M has another nonzero coefficient, c_j. Since there are no other columns with a nonzero product, the coefficient matrix must be of the form

$$\begin{pmatrix} \star \dots & c_i & \dots c_j \dots \star \\ \star \dots & c_{i-\theta}^{q^\theta} & \dots \ 0 \ \dots \star \end{pmatrix}. \tag{25}$$

This, however, results in a nonzero minor. Thus, $c_j = 0$ for all $j \neq i$, and $M = c_i x^{q^i}$ is a linear monomial map. Furthermore, since $c_{i-\theta} \neq 0$, $c_{i-\theta} = c_i$, and so $\theta = 0$. Thus, in this case, $f(x) = cx^2$. Clearly, this case is only nontrivial if q is odd.

In the other case, i.e., the one nonzero coefficient is of the form $c_i c_{j-\theta}^{q^\theta} + c_j c_{i-\theta}^{q^\theta}$, suppose that M has another nonzero coefficient, c_l, for $l \neq i, j$. Since there are no columns with a nonzero product, our coefficient matrix has one of the following forms:

$$\begin{pmatrix} \star \dots c_i \dots & 0 & \dots c_l \dots \star \\ \star \dots \ 0 \ \dots & c_{j-\theta}^{q^\theta} & \dots \ 0 \ \dots \star \end{pmatrix}, \tag{26}$$

or

$$\begin{pmatrix} \star \dots & 0 & \dots c_j \dots c_l \dots \star \\ \star \dots & c_{i-\theta}^{q^\theta} & \dots \ 0 \ \dots \ 0 \ \dots \star \end{pmatrix}. \tag{27}$$

Again, this results in an extra nonzero minor. Therefore, $c_l = 0$ for all $l \neq i, j$. Furthermore, only one of c_i and c_j is nonzero. This fact again implies that Mx is a nonzero linear monomial map. Thus the composition of a quadratic monomial and a nonzero $\mathbb{F}_q$-affine map, M, has the multiplicative symmetry if and only if M is a translation of a linear monomial map.

Therefore, projection indeed does break the symmetry over the large field. The only remaining possible application of the methods of Dubois et al. is if we consider the matrix $M_{a_1,\dots,a_m}$ to be absorbed by U, in which case we must accept that $S = M_{a_1,\dots,a_m}U$ is singular.

This case is fully investigated by Ding et al. in [4] under the same assumptions we make here; namely, we expect each general linear symmetry of the form (6) to be multiplicative, i.e., to be of the form (7). Ding et al. proved in [4] that this is the case when the kernel of the projection is one dimensional, but the general question is still open. While Ding et al. focus on determining when the hidden C^* monomial map maintains a linear symmetry restricted to a subspace of k, we approach the problem somewhat differently, attempting to extend the methods of the original attack by "inverting" the singular map, S.

It is conceivable that the original attack of Dubois et al. may be applied by using a pseudoinverse, S^+, instead of an inverse in the definition, $N_\sigma = S^+ M_\sigma S$. We can then rely on the multiplicative symmetry of the hidden C^* monomial map to continue the original attack. The only restriction is that we require $SS^+ M_\sigma S = M_\sigma S$, which occurs only when the image of S in k, which we denote Sk, is σ-invariant. Since Sk is an $\mathbb{F}_q$-subspace of k containing $\langle\sigma\rangle \leq k^*$, Sk is an

ℓ-subspace of k where ℓ is the smallest intermediate extension of $\mathbb{F}_q$ containing σ. This is the exact necessary condition found in [4], for symmetry to be preserved in a subspace.

Therefore, although Theorem 3 guarantees that projection does remove the multiplicative symmetry from the large field, projection does not exactly "break" the multiplicative symmetry completely; rather, it "pushes down" the symmetry into a subspace over a smaller field. It should be noted that, given a random choice of singular map, S, it is extremely unlikely for Sk to be an ℓ-subspace of k. In particular, Ding et al., in [4], derive an asymptotic upper bound of q^{-n} for the probability of this occurrence. Moreover, as in the case of SFLASH, if k is a prime extension of $\mathbb{F}_q$, then there does not exist a nontrivial intermediate extension, ℓ, and the multiplicative symmetry is completely broken.

6 Conclusion

We conclude from the preceding facts that the method using multiplicative symmetry can be applied only when the hidden permutation polynomial has exactly one nonlinear monomial summand. If this condition is not met, as is the case for the general HFE scheme, the polynomial has no multiplicative symmetry in this sense.

In addition, we extend the theoretical justification for the effectiveness of projection as a means of removing the multiplicative symmetry, proving that a general projection breaks the symmetry over the large field. Projection is a legitimate method of avoiding the new attacks; however, more study is needed to confirm that a projected SFLASH will be secure.

References

1. Dubois, V., Fouque, P.A., Shamir, A., Stern, J.: Practical Cryptanalysis of SFLASH. In: Menezes, A. (ed.) CRYPTO 2007. LNCS, vol. 4622, pp. 1–12. Springer, Heidelberg (2007)
2. Dubois, V., Fouque, P.A., Stern, J.: Cryptanalysis of SFLASH with Slightly Modified Parameters. In: Naor, M. (ed.) EUROCRYPT 2007. LNCS, vol. 4515, pp. 264–275. Springer, Heidelberg (2007)
3. Ding, J., Yang, B.Y., Cheng, C.M., Chen, O., Dubois, V.: Breaking the Symmetry: a Way to Resist the New Differential Attack. Cryptology ePrint Archive, Report 2007/366 (2007), `http://eprint.iacr.org/`
4. Ding, J., Dubois, V., Yang, B.Y., Chen, C.H.O., Cheng, C.M.: Could SFLASH be Repaired? In: Aceto, L., Damgård, I., Goldberg, L.A., Halldórsson, M.M., Ingólfsdóttir, A., Walukiewicz, I. (eds.) ICALP 2008, Part II. LNCS, vol. 5126, pp. 691–701. Springer, Heidelberg (2008)
5. Patarin, J.: Cryptoanalysis of the Matsumoto and Imai Public Key Scheme of Eurocrypt'88. In: Coppersmith, D. (ed.) CRYPTO 1995. LNCS, vol. 963, pp. 248–261. Springer, Heidelberg (1995)
6. Wolf, C., Preneel, B.: Taxonomy of Public Key Schemes Based on the Problem of Multivariate Quadratic Equations. Cryptology ePrint Archive, Report 2005/077 (2005), `http://eprint.iacr.org/`

7. Matsumoto, T., Imai, H.: Public Quadratic Polynominal-Tuples for Efficient Signature-Verification and Message-Encryption. In: Günther, C.G. (ed.) EUROCRYPT 1988. LNCS, vol. 330, pp. 419–453. Springer, Heidelberg (1988)
8. Patarin, J.: Hidden Fields Equations (HFE) and Isomorphisms of Polynomials (IP): Two New Families of Asymmetric Algorithms. In: Maurer, U.M. (ed.) EUROCRYPT 1996. LNCS, vol. 1070, pp. 33–48. Springer, Heidelberg (1996)
9. Mollin, R.A., Small, C.: On Permutation Polynomials over Finite Fields. Internat. J. Math. and Math. Sci. 10, 535–543 (1987)
10. Lidl, R., Niederreiter, H.: Introduction to Finite Fields and their Applications. Cambridge University Press, New York (1986)
11. Patarin, J., Goubin, L., Courtois, N.: C^*_{-+} and HM: Variations Around Two Schemes of T. Matsumoto and H. Imai. In: Ohta, K., Pei, D. (eds.) ASIACRYPT 1998. LNCS, vol. 1514, pp. 35–49. Springer, Heidelberg (1998)
12. Clough, C., Baena, J., Ding, J., Yang, B.Y., Chen, M.S.: Square, a New Multivariate Encryption Scheme. In: Fischlin, M. (ed.) RSA Conference 2009. LNCS, vol. 5473, pp. 252–264. Springer, Heidelberg (2009)

Growth of the Ideal Generated by a Quadratic Boolean Function

Jintai Ding, Timothy J. Hodges, and Victoria Kruglov*

Department of Mathematical Sciences,
University of Cincinnati,
Cincinnati, OH, 45221-0025 USA
jintai.ding@uc.edu, timothy.hodges@uc.edu, kruglov@email.uc.edu

Abstract. We give exact formulas for the growth of the ideal $A\lambda$ for λ a quadratic element of the algebra of Boolean functions over the Galois field $GF(2)$. That is, we calculate $\dim A_k\lambda$ where A_k is the subspace of elements of degree less than or equal to k. These results clarify some of the assertions made in the article of Yang, Chen and Courtois [22,23] concerning the efficiency of the XL algorithm.

1 Introduction

The solution of polynomial equations has been a central question in mathematics since earliest times. Recently this problem has become a central topic in cryptography, in the form of the solution of multivariate polynomial equations over a finite field. For instance, in multivariate public key cryptography [12], the public key is given by a set of polynomials

$$P(x_1, .., x_n) = (P_1(x_1, .., x_n), ..., P_m(x_1, .., x_n))$$

over a finite field. To encrypt a message $(x'_1, .., x'_n)$, one computes the value

$$(y'_1, ...y'_m) = P(x'_1, .., x'_n) = (P_1(x'_1, .., x'_n), ..., P_m(x'_1, .., x'_n)).$$

In order to attack this cipher directly, one needs to solve the system of equations

$$(y'_1, ...y'_m) = P(x_1, .., x_n).$$

Similarly, the algebraic attack [10,3] on symmetric cryptosystems transforms the problem of attacking the cryptosystems into one of solving systems of polynomial equations. For instance in the case of AES, this attack produces a system of 6000 sparse equations in approximately 1600 variables. Though we know that in general solving a set of random nonlinear equations is a NP-complete problem,

* This work grew out of discussions in the Taft Research Seminar on post-quantum cryptography presented at the University of Cincinnati by Bo-Yin Yang. The authors thank Yang for many interesting conversations on this topic. They also thank the Taft Research Center at the University of Cincinnati for its support of the seminar.

N. Sendrier (Ed.): PQCrypto 2010, LNCS 6061, pp. 13–27, 2010.

the understanding of the complexity of solving multivariate equations is still a critical problem which has not only theoretical significance but also serious practical implications.

In 2000, Courtois et al. introduced the XL algorithm [8] to solve such systems of equations. The idea of the XL algorithm, as applied to the solution of a system of m quadratic equations $f_i(\mathbf{x}) = \mathbf{0}$, is to successively eliminate variables by finding linear or 1-variables polynomials inside the ideal generated by the $f_i(\mathbf{x})$. Specifically, one applies an elimination process to the space of functions spanned by the $\mathbf{x}^{\mathbf{b}} f_i(\mathbf{x})$ where $\mathbf{x}^{\mathbf{b}}$ is a monomial of total degree less than or equal to a fixed number D. The key to understanding the complexity of the algorithm is to understand the dimension of this subspace. In [8,9], some heuristic complexity estimates were given for the XL algorithm, but these estimates have been shown to be incorrect [18].

The most commonly quoted estimates of the computational complexity of the XL algorithm use formulas developed in [22], and which were further explored in [24,23]. Yang and Chen produced estimates of the complexity of the XL algorithm based on formulas for the dimension of the space of functions spanned by the $\mathbf{x}^{\mathbf{b}} f_i(\mathbf{x})$. Although the complexity formulas were widely used (for instance, in [21,16,1,2,20,7]), and were in close agreement with experimental evidence, the proofs of the dimension theorems are based on unreliable heuristic arguments and are not correct. Some further exploration of these formulas was also recently done in [19], but based on some heuristic assumptions.

Another fundamental class of algorithms used to solve such systems of equations is the family of Gröbner basis algorithms including the F4 and F5 variants [6,13,14]. F4's implementation in Magma is considered the best in multivariate polynomial solving among all that are publicly available. We also know from [4] that F4 is actually a more efficient algorithm than the XL algorithm **if we assume** that both of them will solve the polynomials systems using Gaussian elimination to solve the systems of linear equations that arise. However, because of the sparse structure of the matrices associated to the XL algorithm, one can solve the linear systems more efficiently using the Wiedermann solver, which has advantages in terms of both speed and memory. It was demonstrated in the attack on the QUAD steam cipher [25] that the Wiedermann XL could indeed outperform the F4 algorithm. Therefore the complexity of the XL algorithm remains of great interests.

Because of the significance of these complexity formulas and their implications in cryptography, we believe that it is important to systematically study this question and to lay a solid mathematical foundation for future developments in this area.

In this paper, we begin with the simplest case, that of a single quadratic polynomial over the field $GF(2)$. Of course, over a field of characteristic zero the answer to the question is easy. The complication when dealing with finite fields is that we are working not in the polynomial ring itself, but in the ring of the functions; that is, the polynomial ring reduced by the related field equations,

$$X_i^q - X_i = 0,$$

where q is the size of the field. This makes our question a highly non-trivial mathematical problem, which turns out to have a surprisingly complex but elegant solution.

The complexity of the Gröbner basis algorithms F4 and F5 was analyzed in [5]. A few words of explanation are in order concerning the difficulty of our results compared to those in [5]. First, we consider here an arbitrary quadratic function, while the results in [5] concern the case of semi-regular sequences. Second we compute the exact dimension at each degree. The arguments in [5] concern the dimensions of the graded components of the ideal generated by the leading terms of the f_i in the associated graded ring (where $X_i^2 = 0$). While this enables one to pull back a certain amount of information to the original algebra of functions, it does not provide the exact dimensions that we calculate here.

2 The Yang-Chen Dimension Formulas

Let F denote the Galois field $GF(2)$. Let $R = F[X_1, \ldots, X_n]$ be the ring of polynomials over F and let

$$A = F[X_1, \ldots, X_n]/(X_1^2 + X_1, \ldots, X_n^2 + X_n)$$

be the ring of Boolean functions.

Let $R_{(d)}$ be the space of homogeneous polynomials of degree d, so that $R = \oplus R_{(d)}$ is the usual grading. Let $R_d = \sum_{i=0}^{d} R_{(i)}$ be the set of polynomials of degree less than or equal to d, so that

$$F = R_0 \subset R_1 \subset \cdots \subset R$$

is the usual filtration by degree. Denote by $\pi : R \to A$ the usual projection and let $A_{(i)} = \pi(R_{(i)})$ and let $A_i = \pi(R_i)$. Then $A = \oplus A_{(d)}$ is a vector space direct sum but not a gradation of rings, but $A_0 \subset A_1 \subset \cdots \subset A_n = A$ is a ring filtration. One may define a concept of degree for an element $\lambda \in A$ by saying that $\deg \lambda = \min\{d \mid \lambda \in A_d\}$. We say that an element is quadratic if it has degree two.

In this article we calculate explicitly $\dim A_k\lambda$ for a quadratic element $\lambda \in A$ and compare this result with that given by Yang and Chen in [22,23]. Let us briefly review the assertions in [23].

Let $\lambda_1, \ldots, \lambda_m \in A$ be a *semi-regular* [5] set of m quadratic elements. Corollary 4 of [23] asserts that

$$T - I = [t^D]\frac{(1+t)^n}{(1+t^2)^m(1-t)}$$

for all $D < D_{reg}$. Here $[t^D](1+t)^n(1+t^2)^{-m}(1-t)^{-1}$ denotes the coefficient of t^D in the powers series expansion of $(1+t)^n(1+t^2)^{-m}(1-t)^{-1}$; $T = \dim A_D$; $I = \dim \sum_i A_{D-2}\lambda_i$; and $D_{reg} = \min\{D \mid [t^D](1+t)^n(1+t^2)^{-m}(1-t)^{-1} \leq 0\}$.

This formula has the following explicit form when $m = 1$. Set

$$\sigma(n,k) = \sum_{j=0}^{k} \binom{n}{j} \quad \text{and} \quad \delta(n,k) = \sum_{i=0}^{\lfloor k/2 \rfloor} (-1)^i \sigma(n, k-2i),$$

Then for $D < D_{reg}$,

$$T - I = [t^D] \frac{(1+t)^n}{(1+t^2)(1-t)} = \delta(n, D)$$

Since $T = \dim A_D = \sigma(n,D)$, this yields $I = \sigma(n,D) - \delta(n,D) = \delta(n, D-2)$. Hence

$$\dim A_{D-2}\lambda = \delta(n, D-2)$$

for any semi-regular quadratic element λ and for any $D < D_{reg}$. While this assertion is suggestive of the actual behavior, the statement of the result is not adequate to include any useful assertions when $m = 1$. It is easily verified that for the definition of D_{reg} given above and in [23], $D_{reg} = \infty$. As can be seen in Theorems 5.3 and 7.1, the assertion that $\dim A_{D-2}\lambda = \delta(n, D-2)$ for all D cannot hold for any λ (except for very small values of n). In fact, no λ can be semi-regular (again except for exceptional cases), so the theorem as stated in [23] is vacuous rather than false in the case $m = 1$. The appropriate formulation of this assertion is that $\dim A_{D-2}\lambda = \delta(n, D-2)$ whenever $D - 2 < \operatorname{rank} \lambda/2$, (Corollary 7.2). In [23], the authors also claim, that in the non-semi-regular case "the value I can only decrease". When $m = 1$, this becomes the assertion that $\dim A_{D-2}\lambda \leq \delta(n, i-2)$ for all $D \leq D_{reg}$. Theorem 5.3 shows that this claim is false.

3 Some Combinatorial Lemmas

Before getting into the details of the man results we present some elementary identities concerning $\sigma(n,k)$ and $\delta(n,k)$ that we will need later.

Lemma 3.1. *The following analogs of the Vandermonde identity hold for $\sigma(n,k)$ and $\delta(n,k)$:*

$$\sigma(n,k) = \sum_{i=0}^{k} \binom{n-r}{i} \sigma(r, k-i) \quad \delta(n,k) = \sum_{i=0}^{k} \binom{n-r}{i} \delta(r, k-i)$$

Proof. The Vandermonde identity for binomial coefficients states that

$$\binom{n}{k} = \sum_{i=0}^{k} \binom{n-r}{i} \binom{r}{k-i}.$$

Hence

$$\begin{aligned}\sum_{i=0}^{k}\binom{n-r}{i}\sigma(r,k-i) &= \sum_{i=0}^{k}\binom{n-r}{i}\sum_{j=0}^{k-i}\binom{r}{j}\\ &= \sum_{i=0}^{k}\sum_{j=0}^{k-i}\binom{n-r}{i}\binom{r}{k-i-j}\\ &= \sum_{j=0}^{k}\sum_{i=0}^{k-j}\binom{n-r}{i}\binom{r}{k-j-i}\\ &= \sum_{j=0}^{k}\binom{n}{k-j} = \sum_{j=0}^{k}\binom{n}{j}\\ &= \sigma(n,k)\end{aligned}$$

Similarly,

$$\begin{aligned}\sum_{i=0}^{k}\binom{n-r}{i}\delta(r,k-i) &= \sum_{i=0}^{k}\binom{n-r}{i}\sum_{j=0}^{\lfloor (k-i)/2\rfloor}(-1)^j\sigma(r,k-i-2j)\\ &= \sum_{i=0}^{k}\sum_{j=0}^{\lfloor (k-i)/2\rfloor}(-1)^j\binom{n-r}{i}\sigma(r,k-2j-i)\\ &= \sum_{j=0}^{\lfloor k/2\rfloor}(-1)^j\sum_{i=0}^{k-2j}\binom{n-r}{i}\sigma(r,k-2j-i)\\ &= \sum_{j=0}^{\lfloor k/2\rfloor}(-1)^j\sigma(n,k-2j)\\ &= \delta(n,k)\end{aligned}$$

Lemma 3.2. *For any* $0 \le k \le n$,

$$\delta(n,k) = \sum_{i=0}^{\lfloor k/4\rfloor}\binom{n}{k-4i} + \sum_{i=0}^{\lfloor (k-1)/4\rfloor}\binom{n}{k-1-4i}.$$

In particular,

$$\delta(n,n) = \sum_{i=0}^{\lfloor n/4\rfloor}\binom{n}{n-4i} + \sum_{i=0}^{\lfloor (n-1)/4\rfloor}\binom{n}{n-1-4i}$$

and

$$\delta(n,n-1) = \sum_{i=0}^{\lfloor (n-1)/4\rfloor}\binom{n}{n-1-4i} + \sum_{i=0}^{\lfloor (n-2)/4\rfloor}\binom{n}{n-2-4i}$$

Proof.

$$\begin{aligned}
\delta(n,k) &= \sum_{i=0}^{\lfloor k/2 \rfloor} (-1)^i \sigma(n, k-2i) \\
&= \sigma(n,k) - \sigma(n,k-2) + \sigma(n,k-4) - \cdots \pm \sigma(n, k-2\lfloor k/2 \rfloor) \\
&= \binom{n}{k} + \binom{n}{k-1} + \binom{n}{k-4} + \binom{n}{k-5} + \binom{n}{k-8} + \binom{n}{k-9} + \cdots \\
&= \binom{n}{k} + \binom{n}{k-4} + \binom{n}{k-8} + \cdots + \binom{n}{k-1} + \binom{n}{k-5} + \cdots \\
&= \sum_{i=0}^{\lfloor k/4 \rfloor} \binom{n}{k-4i} + \sum_{i=0}^{\lfloor (k-1)/4 \rfloor} \binom{n}{k-1-4i}
\end{aligned}$$

Lemma 3.3.

$$\sum_{i=0}^{\lfloor n/4 \rfloor} \binom{n}{4i} = \frac{1}{2}\left(2^{n-1} + 2^{n/2} \cos \frac{n\pi}{4}\right)$$

$$\sum_{i=0}^{\lfloor (n-1)/4 \rfloor} \binom{n}{4i+1} = \frac{1}{2}\left(2^{n-1} + 2^{n/2} \sin \frac{n\pi}{4}\right)$$

$$\sum_{i=0}^{\lfloor (n-2)/4 \rfloor} \binom{n}{4i+2} = \frac{1}{2}\left(2^{n-1} - 2^{n/2} \cos \frac{n\pi}{4}\right)$$

$$\sum_{i=0}^{\lfloor (n-3)/4 \rfloor} \binom{n}{4i+3} = \frac{1}{2}\left(2^{n-1} - 2^{n/2} \sin \frac{n\pi}{4}\right)$$

Proof. See [15, 0.153].

Define

$$\epsilon(k) = \cos\left(\frac{k\pi}{2}\right) + \sin\left(\frac{k\pi}{2}\right)$$

Lemma 3.4. *For any positive integer n,*

1. $\delta(n,n) = 2^{n-1} + \epsilon(n/2)\, 2^{\frac{n}{2}-1}$
2. $\delta(n,n-1) = 2^{n-1} + \epsilon(n/2-1)\, 2^{\frac{n}{2}-1}$

Proof. For part (1) observe that

$$\begin{aligned}
\delta(n,n) &= \sum_{i=0}^{\lfloor n/4 \rfloor} \binom{n}{n-4i} + \sum_{i=0}^{\lfloor (n-1)/4 \rfloor} \binom{n}{n-1-4i} \\
&= \sum_{i=0}^{\lfloor n/4 \rfloor} \binom{n}{4i} + \sum_{i=0}^{\lfloor (n-1)/4 \rfloor} \binom{n}{4i+1} \\
&= 2^{n-1} + \left[\cos \frac{n\pi}{4} + \sin \frac{n\pi}{4}\right] 2^{n/2} \\
&= 2^{n-1} + \epsilon(n/2)\, 2^{n/2}
\end{aligned}$$

Similarly for part (2),

$$\begin{aligned}
\delta(n, n-1) &= \sum_{i=0}^{\lfloor (n-1)/4 \rfloor} \binom{n}{n-1-4i} + \sum_{i=0}^{\lfloor (n-2)/4 \rfloor} \binom{n}{n-2-4i} \\
&= \sum_{i=0}^{\lfloor (n-1)/4 \rfloor} \binom{n}{4i+1} + \sum_{i=0}^{\lfloor (n-2)/4 \rfloor} \binom{n}{4i+2} \\
&= 2^{n-1} + \left[\sin \frac{n\pi}{4} - \cos \frac{n\pi}{4}\right] 2^{n/2} \\
&= 2^{n-1} + \left[\cos \frac{(n-2)\pi}{4} + \sin \frac{(n-2)\pi}{4}\right] 2^{n/2} \\
&= 2^{n-1} + \epsilon(n/2 - 1)\, 2^{n/2}
\end{aligned}$$

4 Equivalence, Rank and Type

The dimension of $A_k\lambda$ is not the same for all quadratic elements λ. However it is obviously invariant under any automorphism that preserves degree. Inside the group of all automorphisms of A we have the subgroup of automorphisms that preserve degree; that is, the subgroup of all automorphisms ϕ such that $\phi(A_1) = A_1$. These are the *affine automorphisms*. We say that two elements of $\lambda, \lambda' \in A$ are equivalent if there exist an affine automorphism ϕ such that $\phi(\lambda) = \lambda'$.

Definition 4.1. *Let $\lambda \in A$. We define the* rank *of λ to be the smallest positive integer r such that λ lies in a subalgebra generated by r linear elements. That is the smallest r such that there exists $\ell_1, \ldots, \ell_r \in A_1$ with $\lambda \in F[\ell_1, \ldots, \ell_r]$.*

It is clear that the rank of an element is invariant under an affine automorphism. In general the set of elements of a given rank and degree is a union of a number of different equivalence classes. For quadratic elements there are two equivalence classes for even rank and one for odd rank.

Theorem 4.2. *Let $\lambda \in A$ be a quadratic element of rank r.*

1. *If r is even, then λ is either equivalent to $x_1x_2 + \cdots + x_{r-1}x_r$ or $x_1x_2 + \cdots + x_{r-1}x_r + 1$. Moreover these two elements are not equivalent.*
2. *If r is odd, then λ is equivalent to $x_1x_2 + \cdots + x_{r-2}x_{r-1} + x_r$.*

Proof. This follows from the classification of quadratic elements in the polynomial ring given in [17].

Thus it suffices to calculate $\dim A_k\lambda$ for the elements listed in the theorem. We begin with the maximal rank case which is the simplest.

5 Even Maximal Rank

The calculation of $\dim A_k\lambda$ in [22] uses the exact sequence:

$$0 \longrightarrow A_k \cap A(\lambda+1) \longrightarrow A_k \longrightarrow A_k\lambda \longrightarrow 0$$

where the map from A_k to $A_k\lambda$ is just multiplication by λ. The kernel of this map is the intersection of $\operatorname{Ann}\lambda = \{b \in A \mid b\lambda = 0\}$ (the annihilator of λ) with A_k. It is well-known and easily verified that $\operatorname{Ann}\lambda = A(\lambda+1)$, so the kernel is $A_k \cap A(\lambda+1)$, yielding the exact sequence above. The kernel $A_k \cap A(\lambda+1)$ clearly contains $A_{k-2}(\lambda+1)$. In order to apply induction we would like $A_k \cap A(\lambda+1) = A_{k-2}(\lambda+1)$. While this often holds, it is not always true. For instance, note that, for r even,

$$(x_1+1)(x_3+1)\dots(x_{r-1}+1)(x_1x_2+\dots+x_{r-1}x_r) = 0$$

so that $(x_1+1)(x_3+1)\dots(x_{r-1}+1) \in A_{r/2} \cap \operatorname{Ann}(x_1x_2+\dots+x_{r-1}x_r) = A_{r/2} \cap A(x_1x_2+\dots+x_{r-1}x_r+1)$ but $(x_1+1)(x_3+1)\dots(x_{r-1}+1) \notin A_{r/2-2}(x_1x_2+\dots+x_{r-1}x_r+1)$. It turns out that these elements are the principal obstructions to the above equality when $r = n$.

Theorem 5.1. *Suppose that n is an even positive integer and suppose that $\lambda = x_1x_2+\dots+x_{n-1}x_n$. Then*

1. *$A_k \cap A(\lambda+1) = A_{k-2}(\lambda+1)$ for all $0 \le k < n/2$ and $n/2+2 \le k \le n+2$*
2. *$A_k \cap A\lambda = A_{k-2}\lambda$ for all $0 \le k \le n+2$.*

Proof. (1) It is clear that $A_{k-2}(\lambda+1) \subseteq A_k \cap A(\lambda+1)$. Thus it suffices to prove that $A_k \cap A(\lambda+1) \subseteq A_{k-2}(\lambda+1)$ for $0 \le k < n/2$ and $n/2+2 \le k \le n+2$. Note that the two extreme cases are easily seen to be true. Since $A = A_n = A_{n+2}$, $A_{n+2} \cap A(\lambda+1) = A \cap A(\lambda+1) = A(\lambda+1) = A_n(\lambda+1)$. On the other hand, $A_{-2} = 0$ and $A_0 = F$. Since $\lambda+1$ is not a unit (because $\lambda(\lambda+1) = 0$), $A_0 \cap A(\lambda+1) = F \cap A(\lambda+1) = 0 = A_{-2}(\lambda+1)$.

We proceed by induction on n. Consider the case when $n = 2$ and $\lambda = x_1x_2$. It remains to show that $A_3 \cap A(\lambda+1) = A_1(\lambda+1)$; that is, that $A(\lambda+1) = A_1(\lambda+1)$. It is easy to verify directly that $\{x_1x_2+1, x_1x_2+x_1, x_1x_2+x_2\}$ forms a basis for $A(\lambda+1)$ and that this basis is contained in $A_1(\lambda+1)$.

We now assume the result is true for $n-2$ variables and deduce that it is true for n variables. Now let $A' = F[x_3, x_4, \dots, x_n]$ and $\lambda' = x_3x_4+\dots+x_{n-1}x_n$ and assume that the assertion is true for λ' and A'. Note that A is a free A'-module with basis $\{1, x_1, x_2, x_1x_2\}$. Thus an arbitrary element of A is of the form $a = a_0' + a_1'x_1 + a_2'x_2 + a_3'x_1x_2$, where $a_i' \in A'$. Since $x_1x_2 = \lambda + \lambda'$ and $\lambda(\lambda+1) = 0$ we see that $x_1x_2(\lambda+1) = \lambda'(\lambda+1)$ and so $a(\lambda+1) = \tilde{a}(\lambda+1)$ where $\tilde{a} = (a_0' + a_3'\lambda') + a_1'x_1 + a_2'x_2$. Hence an arbitrary element of $A(\lambda+1)$ is of the form $a(\lambda+1)$ where $a = a_0' + a_1'x_1 + a_2'x_2$ for some $a_i' \in A'$. Suppose that $a(\lambda+1) \in A_k$. Now

$$\begin{aligned} a(\lambda+1) &= (a_0' + a_1'x_1 + a_2'x_2)(x_1x_2 + \lambda' + 1) \\ &= a_0'(\lambda'+1) + a_1'(\lambda'+1)x_1 + a_2'(\lambda'+1))x_2 + (a_0' + a_1' + a_2')x_1x_2. \end{aligned}$$

Because of the linear independence of the elements $\{1, x_1, x_2, x_1x_2\}$ over A' each of the summands must also lie in A_k. Hence $a_0'(\lambda'+1) \in A_k$; $a_1'(\lambda'+1), a_2'(\lambda'+1) \in A_{k-1}$ and $a_0' + a_1' + a_2' \in A_{k-2}'$.

Suppose that $1 \le k < n/2$. Then $0 \le k-1 < n/2 - 1 = (n-2)/2$. Hence by induction, $A_{k-1}' \cap A'(\lambda'+1)) = A_{k-3}'(\lambda'+1)$. So there exist b_1', $b_2' \in A_{k-3}'$, such that $a_1'(\lambda'+1) = b_1'(\lambda'+1)$ and $a_2'(\lambda'+1) = b_2'(\lambda'+1)$. Let $b_0' = a_0'+a_1'+a_2'+b_1'+b_2'$. Then $b_0' \in A_{k-2}'$ since $a_0' + a_1' + a_2' \in A_{k-2}'$ and $b_1' + b_2' \in A_{k-3}'$. Moreover $b_0'(\lambda'+1) = a_0'(\lambda'+1)$. Now define $b = b_0' + b_1'x_1 + b_2'x_2$. Then, $b \in A_{k-2}$ and

$$\begin{aligned} b(\lambda+1) &= b_0'(\lambda'+1) + b_1'(\lambda'+1)x_1 + b_2'(\lambda'+1))x_2 + (b_0' + b_1' + b_2')x_1x_2 \\ &= a_0'(\lambda'+1) + a_1'(\lambda'+1)x_1 + a_2'(\lambda'+1))x_2 + (a_0' + a_1' + a_2')x_1x_2. \\ &= a(\lambda+1) \end{aligned}$$

Hence $a(\lambda+1) \in A_{k-2}(\lambda+1)$. Thus $A_k \cap A(\lambda+1) \subseteq A_{k-2}(\lambda+1)$, as required.

If on the other hand $n/2 + 2 \le k \le n+1$, then $(n-2)/2 = n/2 - 1 \le k - 1 \le n = (n-2)/2 + 2$. Again we may apply the induction hypothesis to deduce that $A_{k-1}' \cap A'(\lambda'+1)) = A_{k-3}'(\lambda'+1)$. The argument of the previous paragraph can be repeated verbatim to deduce that there exists a $b \in A_{k-2}$ such that $b(\lambda+1) = a(\lambda+1)$. Thus $A_k \cap A(\lambda+1) \subseteq A_{k-2}(\lambda+1)$ if $n/2+2 \le k \le n+2$.

(2) A similar argument proves the second part of the theorem. We need to show that $A_k \cap A(\lambda) \subseteq A_{k-2}(\lambda)$ for $0 \le k \le n+2$. the cases $k = 0$ and $k = n+2$ are easy to see directly just as in part (1).

The key difference lies in the base case $n = 2$. Here $\lambda = x_1x_2$, so $x_1\lambda = \lambda$ and $x_2\lambda = \lambda$. So $A\lambda = A_0\lambda$. Thus $A_0 \cap A\lambda = 0 = A_{-2}\lambda = 0$, $A_1 \cap A\lambda = 0 = A_{-1}\lambda = 0$, $A_2 \cap A\lambda = A_0\lambda$, $A_3 \cap A\lambda = A_0\lambda = A_1\lambda$. Thus the result is true when $n = 2$.

We now assume the result is true for $n-2$ variables and deduce that it is true for n variables. Suppose that $a\lambda \in A_k$. Then $a = a_0' + a_1'x_1 + a_2'x_2 + a_3'x_1x_2$, where $a_i' \in A'$. Since $x_1x_2 + \lambda' = \lambda$, and $\lambda(\lambda+1) = 0$, we have that $x_1x_2\lambda = (\lambda'+1)\lambda$. hence $a\lambda = [a_0' + a_3(\lambda'+1)] + a_1'x_1 + a_2'x_2$. hence we may assume that a is of the form $a = a_0' + a_1'x_1 + a_2'x_2$. Thus

$$\begin{aligned} a\lambda &= (a_0' + a_1'x_1 + a_2'x_2)(x_1x_2 + \lambda') \\ &= a_0'\lambda' + a_1'\lambda'x_1 + a_2'\lambda')x_2 + (a_0' + a_1' + a_2')x_1x_2. \end{aligned}$$

We deduce that $a_0'(\lambda'+1) \in A_k$; $a_1'(\lambda'+1), a_2'(\lambda'+1) \in A_{k-1}$ and $a_0' + a_1' + a_2' \in A_{k-2}'$. We can then use the induction hypothesis and the argument above to deduce that there exists a $b \in A_{k-2}$ such that $a\lambda = b\lambda$. Hence $A_k \cap A\lambda = A_{k-2}\lambda$, as required.

Lemma 5.2. *Let n be even and let $\lambda = x_1x_2 + x_3x_4 + \cdots + x_{n-1}x_n$. Then,*

$$\dim A\lambda = 2^{n-1} - 2^{\frac{n}{2}-1} \quad \textit{and} \quad \dim A(\lambda+1) = 2^{n-1} + 2^{\frac{n}{2}-1}.$$

Proof. Let $\mathcal{Z}(\lambda)$ be the set of zeros of λ. Then $|\mathcal{Z}(\lambda)| = \dim A/A\lambda$. it is well-known that $|\mathcal{Z}(\lambda)| = 2^{n-1} + 2^{\frac{n}{2}-1}$, [17, Theorem 6.32]. Hence $\dim A\lambda = \dim A - |\mathcal{Z}(\lambda)| = 2^n - (2^{n-1} + 2^{\frac{n}{2}-1}) = 2^{n-1} - 2^{\frac{n}{2}-1}$. The second assertion follows from the fact that $|\mathcal{Z}(\lambda)| = 2^{n-1} - 2^{\frac{n}{2}-1}$.

Theorem 5.3. *Suppose that n is even and let $\lambda = x_1x_2 + \cdots + x_{n-1}x_n$. Then*

$$\dim A_k\lambda = \begin{cases} \delta(n,k), & \text{if } k < n/2 \\ \delta(n,k) - (\epsilon(k-n/2)+1)2^{\frac{n}{2}-1}, & \text{if } n/2 \le k \le n \end{cases}$$

$$\dim A_k(\lambda+1) = \begin{cases} \delta(n,k), & \text{if } k < n/2+2 \\ \delta(n,k) - (\epsilon(k-n/2)-1)2^{\frac{n}{2}-1}, & \text{if } n/2 \le k \le n \end{cases}$$

Proof. We first prove the assertion that $\dim A_k\lambda = \delta(n,k) = \dim A_k(\lambda+1)$ for $0 \le k < n/2$ by induction on k. We need two base cases, $k=0$ and $k=1$. When $k=0$, $A_k = F$, and so it is clear that $\dim A_0\lambda = \dim A_0(\lambda+1) = 1 = \delta(n,1)$. When $k=1$ and $n>2$, the maps from A_1 to $A_1\lambda$ and $A_1(\lambda+1)$ are both bijective by Theorem 5.1. So $\dim A_1\lambda = \dim A_1(\lambda+1) = \dim A_1 = \sigma(n,1) = \delta(n,1)$.

Now suppose $1 < k < n/2$. Since $\operatorname{Ann}\lambda = A(\lambda+1)$ and $A_k \cap (\lambda+1) = A_{k-2}(\lambda+1)$ we have the exact sequence

$$0 \longrightarrow A_{k-2}(\lambda+1) \longrightarrow A_k \longrightarrow A_k\lambda \longrightarrow 0$$

Applying the inductive hypothesis yields $\dim A_k\lambda = \dim A_k - \dim A_{k-2}(\lambda+1) = \sigma(n,k) - \delta(n,k-2) = \delta(n,k)$, as desired. A similar argument works for $A_k(\lambda+1)$.

We now prove that for $n/2 \le k \le n$, $\dim A_k\lambda = \delta(n,k) - (\epsilon(k-n/2)+1)2^{\frac{n}{2}-1}$ and $\dim A_k(\lambda+1) = \delta(n,k) - (\epsilon(k-n/2)-1)2^{\frac{n}{2}-1}$ by reverse induction using $k=n$ and $k=n-1$ as base cases. Consider the case $k=n$. Since $A_n = A$, $\dim A_n\lambda = 2^{n-1} - 2^{\frac{n}{2}-1} = \delta(n,n) - \epsilon(n/2)\,2^{n/2} - 2^{\frac{n}{2}-1} = \delta(n,n) - (\epsilon(n/2)+1)2^{\frac{n}{2}-1}$, as required. Similarly, $\dim A_n(\lambda+1) = 2^{n-1} + 2^{\frac{n}{2}-1} = \delta(n,n) - \epsilon(n/2)\,2^{n/2} + 2^{\frac{n}{2}-1} = \delta(n,n) - (\epsilon(n/2)-1)2^{\frac{n}{2}-1}$.

Now consider the case $k = n-1$. Observe that $A_{n-1}\lambda \supset A_{n-2}\lambda = A_n \cap A\lambda = A\lambda$. So $\dim A_{n-1}\lambda = \dim A_n\lambda$. However, using Lemma 3.4 we have that

$$\begin{aligned} \delta(n,n-1) - &(\epsilon(n-1-n/2)+1)2^{\frac{n}{2}-1} \\ &= (2^{n-1} + \epsilon(n/2-1)2^{\frac{n}{2}-1}) - (\epsilon(n/2-1)+1)2^{\frac{n}{2}-1} \\ &= 2^{n-1} - 2^{\frac{n}{2}-1} = \dim A\lambda \end{aligned}$$

A similar argument proves that $A_{n-1}(\lambda+1) = A(\lambda+1)$ and that the formula holds in this case also.

We now assume the formula holds for $k+2$ and prove that it holds for k, provided that $k \ge n/2+2$. Again we have the short exact sequence

$$0 \longrightarrow A_k\lambda \longrightarrow A_{k+2} \longrightarrow A_{k+2}(\lambda+1) \longrightarrow 0$$

So that

$$\begin{aligned} \dim A_k\lambda &= \dim A_{k+2} - \dim A_{k+2}(\lambda+1) \\ &= \sigma(n,k+2) - (\delta(n,k+2) - (\epsilon(k+2-n/2)-1)2^{\frac{n}{2}-1}) \\ &= \delta(n,k) - (\epsilon(k-n/2)+1)2^{\frac{n}{2}-1} \end{aligned}$$

since $\epsilon(k+2) = -\epsilon(k)$. Similarly the exact sequence

$$0 \longrightarrow A_k(\lambda+1) \longrightarrow A_{k+2} \longrightarrow A_{k+2}\lambda \longrightarrow 0$$

yields

$$\begin{aligned}\dim A_k(\lambda+1) &= \dim A_{k+2} - \dim A_{k+2}\lambda \\ &= \sigma(n,k+2) - (\delta(n,k+2) - (\epsilon(k+2-n/2)+1)2^{\frac{n}{2}-1}) \\ &= \delta(n,k) - \epsilon(k-n/2) - 1)2^{\frac{n}{2}-1}\end{aligned}$$

as required.

It remains to deal with the cases when $k = n/2$ and $k = n/2+1$. Using the argument from the upward induction we get in these cases that

$$\dim A_k(\lambda+1) = \dim A_k - \dim A_k(\lambda) = \delta(n,k) = \delta(n,k) - \epsilon(k-n/2) - 1)2^{\frac{n}{2}-1}$$

since $\epsilon(0) = \epsilon(1) = 1$. The downward induction argument above extends to show that $\dim A_k(\lambda) = \dim A_{k+2} - \dim A_{k+2}(\lambda+1) = \delta(n,k) - (\epsilon(k-n/2)+1)2^{\frac{n}{2}-1}$ in these cases.

Note that the values of $\epsilon(k-n/2)+1$ form a sequence of the form $0,0,2,2,0,0,2,\ldots$ and those of $\epsilon(k-n/2)-1$ form the sequence $0,0,-2,-2,0,0,-2,\ldots$. Thus in the first case, when $k > \operatorname{rank}\lambda/2$, the dimension of $A_k\lambda$ varies at or below $\delta(n,k)$, whereas in the second case it varies at or above $\delta(n,k)$. It is asserted in [22,23] that $\dim A_k\lambda \leq \delta(n,k)$ whenever $k-2$ is less than the degree of regularity. This theorem shows that this assertion is false. In fact it is clear from this result that no such universal inequality is likely to hold in general.

6 Odd Maximal Rank

If n is odd and λ is quadratic of rank n, then as observed above, $\lambda \sim x_1x_2 + \cdots + x_{n-2}x_{n-1} + x_n$.

Theorem 6.1. *Suppose that n is odd let $\lambda = x_1x_2 + \cdots + x_{n-2}x_{n-1} + x_n$. Then*

$$A_k \cap A\lambda = A_{k-2}\lambda$$

for $k \neq (n+1)/2$.

Proof. The proof is very similar to the proof of Theorem 5.1. Again, it is clear that $A_{k-2}\lambda \subseteq A_k \cap A\lambda$. Using induction on n, we prove that $A_k \cap A\lambda \subseteq A_{k-2}\lambda$ for $k \neq (n+1)/2$

Consider the case when $n=3$ and $\lambda = x_1x_2 + x_3$. It is easily verified by hand that $A_1 \cap A\lambda = \{0\}$ and that $A\lambda = A_1\lambda$ so that $A_3 \cap A\lambda = A_1\lambda$.

Now suppose that $n \geq 5$. Let $A' = F[x_3, x_4, \ldots, x_n]$ and $\lambda' = x_3x_4 + \cdots + x_{n-2}x_{n-1} + x_n$ and assume the assertion true for λ' and A'. As above, note that

A is a free A'-module with basis $\{1, x_1, x_2, x_1x_2\}$. Again an arbitrary element of $A\lambda$ is of the form $a\lambda$ where $a = a'_0 + a'_1x_1 + a'_2x_2$ for some $a'_i \in A'$.

Let $a\lambda \in A_k$ where a is as above. Now

$$\begin{aligned} a\lambda &= (a'_0 + a'_1x_1 + a'_2x_2)(x_1x_2 + \lambda') \\ &= a'_0\lambda' + a'_1\lambda'x_1 + a'_2\lambda'x_2 + (a'_0 + a'_1 + a'_2)x_1x_2. \end{aligned}$$

Because of the linear independence of the elements $\{1, x_1, x_2, x_1x_2\}$ over A' each of the summands must also lie in A_k. Hence $a'_0\lambda' \in A_k$; $a'_1\lambda', a'_2\lambda' \in A_{k-1}$ and $a'_0 + a'_1 + a'_2 \in A'_{k-2}$.

Suppose that $k \neq (n+1)/2$. Then $k-1 \neq ((n-2)+1)/2$. Hence by induction, $A'_{k-1} \cap A'\lambda' = A'_{k-3}\lambda'$. So there exist $b'_1,\ b'_2 \in A'_{k-3}$, such that $a'_1\lambda' = b'_1\lambda'$ and $a'_2\lambda' = b'_2\lambda'$. Let $b'_0 = a'_0 + a'_1 + a'_2 + b'_1 + b'_2$. Then $b'_0 \in A'_{k-2}$ since $a'_0 + a'_1 + a'_2 \in A'_{k-2}$ and $b'_1 + b'_2 \in A'_{k-3}$. Moreover $b'_0\lambda' = a'_0\lambda'$. Now define $b = b'_0 + b'_1x_1 + b'_2x_2$. Then, $b \in A_{k-2}$ and

$$\begin{aligned} b\lambda &= b'_0\lambda' + b'_1\lambda'x_1 + b'_2\lambda'x_2 + (b'_0 + b'_1 + b'_2)x_1x_2 \\ &= a'_0\lambda' + a'_1\lambda'x_1 + a'_2\lambda'x_2 + (a'_0 + a'_1 + a'_2)x_1x_2. \\ &= a\lambda \end{aligned}$$

Thus $A_k \cap A\lambda \subseteq A_{k-2}\lambda$ as required.

Theorem 6.2. *Suppose that n is odd and let $\lambda = x_1x_2 + \cdots + x_{n-2}x_{n-1} + x_n$. Then*

$$\dim A_k\lambda = \begin{cases} \delta(n,k), & \text{if } k < (n+1)/2 \\ \delta(n,k) - \epsilon(k - n/2)2^{\frac{n}{2}-1}, & \text{if } k \geq (n+1)2 \end{cases}$$

Proof. Since all quadratic elements of A of maximal rank are affine equivalent, the assertion of the theorem is equivalent to the assertion that the result holds for all such elements. In order for the induction to work correctly (that is, to include both the cases of $\dim A_k\lambda$ and $\dim A_k(\lambda + 1)$), we need to work in the framework of this more general assertion. The proof that $\dim A_k\lambda = \delta(n,k)$ if $k < (n+1)/2$ proceeds exactly as for Theorem 5.3 using Theorem 6.1 in place of Theorem 5.1.

It remains to prove that for $(n+1)/2 \leq k \leq n$, $\dim A_k\lambda = \delta(n,k) - \epsilon(k - n/2)2^{\frac{n}{2}-1}$. We again prove the result by reverse induction using $k = n$ and $k = n-1$ as base cases. For the case $k = n$, note first that by the symmetry of λ and $\lambda + 1$, $\dim A_n\lambda = 2^{n/2}$. Moreover,

$$\delta(n,k) - \epsilon(k - n/2)2^{\frac{n}{2}-1} = \delta(n,n) - \epsilon(n/2)2^{\frac{n}{2}-1} = 2^{n/2}$$

by Lemma 3.4. Now consider the case $k = n-1$ and assume that $n > 3$. Observe that $A_{n-1}\lambda = A_{n+1} \cap A\lambda = A\lambda$. So $\dim A_{n-1}\lambda = \dim A_n\lambda$. On the other hand, using Lemma 3.4 we have that

$$\begin{aligned} \delta(n, n-1) - &\epsilon(n - 1 - n/2)2^{\frac{n}{2}-1} \\ &= (2^{n-1} + \epsilon(n/2 - 1)2^{\frac{n}{2}-1}) - \epsilon(n/2 - 1)2^{\frac{n}{2}-1} \\ &= 2^{n-1} = \dim A\lambda \end{aligned}$$

So the result holds in this case also.

We now assume the formula holds for $k+2$ and prove that it holds for k, provided that $(n+1)/2 < k < n-2$. The short exact sequence

$$0 \longrightarrow A_k\lambda \longrightarrow A_{k+2} \longrightarrow A_{k+2}(\lambda+1) \longrightarrow 0$$

implies that

$$\begin{aligned}\dim A_k\lambda &= \dim A_{k+2} - \dim A_{k+2}(\lambda+1)\\ &= \sigma(n,k+2) - (\delta(n,k+2) - \epsilon(k+2-n/2)2^{\frac{n}{2}-1})\\ &= \delta(n,k) - \epsilon(k-n/2)2^{\frac{n}{2}-1}\end{aligned}$$

since $\epsilon(k+2) = -\epsilon(k)$.

7 General Case

Now consider a quadratic element $\lambda \in A$ of arbitrary rank $r \leq n$. Without loss of generality we assume that $\lambda \in A' = F[x_1, \ldots, x_r]$ and that λ has one of the three canonical forms with respect to the variables $x_1, \ldots, x_r$. The dimension of $A_k\lambda$ can be computed from the dimensions of the $A'_{k'}\lambda$. Recall that we make the convention that $A_j = 0$ for $j < 0$,

Theorem 7.1

$$\dim A_k\lambda = \sum_{i=0}^{k} \binom{n-r}{i} \dim A'_{k-i}\lambda$$

Proof Let $S = \{x_{r+1}, \ldots, x_n\}$, let $\mathcal{P}$ be the power set of S. For $T \in \mathcal{P}$ set $x_T = \prod_{i \in T} x_i$. Then the monomials x_T form a basis for A as a free A'-module. Let V_j be the span of the monomials x_T of degree j. Then $A_k = \oplus_{i=0}^{n-r} A'_{k-i}V_i$ and $A_k = \oplus_{i=0}^{k} A'_{k-i}\lambda V_i$ and hence $\dim A_k\lambda = \sum_{i=0}^{k} \dim A'_{k-i}\lambda V_i = \sum_{i=0}^{k} \binom{n-r}{i} \dim A'_{k-i}\lambda$.

Corollary 7.2. *If* $k < \operatorname{rank}\lambda/2$, *then* $\dim A_k\lambda = \delta(n,k)$.

Proof. From Theorem 7.1 we have that $\dim A_k\lambda = \sum_{i=0}^{k} \binom{n-r}{i} \dim A'_{k-i}\lambda$. Since $k-i \leq k < \operatorname{rank}\lambda$ by hypothesis, we can conclude using Theorem 5.3 or Theorem 6.2 that $\dim A'_{k-i}\lambda = \delta(r, k-i)$. Hence

$$\dim A_k\lambda = \sum_{i=0}^{k} \binom{n-r}{i} \dim A'_{k-i}\lambda = \sum_{i=0}^{k} \binom{n-r}{i} \delta(r, k-i) = \delta(n,k)$$

by Lemma 3.1.

Corollary 7.3. *Let* λ *be a quadratic element of rank* r, *then*

$$|\dim A_k\lambda - \delta(n,k)| \leq 2^{n-\frac{r}{2}}$$

Proof. From Theorem 7.1 and Theorems 5.3 and 6.2 we have that

$$\begin{aligned}
|\dim A_k\lambda - \delta(n,k)| &= \left|\sum_{i=0}^{k}\binom{n-r}{i}\dim A'_{k-i}\lambda - \delta(n,k)\right| \\
&\leq \left|\sum_{i=0}^{k}\binom{n-r}{i}\left(\delta(r,k-i)+2^{\frac{r}{2}}\right) - \delta(n,k)\right| \\
&= \left|\delta(n,k) + \sum_{i=0}^{k}\binom{n-r}{i}\left(2^{\frac{r}{2}}\right) - \delta(n,k)\right| \\
&\leq 2^{n-r}2^{\frac{r}{2}} = 2^{n-\frac{r}{2}}
\end{aligned}$$

8 Conclusion

Our results give insight on the validity of [23, Corollary 4]. In particular we show that the formula $\dim A_k\lambda = \delta(n,k)$ is true for any λ provided that k is less than $(\operatorname{rank}\lambda)/2$. Furthermore, we see that the key conditions for the formula to hold involve both the rank and the equivalence class of the element λ. We proved that for large values of k, the value of $\dim A_k$ will oscillate above or below $\delta(n,k)$, depending on the equivalence type of λ. Thus no inequality of the form $\dim A_k\lambda \geq \delta(n,k)$ or $\dim A_k\lambda \leq \delta(n,k)$ can hold universally.

References

1. Afzal, M., Masood, A.: Algebraic Cryptanalysis of A NLFSR Based Stream Cipher. In: The 3 rd International Conference on Information and Communication Technologies: From Theory to Applications, ICTTA 2008 (2008)
2. Albrecht, M., Cid, C.: Algebraic Techniques in Differential Cryptanalysis. In: Dunkelman, O. (ed.) FSE 2009. LNCS, vol. 5665, pp. 193–208. Springer, Heidelberg (2009)
3. Armknecht, F., Krause, M.: Algebraic Attacks on Combiners with Memory. In: Boneh, D. (ed.) CRYPTO 2003. LNCS, vol. 2729, pp. 162–175. Springer, Heidelberg (2003)
4. Ars, G., Faugre, J.C., Imai, H., Kawazoe, M., Sugita, M.: Comparison Between XL and Grobner Basis Algorithms. In: Lee, P.J. (ed.) ASIACRYPT 2004. LNCS, vol. 3329, pp. 338–353. Springer, Heidelberg (2004)
5. Bardet, M., Faugère, J.-C., Salvy, B., Yang, B.-Y.: Asymptotic Expansion of the Degree of Regularity for Semi-Regular Systems of Equations. In: MEGA 2005, Sardinia, Italy (2005)
6. Buchberger, B.: Ein Algorithmus zum Auffinden der Basiselemente des Restklassenringes nach einem nulldimensionalen Polynomideal, University of Innsbruck, PhD thesis (1965)
7. Cid, C., Leurent, G.: An Analysis of the XSL Algorithm. In: Roy, B. (ed.) ASIACRYPT 2005. LNCS, vol. 3788, pp. 333–352. Springer, Heidelberg (2005)

8. Courtois, N.T., Klimov, A.B., Patarin, J., Shamir, A.: Efficient Algorithms for Solving Overdefined Systems of Multivariate Polynomial Equations. In: Preneel, B. (ed.) EUROCRYPT 2000. LNCS, vol. 1807, pp. 392–407. Springer, Heidelberg (2000)
9. Courtois, N., Patarin, J.: About the XL Algorithm over GF(2). In: Joye, M. (ed.) CT-RSA 2003. LNCS, vol. 2612, pp. 141–157. Springer, Heidelberg (2003)
10. Courtois, N.T., Pieprzyk, J.: Cryptanalysis of Block Ciphers with Overdefined Systems of Equations. In: Zheng, Y. (ed.) ASIACRYPT 2002. LNCS, vol. 2501, pp. 267–287. Springer, Heidelberg (2002)
11. Diem, C.: The XL-Algorithm and a Conjecture from Commutative Algebra. In: Lee, P.J. (ed.) ASIACRYPT 2004. LNCS, vol. 3329, pp. 323–337. Springer, Heidelberg (2004)
12. Ding, J., Gower, J., Schmidt, D.: Multivariate Public-Key Cryptosystems. In: Advances in Information Security. Springer, Heidelberg (2006) ISBN 0-387-32229-9
13. Faugère, J.-C.: A new efficient algorithm for computing Gröbner bases (F_4). J. Pure Appl. Algebra 139(1-3), 61–88 (1999)
14. Faugère, J.-C.: A new efficient algorithm for computing Gröbner bases without reduction to zero (F_5). In: Proceedings of the 2002 International Symposium on Symbolic and Algebraic Computation, pp. 75–83. ACM, New York (2002) (electronic)
15. Gradsteyn, S., Ryzhik, I.M.: Table of Integrals, Series, and Products, 7th edn. Academic Press, San Diego (2007)
16. Hu, Y.-H., Chou, C.-Y., Wang, L.-C., Lai, F.: Cryptanalysis of Variants of UOV. In: Katsikas, S.K., López, J., Backes, M., Gritzalis, S., Preneel, B. (eds.) ISC 2006. LNCS, vol. 4176, pp. 161–170. Springer, Heidelberg (2006)
17. Lidl, R., Niederreiter, H.: Finite Fields. In: Encyclopedia of Mathematics and its applications, p. 20. Cambridge University Press, Cambridge (1997)
18. Moh, T.T.: On The Method of "XL" And Its Inefficiency to TTM, IACR eprint server (2001), `http://eprint.iacr.org/2001/047`
19. Rønjom, S., Raddum, H.: Number of Linearly Independent Equations Generated by XL. In: Golomb, S.W., Parker, M.G., Pott, A., Winterhof, A. (eds.) SETA 2008. LNCS, vol. 5203, pp. 239–251. Springer, Heidelberg (2008)
20. Semaev, I.: On solving sparse algebraic equations over finite fields. Journal of Designs, Codes and Cryptography 49(1-3), 47–60 (2008)
21. Wong, K.K.-H., Colbert, B., Batten, L., Al-Hinai, S.: Algebraic Attacks on Clock-Controlled Cascade Ciphers. In: Barua, R., Lange, T. (eds.) INDOCRYPT 2006. LNCS, vol. 4329, pp. 32–47. Springer, Heidelberg (2006)
22. Yang, B.-Y., Chen, J.-M.: Theoretical Analysis of XL over Small Fields. In: Wang, H., Pieprzyk, J., Varadharajan, V. (eds.) ACISP 2004. LNCS, vol. 3108, pp. 277–288. Springer, Heidelberg (2004)
23. Yang, B.-Y., Chen, J.-M., Courtois, N.: On Asymptotic Security Estimates in XL and Grobner Bases-Related Algebraic Cryptanalysis. In: López, J., Qing, S., Okamoto, E. (eds.) ICICS 2004. LNCS, vol. 3269, pp. 401–413. Springer, Heidelberg (2004)
24. Yang, B.-Y., Chen, J.-M.: All in the XL Family: Theory and Practice. In: Park, C.-s., Chee, S. (eds.) ICISC 2004. LNCS, vol. 3506, pp. 67–86. Springer, Heidelberg (2005)
25. Yang, B.-Y., Chen, C.-H., Bernstein, D.J., Chen, J.-M.: Analysis of QUAD. In: Biryukov, A. (ed.) FSE 2007. LNCS, vol. 4593, pp. 290–308. Springer, Heidelberg (2007)

Mutant Zhuang-Zi Algorithm

Jintai Ding[1,3,⋆] and Dieter S. Schmidt[2]

[1] Department of Mathematical Sciences
[2] Department of Computer Science
University of Cincinnati
Cincinnati, OH 45220, USA
[3] Department of Mathematics
Southern Chinese University of Technology
ding@math.uc.edu, dieter.schmidt@uc.edu

Abstract. In this paper we present a new variant of the Zhuang-Zi algorithm, which solves multivariate polynomial equations over a finite field by converting it into a single variable problem over a large extension field. The improvement is based on the newly developed concept of mutant in solving multivariate equations.

Keywords: multivariate polynomials, Hidden Field Equation, polynomial roots, mutant.

1 Introduction

Solving polynomial equations of single or multiple variables has always been a central problem in mathematics. This comes from our desire to understand what is going on with those equations, but more fundamentally it comes from the ubiquitous roles these simple but fundamental problems play in all branches of science and engineering. Though, Babylonians found the first algebraic solution to a single variable quadratic equation [1] more than 3500 years ago, the progress in this area has been very slow. The next successes came 3000 years later with Ferro solving the single variable cubic equation and Ferrari solving the single variable quartic in the 16th century. Galois' theory put an end to finding algebraic formulas for higher order single variable equations.

The situation is much harder in the multivariate case. The real great success came with the Gröbner basis method [2], inspired by ideas of modern algebraic geometry. Recently, a new area of solving multivariate equations over a finite field has attracted a lot of attention, which is inspired by the appearance of multivariate public key cryptography [3]. Here the public key is a set of quadratic polynomials, and in the so called algebraic cryptanalysis one tries to break this cryptosystem by solving a set of multivariate polynomial equations.

Solving a generic set of nonlinear equations over a finite field is not an easy problem, since we know that solving a set of multivariate polynomial equations

⋆ The first author was supported by grants from NSF, NSF China and the Taft Foundation of the University of Cincinnati.

N. Sendrier (Ed.): PQCrypto 2010, LNCS 6061, pp. 28–40, 2010.

over a finite field is, in general, an NP-complete problem [4]. However, much effort has been devoted to search for new methods for solving multivariate polynomial equations over a finite field, along the line of Gröbner bases. Examples include XL [5], the enhanced Gröbner bases methods F_4 and F_5 of Faugère [6,7], the new mutant XL algorithms [8,9,10,11] and the Zhuang-Zi (ZZ) algorithm [12].

Among these algorithms the ZZ algorithm is totally different, since it converts the problem of solving a set of multivariate polynomial equations into solving a polynomial of a single variable over a large extension field. This can be done since any finite n–dimensional vector space over a finite field can be identified as a large finite field of degree n extension over the original finite field. The ZZ algorithm uses the same method as the XL algorithm, except that we try to produce low degree single variable polynomials. Then we solve the low degree polynomial by the very efficient Berlekamp algorithm.

In order to describe the degeneration of multivariate polynomial systems while they are being solved the concept of mutant was introduced recently. It was very successfully applied to improve the XL algorithms [8,9,10,11]. In this paper we will apply the same idea to the ZZ algorithm to produce a new more efficient version of it, which we call the mutant ZZ algorithm.

2 Background

Let k be a finite field with q elements and suppose we have m polynomials $f_0, f_1, \ldots, f_{m-1} \in k[x_0, x_1, \ldots, x_{n-1}]$. We wish to find all $(a_0, a_1, \ldots, a_{n-1}) \in k^n$, such that

$$\begin{aligned} f_0(a_0, a_1, \ldots, a_{n-1}) &= 0 \\ f_1(a_0, a_1, \ldots, a_{n-1}) &= 0 \\ &\vdots \\ f_{m-1}(a_0, a_1, \ldots, a_{n-1}) &= 0 \end{aligned} \tag{1}$$

We may as well work in the ring

$$k[x_0, x_1, \ldots, x_{n-1}]/(x_0^q - x_0, x_1^q - x_1, \ldots, x_{n-1}^q - x_{n-1}),$$

though for convenience we will abuse notation and write $k[x_0, x_1, \ldots, x_{n-1}]$. The key idea of our new algorithm is to shift perspectives from the space of polynomials $k[x_0, x_1, \ldots, x_{n-1}]$ with coefficients in the small field k, to a space of polynomials $K[X]$ with coefficients in some suitably chosen extension field K.

To simplify matters, let us assume that $m = n$. Choose any irreducible polynomial $g(y) \in k[y]$ of degree n. Then $K = k[y]/(g(y))$ is a degree n field extension of k. Let ϕ be the standard k-linear map that identifies K with the n-dimensional vector space k^n, i.e., $\phi : k^n \longrightarrow K$, defined by

$$\phi(a_0, a_1, \ldots, a_{n-1}) = a_0 + a_1 y + \cdots + a_{n-1} y^{n-1} \tag{2}$$

Let $f : k^n \longrightarrow k^n$ be the polynomial map defined by $f = (f_0, f_1, \ldots, f_{n-1})$. We can lift f up to the extension field K using ϕ to create a map $F : K \longrightarrow K$ defined by

$$F = \phi \circ f \circ \phi^{-1}.$$

Using the Lagrangian interpolation formula, we can think of F as a polynomial in $K[X]$, where X is an intermediate. In fact, F has a unique representation in the quotient space $K[X]/(X^{q^n} - X)$. For any given f, the corresponding F can be calculated by solving a set of linear equations. The following theorem tells us the exact form of this representation.

Theorem 1. *Using the notation as defined above, for a linear polynomial map $f = (f_0, f_1, \ldots, f_{n-1})$ we have*

$$F(X) = \sum_{i=0}^{n-1} \beta_i X^{q^i} + \alpha \mod (X^{q^n} - X),$$

for some $\beta_i, \alpha \in K$. If f is a quadratic polynomial map, then

$$F(X) = \sum_{i=0}^{n-1}\sum_{j=i}^{n-1} \gamma_{ij} X^{q^i+q^j} + \sum_{i=0}^{n-1} \beta_i X^{q^i} + \alpha \mod (X^{q^n} - X),$$

for some $\gamma_{ij}, \beta_i, \alpha \in K$. Representations for higher order polynomial maps are similarly described. In the case of $q = 2$, the formulas are slightly different.

In this paper, we will identify the map F with its corresponding representation given in Theorem 1.

It is now clear that we can move freely between multivariate functions and single variable functions, and we will do so in order to solve the original system of equations. This is the basic idea of Matsumoto-Imai, Patarin, Kipnis and Shamir [13,14,15], and is also the basis of our algorithm. Given a system of equations such as (1), the basic strategy will be to lift the associated polynomial map f to the map F in the extension field K. The roots of the representation of F given in Theorem 1 correspond exactly with the solutions to the original system of equations defined over k. Once we have the roots in K, we can descend down to k^n with ϕ^{-1}. It remains to develop techniques for reducing the degree of F, which, if successful, will allow us to use efficient algorithms for solving single variable polynomial equations.

We note a fundamental difference between the ZZ algorithm and others is that the ZZ algorithm can be used only with finite fields and cannot be used with fields of characteristic zero, since the lifting from the multivariate system to a single variable equation works only for a finite field. However, in the case of finite fields, the ZZ algorithm unifies the two problems of solving single variable and multivariate polynomial equations into a single problem. This algorithm is named after Zhuang-Zi, an ancient Chinese philosopher who we believe was one of the first to propose the idea of shifting from a local view of problems to a global view in terms of our mathematical interpretation.

The remainder of this paper is organized as follows. We will explain the basic ZZ algorithm and then our mutant ZZ algorithm. Again, we will present a toy example in order to show how the algorithm works. We then present more meaningful examples and conclude with a discussion of future work.

3 The Zhuang-Zi Algorithm

We will start with the standard case of $m = n$, where we have the same number of variables and equations. The Zhuang-Zi algorithm takes the polynomials $f_0, f_1, \ldots, f_{n-1} \in k[x_0, x_1, \ldots, x_{n-1}]$ and a positive integer D as its input, where D is the upper bound on the degree of a polynomial equation which can be solved efficiently. When successful the algorithm returns all n-tuples $(a_0, a_1, \ldots, a_{n-1}) \in k^n$ such that $f_i(a_0, a_1, \ldots, a_{n-1}) = 0$, for $i = 0, 1, \ldots, n-1$.

- **Step 1:** Choose any degree n irreducible polynomial $g(y) \in k[y]$ and define $K = k[y]/(g(y))$. Let $\phi : k^n \longrightarrow K$ be as defined in (2). Lift the given $f = (f_0, f_1, \ldots, f_{n-1})$ to K by $F = \phi \circ f \circ \phi^{-1}$, and compute the polynomial representation of $F(X)$ modulo $X^{q^n} - X$. If $\deg(F(X)) \leq D$, then go to the last step; otherwise continue to the next step.

- **Step 2:** Let $G = \mathrm{Gal}(K/k)$ be the Galois group of K over k consisting of the Frobenius maps $G_i(X) = X^{q^i}$, for $i = 0, 1, \ldots, n-1$. Calculate

$$F_i(X) = G_i \circ F(X) = F(X)^{q^i} \mod (X^{q^n} - X),$$

  for $i = 0, 1, \ldots, n-1$. Note that $F_0(X) = F(X)$.
- **Step 3:** Let N be the total number of monomials that appear in any $F_i(X)$. For each $F_i(X)$ create a row vector in K^N, where the entries are the coefficients of $F_i(X)$ listed in decreasing order, and construct an $n \times N$ matrix using these row vectors. Then use Gaussian elimination to produce a new set of t basis polynomials $S = \{S_0(X), S_1(X), \ldots, S_{t-1}(X)\}$. In other words eliminate the monomials in the order of the highest degree first. Label the elements of S so that $S_{t-1}(X)$ is the element of lowest degree. If $\deg(S_{t-1}(X)) \leq D$, then go to the last step; otherwise continue to the next step.

- **Step 4:** For each $i = 0, 1, \ldots, t-1$ and $j = 0, 1, \ldots, n-1$ compute

$$X^{q^j} S_i(X) \mod (X^{q^n} - X).$$

  Amend these polynomials to S. As before, apply Gaussian elimination to the matrix associated with this set of polynomials to produce a set S' of new basis polynomials. Let $S'_{t'-1}(X)$ be the polynomial in S' of minimal degree. If $\deg(S'_{t'-1}(X)) \leq D$, then go to the last step; otherwise replace S with S' and repeat this step.

- **Step 5:** At this point we have a polynomial $\Gamma(x)$ with $\deg(\Gamma(x)) \leq D$. Find the roots of $\Gamma(x) = 0$ with a suitable method to obtain a set $V = \{\alpha \in K \mid \Gamma(\alpha) = 0\}$. The solutions of $F(X) = 0$ will be the subset $\{\alpha \in V \mid F(\alpha) = 0\}$.

Since the complexity of any polynomial root finding method depends on the degree of the given polynomial and the size of the field, so too does the complexity of the Zhuang-Zi algorithm. Improvements in the area of polynomial root finding methods will translate directly into an improvement for the Zhuang-Zi algorithm. Efficient methods for finding the roots of a polynomial in a finite field exist and they are described for example in [16,17,18].

Remark 1. The Zhuang-Zi algorithm works also when $m \neq n$. In this case one has to use the maximum of m and n. When $m < n$, there are fewer equations than variables and one simply introduces $n - m$ polynomials identical to 0. If there are more equations than variables ($m > n$) then one can simply introduce $m - n$ fictitious variables $x_n, \ldots, x_{m-1}$.

4 The Mutant Zhuang-Zi Algorithm

Definition 1. *Let X^d with $0 \leq d < q^n$ be the standard basis for the function ring $K[X] \mod (X^{q^n} - X)$. For each monomial X^d define a q-weight as the sum of the coefficients in the q-expansion of the integer d.*

The weight of any polynomial in the ring $K[X] \mod (X^{q^n} - X)$ is the maximal weight of its monomials.

For example, if $q = 3$, the 3-weight of X^{16} is $1 + 2 + 1 = 4$, since

$$16 = 3^2 + 2 \times 3^1 + 1,$$

and the 3-weight of the polynomial $X^{27} + X^{18} + X^{16} + X^{15} + X + 1$ is also 4, since the 3-weight of X^{16} is larger then those of the others. When viewed together with the Frobenius map the weight represents the degree of the original polynomials.

Two procedures for reducing a set of polynomials in X is used several times in the algorithm so that they are defined here in advance:

Definition 2 (Reduce-by-degree(S)). *Let $S=\{S_0(X), S_1(X), \ldots, S_{n-1}(X)\}$ be a set of polynomials in X. Let N be the total number of monomials that appear in any element in S. For each element in S, create a row vector in K^N, where the entries are the coefficients of each element listed in decreasing order, and construct an $n \times N$ matrix using these row vectors. Then use Gaussian elimination to produce a new set of t basis polynomials to replace S: $S = \{S_0(X), S_1(X), \ldots, S_{t-1}(X)\}$. In other words eliminate the monomials in the order of the highest degree first. Label the elements of S so that $S_{t-1}(X)$ is the element of lowest degree on return from the procedure.*

Definition 3 (Reduce-by-weight(S)). *Let $S'=\{S'_0(X), S'_1(X), \ldots, S'_{n-1}(X)\}$ be a set of polynomials in X. Again, let N be the total number of monomials that appear in S'. For each element in S', create a row vector in K^N, where the entries are the coefficients of the elements listed in decreasing order according to the weight (if the same weight, then by the degree), and construct an $n \times N$ matrix using these row vectors. Then use Gaussian elimination to produce and return a new set of t basis polynomials $S' = \{S'_0(X), S'_1(X), \ldots, S'_{t-1}(X)\}$. In other words eliminate the monomials in the order of the weight of the degree first, then the degree.*

We now present the mutant ZZ algorithm. Here we will assume $m = n$ but the polynomials in the set $f = (f_0, f_1, \ldots, f_{n-1})$ can have different degrees. We first select a degree D, such that we can solve a degree D polynomial over a finite field of size q^n efficiently.

- **Step 1:** Choose any degree n irreducible polynomial $g(y) \in k[y]$ and define $K = k[y]/(g(y))$. Let $\phi : k^n \longrightarrow K$ be as defined in (2). Define $f = (f_0, f_1, \ldots, f_{n-1})$, lift this to K by $F = \phi \circ f \circ \phi^{-1}$, and compute the polynomial representation of $F(X)$ modulo $X^{q^n} - X$. If $\deg(F(X)) \leq D$, then go to the last step; otherwise continue to the next step.
- **Step 2:** Let $G = \mathrm{Gal}(K/k)$ be the Galois group of K over k consisting of the Frobenius maps $G_i(X) = X^{q^i}$, for $i = 0, 1, \ldots, n-1$. Calculate

$$F_i(X) = G_i \circ F(X) = F(X)^{q^i} \mod (X^{q^n} - X),$$

 for $i = 0, 1, \ldots, n-1$. Note that $F_0(X) = F(X)$.
 Create two sets of polynomials S and S', and both of them consist of $\{F_0, F_1, \ldots, F_{n-1}\}$ at the moment.
- **Step 3:** Reduce-by-degree(S). If $\deg(S_{t-1}(X)) \leq D$ then go to the last step.
- **Step 4:** Reduce-by-weight(S'). Create a new set R by copying the polynomials in S'. To each polynomial in R assign the index pair $(w_i, 0)$, where w_i is the weight of the polynomial, and the second value will be referred as the multiplication index, denoted by n_i. The set R will be called the root polynomials.
 Create a new set of monomials, which consists of the leading terms of S', and call this set LT. Let W be the weight of the polynomial in R with lowest weight plus 1.
- **Step 5:** Multiply the polynomials R_i of lowest weight by X^{q^j} and amend these polynomials to S' and to S. Change the index of these polynomials in R to $(w_i, 1)$.
- **Step 6:** Reduce-by-degree(S). If $\deg(S_{t-1}(X)) \leq D$ then go to the last step.
- **Step 7:** Reduce-by-weight(S'). Create a new set of monomials, which consists of all leading terms of S', and call this set $\bar{LT}$.
 If the number of monomial whose weight is lower than W are the same in both LT and $\bar{LT}$, replace LT by $\bar{LT}$ and go to **Step 8**.
 If the number of monomials whose weight is lower than W is different in LT and in $\bar{LT}$, pick the polynomials in S' whose leading terms are the ones with weight lower than W and whose leading terms do not belong to LT. Amend these polynomials to the set R with index (weight of this polynomial, 0).

Then replace LT by $\bar{LT}$, and set W to be the lowest weight of all mutants. The newly amended polynomials in R are the mutants.

– **Step 8:** Set $W = W + 1$. For each root polynomial R_i in R if $w_i + n_i < W$, compute

$$X^d R_i(X) \mod (X^{q^n} - X),$$

where the weight of X^d + w_i=W and amend this polynomial to S and S'. Also increase the multiplication index n_i belonging to R_i by 1. Then go to **Step 6**.

– **Step 9:** At this point there exists a polynomial $\Gamma(x)$ with $\deg(\Gamma(x)) \leq D$. Find the roots of $\Gamma(x) = 0$ with a suitable method to obtain a set $V = \{\alpha \in K \mid \Gamma(\alpha) = 0\}$. The solutions of $F(X) = 0$ will be the subset $\{\alpha \in V \mid F(\alpha) = 0\}$.

5 Examples

We present an illustrative and a toy example to see how the mutant Zhuang-Zi algorithm works in practice. We then present two non-trivial examples where Zhuang-Zi succeeds and Gröbner bases fail.

5.1 An Illustrative Example

Let K be the degree 7 extension of $GF(2)$ given by the irreducible polynomial $y^7 + y + 1$. For the final degree require $D = 1$. Use

$$\begin{aligned}
F(X) &= X^5 + 1 = F_0\\
F^2(X) &= X^{10} + 1 = F_1\\
F^4(X) &= X^{20} + 1 = F_2\\
F^8(X) &= X^{40} + 1 = F_3\\
F^{16}(X) &= X^{80} + 1 = F_4\\
F^{32}(X) &= X^{33} + 1 = F_5\\
F^{64}(X) &= X^{66} + 1 = F_6.
\end{aligned}$$

For this case, the Gaussian elimination is done already and $W = 2$. This set also becomes the root polynomials, each with index pair $(2, 0)$. In Step 5 we add the following new polynomials of weight 3.

$$\begin{aligned}
(X^5 + 1)X &= X^6 + X;\\
(X^5 + 1)X^2 &= X^7 + X^2;\\
(X^5 + 1)X^4 &= X^9 + X^4;\\
(X^5 + 1)X^8 &= X^{13} + X^8;\\
(X^5 + 1)X^{16} &= X^{21} + X^{16};\\
(X^5 + 1)X^{32} &= X^{37} + X^{32};\\
(X^5 + 1)X^{64} &= X^{69} + X^{64}.
\end{aligned}$$

$$
\begin{aligned}
(X^{10}+1)X &= X^{11}+X;\\
(X^{10}+1)X^{2} &= X^{12}+X^{2};\\
(X^{10}+1)X^{4} &= X^{14}+X^{4};\\
(X^{10}+1)X^{8} &= X^{18}+X^{8};\\
(X^{10}+1)X^{16} &= X^{26}+X^{16};\\
(X^{10}+1)X^{32} &= X^{42}+X^{32};\\
(X^{10}+1)X^{64} &= X^{74}+X^{64}.
\end{aligned}
$$

$$
\begin{aligned}
(X^{20}+1)X &= X^{21}+X;\\
(X^{20}+1)X^{2} &= X^{22}+X^{2};\\
(X^{20}+1)X^{4} &= X^{24}+X^{4};\\
(X^{20}+1)X^{8} &= X^{28}+X^{8};\\
(X^{20}+1)X^{16} &= X^{36}+X^{16};\\
(X^{20}+1)X^{32} &= X^{52}+X^{32};\\
(X^{20}+1)X^{64} &= X^{84}+X^{64}.
\end{aligned}
$$

$$
\begin{aligned}
(X^{40}+1)X &= X^{41}+X;\\
(X^{40}+1)X^{2} &= X^{42}+X^{2};\\
(X^{40}+1)X^{4} &= X^{44}+X^{4};\\
(X^{40}+1)X^{8} &= X^{48}+X^{8};\\
(X^{40}+1)X^{16} &= X^{56}+X^{16};\\
(X^{40}+1)X^{32} &= X^{72}+X^{32};\\
(X^{40}+1)X^{64} &= X^{104}+X^{64}.
\end{aligned}
$$

$$
\begin{aligned}
(X^{80}+1)X &= X^{81}+X;\\
(X^{80}+1)X^{2} &= X^{82}+X^{2};\\
(X^{80}+1)X^{4} &= X^{84}+X^{4};\\
(X^{80}+1)X^{8} &= X^{88}+X^{8};\\
(X^{80}+1)X^{16} &= X^{96}+X^{16};\\
(X^{80}+1)X^{32} &= X^{112}+X^{32};\\
(X^{80}+1)X^{64} &= X^{17}+X^{64}.
\end{aligned}
$$

$$
\begin{aligned}
(X^{33}+1)X &= X^{34}+X;\\
(X^{33}+1)X^{2} &= X^{35}+X^{2};\\
(X^{33}+1)X^{4} &= X^{37}+X^{4};\\
(X^{33}+1)X^{8} &= X^{41}+X^{8};\\
(X^{33}+1)X^{16} &= X^{49}+X^{16};\\
(X^{33}+1)X^{32} &= X^{65}+X^{32};\\
(X^{33}+1)X^{64} &= X^{97}+X^{64}.
\end{aligned}
$$

$$
\begin{aligned}
(X^{66}+1)X &= X^{67}+X;\\
(X^{66}+1)X^{2} &= X^{68}+X^{2};\\
(X^{66}+1)X^{4} &= X^{70}+X^{4};\\
(X^{66}+1)X^{8} &= X^{74}+X^{8};\\
(X^{66}+1)X^{16} &= X^{82}+X^{16};\\
(X^{66}+1)X^{32} &= X^{98}+X^{32};\\
(X^{66}+1)X^{64} &= X^{3}+X^{64}.
\end{aligned}
$$

At the beginning of step 7 the root polynomials R with their indices are

$$R = \{ X^{80}+1,\ (2,1);\quad X^{66}+1,\ (2,1);\quad X^{40}+1,\ (2,1);\quad X^{20}+1,\ (2,1);\\ X^{33}+1,\ (2,1);\quad X^{10}+1,\ (2,1);\quad X^{5}+1,\ (2,1)\ \}.$$

After Reduce-by-weight(S') the following polynomials with their indices have to be added to R

$$\begin{array}{llll} \{X^{96}+X,\ (2,0); & X^{72}+X,\ (2,0); & X^{68}+X,\ (2,0); & X^{48}+X,\ (2,0); \\ X^{36}+X,\ (2,0); & X^{34}+X,\ (2,0); & X^{24}+X,\ (2,0); & X^{18}+X,\ (2,0); \\ X^{17}+X,\ (2,0); & X^{12}+X,\ (2,0); & X^{9}+X,\ (2,0); & X^{6}+X,\ (2,0); \\ X^{3}+X,\ (2,0); & X^{64}+X,\ (1,0); & X^{32}+X,\ (1,0); & X^{16}+X,\ (1,0); \\ X^{8}+X,\ (1,0); & X^{4}+X,\ (1,0); & X^{2}+X,\ (1,0)\} & \end{array}$$

There are six mutants of weight 1. In step 8 we have $W = 2$ and these six mutants are added to S and S' after multiplying each with X, X^2, X^4, X^8, X^{16}, X^{32}, and X^{64}. When we reduce the new system S' we find $X + 1$ and with it the solution to the system.

In the original ZZ, we would have expanded to weight 4 polynomials and solved the system. But here we went only to weight 3 due to the mutant of weight 1. The example as given could have been solved more easily by other methods, but the details were given in order to illustrate how the mutant ZZ algorithm works.

5.2 A Toy Example

In order to show how the algorithm works in a bigger example we use three quadratic equations in three variables with coefficients in the field $k = GF(3)$. We define the polynomial map $f : k^3 \longrightarrow k^3$ by its components

$$\begin{aligned} f_1(x_1,x_2,x_3) &= 2x_1x_2 + x_1 + x_2^2 + 2x_2 + 2x_3 + 1 \\ f_2(x_1,x_2,x_3) &= x_1^2 + x_1x_2 + 2x_2^2 + x_3 \\ f_3(x_1,x_2,x_3) &= x_1^2 + x_1x_2 + 2x_1 + 2x_2^2 + x_3 + 1 \end{aligned}$$

in $k[x_1, x_2, x_3]$.
One irreducible polynomial of degree two with coefficients in k is

$$g(y) = y^3 + 2y + 1.$$

The mapping $\phi : k^3 \longrightarrow K$ is defined by

$$\phi(x_1,x_2,x_3) = x_1 + x_2y + x_3y^2 = X,$$

while $\phi^{-1} : K \longrightarrow k^3$ is defined by (using matrix notation)

$$\phi^{-1}(X): \quad \begin{pmatrix} x_1 \\ x_2 \\ x_3 \end{pmatrix} = \begin{pmatrix} 2y^2+1 & 2y^2+2y & 2y^2+y \\ 2y & 2y+1 & 2y+2 \\ 2 & 2 & 2 \end{pmatrix} \begin{pmatrix} X \\ X^3 \\ X^9 \end{pmatrix}$$

With this notation, the polynomial map $F = \phi \circ f \circ \phi^{-1}$ is given by

$$\begin{aligned}F(X) = &(2y^2 + y)X^{12} + (2y^2 + 2)X^{10} + (2y^2 + 2y)X^9 \\ &+(y^2 + 1)X^6 + (y^2 + y + 2)X^4 + (2y^2 + 2y + 2)X^3 \\ &+(y^2 + 2y + 1)X^2 + (y^2 + 2y + 2)X + y^2 + 1\end{aligned}$$

Since this is a trivial example, we could factor $F(X)$ directly and obtain

$$\begin{aligned}F(X) = &(X + y^2 + 2) \\ &(X^{11} + (2y^2 + 1)X^{10} + (y^2 + 1)X^9 + (2y + 2)X^8 + (y^2 + 1)X^7 \\ &+(2y^2 + y + 1)X^6 + (y + 2)X^5 + y^2X^4 + (2y^2 + 2y + 1)X^3 \\ &+2yX^2 + (y + 2)X + y^2 + 2y + 1)\end{aligned}$$

from which we can see that $X = 2y^2 + 1$ is the only solution of the equation $F(X) = 0$ in K and with it $x_1 = 1$, $x_2 = 0$ and $x_3 = 2$.

If we set $D = 1$ we want to find the solution directly in the form of a linear function in X. In the original ZZ algorithm, we need to run the algorithm to the extent such that it will generate a space of full span, namely a space of dimension 26 after Gaussian elimination.

If we run the new mutant in ZZ algorithm, we can solve the equation with a space of dimension only 8. The reason for this is that we do linear combinations of the three quadratic equations, and we actually can find a linear equation inside. This means that the set of equations F_0, F_1 and F_2 will produce an equation of the form

$$X^9 + (y^2 + y + 1)X^3 + (2y^2 + 2)X + 2y + 2 = 0,$$

which can be viewed as a mutant. With the help of this mutant, we can solve the set of equations using only 8 equations such that each equation has only 9 monomial at most. This is great improvement in efficiency compared to the original ZZ algorithm.

Someone may say that we are cheating here since we implicitly have a linear equation inside the set of equations. This is true to certain extent, but the point of this example is to illustrate the advantage of the new mutant ZZ algorithm compared to the original ZZ. In larger examples it is more difficult to demonstrate the concept of a mutant when looking at a larger set of equations.

5.3 Non-trivial Examples

The main application of the ZZ algorithms is to the nonlinear multivariate problem where Gröbner bases methods do not succeed. The Zhuang-Zi algorithm requires that we work in a finite field, whereas Göbner bases do not.

When a Gröbner basis is computed in a finite field, it is accomplished usually by augmenting the original set of equations with those defining the finite field. Examples were constructed in [12], where a set of equations can be solved easily by the Zhuang-Zi algorithm, but only with great difficulties via Gröbner bases.

The basic idea of the construction is to select a function $F(X) : K \longrightarrow K$ of low enough degree, so that it can be factored easily, while the corresponding mapping $f : k^n \longrightarrow k^n$ must be complicated, and therefore difficult to solve.

One such that example is the following case: Let $k = GF(2^3)$ and let $K = k[y]/(g(y))$ be a degree n extension of k, for some irreducible $g(y) \in k[y]$. We use a polynomial of low degree in $K[X]$:

$$F(X) = X^{72} + a_1X^{65} + a_2X^{64} + a_3X^{16} + a_4X^9 + a_5X^8 + a_6X^2 + a_7X + a_8, \quad (3)$$

where the coefficients a_j, for $j = 1, \ldots, 8$, are chosen at random from k, treated as a subfield of K via the standard embedding. With $q = 8$, all powers of X in (3) can be written in the form $X^{8^i+8^j}$ or X^{8^i}, and so it is clear that (3) $f = \phi^{-1} \circ F \circ \phi$ is a quadratic polynomial map from k^n to k^n. As in the previous example, it is helpful to write $\phi^{-1} : K \longrightarrow k^n$ using matrix notation

$$\mathsf{A}\mathsf{X} = \mathsf{x},$$

where $\mathsf{X} = (X^{8^0}, X^{8^1}, \ldots, X^{8^{n-1}})^T$, $\mathsf{x} = (x_0, x_1, \ldots, x_{n-1})^T$, and A is an $n \times n$ matrix with entries from K that can easily be found by writing each X^{8^i} as a polynomial in y with coefficients in $k[x_0, x_1, \ldots, x_{n-1}]$.

The polynomial (3) can be factored easily by a computer algebra system like Magma [19], depending on the coefficients $a_1, \ldots, a_8$ of F, and on the value of n. Finding the corresponding solutions directly with the help of a good Gröbner bases program such as Faugère's F_4 version in Magma [6] requires exponential time with increasing n. However this example does not at all demonstrate the advantage of the new improvement since no computation in adding new polynomials is needed.

In [12] another non-trivial example is presented, where $F(X)$ is of a very high degree and therefore cannot be solved with the simplest form of the Zhuang-Zi algorithm. The example is as follows:

Let $q = 4$, $k = GF(q)$. The multiplicative group for the nonzero elements of this field can be generated by the field element a which satisfies $a^2 + a + 1 = 0$. Take $g(y) \in k[y]$ to be the irreducible polynomial

$$g(y) = y^{12} + y^{11} + ay^{10} + ay^9 + y^8 + y^7 + y^5 + a^2y^4 + ay^3 + a^2y^2 + ay + a,$$

and define $K = k[y]/(g(y))$, a degree $n = 12$ extension of k.

Let $F(X) \in K[X]$ be the polynomial

$$\begin{aligned} F(X) =& a^2X^{17664} + X^{5440} + aX^{5376} + X^{4416} + aX^{4096} + aX^{1360} \\ &+ X^{1344} + X^{1280} + a^2X^{1024} + a^2X^{336} + aX^{320} + a^2X^{276} \\ &+ X^{85} + aX^{84} + aX^{64} + aX^{21} + X^{20} + a \end{aligned}$$

Here each exponent of X in $F(X)$ is a sum of powers of four. The exponent with the most powers of four is $5440 = 4^3 + 4^4 + 4^5 + 4^6$. Therefore, the components of $f = \phi^{-1} \circ F \circ \phi$ will be of degree four.

The degree of F prevents us from finding the roots of $F(X) = 0$ directly. Also, the F_4 implementation in Magma failed to find a Gröbner basis for $f_0, f_1, \ldots, f_{n-1}$ due to the fact that memory requirements exceeded the available resources on our PC. The Zhuang-Zi algorithm found the polynomial

$$\Gamma(X) = X^{276} + aX^{85} + a^2X^{84} + a^2X^{64} + a^2X^{21} + aX^{20} + a$$

and with it the solutions $\{1, a\}$ of $F(X) = 0$.

6 Discussion and Conclusion

The ZZ algorithm is not just a new algorithm, but a new way to look at the problem of solving a set of multivariate polynomial equations over a finite field. The ZZ algorithm intends to unify the cases of solving multivariate equations with the cases of solving single variable equations.

In this paper we presented an improvement to the original ZZ algorithm inspired by the idea of mutant, which was discovered recently. Our experiments show that there are cases where the mutant Zhuang-Zi algorithm will work much more efficiently than the old one and in a some cases it can beat other algorithms including the Gröbner bases algorithms like F_4.

Currently there are many directions for further research. One particular interesting direction is to understand when the ZZ algorithm has an advantage over other methods. We believe that the ZZ algorithm is well suited for an attack on MPKCs and it should shed new lights on understanding the security of systems like HFE. We intend to explore this in a subsequent paper, where we can further demonstrate the advantage of the new mutant ZZ algorithm over the ZZ algorithm. We have some small scale examples to show this point, but there is still considerable room to improve and optimize the implementation of the algorithm.

References

1. Smith, D.E.: History of Mathematics, vol. 1, 2. Dover, New York (1951-1952)
2. Buchberger, B.: Ein Algorithmus zum Auffinden der Basiselemente des Restklassenrings nach einem nulldimensionalen Polynomideal. Universität Innsbruck (1965)
3. Ding, J., Gower, J., Schmidt, D.: Multivariate Public Key Cryptography. In: Advances in Information Security. Springer, Heidelberg (2006)
4. Garey, M.R., Johnson, D.S.: Computers and intractability. In: A Guide to the theory of NP-completeness. W.H. Freeman, New York (1979)
5. Courtois, N., Klimov, A., Patarin, J., Shamir, A.: Efficient algorithms for solving overdefined systems of multivariate polynomial equations. In: Preneel, B. (ed.) EUROCRYPT 2000. LNCS, vol. 1807, pp. 392–407. Springer, Heidelberg (2000)
6. Faugère, J.C.: A new efficient algorithm for computing Gröbner bases (F_4). Journal of Pure and Applied Algebra 139, 61–88 (1999)

7. Faugère, J.C.: A new efficient algorithm for computing Gröbner bases without reduction to zero (F_5). In: International Symposium on Symbolic and Algebraic Computation — ISSAC 2002, July 2002, pp. 75–83. ACM Press, New York (2002)
8. Ding, J.: Mutants and its impact on polynomial solving strategies and algorithms. In: Privately distributed research note, University of Cincinnati and Technical University of Darmstadt, 2006 (2006)
9. Ding, J., Carbarcas, D., Schmidt, D., Buchmann, J., Mohamed, M.S.E., Mohamed, W.S.A.E., Tohaneanu, S., Weinmann, R.P.: Mutant XL. In: SCC 2008 (2008)
10. Mohamed, M.S.E., Mohamed, W.S.A.E., Ding, J., Buchmann, J.: MXL2: Solving Polynomial Equations over GF(2) Using an Improved Mutant Strategy. In: Buchmann, J., Ding, J. (eds.) PQCrypto 2008. LNCS, vol. 5299, pp. 203–215. Springer, Heidelberg (2008)
11. Mohamed, M.S.E., Cabarcas, D., Ding, J., Buchmann, J., Bulygin, S.: MXL_3: An efficient algorithm for computing Gröbner bases of zero-dimensional ideals. In: The 12th International Conference on Information Security and Cryptology (ICISC 2009), Seoul, Korea, December 2009. LNCS, Springer, Heidelberg (2009)
12. Ding, J., Gower, J.E., Schmidt, D.: Zhuang-Zi: A new algorithm for solving multivariate polynomial equations over a finite field. In: PQCrypto 2006: International Workshop on Post-Quantum Cryptography, May 23-26. Katholieke Universiteit Leuven, Belgium (2006)
13. Matsumoto, T., Imai, H.: Public quadratic polynomial-tuples for efficient signature verification and message encryption. In: Günther, C.G. (ed.) EUROCRYPT 1988. LNCS, vol. 330, pp. 419–453. Springer, Heidelberg (1988)
14. Patarin, J.: Cryptanalysis of the Matsumoto and Imai public key scheme of Eurocrypt'88. Designs, Codes and Cryptography 20, 175–209 (2000)
15. Kipnis, A., Shamir, A.: Cryptanalysis of the HFE public key cryptosystem by relinearization. In: Wiener, M. (ed.) CRYPTO 1999. LNCS, vol. 1666, pp. 19–30. Springer, Heidelberg (1999)
16. Geddes, K.O., Czapor, S.R., Labahn, G.: Algorithms for Computer Algebra. Kluwer, Amsterdam (1992)
17. Lidl, R., Niederreiter, H.: Finite Fields, 2nd edn. Encyclopedia of Mathematics and its Application, vol. 20. Cambridge University Press, Cambridge (2003)
18. von zur Gathen, J., Gerhard, J.: Modern Computer Algebra, 2nd edn. Cambridge University Press, Cambridge (2003)
19. Computational Algebra Group, University of Sydney: The MAGMA computational algebra system for algebra, number theory and geometry (2005), `http://magma.maths.usyd.edu.au/magma/`

Cryptanalysis of Two Quartic Encryption Schemes and One Improved MFE Scheme

Weiwei Cao[1], Xiuyun Nie[3], Lei Hu[1], Xiling Tang[4], and Jintai Ding[2,4]

[1] State Key Laboratory of Information Security, Graduate University of Chinese Academy of Sciences, Beijing 100049, China
[2] Department of Mathematical Sciences, University of Cincinnati, OH 45221, USA
[3] School of Computer Science and Engineering, University of Electronic Science and Technology of China, Chengdu 610054, China
[4] South China University of Technology, Guangzhou 510640, China
wwcao@is.ac.cn, jintai.ding@uc.edu, hu@is.ac.cn, xynie@uestc.edu.cn

Abstract. MFE, a multivariate public key encryption scheme proposed by Wang et al in CT-RSA 2006, was conquered by second order linearization equation (SOLE) attack by Ding et al in PKC 2007. To resist this attack, many improved schemes were proposed. Wang et al in [WFW09] and Wang in [Wan07] both modified MFE and raised the public key from quadratic to quartic equations. We call the two quartic schemes Quartic-1 and Quartic-2 respectively for convenience. They are indeed immune to the SOLE attack. However, we find that there exist many quadratization equations (QEs), which are quadratic in plaintext variables and linear in ciphertext variables and can be derived from the public keys of Quartic-1 and Quartic-2. In this paper, we utilize QEs to recover the corresponding plaintext for a given ciphertext. For Quartic-1, we firstly find there are at least $2r$ SOLEs, which was regarded as impossible by the original authors, furthermore, we can find at least $35r$ QEs with a complexity $\mathcal{O}((90r^2(15r+1)+180r^2+15r(15r+1)/2+27r+1)^w)$, where r is a small number denoting the degree of extension of finite fields and $w \approx 2.732$. The computational complexity of deriving these equations is about 2^{37}. But to find the original plaintext, there still needs 2^{40} times Gröbner basis computations, which needs practically 1.328 seconds each time. For Quartic-2, we make a theoretical analysis and find $18r$ QEs with a computational complexity $\mathcal{O}((15r+1)6r(12r+1)+180r^2+27r+1)^w$. The complexity is 2^{36} for the parameter proposed in [Wan07], and we can break the scheme practically in 3110.734 seconds. Finally, we show that another improved version of MFE in [WZY07] is insecure against the linearization equation attack although its authors claimed it is secure against high order linearization equation attack. Our attack on the two quartic schemes illustrates that non-linearization equations like quadratization equations which are not degree one in plaintext variables can also be used efficiently to analyze multivariate cryptosystems.

Keywords: multivariate public key encryption, quartic polynomial, quadratic polynomial, linearization attack, quadratization attack.

N. Sendrier (Ed.): PQCrypto 2010, LNCS 6061, pp. 41–60, 2010.

1 Introduction

Public key cryptography (PKC) has opened a new era of cryptography since Diffie and Hellman delivered a new idea in their seminal paper in 1976 [DH76]. The classical trapdoors of PKC are based on the difficulty of integer factorization for RSA and discrete logarithm for ElGamal and ECC. However, with the arrival of quantum computer epoch, cryptosystems based on integer factorization and discrete logarithm will be cracked by quantum computer attack [Sho97]. Therefore, multivariate public key cryptosystem (MPKC), one new public key cryptography, attracts more attention and becomes a hot topic in the last years.

The multivariate public key encryption scheme MFE is proposed by Wang et al in CT-RSA 2006 in [WYH06]. It was designed to be resist against the Patarin attack [Pat95] that utilizes the so-called first order linearization equations (FOLEs) of the form

$$\sum_{i,j} a_{ij}u_iv_j + \sum_i b_iu_i + \sum_j c_jv_j + d = 0,$$

but was conquered by Ding et al in 2007 PKC in [DHN07] by using second order linearization equations (SOLEs), which have a form like

$$\sum_{i,j,k} a_{ijk}u_iv_jv_k + \sum_{i,j} b_{ij}u_iv_j + \sum_{j,k} c_{jk}v_jv_k + \sum_i d_iu_i + \sum_j e_jv_j + f = 0.$$

Here these SOLEs are satisfied by all plaintext variables u_i and their corresponding ciphertext variables v_i and they are derived from the polynomials of the public key. For both first and second order linearization equations, the degrees of plaintext variables are one, and therefore, once the ciphertext variables v_j are evaluated, some plaintext variables can be linearly expressed by the rest plaintext variables, which implies that the range of possible plaintexts is minimized and the number of plaintext variables in public key equations can be reduced. If from the reduced public key equations first or second order linearization equations can be still derived, then the number of plaintext variables can be again reduced. If this number is small enough, we can directly solve out the plaintext variables from the reduced public key equations by XL or Gröbner basis algorithms [Fag99]. With the help of SOLEs, the authors of [DHN07] successfully broke the two instances proposed in [WYH06].

To resist the SOLE attack, Wang et al in [WFW09] and Wang in [Wan07] both modified MFE and raised the public key from quadratic to quartic equations. The increase of degree enlarges the scale of the public key exponentially by the degree of extension of fields r. To bound the length, r has to be very small, like 2 or 3. We call the above two improvements as Quartic-1 and Quartic-2 respectively for convenience. It is indeed the case that the SOLE attack is not practical on them, however, from their quartic public key equations, we can find equations of the form

$$\sum_{i,j,k} a_{ijk}u_iu_jv_k + \sum_{i,j} b_{ij}u_iu_j + \sum_{i,k} c_{ik}u_iv_k + \sum_i d_iu_i + \sum_k e_kv_k + f = 0.$$

We call them as Quadratization Equations (QEs). They are quadratic in plaintext variables and linear in ciphertext variables, hence QEs are still quadratic equations if ciphertext variables are evaluated. QEs can be regarded as a dual of SOLEs in the sense that switching the plaintext and ciphertext variables, QEs are turned into SOLEs. However, QEs can not be used to linearly eliminate plaintext variables, but for our cryptanalysis here, the parameter r in Quartic-1 and Quartic-2 is smaller than that in the original MFE, this means the complexity of searching QEs for Quartic-1 and Quartic-2 is much smaller than that of searching SOLEs for the original MFE.

The main aim of this paper is to illustrate that quadratization equations are helpful for reducing the range of possible plaintexts and can be used to efficiently attack Quartic-1 and Quartic-2. The paper also contains a work of cracking down another improved version of MFE by Wang et al [WZY07]. The improvement maintains public key equations as quadratic and introduces a new operator on matrices in its design for the goal of resisting against high order linearization equation attack. We show that the scheme can be even broken by the first order linearization equation attack.

The paper is organized as follows. In Section 2, we review the original MFE encryption scheme where the notations employed are also used to describe the three improved versions that are analyzed in this paper. In Sections 3 and 4 we present the quadratization equation attack on Quartic-1 and Quartic-2 respectively. Next in Section 5 we give the first order linearization equation attack on the improved MFE scheme of [WZY07]. The last section is the conclusion.

2 MFE Public Key Cryptosystem

2.1 MFE

Let K be a finite field, generally $\mathbb{F}_{2^{16}}$. Let $\mathbb{L}$ be its degree r extension field; $\mathbb{L}$ is considered the "Medium Field", generally $r = 4$ or 5. Its encryption transformation is a composition of three maps L_1, ϕ, and L_2, where $L_1 : K^{12r} \to K^{12r}$ and $L_2 : K^{15r} \to K^{15r}$ are two invertible affine maps and kept as a private key, and the so-called central map $\phi : K^{12r} \to K^{15r}$ is constructed by composing of $15r$ quadratic polynomials in $12r$ variables. The composition map $E = L_2 \circ \phi \circ L_1$ is used as a public key, and it is an ordered set of $15r$ quadratic polynomials in $12r$ variables.

The central map ϕ is publicly known and is constructed as follows. Let $\pi : L \to K^r$ be the natural isomorphism. Namely we take a basis of L over K, $\theta_1, \cdots, \theta_r$, and define π by $\pi(a_1\theta_1 + \cdots + a_r\theta_r) = (a_1, \cdots, a_r)$ for any $a_1, \cdots, a_r \in K$. Let $\tilde{\phi}$ be the polynomial map from L^{12} to L^{15}. Let $\tilde{\phi}(X_1, X_2, ...X_{12}) = (Y_1, Y_2, ...Y_{15})$. Suppose

$$M_1 = \begin{pmatrix} X_1 & X_2 \\ X_3 & X_4 \end{pmatrix}, M_2 = \begin{pmatrix} X_5 & X_6 \\ X_7 & X_8 \end{pmatrix}, M_3 = \begin{pmatrix} X_9 & X_{10} \\ X_{11} & X_{12} \end{pmatrix}.$$

and

$$Z_3 = M_1 M_2 = \begin{pmatrix} Y_4 & Y_5 \\ Y_6 & Y_7 \end{pmatrix}, Z_2 = M_1 M_3 = \begin{pmatrix} Y_8 & Y_9 \\ Y_{10} & Y_{11} \end{pmatrix},$$

$Z_1 = M_2^T M_3 = \begin{pmatrix} Y_{12} & Y_{13} \\ Y_{14} & Y_{15} \end{pmatrix}.$

Then $\tilde{\phi}$ is expressed as

$$\begin{cases} Y_1 = X_1 + \det(M_2) + Q_1 & \\ Y_2 = X_2 + \det(M_3) + Q_2 & \\ Y_3 = X_3 + \det(M_1) + Q_3 & \\ Y_4 = X_1X_5 + X_2X_7 & Y_5 = X_1X_6 + X_2X_8 \\ Y_6 = X_3X_5 + X_4X_7 & Y_7 = X_3X_6 + X_4X_8 \\ Y_8 = X_1X_9 + X_2X_{11} & Y_9 = X_1X_{10} + X_2X_{12} \\ Y_{10} = X_3X_9 + X_4X_{11} & Y_{11} = X_3X_{10} + X_4X_{12} \\ Y_{12} = X_5X_9 + X_7X_{11} & Y_{13} = X_5X_{10} + X_7X_{12} \\ Y_{14} = X_6X_9 + X_8X_{11} & Y_{15} = X_6X_{10} + X_8X_{12} \end{cases} \tag{1}$$

The triple(Q_1, Q_2, Q_3) is a triangular map from K^{3r} to itself as follows. Let $\pi(X_1) = (x_1, \cdots, x_r)$, $\pi(X_2) = (x_{r+1}, \cdots, x_{2r})$, $\pi(X_3) = (x_{2r+1}, \cdots, x_{3r})$, and let $q_i \in K[x_1, \cdots, x_{i-1}]$, $2 \le i \le 3r$. Then

$$\begin{cases} Q(X_1) = \sum_{i=2}^{r} q_i(x_1, \cdots, x_{i-1})\theta_i \\ Q(X_1, X_2) = \sum_{i=1}^{r} q_{r+i}(x_1, \cdots, x_{i-1}\theta_i) \\ Q(X_1, X_2, X_3) = \sum_{i=1}^{r} q_{2r+i}(x_1, \cdots, x_{i-1}\theta_i) \end{cases}$$

The q_i can be any randomly chosen quadratic polynomials. The public key $E = L_2 \circ \pi \circ \tilde{\phi} \circ \pi^{-1} \circ L_1$. The encryption of MFE is the evaluation of public key polynomials, namely given a plaintext $(u_1, \cdots, u_{12r})$, its ciphertext is

$$(v_1, \cdots, v_{15r}) = (h_1(u_1, \cdots, u_{12r}), \cdots, h_{15r}(u_1, \cdots, u_{12r}))$$

For a legal user, having known L_1, L_2, the key point of decryption is efficiently inverse $\tilde{\phi}$. For a given $(Y_1, \cdots, Y_{15})$, we can easily compute $\det(Z_1)$, $\det(Z_2)$, $\det(Z_3)$, and by

$$\begin{cases} \det(Z_3) = \det(M_1)\det(M_2) \\ \det(Z_2) = \det(M_1)\det(M_3) \\ \det(Z_1) = \det(M_2)\det(M_3) \end{cases} \tag{2}$$

if M_1,M_2 and M_3 are invertible, we can compute the value of $\det(M_1)$,$\det(M_2)$ and $\det(M_3)$. In this case, by the former three equations of (1), X_1, X_2 and X_3 are solved out. If $X_1 \neq 0$, from $X_1X_4 + X_2X_3 = \det(M_1)$, we can get the value of X_4. With X_1, X_2, X_3 and X_4 evaluated, the latter 12 equations of (1) form a triangular structure, so $X_4, \cdots, X_{12}$ are subsequently attained. Appendix B of

[WYH06] presents the method of computing the X_1 in the case when $X_1 = 0$. It is slightly easier than the case of $X_1 \neq 0$. Since the possibility that M_1,M_2 and M_3 are invertible is close to 1, then we can assume that we can always successfully decrypt a valid ciphertext in the above way.

There are two typical instances of MFE proposed by the designers of MFE.

1. MFE-1, where $K = F_{2^{16}}$ and $r = 4$. The public key has 60 quadratic polynomials with 48 variables.
2. MFE-1′,where $K = F_{2^{16}}$ and $r = 5$. The public key has 75 quadratic polynomials with 60 variables.

2.2 SOLE Attack on MFE

Denote M^* as the associated matrix of a square matrix M; then $MM^* = \det(M)I$, where I is a square identity matrix. we have

$$Z_3 = M_1 M_2, Z_2 = M_1 M_3$$

From these, we can derive

$$M_3 M_3^* M_1^* M_1 M_2 = M_3 Z_2^* Z_3 = \det(Z_2) M_2$$

That is

$$M_3 Z_2^* Z_3 = \det(Z_2) M_2$$

Expand the relation into the matrix form, we can get 4 equations on each entry of the form

$$\sum_{i,j,k} A_{ijk} X_i Y_j Y_k = 0, A_{ijk} \in L \tag{3}$$

In [DHN07], using the same technique, 24 equations of this form can be found. Applying $(X_1, \cdots, X_{12}) = \pi^{-1} L_1(v_1, \cdots, v_{12r})$ and $(Y_1, \cdots, Y_{15}) = \pi^{-1} L_2^{-1}(u_1, \cdots, u_{15r})$ to (3), we can get $24r$ equations of the form

$$\sum_{ijk} a_{ijk} u_i v_j v_k + \sum_{i,j} b_{ij} u_i v_j + \sum_{jk} c_{jk} v_j v_k + \sum_{i} d_i u_i + \sum_{j} e_j v_j + c = 0$$

where $a_{ijk}, b_{ij}, c_{jk}, d_i, e_j, c \in K$. These equations are SOLEs. Once the ciphertext variables are evaluated, these equations are linear in u_i, so some plaintext variables can be linearly expressed by the rest plaintext variables, which implies that the number of plaintext variables in public key equations will be reduced. If the number is small enough, we can directly solve out the plaintext variables from the reduced public key equations by XL or Gröebner Basis. With the help of these SOLEs, authors of [DHN07] successfully broke the above two instances.

3 Quadratization Equation Attack on the Quartic-1 Scheme

3.1 The Quartic-1 Scheme

Having noticed the existence of SOLEs, the authors of [WFW09] design Z_1, Z_2 and Z_3 in the following strategy. Here M_1, M_2, M_3 are the same as those in the original MFE.

$$M_1 = \begin{pmatrix} X_1 & X_2 \\ X_3 & X_4 \end{pmatrix}, M_2 = \begin{pmatrix} X_5 & X_6 \\ X_7 & X_8 \end{pmatrix}, M_3 = \begin{pmatrix} X_9 & X_{10} \\ X_{11} & X_{12} \end{pmatrix}.$$

Set

$$Z_3 = X_2X_3M_1M_2 = \begin{pmatrix} Y_4 & Y_5 \\ Y_6 & Y_7 \end{pmatrix},$$

$$Z_2 = X_1X_2M_1M_3 = \begin{pmatrix} Y_8 & Y_9 \\ Y_{10} & Y_{11} \end{pmatrix},$$

and

$$Z_1 = X_1X_3M_2^TM_3 = \begin{pmatrix} Y_{12} & Y_{13} \\ Y_{14} & Y_{15} \end{pmatrix}.$$

The corresponding central map $\tilde{\phi} : L^{12} \to L^{15}$ is given as follows:

$$\begin{cases} Y_1 = X_1 + X_1^2\det(M_3) + Q_1 \\ Y_2 = X_2 + X_2^2\det(M_1) + Q_2 \\ Y_3 = X_3 + X_3^2\det(M_2) + Q_3 \\ Y_4 = X_2X_3(X_1X_5 + X_2X_7) \quad Y_5 = X_2X_3(X_1X_6 + X_2X_8) \\ Y_6 = X_2X_3(X_3X_5 + X_4X_7) \quad Y_7 = X_2X_3(X_3X_6 + X_4X_8) \\ Y_8 = X_1X_2(X_1X_9 + X_2X_{11}) \quad Y_9 = X_1X_2(X_1X_{10} + X_2X_{12}) \\ Y_{10} = X_1X_2(X_3X_9 + X_4X_{11}) \quad Y_{11} = X_1X_2(X_3X_{10} + X_4X_{12}) \\ Y_{12} = X_1X_3(X_5X_9 + X_7X_{11}) \quad Y_{13} = X_1X_3(X_5X_{10} + X_7X_{12}) \\ Y_{14} = X_1X_3(X_6X_9 + X_8X_{11}) \quad Y_{15} = X_1X_3(X_6X_{10} + X_8X_{12}) \end{cases} \tag{4}$$

The triple (Q_1, Q_2, Q_3) is constructed in the same way as in MFE [WYH06]. The decryption process follows the same line of that of MFE. Given a valid ciphertext, we can get $\det(Z_1)$, $\det(Z_2)$, and $\det(Z_3)$ as follows. Since we have

$$\begin{cases} \det(Z_3) = X_2^2X_3^2\det(M_1)\det(M_2) \\ \det(Z_2) = X_1^2X_2^2\det(M_1)\det(M_3) \\ \det(Z_1) = X_1^2X_3^2\det(M_2)\det(M_3) \end{cases} \tag{5}$$

when M_1,M_2 and M_3 are invertible and none of X_1,X_2 and X_3 is zero, we can get values of $X_1^2\det(M_3)$, $X_3^2\det(M_2)$ and $X_2^2\det(M_1)$ as follows:

$$\begin{cases} X_1^2\det(Z_3) = \sqrt{\det(Z_2)\det(Z_1)\det(Z_3)^{-1}} \\ X_3^2\det(Z_2) = \sqrt{\det(Z_1)\det(Z_3)\det(Z_2)^{-1}} \\ X_2^2\det(Z_1) = \sqrt{\det(Z_2)\det(Z_3)\det(Z_1)^{-1}} \end{cases}$$

The square root operation is easy to handle over a characteristic two field. Substituting $X_1^2\det(M_3)$, $X_3^2\det(M_2)$ and $X_2^2\det(M_1)$ into the first three equations of (4), X_1, X_2 and X_3 are solved out. From $X_2^2\det(M_1) = X_2^2(X_1X_4 + X_2X_3)$, we can get X_4. Substituting X_1,X_2,X_3 and X_4 into the last twelve equations of (4), a triangular structure is formed so that $X_5, \cdots, X_{12}$ can be subsequently attained.

This new encryption scheme Quartic-1 raises the polynomials of the public key to be degree four, namely they are quartic polynomials in plaintext variables. To bound the size of public key, the authors in [WFW09] has to reduce the size of K and the extension degree r. There are two sets of parameters proposed:

1. Quartic-1, where $K = \mathbb{F}_{2^8}$ and $r = 2$. The public key has 30 quartic polynomials with 24 variables.
2. Quartic-1′,where $K = \mathbb{F}_{2^4}$ and $r = 3$. The public key has 45 quartic polynomials with 36 variables.

3.2 Cryptanalysis of Quartic-1

In [WFW09], the authors claim that SOLEs do not exist for the Quartic-1 system, however, our experiments show that at least $2r$ SOLEs always exist. We find two equations that hold on $\tilde{\phi}$:

$$\begin{cases} X_2Y_{12}Y_{15} + X_2Y_{13}Y_{14} + X_9Y_4Y_{15} + X_9Y_5Y_{13} + X_{10}Y_4Y_{14} + X_{10}Y_5Y_{12} = 0 \\ X_5Y_{10}Y_{15} + X_5Y_{11}Y_{14} + X_6Y_{10}Y_{13} + X_6Y_{11}Y_{12} + X_9Y_4Y_{15} + X_9Y_5Y_{13} \\ \qquad +X_{10}Y_4Y_{14} + X_{10}Y_5Y_{12} = 0 \end{cases} \tag{6}$$

Substituting $(X_1, \cdots, X_{12}) = \pi^{-1}L_1(v_1, \cdots, v_{12r})$ and $(Y_1, \cdots, Y_{15}) = \pi^{-1}L_2^{-1}$ $(u_1, \cdots, u_{15r})$ to (6), we can get $2r$ equations of the form:

$$\sum_{i,j,k} a_{ijk}u_iv_jv_k + \sum_{i,j} b_{ij}u_iv_j + \sum_{j,k} c_{jk}v_jv_k + \sum_i d_iu_i + \sum_j e_jv_j + f = 0 \tag{7}$$

where $a_{ijk}, b_{ij}, c_{jk}, d_i, e_j, c \in K$. They are SOLEs and can help us to reduce the number of plaintext variables for a ciphertext-only attack. The complexity of recovering the coefficient vectors $(a_{ijk}, b_{ij}, c_{jk}, d_i, e_j, c)$ is $(90r^2(15r + 1) + 180r^2 + 15r(15r + 1)/2 + 27r + 1)^w$, $w \approx 2.732$. For the parameter specification of Quartic-1, this complexity is about 2^{37}; for the parameter of Quartic-1′, this complexity is about 2^{41}.

Unfortunately, these SOLEs can only reduce $2r$ plaintext variables, and they help little to simplify the central map in order to derive more SOLEs, moreover, substituting them into the central map $\tilde{\phi}$ would destroy its compact expression.

However, we can easily find plenty of quadratization equations from $\tilde{\phi}$. Taking Y_4, Y_5, Y_6, Y_7 into consideration, it is obvious that there holds a QE between any two of them. Take Y_4, Y_5 as example, it is

$$(X_1X_5 + X_2X_7)Y_5 = (X_1X_6 + X_2X_8)Y_4$$

In fact, there are at least 9 independent Quadratic Equation. They are as follows:

$$\begin{cases} (X_1X_6 + X_2X_8)Y_4 + (X_1X_5 + X_2X_7)Y_5 = 0 \\ (X_3X_5 + X_4X_7)Y_4 + (X_1X_5 + X_2X_7)Y_6 = 0 \\ (X_3X_6 + X_4X_8)Y_4 + (X_1X_5 + X_2X_7)Y_7 = 0 \\ (X_3X_5 + X_4X_7)Y_5 + (X_1X_6 + X_2X_8)Y_6 = 0 \\ (X_3X_6 + X_4X_8)Y_5 + (X_1X_6 + X_2X_8)Y_7 = 0 \\ (X_3X_6 + X_4X_8)Y_6 + (X_3X_5 + X_4X_7)Y_7 = 0 \\ X_3X_6Y_4 + X_4X_7Y_5 + X_1X_6Y_6 + X_2X_7Y_7 = 0 \\ X_3X_8Y_4 + X_3X_7Y_5 + X_1X_8Y_6 + X_1X_7Y_7 = 0 \\ X_4X_6Y_4 + X_4X_5Y_5 + X_2X_6Y_6 + X_2X_5Y_7 = 0 \end{cases} \tag{8}$$

If Y_4, Y_5, Y_6, Y_7 are substituted by a ciphertext, we will get 6 independent quadratic equations in (8) if $Y_4Y_5 \neq 0$, since we can find a 6×6 invertible coefficient submatrix

$$\begin{pmatrix} Y_5 & 0 & 0 & 0 & 0 & 0 \\ Y_6 & Y_4 & Y_4 & 0 & 0 & 0 \\ Y_7 & 0 & 0 & Y_4 & 0 & 0 \\ 0 & 0 & Y_5 & Y_4 & 0 & 0 \\ 0 & 0 & 0 & 0 & Y_4 & 0 \\ 0 & 0 & 0 & 0 & 0 & Y_4 \end{pmatrix}$$

with determinant equal to $Y_4^4Y_5^2$. Here consider every term X_iX_j presented in (8) as a single variable. Since $Y_4Y_5 \neq 0$ holds with a probability almost being 1, we can always get 6 independent quadratic equations.

Similarly to (8), we can find at least 9 independent QEs from Y_8, Y_9, Y_{10}, Y_{11} and another 9 independent quadratic equations from $Y_{12}, Y_{13}, Y_{14}, Y_{15}$. These three sets of QEs are composed of different terms, hence we can get 27 QEs, and they become 18 independent quadratic equations if variables Y_i are fixed by ciphertext values.

Besides, observe the relation between Y_4, Y_5, Y_{12} and Y_{14} and the relation between Y_4, Y_5, Y_{13} and Y_{15}, we have

$$\begin{cases} X_8X_9Y_4 + X_7X_9Y_5 + X_2X_8Y_{12} + X_2X_7Y_{14} = 0 \\ X_8X_{11}Y_4 + X_7X_{11}Y_5 + X_2X_6Y_{12} + X_2X_5Y_{14} = 0 \\ X_8X_{10}Y_4 + X_7X_{10}Y_5 + X_2X_8Y_{13} + X_2X_7Y_{15} = 0 \\ X_8X_{12}Y_4 + X_7X_{12}Y_5 + X_2X_6Y_{13} + X_2X_5Y_{15} = 0. \end{cases} \tag{9}$$

Similarly, we can also find another two QEs from Y_{10}, Y_{11}, Y_{12} and Y_{13}, and 2 QEs from Y_{10}, Y_{11}, Y_{14} and Y_{15}. So totally there are 35 QEs derived from the central map, and at least 18 of them are independent.

Substituting $(X_1, \cdots, X_{12}) = \pi^{-1}L_1(v_1, \cdots, v_{12r})$ and $(Y_1, \cdots, Y_{15}) = \pi^{-1}$ $L_2^{-1}(u_1, \cdots, u_{15r})$ into (8) and (9), we can get $35r$ QEs over K of the form

$$\sum_{i,j,k} a_{ijk}u_iu_jv_k + \sum_{i,j} b_{ij}u_iu_j + \sum_{i,k} c_{ik}u_iv_k + \sum_i d_iu_i + \sum_k e_kv_k + f = 0, \tag{10}$$

where $a_{ijk}, b_{ij}, c_{jk}, d_i, e_j, c \in K$. Since (8) and (9) exist for all corresponding plaintext and ciphertext variables, recovering a basis of these QE's coefficient vectors $(a_{ijk}, b_{ij}, c_{jk}, d_i, e_j, c)$ is a precomputation. The computational complexity is $\mathcal{O}((15r+1)6r(12r+1)+180r^2+27r+1)^w$, $w \approx 2.732$. This complexity is about 2^{36} for the parameter in Quartic-1; and 2^{40} for the parameter in Quartic-1$'$.

Given a ciphertext, if it is substituted into (8) and (9), we can get a system of at least $35r$ quadratic equations, denote it as $\mathcal{S}$. If we can work out a Gröbner basis of $\mathcal{S}$ with a small dimension, say s, we can find the original plaintext by $|K|^s$ exhausted search.

3.3 Dimension of $\mathcal{S}$

Since the scale of $\mathcal{S}$ is impractical for directly computing its Gröber basis, when $r = 2$, $|\mathcal{S}| \geq 70$. Experiment shows that it is really time consuming, so after obtaining $\mathcal{S}$, how to determine its dimension s? We apply an intermediate way to find s. Suppose we fix the last t variables by randomly chosen elements in K, and compute the corresponding Gröbner basis by an equation solving algorithm like F_4. By experiment, we find the following three results can be efficiently obtained:

1. if $t > s$, it always output GB=$\{1\}$.
2. if $t = s$, it always output a zero-dimensional GB.
3. if $t < s$, it always output a positive-dimensional GB.

This observation help us to make a strategy to determine s. We can choose a fairly big t, if it outputs GB=$\{1\}$ by F_4, then t decrease by 1; if it outputs a zero-dimensional GB, returns t and stops.

Using the above strategy we can efficiently determine the dimension of $\mathcal{S}$, i.e., s. The last step is to search the last s ciphertext variables $|K|^s$ times and compute the Gröbner basis for each time. It would be a disaster for a normal computer, but this set-back can be greatly improved by sufficiently many parallel computers.

3.4 Experiment Results

In order to compare Quartic-1 and Quartic-2, which will be analyzed in the following section, we take the parameter of Quartic-1 in section 3.1, $K = \mathbb{F}_{2^8}$, $r = 2$, which is the same as Quartic-2 given in Section 4.1. We chose 10 different pairs of L_1 and L_2 and, and for each of them, we chose 100 different valid ciphertext for experiments.

The precomputation is to recover SOLEs and QEs from the public key of Quartic-1. To recover (7), we randomly selected 13400 plain/cipher-text pairs and substituted them into the public key. Then the main task is a Gaussian elimination on a 13400×13400 matrix on $\mathbb{F}_{2^8}$. On a normal computer, with Genuine Intel(R) CPU T2300@1.66GHz, 504MB RAM, the time running in a magma procedure is about 3595.125 seconds; To recover (10), use the same technique as for (7) to recover the coefficients in (10) and the running time is about 2316.750 seconds.

Using the strategy mentioned in the previous subsection, we can efficiently determine the dimension of $\mathcal{S}$, $s = 5$. We find it just need 0.531 seconds when $t > s$, and 1.328 seconds when $t = s$. However, doing 2^{40} times GB computation would still be a disaster for the above normal computer. If we have sufficiently many fast-speed parallel computers, then we can run Gröbner basis algorithm independently on multiple machines, so that the cost of time in this search process can be greatly saved.

4 Quadratization Equation Attack on the Quartic-2 Scheme

4.1 The Quartic-2 Scheme

To resist SOLEs, the author of [Wan07] proposed to construct the Z_1,Z_2 and Z_3 in the MFE scheme as follows: $Z_3 = M_1M_2^2 = \begin{pmatrix} Y_4 & Y_5 \\ Y_6 & Y_7 \end{pmatrix}$, $Z_2 = M_1M_3^2 = \begin{pmatrix} Y_8 & Y_9 \\ Y_{10} & Y_{11} \end{pmatrix}$, $Z_1 = M_3^2(M_2^T)^2 = \begin{pmatrix} Y_{12} & Y_{13} \\ Y_{14} & Y_{15} \end{pmatrix}$. Here M_1, M_2, M_3 are defined as the same as those in MFE.

Write the above three matrix equations into equations on their each entry, the central map $\tilde{\phi} : L^{12} \rightarrow L^{15}$ is then defined as follows:

$$\begin{cases} Y_1 = X_1 + \det(M_2) + Q_1 \\ Y_2 = X_2 + \det(M_3) + Q_2 \\ Y_3 = X_3 + \det(M_1) + Q_3 \\ Y_4 = X_1X_5^2 + X_1X_6X_7 + X_2X_5X_7 + X_2X_7X_8 \\ Y_5 = X_1X_5X_6 + X_1X_6X_8 + X_2X_6X_7 + X_2X_8^2 \\ Y_6 = X_3X_5^2 + X_3X_6X_7 + X_4X_5X_7 + X_4X_7X_8 \\ Y_7 = X_3X_5X_6 + X_3X_6X_8 + X_4X_6X_7 + X_4X_8^2 \\ Y_8 = X_1X_9^2 + X_1X_{10}X_{11} + X_2X_9X_{11} + X_2X_{11}X_{12} \\ Y_9 = X_1X_9X_{10} + X_1X_{10}X_{12} + X_2X_{10}X_{11} + X_2X_{12}^2 \\ Y_{10} = X_3X_9^2 + X_3X_{10}X_{11} + X_4X_9X_{11} + X_4X_{11}X_{12} \\ Y_{11} = X_3X_9X_{10} + X_3X_{10}X_{12} + X_4X_{10}X_{11} + X_4X_{12}^2 \\ Y_{12} = (X_9^2 + X_{10}X_{11})(X_5^2 + X_6X_7) + (X_9X_{10} + X_{10}X_{12})(X_5X_6 + X_6X_8) \\ Y_{13} = (X_9^2 + X_{10}X_{11})(X_5X_7 + X_7X_8) + (X_9X_{10} + X_{10}X_{12})(X_6X_7 + X_8^2) \\ Y_{14} = (X_9X_11 + X_{11}X_{12})(X_5^2 + X_6X_7) + (X_{10}X_{11} + X_{12}^2)(X_5X_6 + X_6X_8) \\ Y_{15} = (X_9X_{11} + X_{11}X_{12})(X_5X_7 + X_7X_8) + (X_{10}X_{11} + X_{12}^2)(X_6X_7 + X_8^2) \end{cases} \tag{11}$$

The triple (Q_1, Q_2, Q_3) is constructed in the same way as in MFE. The decryption of a valid ciphertext is a little complex comparing with that of the original MFE. As limit of space, and that the subsequent analysis do not rely on how to decrypt, there is no need to elaborate the whole decryption process, so we only give how to get $\det(M_1)$,$\det(M_2)$, and $\det(M_3)$ given a valid ciphertext. Given a valid ciphertext, we can get $\det(Z_1)$, $\det(Z_2)$, $\det(Z_3)$. Since we have

$$\begin{cases} \det(Z_3) = \det(M_1)\det(M_2)^2 \\ \det(Z_2) = \det(M_1)\det(M_3)^2 \\ \det(Z_1) = \det(M_2)^2\det(M_3)^2 \end{cases} \tag{12}$$

when M_1,M_2 and M_3 are invertible and none of X_1,X_2 and X_3 is zero, we can get values of $\det(M_3)$, $\det(M_2)$ and $\det(M_1)$ as follows:

$$\begin{cases} \det(M_1) = \sqrt{\det(Z_2)\det(Z_3)\det(Z_1)^{-1}} \\ \det(M_2) = \sqrt[4]{\det(Z_3)\det(Z_1)\det(Z_2)^{-1}} \\ \det(M_3) = \sqrt[4]{\det(Z_1)\det(Z_2)\det(Z_3)^{-1}} \end{cases}$$

Note that square root operation here is easy to handle over a characteristic two field.

Since the public key equations of Quartic-2 are raised up to quartic, to bound the size of public key, the authors has to decrease the size of K and the extension degree r. There is one set of parameters proposed in [Wan07]:

1. Quartic-2, where $K = \mathbb{F}_{2^8}$ and $r = 2$. The public key has 30 quartic polynomials with 24 variables.

4.2 Cryptanalysis of Quartic-2

The designer of Quartic-2 noted that Quartic-2 is free from SOLE attack, this is indeed the case by experiment. However, we can utilize Quadratization Equations derived from quartic public key equations to attack Quartic-2.

From

$$Z_3 = M_1 M_2^2, Z_2 = M_1 M_3^2, Z_1 = M_3^2 (M_2^T)^2,$$

we can derive that

$$\begin{cases} M_1 Z_1^T = Z_3 (M_3^T)^2 \\ Z_2 (M_2^T)^2 = M_1 Z_1 \end{cases} \tag{13}$$

From matrix equations in (13), we can find 8 quadratic equations on each entry over L of the form

$$\sum_{i,j,k} A_{ijk} X_i X_j Y_k + \sum_{i,k} B_{i,k} X_i Y_k = 0 \tag{14}$$

where $A_{ijk}, B_{j,k} \in L$. Obviously they become quadratic in plaintext variables once the ciphertext variables are fixed. Consider all the QEs as a vector space spanned by the coefficients of terms. If Z_3, Z_2 are invertible (the probablity is almost 1), then these 8 equations are linearly independent.

Moreover, we can find other 6 quadratic equations exsit on $\tilde{\phi}$. They are as follows:

$$\begin{cases} X_3X_6Y_4 + X_4X_7Y_5 + X_1X_6Y_6 + X_2X_7Y_7 = 0 \\ X_3X_{10}Y_8 + X_4X_{11}Y_9 + X_1X_{10}Y_{10} + X_2X_{11}Y_{11} = 0 \\ X_4X_6Y_4 + (X_3X_6 + X_4X_5 + X_4X_8)Y_5 + X_2X_6Y_6 + (X_1X_6 + X_2X_5 + X_2X_8)Y_7 = 0 \\ (X_3X_5 + X_3X_8 + X_4X_7)Y_4 + X_3X_7Y_5 + (X_1X_5 + X_1X_8 + X_2X_7)Y_6 + X_1X_7Y_7 = 0 \\ (X_3X_9 + X_3X_{12} + X_4X_{11})Y_8 + X_3X_{11}Y_9 + (X_1X_9 + X_1X_{12} + X_2X_{11})Y_{10} + X_1X_{11}Y_{11} = 0 \\ X_4X_{10}Y_8 + (X_3X_{10} + X_4X_9 + X_4X_{12})Y_9 + X_2X_{10}Y_{10} + (X_1X_{10} + X_2X_9 + X_2X_{12})Y_{11} = 0 \end{cases} \quad (15)$$

Substituting $(X_1, \cdots, X_{12}) = \pi^{-1}L_1(v_1, \cdots, v_{12r})$ and $(Y_1, \cdots, Y_{15}) = \pi^{-1}$ $L_2^{-1}(u_1, \cdots, u_{15r})$ into (13) and (4.2), we can get $14r$ QEs over K of the form

$$\sum_{i,j,k} a_{ijk}u_iu_jv_k + \sum_{i,j} b_{ij}u_iu_j + \sum_{i,k} c_{ik}u_iv_k + \sum_i d_iu_i + \sum_k e_kv_k + f = 0 \quad (16)$$

where $a_{ijk}, b_{ij}, c_{jk}, d_i, e_j, c \in K$. Since (13) and (4.2) exist for all corresponding plaintext and ciphertext variables, and recovering a basis of these QE's coefficient vectors $(a_{ijk}, b_{ij}, c_{jk}, d_i, e_j, c)$ is a precomputation. The complexity is $\mathcal{O}((15r + 1)6r(12r+1) + 180r^2 + 27r + 1)^w$, $w \approx 2.732$. It is about 2^{36} for the parameter given in the previous subsection.

Assume we have found the above $14r$ QEs in (16), now for a given ciphertext $(v_1', \cdots, v_{15r}')$, after substituting v_i' into (16), we get $14r$ quadratic equations in $12r$ plaintext variables, denoted as $(16)'$. Instead of solving the public quartic equations by XL or F$_4$, we can turn to solve $(16)'$. Since $(16)'$ are quadratic and r is as small as 2, it is realistic to save much more time and memory. It also means that we can find the variety of $(16)'$, denoted as $\mathcal{V}$. Next we will show there still exist Quadratic Equations that holds on $\mathcal{V}$.

Let $(Y_1', \cdots, Y_{15}') = \pi^{-1}L_2^{-1}(v_1', \cdots, v_{15r}')$ and $(X_1, \cdots, X_{12}) = \pi^{-1}L_1(u_1, \cdots, u_{12r})$. Note that here $(v_1', \cdots, v_{15r}')$ is known, and $(u_1, \cdots, u_{12r})$ is unknown. By (13), we have

$$M_1Z_1'^T = Z_3'(M_3^T)^2 \quad Z_2'(M_2^T)^2 = M_1Z_1'. \quad (17)$$

Here Z_1', Z_2' and Z_3' are constant matrices. Suppose after adding these two relations (17) into the $\tilde{\phi}$ results into another $\tilde{\phi}'$. The relation $Z_2 = M_1M_3^2$, $Z_3 = M_1M_2$ which originally hold on $\tilde{\phi}$, definitely still hold on $\tilde{\phi}'$. From $\tilde{\phi}'$, we get

$$Z_2Z_3'^T = M_1Z_1'M_1^T. \quad (18)$$

holds on $\tilde{\phi}'$. From this matrix equation, we can get 4 quadratic equations over L of the form

$$\sum_{i,j} A_{ij}X_iX_j + \sum_k B_kY_k = 0 \quad (19)$$

where $A_{ij}, B_k \in L$. If Z_1' is invertible (the possiblity is almost 1), these 4 quadratic equations are linearly independent. Substituting $(X_1, \cdots, X_{12}) = \pi^{-1}$ $L_1(v_1, \cdots, v_{12r})$ and $(Y_1, \cdots, Y_{15}) = \pi^{-1}L_2^{-1}(u_1, \cdots, u_{15r})$ into (19), we can get another $4r$ independent quadratic equations in plaintext variables over K of the form

$$\sum_{i,j} a_{ij}u_iu_j + \sum_i b_iu_i + \sum_k c_kv_k + c = 0 \tag{20}$$

where $a_{ij}, b_i, c_k, c \in K$. To recover the coefficients of (20), the complexity is $\mathcal{O}(6r(12r+1)+27r+1)^w$. It is about 2^{23} for the parameter given in the previous subsection.

From the above analysis, given a ciphertext, (16) and (20) theoretically give $18r$ quadratic equations, of which at least $12r$ have linearly independent coefficient vectors. The complexity of recovering all these quadratic equations is mainly depend on the precomputation of recovering (16), and it is about 2^{36} for the parameter given in section 4.1.

Given a ciphertext, after finding quadratic equations $(16)'$ and $(20)'$, here (20) becomes $(20)'$ after ciphertext variabes are evaluated, the last step is to find the plaintext by solving these quadratic equations. Experiment results show that it efficiently works using equation solving algorithm to compute Gröbner basis as r is small. So we conclude that ciphertext-only attack on Quartic-2 can be reduced to solving quadratic equations derived from $(16)'$ and $(20)'$ with complexity $\mathcal{O}((15r+1)6r(12r+1)+180r^2+27r+1)^w$, it is 2^{36} for the parameter mentioned above.

4.3 Experiment Results

As the parameter set proposed in [Wan07], we set $K = \mathbb{F}_{2^8}$ and $r = 2$. We chose 10 different pairs of L_1 and L_2, and for each of them we chose 100 different valid ciphertext for experiments.

The first step of our attack is recovering (16). To recover (16), we randomly selected 10075 plain/cipher-text pairs and substituted them into the public key. Then the main task is a Gaussian elimination on a 10075×11075 matrix on $\mathbb{F}_{2^8}$. On a normal computer, with Genuine Intel(R) CPU T2300@1.66GHz, 504MB RAM, a Magma procedure run averagely in 1779.656 seconds. The number of (16) is always much bigger than $14r$, which is 28 for our parameter, and it is always up to 49. The second step is to use equation solving algorithms like F_4 to find $\mathcal{V}$ in order to deduce more quadratic equations in (20). This step takes up a long time as 3110.734 seconds on average. Actually, our experiment results show that only through solving quadratic equations from $(16)'$, we can always find the original plaintext, which means we do not need to take the further step to find (20).

5 The Improved MFE Public Key Cryptosystem

5.1 The Improved MFE

To resist SOLE, the authors of [WZY07] proposed an improved MFE encryption transformation. The public key polynomials are still of degree 2. Let

$\tilde{\phi}(X_1, X_2, \cdots, X_8) = (Y_1, Y_2, \cdots, Y_{10})$, the central map $\tilde{\phi}$: $L^8 \to L^{10}$ is defined as follows.

$$\begin{cases} Y_1 = X_1 + X_5X_8 + X_6X_7 + Q_1; \\ Y_2 = X_2 + X_1X_4 + X_2X_3 + Q_2; \\ Y_3 = X_1X_5 + X_2X_7; \qquad Y_4 = X_1X_6 + X_2X_8; \\ Y_5 = X_3X_5 + X_4X_7; \qquad Y_6 = X_3X_6 + X_4X_8; \\ Y_7 = X_1X_5 + X_3X_7; \qquad Y_8 = X_2X_5 + X_4X_7; \\ Y_9 = X_1X_6 + X_3X_8; \qquad Y_{10} = X_2X_6 + X_4X_8; \end{cases} \tag{21}$$

Here the definitions of Q_1, Q_2 is similar to Q_1, Q_2, Q_3 in section 2. Q_1, Q_2 form a triangular map from K^{2r} to itself. Suppose

$$M_1 = \begin{pmatrix} X_1 & X_2 \\ X_3 & X_4 \end{pmatrix}, \quad M_2 = \begin{pmatrix} X_5 & X_6 \\ X_7 & X_8 \end{pmatrix},$$

and

$$Z_1 = M_1^{\hat{l}} M_2 = \begin{pmatrix} Y_3 & Y_4 \\ Y_5 & Y_6 \end{pmatrix}, \quad Z_2 = M_2^T M_1 = \begin{pmatrix} Y_7 & Y_8 \\ Y_9 & Y_{10} \end{pmatrix}.$$

Here, the operator "ˆ" is defined as follows:

$$M^{\hat{l}} = \begin{pmatrix} a & b \\ c & d \end{pmatrix}^{\hat{l}} = \begin{pmatrix} a^l & b^l \\ c^l & d^l \end{pmatrix}.$$

Given a valid ciphertext $(v_1, \cdots, v_{10r})$, the decryption of the scheme follows the same line of decrypting MFE, and the key point is to recover M_1 and M_2. From Z_1, Z_2, we have

$$\begin{cases} [\det(M_1)]^l \cdot \det(M_2) = \det(Z_1) \\ \det(M_2) \cdot \det(M_1) = \det(Z_2) \end{cases} \tag{22}$$

Hence,

$$\begin{aligned} \det(M_1) &= \left(\frac{\det(Z_1)}{\det(Z_2)}\right)^{\frac{1}{l-1}} \\ \det(M_2) &= \frac{\det(Z_2)}{\det(M_1)} \end{aligned} \tag{23}$$

Then, the values of $X_1, \cdots, X_8$ can be derived in turn.

Remark: Because for any $X \in L$, we have $X^l = X$. Then,

$$M_1^{\hat{l}} = \begin{pmatrix} X_1 & X_2 \\ X_3 & X_4 \end{pmatrix}^{\hat{l}} = \begin{pmatrix} X_1^l & X_2^l \\ X_3^l & X_4^l \end{pmatrix} = \begin{pmatrix} X_1 & X_2 \\ X_3 & X_4 \end{pmatrix} = M_1$$

So the left sides of two equations in system (22) are equal, and consequently the value of $\det(M_1)$ can not be gotten from (23). That means the decryption fails to recovering ciphertext. There is no recommended parameter in [WZY07], to assure the safety, we use $K = F_8, r = 10$ for experiment in our paper.

5.2 Linearization Equation Attack

Through analysis, we found that there are many FOLEs satisfied by the above improved MFE. Since $Z_2 = M_2^T M_1$, multipling M_2 on both sides, we have $Z_2 M_2 = M_2^T M_1 M_2 = M_2^T Z_1$, so,

$$Z_2 M_2 = M_2^T Z_1$$

Expanding it, we have

$$\begin{pmatrix} Y_7 & Y_8 \\ Y_9 & Y_{10} \end{pmatrix} \begin{pmatrix} X_5 & X_6 \\ X_7 & X_8 \end{pmatrix} = \begin{pmatrix} X_5 & X_7 \\ X_6 & X_8 \end{pmatrix} \begin{pmatrix} Y_3 & Y_4 \\ Y_5 & Y_6 \end{pmatrix}$$

then

$$\begin{pmatrix} X_5Y_7 + X_7Y_8 & X_6Y_7 + X_8Y_8 \\ X_5Y_9 + X_7Y_{10} & X_6Y_9 + X_8Y_{10} \end{pmatrix} = \begin{pmatrix} X_5Y_3 + X_7Y_5 & X_5Y_4 + X_7Y_6 \\ X_6Y_3 + X_8Y_5 & X_6Y_4 + X_8Y_6 \end{pmatrix}$$

that is,

$$\begin{cases} X_5Y_7 + X_7Y_8 = X_5Y_3 + X_7Y_5; \\ X_6Y_7 + X_8Y_8 = X_5Y_4 + X_7Y_6; \\ X_5Y_9 + X_7Y_{10} = X_6Y_3 + X_8Y_5; \\ X_6Y_9 + X_8Y_{10} = X_6Y_4 + X_8Y_6. \end{cases} \tag{24}$$

On the other hand, from $Z_1 = M_1 M_2$, take transpose on it and then right multiply $(M_1^T)^{-1}$ on both sides, we have

$$Z_1^T \left(M_1^T\right)^{-1} = M_2^T \tag{25}$$

From $Z_2 = M_2^T M_1$, right multiply $(M_1)^{-1}$ on both sides, we get

$$Z_2 M_1^{-1} = M_2^T. \tag{26}$$

From (25) and (26), we can deduce

$$Z_1^T \left(M_1^T\right)^* = Z_2 M_1^* \tag{27}$$

Expanding it, we derive

$$\begin{cases} X_4Y_3 + X_2Y_5 = X_4Y_7 + X_3Y_8; \\ X_3Y_3 + X_1Y_5 = X_2Y_7 + X_1Y_8; \\ X_4Y_4 + X_2Y_6 = X_4Y_9 + X_3Y_{10}; \\ X_3Y_4 + X_1Y_6 = X_2Y_9 + X_1Y_{10}. \end{cases} \tag{28}$$

Substituting $(X_1, \cdots, X_8) = \pi_1 \circ \phi_1(u_1, \cdots, u_{8r})$ and $(Y_1, \cdots, Y_{10}) = \pi_2^{-1} \circ \phi_3^{-1}(v_1, \cdots, v_{10r})$ into (24) and (28), we get $8r$ equations of the form

$$\sum_{i,j} a_{ij} m_i z_j + \sum_i b_i m_i + \sum_j c_j z_j + d = 0 \tag{29}$$

where the coefficients $a_{ij}, b_i, c_j, d \in K$, and they are first order linearization equations (FOLEs). The complexity of recovering coefficients in these equations is $(80r^2 + 18r + 1)^w$., which is $(8200)^3 \leq 2^{40}$ for the parameter we choosen. So there are at least $8r$ FOLEs.

Through analysis,we find that the ranks of systems (24) and (28) coefficients matrix are both equal to 3. Hence, after substituting ciphertext variables into them, we can at least get $6r$ independent linear equations. So all the plaintext variables can be represented by $2r$ plaintext variables. Actually, from (24) and (28), X_1, X_2, X_3, X_4 can be expressed by the multiple of one variable (say S_1) of them and X_5, X_6, X_7, X_8 can be expressed by the multiple of one variable (say S_2) of them. The central map of new quadratic functions can be changed to:

$$\begin{cases} \tilde{Y_1} = C_1 S_1 + C_2 S_2^2 + Q_1 \\ \tilde{Y_2} = C_3 S_1 + C_4 S_1^2 + Q_2 \\ \tilde{Y_3} = C_5 S_1 S_2 \end{cases} \tag{30}$$

So, there are only $2r$ unknowns and $3r$ linearly independent equations in system (30). We can solve this system directly by Gröbner algorithm.

5.3 Experiment Results

In our experiments, we choose $K = \mathbb{F}_{2^8}$, $r = 10$. We chose 10 different pairs of L_1 and L_2, and for each of them we chose 100 different valid ciphertext for experiments.

The first step is recovering FOLEs in (29). To recover (29), we randomly selected 8200 plain/cipher-text pairs and substituted them into the public key. Then the main task is a Gaussian elimination on a 8200×8200 matrix on $\mathbb{F}_{2^8}$, and it takes 22 minutes. The number of (29) is always much bigger than $8r$, and it is always 110 in our experiment. Since this step is independent of the value of the ciphertext, then this step is a precomputation.

The second step is that given a ciphertext $(v_1', \cdots, v_{10r}')$, find corresponding plaintext $(u_1', \cdots, u_{8r}')$. Substitute $(v_1', \cdots, v_{10r}')$ into (29), suppose we can get s independent linear equations. Our experiments show $s = 60$ exactly the same as the theoretical analysis in the above section.

The third step is to substitute the 60 linear expressions into the public key polynomials and get a system of reduced linear public key polynomials as (30). Our experiments show, it takes about 6 second to solve the system by F_4 and recover the corresponding plaintext.

5.4 Extension of Improved MFE and Its Analysis

We extend the improvement in [WZY07]. Use the same notation as in [WZY07], we extended the central map $\tilde{\phi}_2(X_1, X_2, \cdots, X_8) = (Y_1, Y_2, \cdots, Y_{10})$ as following form.

$$\begin{cases} Y_1 = X_1 + X_5X_8 + X_6X_7 + Q_1 \\ Y_2 = X_2 + X_1X_4 + X_2X_3 + Q_2 \\ Y_3 = X_1^{q^t}X_5 + X_2^{q^t}X_7 \qquad Y_4 = X_1^{q^t}X_6 + X_2^{q^t}X_8 \\ Y_5 = X_3^{q^t}X_5 + X_4^{q^t}X_7 \qquad Y_6 = X_3^{q^t}X_6 + X_4^{q^t}X_8 \\ Y_7 = X_1X_5 + X_3X_7 \qquad Y_8 = X_2X_5 + X_4X_7 \\ Y_9 = X_1X_6 + X_3X_8 \qquad Y_{10} = X_2X_6 + X_4X_8 \end{cases}$$

where $1 \leq t < l$.

The matrix forms are listed as follows.

$$M_1 = \begin{pmatrix} X_1 & X_2 \\ X_3 & X_4 \end{pmatrix}, M_2 = \begin{pmatrix} X_5 & X_6 \\ X_7 & X_8 \end{pmatrix}.$$

$$Z_1 = M_1^{\hat{t}} M_2 = \begin{pmatrix} Y_3 & Y_4 \\ Y_5 & Y_6 \end{pmatrix}, Z_2 = M_2^T M_1 = \begin{pmatrix} Y_7 & Y_8 \\ Y_9 & Y_{10} \end{pmatrix}.$$

From

$$\begin{cases} [\det(M_1)]^{q^t} \cdot \det(M_2) = \det(Z_1) \\ \det(M_2) \cdot \det(M_1) = \det(Z_2) \end{cases}$$

we can obtain the values $\det(M_1)$ and $\det(M_2)$, then we can get $X_1, \cdots, X_8$ in turn.

Unfortunately, this scheme also satisfy FOLEs, but in this case we can only derive $4r$ FOLEs in first step.

Lemma 1. Let k be a finite field with characteristic q, the operator "^" defined on k is homomorphic, that is

$$\begin{pmatrix} a_1 & b_1 \\ c_1 & d_1 \end{pmatrix}^{\hat{q}^t} \begin{pmatrix} a_2 & b_2 \\ c_2 & d_2 \end{pmatrix}^{\hat{q}^t} = \left(\begin{pmatrix} a_1 & b_1 \\ c_1 & d_1 \end{pmatrix} \begin{pmatrix} a_2 & b_2 \\ c_2 & d_2 \end{pmatrix} \right)^{\hat{q}^t}$$

where$a_1, a_2, b_1, b_2, c_1, c_2, d_1, d_2 \in k$.

Proof. In finite field k with characteristic q,

$$(a+b)^q = a^q + b^q, a, b \in k.$$

Then

$$\begin{aligned} \begin{pmatrix} a_1 & b_1 \\ c_1 & d_1 \end{pmatrix}^{\hat{q}^t} \begin{pmatrix} a_2 & b_2 \\ c_2 & d_2 \end{pmatrix}^{\hat{q}^t} &= \begin{pmatrix} a_1^{q^t} & b_1^{q^t} \\ c_1^{q^t} & d_1^{q^t} \end{pmatrix} \begin{pmatrix} a_2^{q^t} & b_2^{q^t} \\ c_2^{q^t} & d_2^{q^t} \end{pmatrix} \\ &= \begin{pmatrix} a_1^{q^t}a_2^{q^t} + b_1^{q^t}c_2^{q^t} & a_1^{q^t}b_2^{q^t} + b_1^{q^t}d_2^{q^t} \\ c_1^{q^t}a_2^{q^t} + d_1^{q^t}c_2^{q^t} & c_1^{q^t}b_2^{q^t} + d_1^{q^t}d_2^{q^t} \end{pmatrix} \\ &= \begin{pmatrix} (a_1a_2 + b_1c_2)^{q^t} & (a_1b_2 + b_1d_2)^{q^t} \\ (c_1a_2 + d_1c_2)^{q^t} & (c_1b_2 + d_1d_2)^{q^t} \end{pmatrix} \end{aligned}$$

$$= \begin{pmatrix} a_1a_2 + b_1c_2 & a_1b_2 + b_1d_2 \\ c_1a_2 + d_1c_2 & c_1b_2 + d_1d_2 \end{pmatrix}^{\hat{q}^t}$$
$$= \left(\begin{pmatrix} a_1 & b_1 \\ c_1 & d_1 \end{pmatrix} \begin{pmatrix} a_2 & b_2 \\ c_2 & d_2 \end{pmatrix} \right)^{\hat{q}^t}$$

□

According to Lemma 1, we have

$$Z_2^{\hat{q}^t} = (M_2^T M_1)^{\hat{q}^t} = (M_2^T)^{\hat{q}^t} M_1^{\hat{q}^t}$$

Multiplying M_2 on both sides,

$$Z_2^{\hat{q}^t} M_2 = (M_2^T)^{\hat{q}^t} M_1^{\hat{q}^t} M_2 = (M_2^T)^{\hat{q}^t} Z_1$$

Expanding it, we get 4 equation below,

$$\begin{cases} X_5 Y_7^{q^t} + X_7 Y_8^{q^t} = X_5^{q^t} Y_3 + X_7^{q^t} Y_5; \\ X_6 Y_7^{q^t} + X_8 Y_8^{q^t} = X_5^{q^t} Y_4 + X_7^{q^t} Y_6; \\ X_5 Y_9^{q^t} + X_7 Y_{10}^{q^t} = X_6^{q^t} Y_3 + X_8^{q^t} Y_5; \\ X_6 Y_9^{q^t} + X_8 Y_{10}^{q^t} = X_6^{q^t} Y_4 + X_8^{q^t} Y. \end{cases} \tag{31}$$

If we use K-linear isomorphisms on map $Y = X^{q^t}$, $X, Y \in L$, it should be linear map on K, see [DGS06]. Hence,we can find there exit at least $4r$ FOLEs satisfied by this scheme.

On the other hand, from $Z_2^T = M_1^T M_2$, $Z_1 = M_1^{\hat{q}^t} M_2$, we can derive

$$\left(M_1^{\hat{q}^t}\right)^{-1} Z_1 = (M_1^T)^{-1} Z_2^T$$

Namely,

$$\det(M_1) \left(M_1^{\hat{q}^t}\right)^* Z_1 = [\det(M_1)]^{q^t} (M_1^T)^* Z_2^T. \tag{32}$$

However, (32) is of degree 3 in plaintext variables. Hence, they can not help to do plaintext variables elimination on public key from these equations.

Having (31), we can represent s variables of $u_1, \cdots, u_{8r}$ by linear combinations of other $8r - s$. Our experiments show $s = 3r$. However, when we substitute s variables by their expression on other $8r - s$, we find other $4r$ FOLEs by experiments and we can eliminate $3r$ variables on public key furthermore. For the reminder equations with $2r$ variables, we can solve it directly by Gröbner basis algorithm.

We use parameters $r = 10$, $K = \mathbb{F}_{2^8}$ for experiment, it takes 918.783 seconds to derive the first $4r$ FLOEs and 1021.183 seconds for second $4r$ FLOEs. In the last step, we recover corresponding plaintext for a given ciphertext using Gröbner basis algorithm in 2.621 seconds.

All of our experiments were performed on a normal computer, with Genuine Intel(R) CPU T2300@1.66GHz, 504MB RAM by magma.

6 Conclusion

In this paper, we give a new cryptanalysis on the two improved MFE schemes, Quartic-1 and Quartic-2, by utilizing quadratization equations which are quadratic in plaintext variables. For a given ciphertext, cracking down Quartic-1 with the same parameter as in Quartic-2 needs 2^{40} times Gröbner basis computations (about 1.328 seconds each time), while the Quatic-2 instance can be broken by quadratization equations in 3110.734 seconds. They both have weak points in their central map design. We also use the first order Linearization attack method to break another improved MFE scheme proposed in [WZY07]. Our analysis on the two quartic schemes is an example that non-linearization equations in plaintext variables like quadratization equations can be used efficiently in the cryptanalysis of multivariate cryptography.

Acknowledgement

This work is supported by the National Natural Science Foundation of China under Grant Numbers 60773134, 60973131 and 10990011, the National High Technology Research and Development (863) Program of China under Grant No. 2006AA01Z416, and the National Basic Research (973) Program of China under Grant No. 2007CB311201. The first two authors also thank a partial support from NSF and Taft Foundation.

References

[DH76] Diffie, W., Hellman, M.: New Directions in Cryptography. IEEE Transactions on Information Theory 22, 644–654 (1976)

[DGS06] Ding, J., Gower, J., Schmidt, D.: Multivariate Public-Key Cryptosystems. In: Advances in Information Security. Springer, Heidelberg (2006) ISBN 0-387-32229-9

[DHN07] Ding, J., Hu, L., Nie, X., Li, J., Wagner, J.: High Order Linearization Equation (HOLE) Attack on Multivariate Public Key Cryptosystems. In: Okamoto, T., Wang, X. (eds.) PKC 2007. LNCS, vol. 4450, pp. 233–248. Springer, Heidelberg (2007)

[Fag99] Faugère, J.: A New Efficient Algorithm for Computing Gröbner Bases (F4). Journal of Applied and Pure Algebra 139, 61–88 (1999)

[Pat95] Patarin, J.: Cryptanalysis of the Matsumoto and Imai Public Key Scheme of Eurocrypt'88. In: Coppersmith, D. (ed.) CRYPTO 1995. LNCS, vol. 963, pp. 248–261. Springer, Heidelberg (1995)

[Sho97] Shor, P.: Polynomial-time Algorithms for Prime Factorization and Discrete Logarithms on a Quantum Computer. SIAM Journal on Computing 26, 1484–1509 (1997)

[Wan07] Wang, Z.: An Improved Medium-Field Equation (MFE) Multivariate Public Key Encryption Scheme. In: IIH-MISP (2007), http://bit.kuas.edu.tw/ iihmsp07/accepted_list_general_session.html

[WFW09] Wang, X., Feng, F., Wang, X., Wang, Q.: A More Secure MFE Multivariate Public Key Encryption Scheme. International Journal of Computer Science and Applications 6(3), 1–9 (2009), http://www.tmrfindia.org/ijcsa/v6i31.pdf

[WYH06] Wang, L., Yang, B., Hu, Y., Lai, F.: A Medium-Field Multivariate Public Key Encryption Scheme. In: Pointcheval, D. (ed.) CT-RSA 2006. LNCS, vol. 3860, pp. 132–149. Springer, Heidelberg (2006)

[WZY07] Wang, Z., Zheng, S., Yang, Y., et al.: Improved Medium- Field Multivariate Public Key Encryption. Journal of University of Electonic Science an Technology of China 36(6), 1152–1154 (2007) (in Chinese)

Cryptanalysis of the Niederreiter Public Key Scheme Based on GRS Subcodes

Christian Wieschebrink

Federal Office for Information Security (BSI),
Godesberger Allee 185-189, 53175 Bonn, Germany
christian.wieschebrink@bsi.bund.de

Abstract. In this paper a new structural attack on the McEliece/Niederreiter public key cryptosystem based on subcodes of generalized Reed-Solomon codes proposed by Berger and Loidreau is described. It allows the reconstruction of the private key for almost all practical parameter choices in polynomial time with high probability.

Keywords: Public key cryptography, McEliece encryption, Niederreiter encryption, error-correcting codes, generalized Reed-Solomon codes, Sidelnikov-Shestakov attack.

1 Introduction

Public key cryptosystems based on the difficulty of the (syndrome) decoding problem for linear codes have been discussed since the work by McEliece [1] in 1977. Although the McEliece cryptosystem remains unbroken till today (for suitable parameter choices) and efficient quantum computer attacks are unknown in practice it could not stand up to encryption schemes such as RSA or schemes based on the discrete logarithm problem. This is partly due to the large (public) key sizes needed in the McEliece scheme. For example in terms of security a RSA public key of size 1024 bit is comparable to a 69 kB key in the McEliece scheme [2].

In order to reduce key sizes several alternative approaches for code based cryptography were proposed. In most of these approaches the Goppa code which is used in the McEliece cryptosystem is replaced by other codes which allow polynomial-time bounded distance decoding such as Reed-Muller codes, Gabidulin codes or generalized Reed-Solomon codes. However most of these basic variants turn out to be insecure [3,4,5].

Recently Berger and Loidreau presented a public key scheme based on subcodes of generalized Reed-Solomon codes [6]. It was partially cryptanalyzed in [7] where it was shown that the secret key can be recovered in manageable time if the subcode is chosen too large. However the attack quickly becomes infeasible for smaller subcodes. In the present paper we describe a new structural attack on the Berger-Loidreau scheme which works for almost all practical parameter choices. It is shown that even if relatively few (linear independent) codewords of a generalized Reed-Solomon code are given the complete code can be recovered with high probability which allows the reconstruction of the secret code parameters.

N. Sendrier (Ed.): PQCrypto 2010, LNCS 6061, pp. 61–72, 2010.

In the subsequent sections 2 and 3 we introduce some basic properties of generalized Reed-Solomon codes and the cryptosystems using those. In section 4 we review some known attacks and in section 5 we continue with the description of the new attack. A experimental analysis is given in section 6.

2 Basic Facts about Generalized Reed-Solomon Codes

Let $\mathbb{F}$ be a finite field with q elements. We will assume a field of characteristic 2, i.e. $q = 2^e$. For a matrix M let $<M>$ denote the linear code generated by the rows of M. Let $k, n \in \mathbb{N}$, $k \le n$, $\alpha = (\alpha_1, \ldots, \alpha_n) \in \mathbb{F}^n, x = (x_1, \ldots, x_n) \in (\mathbb{F}\backslash\{0\})^n$, where the α_i are pairwise distinct. The *generalized Reed-Solomon code (or GRS code)* $GRS_{n,k}(\alpha, x)$ is a linear code of length n and dimension k over $\mathbb{F}$ given by the generator matrix

$$G_{\alpha,x} = \begin{pmatrix} x_1 & x_2 & \cdots & x_n \\ x_1\alpha_1 & x_2\alpha_2 & \cdots & x_n\alpha_n \\ \vdots & & \ddots & \\ x_1\alpha_1^{k-1} & x_2\alpha_2^{k-1} & \cdots & x_n\alpha_n^{k-1} \end{pmatrix}, \tag{1}$$

i.e. $GRS_{n,k}(\alpha, x) = <G_{\alpha,x}>$. Typically we will assume that $GRS_{n,k}(\alpha, x)$ has full length, i.e. $n = q$. It is easy to see that $GRS_{n,k}(x, \alpha)$ consists exactly of those codewords $c \in \mathbb{F}^n$ for which a (unique) polynomial $f_c \in \mathbb{F}[x]$ of degree at most $k - 1$ exists such that

$$c = (x_1 f_c(\alpha_1), x_2 f_c(\alpha_2), \ldots, x_n f_c(\alpha_n)) .$$

We call f_c the *polynomial associated to c*. GRS codes allow efficient error correction. Up to $\lfloor \frac{n-k}{2} \rfloor$ errors can be corrected using the Berlekamp-Welch algorithm [8]. By applying so called list-decoding techniques even up to $n - \sqrt{(k-1)n}$ errors can be corrected [9] in polynomial time.

A useful fact about GRS codes is stated in the following

Proposition 1. *Let α, x be defined as above. Then*

$$GRS_{n,k}(\alpha, x) = GRS_{n,k}((a\alpha_1 + b, \ldots, a\alpha_n + b), (cx_1, \ldots, cx_n))$$

for all $a, b, c \in \mathbb{F}$, $a, c \neq 0$.

A proof can be found in [10]. It follows for example that α_1 and α_2 can be fixed to arbitrary distinct values in $\mathbb{F}$.

The dual of a GRS code is also a GRS code:

Proposition 2. *Let α, x be defined as above and $u := (u_1, \ldots u_n)$ where $u_i := x_i^{-1} \prod_{j \neq i} (\alpha_i - \alpha_j)^{-1}$. Then the dual code of $GRS_{n,k}(\alpha, x)$ is given by*

$$GRS_{n,k}(\alpha, x)^\perp = GRS_{n,n-k}(\alpha, u) .$$

Proof. See [10]. □

3 Cryptosystems Based on GRS Codes

Niederreiter was the first to suggest a public-key scheme based on GRS codes [11]. It can be described as follows:

Key generation. Given n, k $(k < n)$ randomly choose α, x with above properties and let $G_{\alpha,x}$ be the generator matrix (1) of the corresponding GRS code. Furthermore choose a random nonsingular $k \times k$-matrix H over $\mathbb{F}$ and compute $M := H \cdot G_{\alpha,x}$. Let $t := \lfloor \frac{n-k}{2} \rfloor$. The public key ist given by (M, t), the private key by (α, x).

Encryption. Suppose Alice wants to send a message $b \in \mathbb{F}^k$ to Bob using his public key (M, t). Therefore she chooses a random $e \in \mathbb{F}^n$ of Hamming weight at most t and computes the ciphertext $v := b \cdot M + e$.

Decryption. Using α, x Bob applies the Berlekamp-Welch algorithm to the received ciphertext v obtaining $b' := b \cdot M$. Let M^{-1} be a right side inverse on M. The plaintext is given by $b = b' \cdot M^{-1}$.

As we will see below the Niederreiter scheme is insecure due to the Sidelnikov-Shestakov attack.

The Berger-Loidreau cryptosystem [6] is a variant of the Niederreiter scheme which resists the Sidelnikov-Shestakov attack:

Key generation. Let n, k, α, x and $G_{\alpha,x}$ be as above and $l \in \mathbb{N}^{\leq k}$. Now choose a random $(k - l) \times k$-matrix H over $\mathbb{F}$ of rank $k - l$ and compute $M := H \cdot G_{\alpha,x}$. Let $t := \lfloor \frac{n-k}{2} \rfloor$. The public key ist given by (M, t), the private key by (α, x).

Encryption. The plaintext $b \in \mathbb{F}^{k-l}$ is encrypted by choosing a random $e \in \mathbb{F}^n$ of Hamming weight at most t and computing the ciphertext $v := b \cdot M + e$.

Decryption. Decryption works the same way as in the Niederreiter scheme. The Berlekamp-Welch algorithm is applied to v giving $b' := b \cdot M$. Finally b can be calculated from b' as above.

Obviously in the Berger-Loidreau scheme the public matrix M is the generator matrix of a subcode of $GRS_{n,k}(\alpha, x)$. In [6] the example parameters $(n, k, l) = (255, 133, 4)$ are given. In this case the work factor of a decoding attack is $> 2^{100}$.

4 Existing Attacks

4.1 The Sidelnikov-Shestakov Attack

As mentioned above the Niederreiter cryptosystem based on GRS codes was broken by Sidelnikov and Shestakov [5]. They show that the parameters α, x of the chosen GRS code can be recovered from the public key in polynomial time. The basic idea of their attack can be described as follows. Let $M = HG_{\alpha,x}$ be the public key. In a first step α is reconstructed. Compute the echelon form $E(M)$ of M:

$$E(M) = \begin{pmatrix} 1 & 0 & \cdots & 0 & b_{1,k+1} & \cdots & b_{1,n} \\ 0 & 1 & \cdots & 0 & b_{2,k+1} & \cdots & b_{2,n} \\ & & \ddots & & \vdots & & \vdots \\ 0 & \cdots & 0 & 1 & b_{k,k+1} & \cdots & b_{k,n} \end{pmatrix}$$

Consider the i-th row b_i of $E(M)$ and the associated polynomial f_{b_i}. Since the entries $b_{i,1}, \ldots, b_{i,i-1}$ and $b_{i,i+1}, \ldots, b_{i,k}$ of b_i are equal to zero and f_{b_i} has degree at most $k-1$ the polynomial must have the form

$$f_{b_i}(y) = c_{b_i} \cdot \prod_{j=1, j \neq i}^{k} (y - \alpha_j) \tag{2}$$

with $c_{b_i} \in \mathbb{F} \backslash \{0\}$. Now pick two arbitrary rows of $E(M)$, for example b_1 and b_2, and divide the entries of the first row by the corresponding entries in the second row as long as these are different from zero. Using (2) we get

$$\frac{b_{1,j}}{b_{2,j}} = \frac{x_j \cdot f_{b_1}(\alpha_j)}{x_j \cdot f_{b_2}(\alpha_j)} = \frac{c_{b_1}(\alpha_j - \alpha_2)}{c_{b_2}(\alpha_j - \alpha_1)} \tag{3}$$

for $j = k+1, \ldots, n$. By Proposition 1 we can assume that $\alpha_1 = 0$ and $\alpha_2 = 1$. Since the $\frac{b_{1,j}}{b_{2,j}}$ are known, the α_j can uniquely be reconstructed from (3), if $\frac{c_{b_1}}{c_{b_2}}$ is guessed correctly. It remains to find $\alpha_3, \ldots, \alpha_k$. Therefore we replace the row b_2 by b_i $(i = 3, \ldots, k)$ in the above equation (3) and get

$$\frac{b_{1,j}}{b_{i,j}}(\alpha_j - \alpha_1) = \frac{c_{b_1}}{c_{b_i}}(\alpha_j - \alpha_i) . \tag{4}$$

Here $\frac{c_{b_1}}{c_{b_i}}$ and α_i are unknown, but by letting $j = k+1, k+2$ for example, those values can uniqely be reconstructed by solving a system of two linear equations.

In total α can be calculated using $O(k^2 n)$ arithmetic operations in $\mathbb{F}$ (assuming that $\frac{c_{b_1}}{c_{b_2}}$ has been guessed correctly).

Now in a second step x (and the matrix H as a byproduct) can be recovered. First find a non-trivial solution $c = (c_1, \ldots, c_{k+1})$ of the linear system

$$M' \cdot c = 0 ,$$

where M' is the $k \times (k+1)$-matrix consisting of the $k+1$ leftmost columns of the public key M. Let G' be the $k \times (k+1)$-matrix consisting of the $k+1$ leftmost columns of $G_{\alpha,x}$. Because of $M' = HG'$ c also solves

$$G' \cdot c = 0$$

and therefore the first $k+1$ entries $x_1, \ldots, x_{k+1}$ of x solve

$$\begin{pmatrix} c_1\alpha_1^0 & c_2\alpha_2^0 & \cdots & c_{k+1}\alpha_{k+1}^0 \\ c_1\alpha_1^1 & c_2\alpha_2^1 & \cdots & c_{k+1}\alpha_{k+1}^1 \\ \vdots & & \ddots & \vdots \\ c_1\alpha_1^{k-1} & c_2\alpha_2^{k-1} & \cdots & c_{k+1}\alpha_{k+1}^{k-1} \end{pmatrix} \begin{pmatrix} x_1 \\ x_2 \\ \vdots \\ x_{k+1} \end{pmatrix} = 0 .$$

By assuming $x_1 = 1$ the solution is uniquely determined. Now the matrix G' is completely known. Let G'' be the matrix consisting of the first k columns of G' and M'' the matrix consisting of the first k columns of M. We have $H = M''(G'')^{-1}$. Finally $G = H^{-1}M$ (and thereby the remaining x_i) can be computed. The second step can be completed with $O(k^3 + k^2 n)$ operations in $\mathbb{F}$. The attack works if $2 \leq k \leq n-2$.

The above attack proves the following

Proposition 3. *Let $2 \leq k \leq n-2$ and α, x be as above. There are at most $q(q-1)^2$ pairwise distinct vectors $\alpha' \in \mathbb{F}^n$ for which a $x' \in \mathbb{F}^n$ exists, s.t.*

$$GRS_{n,k}(\alpha, x) = GRS_{n,k}(\alpha', x') \ . \tag{5}$$

If two arbitrary entries of α' are fixed, the number of different α' for which x' with (5) exists is upper bounded by $(q-1)$.

Proof. Equation (3) shows that $\alpha_{k+1}, \dots, \alpha_n$ are uniquely determined if $\alpha_1, \alpha_2, \frac{c_{b_1}}{c_{b_2}}$ are given (since the GRS code has minimum weight $n-k+1$ we know that $\frac{b_{1,j}}{b_{2,j}} \neq 0$). Furthermore, if $\alpha_{k+1}, \alpha_{k+2}$ are uniquely determined, so are $\alpha_3, \dots, \alpha_k$: considering (4) for $j = k+1, k+2$ define

$$\gamma_1 := \frac{b_{i,k+1}}{b_{1,k+1}(\alpha_{k+1} - \alpha_1)}, \ \gamma_2 := \frac{b_{i,k+2}}{b_{1,k+2}(\alpha_{k+2} - \alpha_1)} \ .$$

It follows

$$\frac{c_{b_i}}{c_{b_1}} = \gamma_1(\alpha_{k+1} - \alpha_i) = \gamma_2(\alpha_{k+2} - \alpha_i)$$

and thereby

$$\gamma_1 \alpha_{k+1} - \gamma_2 \alpha_{k+2} = (\gamma_1 - \gamma_2)\alpha_i \ .$$

As a consequence $\gamma_1 - \gamma_2 \neq 0$ since otherwise $\alpha_{k+1} = \alpha_{k+2}$. This means α_i is uniquely determined for $i = 3, \dots, k$ if $\alpha_{k+1}, \alpha_{k+2}$ are given.

The proof is complete by noting that there are at most $q(q-1)^2$ different choices for $(\alpha_1, \alpha_2, \frac{c_{b_1}}{c_{b_2}})$.

4.2 An Attack on the Berger-Loidreau Cryptosystem

The attack on the Berger-Loidreau cryptosystem presented in [7] can be considered as an extension of the above method by Sidelnikov and Shestakov. We give a brief overview. Let $E(M) = [1_{k-l}|B] = (t_{i,j})$ be the echelon form of the public matrix M of the Berger-Loidreau scheme. Generalizing the above argument for every pair $(c,d) \in \{1, \dots, k-l\}^2$ there exist polynomials $P_c, P_d \in \mathbb{F}[x]$ of degree $\leq l$ such that

$$\frac{t_{c,j}}{t_{d,j}} = \frac{(\alpha_j - \alpha_d)P_c(\alpha_j)}{(\alpha_j - \alpha_c)P_d(\alpha_j)} \tag{6}$$

for all $j = k-l+1, \dots, n$ with $t_{d,j} \neq 0$. Now let $d = k - l =: m$ and define

$$\tilde{P}_c(x) := (x - \alpha_m)P_c(x), \tilde{Q}_c(x) := (x - \alpha_c)P_m(x) \ ,$$

s.t. (6) becomes

$$\frac{t_{c,j}}{t_{d,j}} = \frac{\tilde{P}_c(\alpha_j)}{\tilde{Q}_c(\alpha_j)} \ .$$

Suppose (for a moment) that $\alpha_{m+1}, \ldots, \alpha_{m+2l+3}$ are known. In this case the polynomials $\tilde{P}_c, \tilde{Q}_c$ can be calculated by solving a linear system. (The polynomials are uniqely determined if we assume that they are relatively prime and $\tilde{Q}_c$ is monic.) By extracting the linear factors of $\tilde{Q}_c$, where c ranges over $1, \ldots, m-1$ the $\alpha_1, \ldots, \alpha_{m-1}$ can be recovered. By appropriately permuting the columns of M and applying the just described method to the permuted matrix the remaining $\alpha_m, \alpha_{m+2l+4}, \ldots, \alpha_n$ can be found. Once α is found, x can easily be determined: since $<M>$ is a subcode of $GRS_{n,k}(\alpha, x)$ it follows from Proposition 2 that

$$M_{i,1}\alpha_1^j u_1 + \cdots + M_{i,n}\alpha_n^j u_n = 0$$

for all $i = 1, \ldots, k-l$ and $j = 0, \ldots, n-k-1$, where $M = (M_{i,j})$. So the values $u_1, \ldots, u_n$ can be recovered by solving a system of $(k-l)(n-k)$ linear equations. Typically $(k-l)(n-k) > n$ so $(u_1, \ldots, u_n)$ is expected to be uniqely determined if we require $u_1 = 1$. Finally x can be computed from $(u_1, \ldots, u_n)$.

Since $\alpha_{m+1}, \ldots, \alpha_{m+2l+3}$ are unknown (we can assume $\alpha_{m+1} = 0$ and $\alpha_{m+2} = 1$ however) all $(q-2) \cdot \ldots \cdot (q-2l-2)$ possible assignments have to be checked. In total the procedure to reconstruct α can be completed with $O(m^2 n + q^{2l+1} m l^3)$ arithmetic operations in $\mathbb{F}$, so is feasible if l and q are small. However if for example $q \geq 64$ and $l \geq 8$ the attack becomes impractical.

The described method can be improved by finding two codewords in $<M>$ which have many (i.e. more than $m-2$) zero entries in common positions. For details we refer to [7].

5 An Improved Attack on the Berger-Loidreau Cryptosystem

Let $M = H \cdot G_{\alpha,x}$ be the public matrix of the Berger-Loidreau cryptosystem, which is the generator matrix of a $(k-l)$-dimensional subcode of $GRS_{n,k}(\alpha, x)$. We present an algorithm to recover the secret parameters α, x from M which is feasible even for larger l.

Let $r_1, \ldots, r_m$ be the rows of M and $f_1, \ldots, f_m$ $(m = k-l)$ be the polynomials associated to these rows. For two row vectors $a, b \in \mathbb{F}^n$ we define the componentwise product $a * b \in \mathbb{F}^n$ to be

$$a * b := (a_1 \cdot b_1, a_2 \cdot b_2, \ldots, a_n \cdot b_n) \ .$$

For our attack we distinguish two cases. First we consider the case $2k-1 \leq n-2$. Then the attack works as follows. Calculate $r_i * r_j$ for all $i, j \in \{1, \ldots, m\}, i \leq j$. Obviously $r_i * r_j$ has the form

$$r_i * r_j = (x_1^2 f_i(\alpha_1) \cdot f_j(\alpha_1), \ldots, x_n^2 f_i(\alpha_n) \cdot f_j(\alpha_n)) \ ,$$

and since $\deg f_i \cdot f_j \leq 2k-2$ the code C generated by the $r_i * r_j$ is a subcode of $GRS_{n,2k-1}(\alpha, x')$, where $x' = (x_1^2, \dots, x_n^2)$. If $C = GRS_{n,2k-1}(\alpha, x')$ then the Sidelnikov-Shestakov attack can be applied to an generator matrix of C returning x', α. If char $\mathbb{F} = 2$ the vector x can be computed from x' directly (by applying the inverse Frobenius operator), otherwise x can be recovered from M with the method described in section 4.2.

Otherwise if $C \neq GRS_{n,2k-1}(\alpha, x')$ we consider this attack to have failed. Since the running time of the attack of section 4.2 largely depends on $l = k-m$ at least we can apply 4.2 to a generator matrix of C if $0 < 2k-1-$ dim $C < l$. Note however that for not too large l the probability that C equals $GRS_{n,2k-1}(\alpha, x')$ seems to be very high (see section 6).

For typical instances of the Berger-Loidreau cryptosystem the case $2k-1 > n-2$ may apply. The above attack does not work here in general since the Sidelnikov-Shestakov algorithm cannot be applied or the code generated by the $r_i * r_j$ may be equal to $\mathbb{F}^n$. However the idea of multiplying codewords componentwise can be applied to a shortened code of $<M>$.

Definition 1. *Let $C \subset \mathbb{F}^n$ be a linear code of length n and dimension k and let $d \in \mathbb{N}^{\leq k}$. The* shortened code *$S_d(C)$ consists of all codewords $(s_1, \dots, s_{n-d}) \in \mathbb{F}^{n-d}$ such that*

$$(\underbrace{0, \dots, 0}_{d\ times}, s_1, \dots, s_{n-d}) \in C \ .$$

Given the generator matrix $G_C = [1_k|E]$ of C in echelon form (where E denotes a $k \times (n-k)$-matrix) a basis of $S_d(C)$ can easily be obtained by extracting the $n-d$ rightmost components of the last $k-d$ rows of G_C.

Now let M again be the public $(m \times n)$-matrix of the Berger-Loidreau cryptosystem and S be a generator matrix of $S_d(<M>)$. For a row $s = (s_1, \dots s_{n-d})$ of S we have

$$(0, \dots, 0, s_1, \dots, s_{n-d}) \in GRS_{n,k}(\alpha, x) \ ,$$

so s can be written

$$s = (x_{d+1} f(\alpha_{d+1}), \dots, x_n f(\alpha_n)) \ ,$$

where $f(x) \in \mathbb{F}[x]$ has the form

$$f(x) = g(x) \prod_{j=1}^{d} (x - \alpha_j)$$

with $\deg g(x) \leq k-d-1$. Letting $z := (x_{d+i} \prod_{j=1}^{d} (\alpha_{d+i} - \alpha_j))_{i=1,\dots,n-d}$ and $\alpha' := (\alpha_{d+1}, \dots, \alpha_n)$ obviously we have

$$S_d(<M>) = <S> \subset GRS_{n-d,k-d}(\alpha', z) \ .$$

If d can be chosen such that $d \leq m-1$ and $2(k-d)-1 \leq n-d-2$ the above algorithm can be applied to S which in case of success delivers at most $q(q-1)^2$

candidates for α' according to proposition 3 ($q-1$ candidates at most if we assume $\alpha'_{n-1}=1, \alpha'_n=0$ for example). Let T be the set of these solutions. Once T is known the remaining $\alpha_1,\ldots,\alpha_d$ could be computed with similiar methods as described in [7]. In the following an alternative approach is given.

Let $m^{(1)},\ldots,m^{(n)}$ be the column vectors of matrix M and $\pi:\{1,\ldots,n\}\rightarrow\{1,\ldots,n\}$ be a permutation. Let M_π denote the matrix obtained from M by permuting the columns according to π, i.e. $M_\pi=(m^{(\pi(1))},\ldots,m^{(\pi(n))})$. Similiarly for $y:=(y_1,\ldots,y_n)\in\mathbb{F}^n$ we define $y_\pi:=(y_{\pi(1)},\ldots,y_{\pi(n)})$. Obviously we have

$$<M_\pi>\subset GRS_{n,k}(\alpha_\pi, x_\pi)\ . \tag{7}$$

For simplicity we assume $2d\le n-3$ (for typical instances d can be chosen this way, however the following method can easily be extended to the general case). Now let $\pi:\{1,\ldots,n\}\rightarrow\{1,\ldots,n\}$ be given by

$$\pi(i)=\left\{\begin{matrix} i+d,\ 1\le i\le d \\ i-d,\ d+1\le i\le 2d \\ i,\quad 2d+1\le i\le n \end{matrix}\right\}\ .$$

Apply the above algorithm to M_π, i.e. compute a generator matrix S' of $S_d(<M_\pi>)$ and multiply every pair of rows of S' componentwise. Because of (7) we find a set T' of candidates for $(\alpha_{\pi(d+1)},\ldots,\alpha_{\pi(n)})$. A solution for α can be reconstructed by finding $\sigma\in T$ and $\tau\in T'$ with $\sigma_{d+1}=0, \sigma_{d+2}=1$ and $\sigma_i=\tau_i$ for $i=d+1,\ldots,n-d$ and setting

$$\begin{aligned} \alpha_i &= \tau_i && \text{for } 1\le i\le d,\\ \alpha_i &= \sigma_{i-d} && \text{for } d+1\le i\le 2d,\\ \alpha_i &= \sigma_{i-d}=\tau_{i-d} && \text{for } 2d+1\le i\le n\ . \end{aligned}$$

The above algorithm is summarized in Algorithms 1 and 2. The procedure *SidelnikovShestakovAlpha(P)* in line 13 of algorithm 1 represents the Sidelnikov-Shestakov algorithm and returns the set of all possible α for a given generator matrix P of a GRS code.

6 Analysis and Experimental Results

Let us consider the case $2k\le n-1$. The above attack is successful if the products r_i*r_j generate the code $GRS_{n,2k-1}(\alpha,x')$. The number of different products is at most $\frac{m(m+1)}{2}$. If l is chosen small (as it is suggested in [6]) then $\frac{m(m+1)}{2}>2k-1$. For randomly chosen subcodes it is expected that indeed the above GRS code is generated. In this case the algorithm takes $O(m^4n+k^2n+m^2(n-k)^2n)$ operations in $\mathbb{F}$ in the worst case, i.e. we have a polynomial running time in the code length n.

In case $2k>n-1$ the attack is sucessful if there is a d with

$$2k-n+1\le d\le m-1 \tag{8}$$

Algorithm 1. *partAlpha(d,M)*

Input: d, generator matrix M with $m = k - l$ rows s.t. $<M> \subset GRS_{n,k}(\alpha, x)$
Output: Set A of candidates for $(\alpha_{d+1}, \ldots, \alpha_n)$

$G = (G_{i,j}) \leftarrow$ echelon form of M
$S \leftarrow (G_{i,j})_{\substack{i=d+1,\ldots,m \\ j=d+1,\ldots,n}}$
$s_1, \ldots, s_{m-d} \leftarrow$ rows of S
$r \leftarrow 1$
for $i \leftarrow 1, \ldots, m-d$ **do**
  for $j \leftarrow i, \ldots, m-d$ **do**
    $p_r \leftarrow s_i * s_j$
    $r \leftarrow r + 1$
  end for
end for
$P \leftarrow$ generator matrix of the code spanned by the p_r
if dim $<P> = 2(k-d) - 1$ **then**
  $A \leftarrow$ *SidelnikovShestakovAlpha(P)*
  return A
else
  return FAIL
end if

such that the componentwise products of the rows of the generator matrices of $S_d(<M>)$ and $S_d(<M_\pi>)$ generate the corresponding GRS codes. A necessary condition for this is

$$\frac{(m-d)(m-d+1)}{2} \geq 2(k-d) - 1 \; . \tag{9}$$

In this case we need $O((m-d)^4 n + (k-d)^2 n + n^3 + m^2(n-k)^2 n)$ operations for the complete attack (assuming $q = n$).

The above attack was implemented in MAGMA and verified experimentally. To this end 100 random instances of the public key for four different parameter sets were created. It turned out that for all 400 created instances the private key could be reconstructed. The average times t_α and t_x to reconstruct the vectors α and x respectively are given in table 1. (Experiments were made using MAGMA V2.11-6 on a 1.83 GHz Core 2 Duo machine.) The first line in table 1 represents the suggested parameters in [6]. The results clearly show that even if the dimension m of the subcode is small the parameters of the GRS code can easily be obtained.[1] For most practical parameter sets the scheme of [6] is insecure.

However it is not difficult to construct instances of the Berger-Loidreau scheme where the above attack fails in the sense that $GRS_{n,2k-1}(\alpha, x')$ cannot be completely generated. For example let $k < \frac{n-3}{2}$, $b, c \in \mathbb{N}$ with $1 < c < k$ and

[1] Note that small m are insecure anyway due to possible decoding attacks.

Algorithm 2. Reconstruction of α and x

Input: Public generator matrix M of the Berger-Loidreau scheme with $m = k - l$ rows and n columns
Output: Parameters α, x, s.t. $<M> \subset GRS_{n,k}(\alpha, x)$

$d \leftarrow 2k - n + 2$
if $d > m - 1$ **then**
  return FAIL
end if
if $d < 0$ **then**
  $d \leftarrow 0$
end if
$A_1 \leftarrow$ *partAlpha(d,M)*
if $d = 0$ **then**
  $\alpha \leftarrow$ random element of A_1
end if
if $d > 0$ **then**
  for $i \leftarrow 1, \ldots, n$ **do**
    if $1 \leq i \leq d$ **then**
      $\pi(i) \leftarrow d + i$
    end if
    if $d + 1 \leq i \leq 2d$ **then**
      $\pi(i) \leftarrow i - d$
    end if
    if $2d + 1 \leq i \leq n$ **then**
      $\pi(i) \leftarrow i$
    end if
  end for
  $A_2 \leftarrow$ *partAlpha(d, M_π)*
  Find $(\sigma, \tau) \in A_1 \times A_2$ with $\sigma_{d+1} = 0, \sigma_{d+2} = 1, \sigma_i = \tau_i$ for $i = d + 1, \ldots, n - d$
  for $i \leftarrow 1, \ldots, n$ **do**
    if $1 \leq i \leq d$ **then**
      $\alpha_i \leftarrow \tau_i$
    end if
    if $d + 1 \leq i \leq n$ **then**
      $\alpha_i \leftarrow \sigma_{i-d}$
    end if
  end for
end if
$X \leftarrow$ solution space of the linear system

$$M_{i,1}\alpha_1^j u_1 + \cdots + M_{i,n}\alpha_n^j u_n = 0$$

  for $i = 1, \ldots, m$ and $j = 0, \ldots, n - k$.
$(u_1, \ldots, u_n) \leftarrow$ random nonzero element of X
for $i \leftarrow 1, \ldots, n$ **do**
  $x_i \leftarrow (u_i \prod_{j \neq i}(\alpha_i - \alpha_j))^{-1}$
end for
return α, x

Table 1. Running times of the attack

q	n	k	m	t_α (sec)	t_x (sec)
2^8	256	133	129	337	209
2^8	256	126	45	176	105
2^7	128	60	16	23	10
2^7	128	70	34	40	14

$\frac{b(b-1)}{2} < c$. Let M be an instance of the public matrix with rows m_i where the polynomials f_i associated to the m_i have the form

$$f_i(y) = a_i(y)g(y) + r_i(y)$$

with $i = 1, \ldots, m$ ($m < k$) for a fixed $g(y)$ where deg $g(y) = c$, deg $a_i(y) \leq k - c - 1$, deg $r_i(y) < c$ and

$$r_b(y) = r_{b+1}(y) = \ldots = r_m(y) = 0 .$$

We have

$$f_i \cdot f_j = a_i a_j g^2 + (a_i r_j + a_j r_i)g + r_i r_j .$$

Since there are at most $\frac{b(b-1)}{2}$ different $r_i r_j \neq 0$ the subspace of $\mathbb{F}[y]$ generated by the $f_i f_j$ cannot cover all possible remainders mod g, which means the $f_i f_j$ cannot generate the linear space $\mathbb{F}^{2k-2}[y]$ of all polynomials over $\mathbb{F}$ of degree at most $2k-2$ and thus the $m_i * m_j$ cannot generate $GRS_{n,2k-1}(\alpha, x')$.

7 Conclusion and Future Work

A new attack on the Berger-Loidreau public key cryptosystem which allows the reconstruction of the private key was presented. Experimental evidence of its correctness was given. The presented attack is much more efficient than previously known structural attacks. It is possible to construct instances of the scheme which resist the attack however it seems doubtful that these are secure.

Finally we make some remarks about possible implications for the security of the original McEliece scheme [1]. The original McEliece cryptosystem is one of the few unbroken code-based public key schemes. It is analogous to the Niederreiter scheme presented in section 3 where the GRS code is replaced by a binary irreducible Goppa code. This type of code belongs to the class of alternant codes. More specifically let $n := 2^e$, $(\alpha_1, \ldots, \alpha_n)$ a permutation of the elements of $\mathbb{F} := GF(n)$ and $G(x) \in \mathbb{F}[x]$ an irreducible polynomial. Then the binary linear code in $GF(2)^n$ given by

$$GRS_{n,\deg G}((\alpha_1, \ldots, \alpha_n), (G(\alpha_1)^{-1}, \ldots, G(\alpha_n)^{-1})^{\perp} \cap GF(2)^n ,$$

is called binary irreducible Goppa code. So given a (scrambled) generator matrix M of such a code (which represents the public key of the McEliece scheme), M

can be considered as a generator matrix of a subcode of a GRS code. However the attack of section 5 fails in this case, since typically we have for the dimension m of the Goppa code

$$m \approx n - e \cdot \deg G = 2k - n - (e-2)\deg G \ ,$$

where $k = n - \deg G$. As $(e-2)\deg G > 0$ there is no suitable d with (8). Of course another reason is that the component-wise products of the rows of M are elements of $GF(2)^n$, so they cannot generate a non-trivial GRS code in $\mathbb{F}^n$. There seems to be no straightforward way to generalize the attack to this case, however a more detailed analysis of the attack in this respect remains part of future work.

References

1. McEliece, R.: A public-key cryptosystem based on algebraic coding theory. DSN Progress Report, Jet Prop. Lab., California Inst. Tech. 42-44, 114–116 (1978)
2. van Tilborg, H.: Encyclopedia of Cryptography and Security. Springer, Heidelberg (2005)
3. Minder, L., Shokrollahi, A.: Cryptanalysis of the Sidelnikov cryptosystem. In: Naor, M. (ed.) EUROCRYPT 2007. LNCS, vol. 4515, pp. 347–360. Springer, Heidelberg (2007)
4. Gibson, K.: The security of the Gabidulin public-key cryptosystem. In: Maurer, U.M. (ed.) EUROCRYPT 1996. LNCS, vol. 1070, pp. 212–223. Springer, Heidelberg (1996)
5. Sidelnikov, V., Shestakov, S.: On insecurity of cryptosystems based on generalized Reed-Solomon codes. Discrete Math. Appl. 2, 439–444 (1992)
6. Berger, T., Loidreau, P.: How to mask the structure of codes for a cryptographic use. Designs, Codes and Cryptography 35, 63–79 (2005)
7. Wieschebrink, C.: An attack on a modified Niederreiter encryption scheme. In: Yung, M., Dodis, Y., Kiayias, A., Malkin, T.G. (eds.) PKC 2006. LNCS, vol. 3958, pp. 14–26. Springer, Heidelberg (2006)
8. Berlekamp, E., Welch, L.: Error correction of algebraic block codes, US Patent No. 4,633,470 (1986)
9. Guruswami, V., Sudan, M.: Improved decoding of Reed-Solomon and algebraic-geometric codes. In: Proceedings of 39th Annual Symposium on Foundations of Computer Science, pp. 28–37 (1998)
10. MacWilliams, F., Sloane, N.: The Theory of Error-Correcting Codes. North-Holland, Amsterdam (1997)
11. Niederreiter, N.: Knapsack-type cryptosystems and algebraic coding theory. Problems of Control and Information Theory 15, 159–166 (1986)

Grover vs. McEliece

Daniel J. Bernstein*

Department of Computer Science (MC 152)
The University of Illinois at Chicago
Chicago, IL 60607–7053
djb@cr.yp.to

Abstract. This paper shows that quantum information-set-decoding attacks are asymptotically much faster than non-quantum information-set-decoding attacks.

Keywords: code-based cryptography, post-quantum cryptography.

1 Introduction

Assume that large quantum computers are built, and that they scale as smoothly as one could possibly hope. Shor's algorithm and its generalizations will then completely break RSA, DSA, ECDSA, and many other popular cryptographic systems: for example, a quantum computer will find an RSA user's secret key at essentially the same speed that the user can apply the key. See [21] for Shor's original algorithm, [24] for a detailed complexity analysis, and [16] for a survey of generalizations.

It seems inconceivable, however, that Shor's period-finding idea will ever have any relevance to the vast majority of "one-way" cryptographic systems: secret-key stream ciphers, hash-based public-key signature systems, etc. There are, furthermore, several well-known "trapdoor one-way" cryptographic systems—most importantly, public-key encryption systems—that seem immune to Shor's algorithm. The oldest example is the code-based public-key system introduced by McEliece in [19] thirty years ago.

The conventional wisdom is that all of these systems will nevertheless need to double their key sizes in order to survive quantum computers. Shor's algorithm is not the only application of quantum computers! A quantum searching algorithm introduced by Grover in [13] and [14] finds (e.g.) a 256-bit AES key in only about 2^{128} quantum operations, given a few known plaintexts encrypted under that key. Users who want to push the attacker's cost significantly higher than 2^{128}—the original motivation for 256-bit AES—will need a cipher with significantly more than a 256-bit key.

* Permanent ID of this document: e2bbcdd82c3e967c7e3487dc945f3e87. Date of this document: 2010.03.02. This work was supported in part by the National Science Foundation under grant ITR–0716498, and in part by Cisco's University Research Program.

N. Sendrier (Ed.): PQCrypto 2010, LNCS 6061, pp. 73–80, 2010.

There is, however, no reason to think that the doubled key size for a secret-key cipher will be matched by a doubled hash-function output length, a doubled key size for McEliece, etc. Consider the following examples:

- A frequently cited Brassard–Høyer–Tapp paper "Quantum cryptanalysis of hash and claw-free functions" [8] argues that quantum computers force a 1.5× expansion in the output length of a collision-resistant black-box hash function. My new paper [3] argues that quantum computers actually have no impact on the difficulty of finding black-box hash collisions.
- Quantum computers obviously have no impact on the key length required for the Gilbert–MacWilliams–Sloane authenticator [11] and other information-theoretically secure cryptographic systems.
- Overbeck and Sendrier argue in [20, Section 3.5] that quantum computers have only a small impact on the McEliece public-key system, reducing the attacker's decoding cost from (e.g.) 2^{140} to 2^{133} for a code of length 4096 and dimension $4096 - 45 \cdot 12 = 3556$.

Grover's algorithm takes only square-root time compared to a brute-force key search, but this does not mean that it takes less time than the more sophisticated algorithms used to find hash collisions, McEliece error vectors, etc. Sometimes Grover's idea can be used to speed up the more sophisticated algorithms, but understanding the extent of the speedup requires careful analysis.

Contents of this paper. This paper points out a way to attack the McEliece system with Grover's algorithm. This attack is asymptotically much faster than the approach analyzed in [20, Section 3.5].

Fix a rational number R with $0 < R < 1$. State-of-the-art information-set-decoding algorithms take time just $c^{(1+o(1))n/\lg n}$ to break a length-n rate-R code; here $c = 1/(1-R)^{1-R}$, and $o(1)$ is a function of n that converges to 0 as $n \to \infty$. See [6] for a much more detailed analysis. What this paper shows is that quantum versions of the same information-set-decoding algorithms take time only $c^{(1/2+o(1))n/\lg n}$. Protecting against this attack requires replacing n by $(2+o(1))n$, essentially *quadrupling* the McEliece key size.

Users who were already making the worst-case assumption regarding the impact of Grover's algorithm, namely a square-root speedup in all attacks, will not be affected by this paper. However, users who were making more optimistic assumptions to reduce key size, decryption time, etc. will need to change their parameters in the McEliece system and in other code-based systems to survive quantum computers.

2 Review of Attacks against the McEliece System

This section reviews the McEliece public-key cryptosystem; information-set-decoding attacks against the system; and some claims in the literature regarding the applicability of quantum computers to information-set decoding.

Review of McEliece encryption. Recall that the McEliece public key is a "random" full-rank $k \times n$ matrix G with entries in $\mathbf{F}_2$. Here k and n are system parameters. McEliece originally suggested $k = 524$ and $n = 1024$, aiming for 64-bit security, but these parameters were broken in [5]. Users today take much larger parameters, such as $k = 3556$ and $n = 4096$.

The matrix G specifies a linear map from $\mathbf{F}_2^k$ to $\mathbf{F}_2^n$. The sender encrypts a suitably randomized message $m \in \mathbf{F}_2^k$, together with a uniform random vector $e \in \mathbf{F}_2^n$ of Hamming weight t, as $Gm + e \in \mathbf{F}_2^n$. Here t is another system parameter. Typically $t = (n-k)/\lceil \lg n \rceil$.

The receiver secretly generates G as a scrambled Goppa matrix, and uses this structure to quickly decode $Gm + e$, obtaining m and e. This structure means that G is not actually a uniform random full-rank matrix. However, all known "structural attacks" that discover the secret, or that merely distinguish G from uniform random, are much slower than the information-set-decoding attacks discussed below.

Review of basic information-set decoding. Basic information-set decoding works as follows. Choose a uniform random size-k subset $S \subseteq \{1, 2, \ldots, n\}$, and consider the natural projection $\mathbf{F}_2^n \to \mathbf{F}_2^S$ that extracts the coordinates indexed by S, discarding all other coordinates. Assume that the following two events occur simultaneously:

- The error vector e projects to $0 \in \mathbf{F}_2^S$; i.e., the entries of e indexed by S are all 0.
- The composition $\mathbf{F}_2^k \xrightarrow{G} \mathbf{F}_2^n \to \mathbf{F}_2^S$ is invertible; i.e., the columns of G indexed by S form an invertible $k \times k$ matrix.

Obtain m by applying the inverse to the projection of $Gm + e$, and obtain e by subtracting Gm from $Gm + e$. If this fails—i.e., if the composition is not invertible, or if the resulting e does not have Hamming weight t—then go back to the beginning and try another set S.

The first event occurs for exactly $\binom{n-t}{k}$ out of the $\binom{n}{k}$ choices of S, so it occurs on average after $\binom{n}{k}/\binom{n-t}{k}$ iterations. If $k = Rn$ and $t \approx (1-R)n/\lg n$ then

$$\frac{\binom{n}{k}}{\binom{n-t}{k}} = \frac{n \cdots (n-t+1)}{(n-k) \cdots (n-k-t+1)} \approx \left(\frac{n}{n-k}\right)^t = \left(\frac{1}{1-R}\right)^t \approx c^{n/\lg n}$$

where $c = 1/(1-R)^{1-R}$. These approximations are quite crude, but a more careful analysis shows that $\binom{n}{k}/\binom{n-t}{k} \in c^{(1+o(1))n/\lg n}$ when t is sufficiently close to $(1-R)n/\lg n$.

For any particular S, the second event occurs for approximately 29% of all matrices G, since approximately 29% of all $k \times k$ matrices over $\mathbf{F}_2$ are invertible. It is tempting to leap to the conclusion that, for any particular G, the second event occurs for approximately 29% of all choices of S, and that the combination of events occurs for approximately $0.29\binom{n-t}{k}$ out of the $\binom{n}{k}$ choices of S. This conclusion is wrong for some choices of G but does appear to be correct for McEliece public keys. For further discussion of this point see [6, Section 2, under "Model of the number of iterations"].

Review of advanced information-set decoding. More advanced forms of information-set decoding complicate each iteration but decrease the number of iterations required, for example by allowing e to have a few bits set within S and combinatorially searching for those bits. There are also many techniques to reduce the cost of finding appropriate sets S, computing inverses, checking whether m is correct, etc. See generally [5].

The analysis in [6] shows that these improvements collectively reduce the cost of information-set decoding by more than a constant power of n but that the final cost is still $c^{(1+o(1))n/\lg n}$.

Review of previous analyses of quantum decoding attacks. I am aware of two previous attempts to quantify the impact of quantum computers upon information-set decoding. The first is by Barg and Zhou in [2, Section 1]. The second is by Overbeck and Sendrier in [20, Section 3.5], as mentioned above.

The Barg–Zhou analysis is a brief sentence claiming that Grover's algorithm can decode any length-n code C, linear or not, "on a quantum computer of circuit size $O(n|C|^{1/2})$ in time $O(n|C|^{1/2})$, which is essentially optimal following a result in [1997 Bennett et al.]." Note that if C has rate R then $|C| = 2^{Rn}$ and $|C|^{1/2} = 2^{Rn/2}$.

There are many reasons to question the Barg–Zhou claim. Specifying an arbitrary non-linear code of length n and rate R requires almost $2^{Rn}n$ bits of information; there is no theoretical obstacle to this information being packed into only $O(2^{Rn/2}n)$ qubits, but Barg and Zhou give no explanation of how to extract the information again from those qubits, never mind the question of what this has to do with Grover's algorithm.

There is no difficulty in building a small computer to enumerate a large *linear* code. In this case a naive application of Grover's algorithm would take essentially $2^{Rn/2}$ iterations but would require only a polynomial-size quantum computer, far below the "optimal" circuit size claimed by Barg and Zhou. Furthermore, information-set decoding takes time only about $c^{n/\lg n}$ on a small non-quantum computer, asymptotically far below the "optimal" time $2^{Rn/2}$ claimed by Barg and Zhou.

The Overbeck–Sendrier analysis is more detailed and is aimed at giving an "intuition why Grover's algorithm is not able [to] give a significant speed-up for the existing attacks." Overbeck and Sendrier begin with "the simplifying assumption that by Grover's algorithm we are able to search a set of size N in $O(\sqrt{N})$ operations on a quantum computer with at least $\log_2(N)$ QuBits." They say that the combinatorial search in advanced forms of information-set decoding (e.g., the collision search introduced by Stern in [23]) "achieves the same speed-up as Grover's algorithm would achieve."

Overbeck and Sendrier also briefly consider, but dismiss, the idea of using Grover's algorithm for "the guessing phase," i.e., to search for sets S having both of the desired properties. They say that "this would either require an iterative application of Grover's algorithm (which is not possible) or a memory of size of the whole search space, as the search function in the second step depends on the first step. This would clearly ruin the 'divide-and-conquer' strategy and is thus not possible either."

This paper shows the opposite: Grover's searching algorithm can be used to drastically speed up the search for sets S. One might speculate that previous authors were misled by Grover's often-repeated description of his algorithm as searching a "database." See the next section of this paper for further discussion of what Grover's algorithm actually does.

3 Quantum Information-Set Decoding

Grover's algorithm is properly understood not as searching through a "database" but as searching for roots of a function. It is easy, from this perspective, to see how to apply Grover's algorithm to information-set decoding. This section spells out the details.

Grover's algorithm. Grover's algorithm is actually a generic constructive transformation from conventional circuits into quantum root-finding circuits. The input to the transformation is a circuit that computes a function $f : \mathbf{F}_2^b \to \mathbf{F}_2$. The output is a quantum circuit that computes a root of f (if one exists): a b-bit string x such that $f(x) = 0$.

In this paper I will be satisfied with a limited class of b-bit-to-1-bit circuits, namely "combinatorial" circuits: i.e., directed acyclic graphs where each node has two incoming edges and computes the NAND of its predecessor nodes. There is a loss of space efficiency from unrolling a long computation into a combinatorial circuit, but the specific functions used in this paper do not take very long to compute, at least compared to the speedups discussed in this paper.

To build a quantum circuit for f one must first build a "reversible" circuit for f: a non-erasing circuit built from Toffoli gates $(x, y, z) \mapsto (x, y, z + xy)$ rather than NANDs. This costs small constant factors in the number of input bits and in the size of the circuit. Replacing the bits by qubits, and replacing the Toffoli gates by quantum Toffoli gates, then produces a circuit of essentially the same size, and essentially the same speed, that computes f on a quantum *superposition* of inputs.

Grover assumes for simplicity that f has a unique root; combines a quantum circuit for f with a quantum rotation and a Hadamard transformation; and iterates the resulting quantum circuit approximately $\sqrt{2^b}$ times, obtaining the root of f with high probability. The rotation and the Hadamard transformation take negligible time and space compared to typical functions f.

Boyer, Brassard, Høyer, and Tapp in [7] presented a generalization of Grover's algorithm using $\sqrt{2^b/r}$ iterations to handle a function f having r roots. The number r need not be known in advance. The generalization in [7] is not actually necessary: one can simply apply Grover's algorithm to random restrictions of f having 1 input, 2 inputs, 4 inputs, etc. With either approach, the number of iterations used by quantum search is only about the square root of the number of iterations used by a traditional brute-force search.

Basic quantum information-set decoding. Fix $y \in \mathbf{F}_2^n$, and fix a $k \times n$ matrix G. Consider the function that, given a size-k subset $S \subseteq \{1, 2, \ldots, n\}$,

- inverts the composition $\mathbf{F}_2^k \xrightarrow{G} \mathbf{F}_2^n \to \mathbf{F}_2^S$, giving up if the composition is not invertible;
- applies the inverse to the image of y in $\mathbf{F}_2^S$, obtaining a vector $m \in \mathbf{F}_2^k$;
- computes $Gm \in \mathbf{F}_2^n$;
- gives up if $Gm - y$ does not have Hamming weight t; and, finally,
- returns 0.

This function can easily be computed by a combinatorial circuit consisting of $O(n^3)$ bit operations.

Recall that basic information-set decoding searches randomly for a root of this function. The search uses approximately $\binom{n}{k}/0.29\binom{n-t}{k} \approx c^{n/\lg n}$ function evaluations on average.

This paper's basic quantum information-set-decoding algorithm finds a root of exactly the same function by Grover's algorithm. Grover's algorithm uses only about $\sqrt{\binom{n}{k}/0.29\binom{n-t}{k}} \approx c^{(1/2)n/\lg n}$ iterations. Each iteration is a quantum function evaluation performing $O(n^3)$ qubit operations; each iteration thus takes time $n^{O(1)}$ on a quantum computer of size $n^{O(1)}$. The total time to find S is $c^{(1/2+o(1))n/\lg n}$ on a quantum computer of size $n^{O(1)}$. Having found S one can compute m and $e = Gm - y$ with negligible extra effort.

Consider again the example $(n, k, t) = (4096, 3556, 45)$ from [20, Section 3.5]. Basic quantum information-set decoding performs only about 2^{68} evaluations of this function. Each function evaluation takes a few billion bit operations, so the total cost is approximately 2^{100} qubit operations. Evidently these parameters are far below a safe 128-bit security level, contrary to the analysis in [20].

Advanced quantum information-set decoding. Recall that more advanced forms of information-set decoding evaluate more complicated functions that have more roots S. One can—and, to properly optimize parameters, should—consider analogous forms of quantum information-set decoding.

Beware that optimization of quantum information-set decoding is not the same as optimization of non-quantum information-set decoding. A 100× increase in the cost of function evaluation has a 100× impact in both settings, but a 100× increase in the number of roots has only a 10× impact in the quantum setting.

For example, the improvement introduced by Lee and Brickell in [17] increases the number of roots by a factor $n^{2+o(1)}$, while increasing the cost of each iteration by only a constant factor. See [6, Section 3] for a detailed analysis of these factors. This improvement therefore saves a factor $n^{1+o(1)}$ in quantum information-set decoding.

The improvement introduced by Stern in [23] increases the number of roots by a larger factor. However, it also increases the cost of each iteration by more than the square root of the same factor. I do not see how Stern's collision-searching idea can save time in quantum information-set decoding.

References

[1] Proceedings of the twenty-eighth annual ACM sy puting, held in Philadelphia, PA, May 22-24. Ass ery (1996), ISBN 0-89791-785-5. MR 97g:68005.

[2] Barg, A., Zhou, S.: A quantum decoding algoritl ceedings of the 36th Annual Allerton Conference Computing, Monticello, IL, September 23-25 (19 http://www.enee.umd.edu/~abarg/reprints/ri Citations in this document: §2

[3] Bernstein, D.J.: Cost analysis of hash collisions: Will quantum computers make SHARCS obsolete? In: Workshop Record of SHARCS '09: Special-purpose Hardware for Attacking Cryptographic Systems (2009), http://cr.yp.to/papers.html#collisioncost; Citations in this document: §1

[4] Bernstein, D.J., Buchmann, J., Dahmen, E. (eds.): Post-quantum cryptography. Springer, Heidelberg (2009), ISBN 978–3–540–88701–0.See [16], [20]

[5] Bernstein, D.J., Lange, T., Peters, C.: Attacking and defending the McEliece cryptosystem. In: [9], pp. 31–46 (2008), http://eprint.iacr.org/2008/318; Citations in this document: §2, §2

[6] Bernstein, D.J., Lange, T., Peters, C., van Tilborg, H.: Explicit bounds for generic decoding algorithms for code-based cryptography. In: WCC 2009 (2009); Citations in this document: §1, §2, §2, §3

[7] Boyer, M., Brassard, G., Høyer, P., Tapp, A.: Tight bounds on quantum searching (1996), http://arxiv.org/abs/quant-ph/9605034v1; Citations in this document: §3, §3

[8] Brassard, G., Høyer, P., Tapp, A.: Quantum cryptanalysis of hash and claw-free functions. In: [18], pp. 163–169 (1998); MR 99g:94013. Citations in this document: §1

[9] Buchmann, J., Ding, J. (eds.): PQCrypto 2008. LNCS, vol. 5299. Springer, Heidelberg (2008); See [5]

[10] Cohen, G.D., Wolfmann, J. (eds.): Coding Theory 1988. LNCS, vol. 388. Springer, Heidelberg (1989)

[11] Gilbert, E.N., MacWilliams, F.J., Sloane, N.J.A.: Codes which detect deception. Bell System Technical Journal 53, 405–424 (1974), ISSN 0005–8580. MR 55:5306, http://cr.yp.to/bib/entries.html#1974/gilbert. Citations in this document: §1

[12] Goldwasser, S. (ed.): 35th annual IEEE symposium on the foundations of computer science. Proceedings of the IEEE symposium held in Santa Fe, NM, November 20-22. IEEE, Los Alamitos (1994), ISBN 0-8186-6580-7. MR 98h:68008. See [21]

[13] Grover, L.K.: A fast quantum mechanical algorithm for database search. In: [1], pp. 212–219 (1996); MR 1427516. Citations in this document: §1

[14] Grover, L.K.: Quantum mechanics helps in searching for a needle in a haystack. Physical Review Letters 79, 325–328 (1997); Citations in this document: §1

[15] Günther, C.G. (ed.): EUROCRYPT 1988. LNCS, vol. 330. Springer, Heidelberg (1988), ISBN 3–540–50251–3. MR 90a:94002. See [17]

[16] Hallgren, S., Vollmer, U.: Quantum computing. In: [4], pp. 15–34 (2009); Citations in this document: §1

[17] Lee, P.J., Brickell, E.F.: An observation on the security of McEliece's public-key cryptosystem. In: [15], pp. 275–280 (1988); Citations in this document: §3

L., Moura, A.V. (eds.): LATIN 1998. LNCS, vol. 1380. Springer, Hei-
1998), ISBN 3-540-64275-7. MR 99d:68007. See [8]

ce, R.J.: A public-key cryptosystem based on algebraic coding theory. JPL Progress Report, 114–116 (1978), tp://ipnpr.jpl.nasa.gov/progress_report2/42-44/44N.PDF; Citations in this document: §1

0] Overbeck, R., Sendrier, N.: Code-based cryptography. In: [4], pp. 95–145 (2009); Citations in this document: §1, §1, §2, §3, §3

[21] Shor, P.W.: Algorithms for quantum computation: discrete logarithms and factoring. In: [12], pp. 124–134 (1994), see also newer version [22]. MR 1489242. Citations in this document: §1

[22] Shor, P.W.: Polynomial-time algorithms for prime factorization and discrete logarithms on a quantum computer. SIAM Journal on Computing 26, 1484–1509 (1997), see also older version [21]. MR 98i:11108

[23] Stern, J.: A method for finding codewords of small weight. In: [10], pp. 106–113 (1989); Citations in this document: §2, §3

[24] Zalka, C.: Fast versions of Shor's quantum factoring algorithm (1998), http://arxiv.org/abs/quant-ph/9806084; Citations in this document: §1

Information-Set Decoding for Linear Codes over $\mathbf{F}_q$

Christiane Peters*

Department of Mathematics and Computer Science
Technische Universiteit Eindhoven, P.O. Box 513, 5600 MB Eindhoven, Netherlands
c.p.peters@tue.nl

Abstract. The best known non-structural attacks against code-based cryptosystems are based on information-set decoding. Stern's algorithm and its improvements are well optimized and the complexity is reasonably well understood. However, these algorithms only handle codes over $\mathbf{F}_2$.

This paper presents a generalization of Stern's information-set-decoding algorithm for decoding linear codes over arbitrary finite fields $\mathbf{F}_q$ and analyzes the complexity. This result makes it possible to compute the security of recently proposed code-based systems over non-binary fields.

As an illustration, ranges of parameters for generalized McEliece cryptosystems using classical Goppa codes over $\mathbf{F}_{31}$ are suggested for which the new information-set-decoding algorithm needs 2^{128} bit operations.

Keywords: Generalized McEliece cryptosystem, security analysis, Stern attack, linear codes over $\mathbf{F}_q$, information-set decoding.

1 Introduction

Quantum computers will break the most popular public-key cryptosystems. The McEliece cryptosystem — introduced by McEliece in 1978 [12] — is one of the public-key systems without known vulnerabilities to attacks by quantum computers. Grover's algorithm can be countered by doubling the key size (see [8], [14]). Its public key is a random-looking algebraic code over a finite field. Encryption in McEliece's system is remarkably fast. The sender simply multiplies the information vector with a matrix and adds some errors. The receiver, having generated the code by secretly transforming a Goppa code, can use standard Goppa-code decoders to correct the errors and recover the plaintext.

The security of the McEliece cryptosystem relies on the fact that the published code does not come with any known structure. An attacker is faced with the *classical decoding problem*: Find the closest codeword in a linear code C to a given vector in the ambient space of C, assuming that there is a unique

* Date of this document: 2010.02.28. This work has been supported in part by the European Commission through the ICT Programme under Contract ICT–2007–216676 ECRYPT II.

N. Sendrier (Ed.): PQCrypto 2010, LNCS 6061, pp. 81–94, 2010.

closest codeword. This is a well known-problem. Berlekamp, McEliece, and van Tilborg [3] showed that the general decoding problem for linear binary codes is NP-complete. The classical decoding problem is assumed to be hard on average.

Information-set decoding. An attacker does not know the secret code and thus has to decode a random-looking code without any obvious structure. The best known algorithms which do not exploit any code structure rely on information-set decoding, an approach introduced by Prange in [15]. The idea is to find a set of coordinates of a garbled vector which are error-free and such that the restriction of the code's generator matrix to these positions is invertible. Then, the original message can be computed by multiplying the encrypted vector by the inverse of the submatrix. Improvements of this simplest form of information-set decoding were devised by Lee and Brickell [10], Leon [11], and Stern [16] — all for binary linear codes.

Best known attacks against binary McEliece. At PQCrypto 2008 Bernstein, Lange and Peters [4] presented several improvements to Stern's attack and gave a precise analysis of the complexity. Finiasz and Sendrier [7] presented a further improvement which can be combined with the improvements in [4] but did not analyze the combined attack. For 128-bit security [4] suggests the use of binary Goppa codes of length 2960 and dimension 2288 with a degree-56 Goppa polynomial and 57 added errors.

Decreasing public-key sizes by using larger fields. Several papers have suggested to use base fields other than $\mathbf{F}_2$, e.g. [9], [2], and more recently [1] and [13]. This idea is interesting as it has the potential to reduce the public-key size. One could hope that using a code over $\mathbf{F}_q$ saves a factor of $\log_2 q$: row and column dimension of the generator matrix both shrink by a factor of $\log_2 q$ at the cost of the matrix entries having size $\log_2 q$. However, information-set-decoding algorithms do not scale as brute force attacks. It is important to understand the implications of changing from $\mathbf{F}_2$ to $\mathbf{F}_q$ for arbitrary prime powers q on the attacks. Note that some papers claim structural attacks against [13] but they are using that the codes are dyadic and do not attack the general principle of using larger base fields.

Contributions of this paper. This paper generalizes Lee–Brickell's algorithm and Stern's algorithm to decoding algorithms for codes over arbitrary fields and extends the improvements from [4] and [7]. The algorithms are both stated as fixed-distance-decoding algorithms as in [5]. In particular, the algorithm using Stern's idea can be directly used for decoding a fixed number of errors. The most important contribution of this paper is a precise analysis of these improved and generalized algorithms. For $q = 31$, code parameters (length n, dimension k, and degree t of the Goppa polynomial) are presented that require 2^{128} bit operations to compute the closest codeword.

2 The McEliece Cryptosystem

This section gives the background on the McEliece cryptosystem and introduces notation for linear codes which is used throughout this paper.

Linear codes. Let $\mathbf{F}_q$ be a finite field with q elements. An $[n, k]$ code C is a linear code of length n and dimension k. A *generator matrix* for C is a $k \times n$ matrix G such that $C = \left\{\mathbf{m}G : \mathbf{m} \in \mathbf{F}_q^k\right\}$. The matrix G corresponds to a map $\mathbf{F}_q^k \to \mathbf{F}_q^n$ sending a message $\mathbf{m}$ of length k to an element in $\mathbf{F}_q^n$.

Setup of the McEliece cryptosystem. The *secret key* of the McEliece cryptosystem consists of a classical Goppa code Γ over a finite field of $\mathbf{F}_q$ of length n and dimension k with an error-correction capacity of w errors. A generator matrix G for the code Γ as well as an $n \times n$ permutation matrix P, and an invertible $k \times k$ matrix S are randomly generated and kept secret as part of the secret key.

The parameters n, k, and w are *public system parameters*. The *McEliece public key* is the $k \times n$ matrix $\hat{G} = SGP$ and the error weight w.

McEliece encryption of a message $\mathbf{m} \in \mathbf{F}_q^k$: Compute $\mathbf{m}\hat{G}$. Then hide the message by adding a random error vector $\mathbf{e}$ of length n and weight w. Send $\mathbf{y} = \mathbf{m}\hat{G} + \mathbf{e}$.

McEliece decryption: Compute $\mathbf{y}P^{-1} = \mathbf{m}SG + \mathbf{e}P^{-1}$. Use the decoding algorithm for Γ to find $\mathbf{m}S$ and thereby $\mathbf{m}$.

The decryption algorithm works since $\mathbf{m}SG$ is a codeword in Γ and the vector $\mathbf{e}P^{-1}$ has weight w.

An attacker who got hold of an encrypted message $\mathbf{y}$ has two possibilities in order to retrieve the original message $\mathbf{m}$.

- Find out the secret code; i.e., find G given $\hat{G}$, or
- Decode $\mathbf{y}$ without knowing an efficient decoding algorithm for the public code given by $\hat{G}$.

Attacks of the first type are called *structural attacks*. If G or an equivalently efficiently decodable representation of the underlying code can be retrieved in subexponential time, this code should not be used in the McEliece cryptosystem. Suitable codes are such that the best known attacks are decoding random codes. In the next section we will describe how to correct errors in a random-looking code with no obvious structure.

3 Generalizations of Information-Set-Decoding Algorithms

This section generalizes two information-set-decoding algorithms. Lee–Brickell's algorithm and Stern's algorithm — both originally designed for binary codes — are stated for arbitrary finite fields $\mathbf{F}_q$. Stern's algorithm is more efficient and supersedes Lee–Brickell's algorithm but the latter is easier to understand and the generalization of it can be used as a stepping stone to the generalization of Stern's.

The preliminaries are the following: Let C be an $[n, k]$ code over a finite field $\mathbf{F}_q$. Let G be a generator matrix for C. Let I be a non-empty subset of $\{1, \ldots, n\}$. Denote by G_I the restriction of G to the columns indexed by I. For any vector $\mathbf{y}$ in $\mathbf{F}_q^n$ denote by $\mathbf{y}_I$ the restriction of $\mathbf{y}$ to the coordinates indexed by I.

Let $\mathbf{y}$ be a vector in $\mathbf{F}_q^n$ at distance w from the code C. The goal of this section is to determine a vector $\mathbf{e} \in \mathbf{y} + \mathbf{F}_q^k G$ of weight w given G, $\mathbf{y}$ and w. Note that $\mathbf{y} + \mathbf{F}_q^k G$ is the coset of C containing $\mathbf{e}$.

We start with the definition of an information set.

Information-set decoding. Let G^{sys} be a generator matrix for C in *systematic form*, i.e., $G^{sys} = (I_k|Q)$ where Q is a $k \times (n-k)$ matrix, and consider $\mathbf{c} = \mathbf{m}G^{sys}$ for some vector $\mathbf{m}$ in $\mathbf{F}_q^k$. Since the first k columns of G^{sys} form the identity matrix the first k positions of $\mathbf{c}$ equal $\mathbf{m}$. The first k symbols of $\mathbf{m}G^{sys}$ are therefore called *information symbols.*

The notion of information symbols leads to the concept of information sets as follows. Let G be an arbitrary generator matrix of C. Let I be a size-k subset of $\{1, \ldots, n\}$. The columns indexed by I form a $k \times k$ submatrix of G which is denoted by G_I. If G_I is invertible the I-indexed entries of any codeword $\mathbf{m}G_I^{-1}G$ are information symbols and the set I is called an *information set.* Note that $G_I^{-1}G$ and G generate the same code.

Information-set decoding in its simplest form takes as input a vector $\mathbf{y}$ in $\mathbf{F}_q^n$ which is known to have distance w from C. Denote the closest codeword by $\mathbf{c}$. Let I be an information set. Assume that $\mathbf{y}$ and $\mathbf{c}$ coincide on the positions indexed by I, i.e., no errors occurred at these positions. Then, $\mathbf{y}_I G_I^{-1}$ is the preimage of $\mathbf{c}$ under the linear map induced by G and we obtain $\mathbf{c}$ as $(\mathbf{y}_I G_I^{-1})G$.

The following subsection presents Lee–Brickell's algorithm which is a classical information-set-decoding algorithm and serves as a basis for all further improvements.

Notation: for any a in an information set I let $\mathbf{g}_a$ denote the unique row of $G_I^{-1}G$ where the column indexed by a has a 1.

Lee–Brickell's algorithm. Let p be an integer with $0 \leq p \leq w$.

1. Choose an information set I.
2. Replace $\mathbf{y}$ by $\mathbf{y} - \mathbf{y}_I G_I^{-1} G$.
3. For each size-p subset $A = \{a_1, \ldots, a_p\} \subset I$ and for each $\mathbf{m} = (m_1, \ldots, m_p)$ in $(\mathbf{F}_q^*)^p$ compute $\mathbf{e} = \mathbf{y} - \sum_{i=1}^{p} m_i \mathbf{g}_{a_i}$. If $\mathbf{e}$ has weight w print $\mathbf{e}$. Else go back to Step 1.

Step 1 can be performed by choosing k indices in $\{1, \ldots, n\}$ uniformly at random and then performing Gaussian elimination on G in order to see if its I-indexed columns form an invertible submatrix G_I. A better way of determining an information set I is to choose k columns one by one: check for each newly selected column if it does not linearly depend on the already selected columns.

If $p = 0$ Step 3 only consists of checking whether $\mathbf{y} - \mathbf{y}_I G_I^{-1} G$ has weight w. If $p > 0$ Step 3 requires going through all possible weighted sums of p rows of G which need to be subtracted from $\mathbf{y} - \mathbf{y}_I G_I^{-1} G$ in order to make up for the p errors permitted in I. In Section 4 we will explain how to generate all vectors needed using exactly one row addition for each combination.

Steps 1–3 form one iteration of the generalized Lee–Brickell algorithm. If the set I chosen in Step 1 does not lead to a weight-w word in Step 3 another iteration has to be performed.

The parameter p is chosen to be a small number to keep the number of size-p subsets small in Step 3. In the binary case $p = 2$ is optimal; see e.g., [5].

Lee–Brickell, Leon, Stern. Stern's algorithm was originally designed to look for a codeword of a given weight in a binary linear code. The algorithm presented here builds on Stern's algorithm but works for codes over arbitrary fields $\mathbf{F}_q$. It is stated as a fixed-distance-decoding algorithm following [5]: Given $\mathbf{y}$ in $\mathbf{F}_q^n$, G and w, find $\mathbf{e}$ of weight w such that $\mathbf{e}$ lies in $\mathbf{y} + \mathbf{F}_q^k G$. This algorithm still can be used to determine codewords of a given weight w: just choose $\mathbf{y}$ to be the zero-codeword in $\mathbf{F}_q^n$. See Sections 4 and 8 for a discussion of stating this algorithm in a fixed-distance-decoding fashion.

The basic Stern algorithm uses two parameters p and ℓ whose size are determined later on. In each round an information set I is chosen. Stern's algorithm uses the idea of Lee and Brickell to allow a fixed number of errors in the information set. The algorithm also uses the idea of Leon's minimum-weight-word-finding algorithm [11] to look for the error vector $\mathbf{e}$: since $\mathbf{e}$ is a low-weight vector one restricts the number of possible candidates to those vectors having ℓ zeros outside the I-indexed columns.

Stern's algorithm divides the information set I into two equal-size subsets X and Y and looks for words having exactly weight p among the columns indexed by X, exactly weight p among the columns indexed by Y, and exactly weight 0 on a fixed uniform random set of ℓ positions outside the I-indexed columns.

Stern's algorithm. Let p be an integer with $0 \le p \le w$. Let ℓ be an integer with $0 \le \ell \le n - k$. For simplicity assume that k is even.

1. Choose an information set I.
2. Replace $\mathbf{y}$ by $\mathbf{y} - \mathbf{y}_I G_I^{-1} G$.
3. Choose a uniform random subset $X \subset I$ of size $k/2$.
4. Set $Y = I \setminus X$.
5. Select a uniform random size-ℓ subset Z in $\{1, \ldots, n\} \setminus I$.
6. For any size-p subset $A = \{a_1, \ldots, a_p\} \subset X$ consider the set $\mathcal{V}_A = \left\{\mathbf{y} - \sum_{i=1}^{p} m_i \mathbf{g}_{a_i} : \mathbf{m} = (m_1, \ldots, m_p) \in (\mathbf{F}_q^*)^p\right\}$. For each $\phi \in \mathcal{V}_A$ compute the vector $\phi(Z) \in \mathbf{F}_q^\ell$: the Z-indexed entries of ϕ.
7. For any size-p subset $B = \{b_1, \ldots, b_p\} \subset Y$ consider the set $\mathcal{V}_B = \left\{\sum_{j=1}^{p} m'_j \mathbf{g}_{b_j} : \mathbf{m}' = (m'_1, \ldots, m'_p) \in (\mathbf{F}_q^*)^p\right\}$. For each $\psi \in \mathcal{V}_B$ compute the vector $\psi(Z) \in \mathbf{F}_q^\ell$: the Z-indexed entries of ψ.

8. For each pair (A, B) where there is a pair of vectors $\phi = \mathbf{y} - \sum_i m_i \mathbf{g}_{a_i}$ and $\psi = \sum_j m'_j \mathbf{g}_{b_j}$ such that $\phi(Z) = \psi(Z)$ compute $\mathbf{e} = \phi - \psi$. If $\mathbf{e}$ has weight w print $\mathbf{e}$. Else go back to Step 1.

This algorithm finds a weight-w vector $\mathbf{e}$ in $\mathbf{y} + \mathbf{F}_q^k G$ if an information set I together with sets X, Y, and Z can be found such that $\mathbf{e}$ has weights p, p, 0 on the positions indexed by X, Y, and Z, respectively. Steps 1–8 form one iteration of the generalized Stern algorithm. If the set I chosen in Step 1 does not lead to a weight-w word in Step 8 another iteration has to be performed.

4 Analysis of an Improved Version of Stern's Algorithm for Prime Fields

This section analyzes the cost for the generalization of Stern's algorithm as presented in Section 3. In this section the field $\mathbf{F}_q$ is restricted to prime fields. The general case is handled in the next section.

Note that the Stern algorithm stated in Section 3 is the basic algorithm. The following analysis takes several speedups into account that were introduced in [4] for the binary case.

Reusing additions. In Step 6 one has to compute $\binom{k/2}{p}(q-1)^p$ vectors $\mathbf{y} - \sum_{i=1}^{p} m_i \mathbf{g}_{a_i}$ on ℓ positions. Computing those vectors naively one by one would require $p\ell$ multiplications and $p\ell$ additions in $\mathbf{F}_q$ per vector. However, each sum $\sum_{i=1}^{p} m_i \mathbf{g}_{a_i}$ can be computed with exactly one row operation using intermediate sums. The sums in Step 6 additionally involve adding $\mathbf{y}$. The naive approach is to subtract each $\sum_i m_i \mathbf{g}_{a_i}$ from $\mathbf{y}$. Recall that for $i \in I$ the vector $\mathbf{g}_i$ is the unique row of $G_I^{-1}G$ where the column indexed by i has a 1. Observe that each $\mathbf{y} - \sum_i m_i \mathbf{g}_{a_i}$ includes at least one vector $\mathbf{y} - \mathbf{g}_i$ for $k/2 - p + 1$ rows $\mathbf{g}_i$ with $i \in X$. So it is sufficient to carry out only $k/2 - p + 1$ additions for $\mathbf{y}$.

In Step 7 all vectors induced by size-p subsets of Y on the Z-indexed columns are also computed using intermediate sums.

Collisions. The expected number of colliding vectors $\phi(Z)$, $\psi(Z)$ in Step 8 is about

$$\left(\binom{k/2}{p}(q-1)^p\right)^2 \Big/ q^\ell.$$

For each collision one computes $\mathbf{y}$ minus the sum of $2p$ weighted rows on all positions outside X, Y, and Z. Naive computation of one such a vector would take $2p$ multiplications and $2p$ additions on $n-k-\ell$ positions. However, first of all one can discard multiplications by 1, leaving $2p$ additions and $(2p)(q-2)/(q-1)$ multiplications. Looking more carefully one observes that each entry has a chance of $(q-1)/q$ to be a non-zero entry. In order to save operations, one computes the result in a column-by-column fashion and uses an early abort: after about $(q/(q-1))(w-2p+1)$ columns are handled it is very likely that the resulting row vector has more than the allowed $w - 2p$ non-zero entries and can be discarded.

This means that partial collisions that do not lead to a full collision consume only $(q/(q-1))(w-2p+1)$ operations.

If $\mathbf{y}$ is the all-zero codeword the algorithm looks for a weight-w codeword. Then the cost for adding $\mathbf{y}$ to weighted rows $\mathbf{g}_a$ coming from sets A in Steps 6 and 8 can be neglected.

Updating the matrix G with respect to I. At the beginning of each iteration a new information set I needs to be chosen. Then one has to reduce — using Gaussian elimination — the I-indexed columns of the matrix G to the $k \times k$ identity matrix. A crude estimate of the cost for this step is given by $(n-k)^2(n+k)$ operations.

Note that for large fields the cost for Gaussian elimination become negligible in comparison to the cost of Steps 6–8. The same holds if the code length goes to infinity as shown in [5]. However, for small fields the following improvements should be taken into account.

Reusing parts of information sets and precomputations. Canteaut and Chabaud in [6] proposed to use a column-swapping technique for Stern's algorithm in order to cut down on Gaussian elimination cost. If an information set I does not lead to a weight-w vector $\mathbf{e}$ then instead of abandoning the whole set I reuse $k-1$ columns and select a new column out of the remaining $n-k$ non-selected columns of G. The submatrix $G_{I'}$ has to be updated for this new information set I'. Bernstein, Lange, and Peters pointed out in [4] that selecting only a single new column increases the number of iterations of Stern's algorithm significantly and proposed to swap more than one column in each round: reuse $k-c$ columns from the previous iteration and select c new linearly independent columns out of the non-selected $n-k$ columns. The value c has to be chosen with respect to the code length n, its dimension k and the error weight w.

At the beginning of each new iteration there are k columns from the previous iteration in row echelon form. Exchanging c columns means that Gaussian elimination has to be performed on those c columns.

Updating the matrix and looking for pivots in c columns with respect to the chosen columns is done using precomputations. Since sums of certain rows are used multiple times those sums are precomputed. Following [4, Section 4] pick e.g., the first r rows and compute all possible sums of those rows. The parameter r needs to be tuned with respect to the field size q and the code dimension k. In particular, $r \leq c$. Starting with r columns one has to precompute $q^r - r - 1$ sums of r rows. Each of the remaining $k-r$ rows requires on average $1 - 1/q^r$ vector additions. Choosing $r > 1$ yields good speedups for codes over small fields.

We covered most of the improvements suggested in [4] but we omitted choosing multiple sets Z of size ℓ. This step amortizes the cost of Gaussian elimination over more computations in the second part. As noted before, for larger q Gaussian elimination is even less of a bottleneck than in binary fields and we thus omitted this part here.

To estimate the cost per iteration we need to express the cost in one measure, namely in additions in $\mathbf{F}_q$. We described Steps 6–8 using multiplications. Since we consider only quite small fields $\mathbf{F}_q$ multiplications can be implemented as table lookups and thus cost the same as one addition.

Cost for one iteration of Stern's algorithm. Stern's algorithm in the version presented here uses parameters p, ℓ, and additional parameters c and r.

The cost of one iteration of Stern's algorithm is as follows:

$$(n-1)\left((k-1)\left(1-\frac{1}{q^r}\right)+(q^r-r)\right)\frac{c}{r}$$
$$+\left(\left(\frac{k}{2}-p+1\right)+2\binom{k/2}{p}(q-1)^p\right)\ell$$
$$+\frac{q}{q-1}(w-2p+1)2p\left(1+\frac{q-2}{q-1}\right)\frac{\binom{k/2}{p}^2(q-1)^{2p}}{q^\ell}.$$

For large fields the improvements regarding Gaussian elimination do not result in significantly lower cost. In this case the reader can also replace the first line with $(n-k)^2(n+k)$.

Success probability of the first iteration. Let I be an information set chosen uniformly at random. A random weight-w word $\mathbf{e}$ has weight $2p$ among the columns indexed by I with probability $\binom{k}{2p}\binom{n-k}{w-2p}/\binom{n}{w}$.

Let X, Y be disjoint size-$(k/2)$ subsets of I chosen uniformly at random. The conditional probability of the $2p$ errors of I-indexed positions in $\mathbf{e}$ appearing as p errors among the positions indexed by X and p errors among the positions indexed by Y is given by $\binom{k/2}{p}^2/\binom{k}{2p}$.

Let Z be a size-ℓ subset in $\{1,\ldots,n\}\setminus I$ chosen uniformly at random. The conditional probability of $\mathbf{e}$ having $w-2p$ errors outside the information set avoiding the positions indexed by Z is given by $\binom{n-k-(w-2p)}{\ell}/\binom{n-k}{\ell}$.

The product of these probabilities equals $\binom{k/2}{p}^2\binom{n-k-\ell}{w-2p}/\binom{n}{w}$ and is the chance that Stern's algorithm finds $\mathbf{e}$ after the first round.

Number of iterations. The iterations of Stern's algorithm are independent if the set I is chosen uniformly at random in each round. Then the average number of iterations of Stern's algorithm is the multiplicative inverse of the success probability of the first round.

However, the iterations are not independent if $k-c$ columns are reused. In fact, each iteration depends exactly on the preceding iteration. Thus the number of iterations can be computed using a Markov chain as in [4]. The chain has $w+2$ states, namely

- 0: The chosen information set contains 0 errors.
- 1: The chosen information set contains 1 error.
- ...
- w: The chosen information set contains w errors.
- Done: The attack has succeeded.

An iteration chooses c distinct positions in the information set I of the preceding iteration and c distinct positions outside I which are then swapped. An iteration of the attack moves from state u to state $u+d$ with probability

$$\sum_i \binom{w-u}{i}\binom{n-k-w+u}{c-i}\binom{u}{d+i}\binom{k-u}{c-d-i}\Big/\binom{n-k}{c}\binom{k}{c}.$$

Then the iteration checks for success: in state $2p$ it moves to state "Done" with probability

$$\beta = \frac{\binom{k/2}{p}^2}{\binom{k}{2p}} \frac{\binom{n-k-(w-2p)}{\ell}}{\binom{n-k}{\ell}},$$

and stays the same in any of the other states.

Choice of parameters for Stern's algorithm. The parameter p is chosen quite small in order to minimize the cost of going though all subsets A, B of X and Y. The parameter ℓ is chosen to balance the number of all possible length-ℓ vectors $\phi(Z)$ and $\psi(Z)$, $2\binom{k/2}{p}(q-1)^p$ with the number of expected collisions on ℓ positions, $\binom{k/2}{p}^2(q-1)^{2p}\Big/q^\ell$. A reasonable choice is

$$\ell = \log_q\binom{k/2}{p} + p\log_q(q-1).$$

5 Analysis of an Improved Version of Stern's Algorithm for Extension Fields

We presented a generalization for information-set decoding over arbitrary finite fields $\mathbf{F}_q$. However, the cost analysis in the previous section was restricted to prime values of q. Here we point out the differences in handling arbitrary finite fields.

The main difference in handling arbitrary finite fields is in Steps 6 and 7 of the generalized Stern algorithm when computing sums of p rows coming from subsets A of X, and sums of p rows coming from subsets B of Y. In prime fields all elements are reached by repeated addition since 1 generates the additive group. If q is a prime power 1 does not generate the additive group.

Let $\mathbf{F}_q$ be represented over its prime field via an irreducible polynomial $h(x)$. To reach all elements we also need to compute x times a field element, which is essentially the cost of reducing modulo h. In turn this means several additions of the prime field elements. Even though these operations technically are not additions in $\mathbf{F}_q$, the costs are essentially the same. This means that the costs of these steps are the same as before.

In the analysis of Step 8 we need to account for multiplications with the coefficient vectors $(m_1, \ldots, m_p)$ and $(m'_1, \ldots, m'_p)$. This is the same problem that we faced in the previous section and thus we use the same assumption, namely that one multiplication in $\mathbf{F}_q$ has about the same cost as one addition in $\mathbf{F}_q$.

This means that a good choice of ℓ again is given by

$$\ell = \log_q \binom{k/2}{p} + p \log_q(q-1).$$

6 Increasing the Collision Probability in Stern's Algorithm

In [7] Finiasz and Sendrier propose a speedup of Stern's algorithm. This section generalizes this approach to codes over arbitrary finite fields.

Stern splits an information set I into two disjoint sets X and Y, each of size $\binom{k/2}{p}$ and searches for collisions among size-p subsets taken from X and Y.

Finiasz and Sendrier propose not to split the information set I into two disjoint sets but to look more generally for collisions. The split of I into two disjoint size-$(k/2)$ sets is omitted at the benefit of creating more possible words having weight $2p$ among the information set.

This version of Stern's algorithm uses parameters p, ℓ, N, and N' whose size is determined in Section 7.

Stern's algorithm with overlapping sets. Let p be an integer with $0 \leq p \leq w$. Let ℓ be an integer with $0 \leq \ell \leq n-k$. Let N, N' be integers with $0 \leq N, N' \leq \binom{k}{p}$.

1. Choose an information set I.
2. Replace $\mathbf{y}$ by $\mathbf{y} - \mathbf{y}_I G_I^{-1} G$.
3. Select a uniform random size-ℓ subset Z in $\{1, \dots, n\} \setminus I$.
4. Repeat N times: Choose a size-p subset $A = \{a_1, \dots, a_p\} \subset I$ uniformly at random and consider the set
$\mathcal{V}_A = \left\{\mathbf{y} - \sum_{i=1}^{p} m_i \mathbf{g}_{a_i} : \mathbf{m} = (m_1, \dots, m_p) \in (\mathbf{F}_q^*)^p\right\}$.
For each $\phi \in \mathcal{V}_A$ compute the vector $\phi(Z) \in \mathbf{F}_q^\ell$: the Z-indexed entries of ϕ.
5. Repeat N' times: Choose a size-p subset $B = \{b_1, \dots, b_p\} \subset I$ uniformly at random and consider the set
$\mathcal{V}_B = \left\{\sum_{j=1}^{p} m'_j \mathbf{g}_{b_j} : \mathbf{m}' = (m'_1, \dots, m'_p) \in (\mathbf{F}_q^*)^p\right\}$.
For each $\psi \in \mathcal{V}_B$ compute the vector $\psi(Z) \in \mathbf{F}_q^\ell$: the Z-indexed entries of ψ.
6. For each pair (A, B) where there is a pair of vectors $\phi = \mathbf{y} - \sum_i m_i \mathbf{g}_{a_i}$ and $\psi = \sum_j m'_j \mathbf{g}_{b_j}$ such that $\phi(Z) = \psi(Z)$ compute $\mathbf{e} = \phi - \psi$.
If $\mathbf{e}$ has weight w print $\mathbf{e}$. Else go back to Step 1.

This algorithm finds a weight-w vector $\mathbf{e}$ in $\mathbf{y} + \mathbf{F}_q^k G$ if there is a vector $\mathbf{e}$ having weight $2p$ on positions indexed by the information set and weight 0 on the positions indexed by Z. Steps 1–6 form one iteration. If the set I chosen in Step 1 does not lead to a weight-w word in Step 6 another iteration has to be performed.

It is possible that a subset chosen in Step 4 is also chosen in Step 5. This case is allowed in order to benefit from a larger set of possible sums of p rows. The choice of N and N' is adjusted so that the number of overlapping sets is minimal.

7 Cost of Stern's Algorithm with Finiasz–Sendrier's Improvement

The analysis of the cost for the algorithm presented in Section 6 is done analogously to the analysis in Section 4 and Section 5.

In Step 4 one has to compute $N(q-1)^p$ vectors $\mathbf{y} - \sum_{i=1}^{p} m_i \mathbf{g}_{a_i}$ and in Step 5 one has to compute $N'(q-1)^p$ vectors — each vector on ℓ positions. First compute $k-p+1$ vectors $\mathbf{y} - \mathbf{g}_i$ with $i \in I$ and use intermediate sums so that each sum of p rows is computed using only one row addition, i.e., only ℓ additions in $\mathbf{F}_q$. The expected number of collisions in Step 6 is about $NN'(q-1)^{2p}/q^\ell$.

The total cost for one iteration of the algorithm is

$$\begin{aligned}&(n-1)\left((k-1)\left(1-\frac{1}{q^r}\right)+(q^r-r)\right)\frac{c}{r}\\&+((k-p+1)+(N+N')(q-1)^p)\,\ell\\&+\frac{q}{q-1}(w-2p)2p\left(1+\frac{q-2}{q-1}\right)\frac{NN'(q-1)^{2p}}{q^\ell}.\end{aligned}$$

Success probability of the first iteration. There are $\binom{2p}{p}$ different possibilities of splitting $2p$ errors into two disjoint subsets of cardinality p each. The probability of not finding an error vector $\mathbf{e}$, which has $2p$ errors in I, by a fixed set A and a fixed set B is $1 - \binom{2p}{p}/\binom{k}{p}^2$. If one chooses N sets A and N' sets B uniformly at random the probability of $\mathbf{e}$ not being found by any pair (A, B) equals $\left(1-\binom{2p}{p}\big/\binom{k}{p}^2\right)^{NN'} \approx \exp\left(-NN'\binom{2p}{p}\big/\binom{k}{p}^2\right)$.

The probability of the first iteration to succeed is thus

$$\frac{\binom{k}{2p}\binom{n-k-\ell}{w-2p}}{\binom{n}{w}}\left(1-\left(1-\frac{\binom{2p}{p}}{\binom{k}{p}^2}\right)^{NN'}\right).$$

Compute the number of iterations. The same Markov chain computation applies as in Section 4. Note that an iteration moves from state $2p$ to state "Done" with probability

$$\beta = \left(1-\left(1-\frac{\binom{2p}{p}}{\binom{k}{p}^2}\right)^{NN'}\right)\frac{\binom{n-k-(w-2p)}{\ell}}{\binom{n-k}{\ell}}.$$

Choice of parameters. As in Stern's algorithm the parameter p is chosen to be a small number. Note that one could try to outweigh the extra cost for adding $\mathbf{y}$ to rows induced by sets A in Step 4 by choosing N' to be a little larger than N. The parameter ℓ is chosen to balance the number of all computed length-ℓ vectors $\phi(Z)$ and $\psi(Z)$, $(N+N')(q-1)^p$, with the number of expected collisions on ℓ positions being $NN'(q-1)^{2p}/q^{\ell}$. Assuming N and N' are about the same a reasonable choice is $\ell = \log_q N + p\log_q(q-1)$.

This algorithm works for any numbers N and N' less than or equal to $\binom{k}{p}$, the number of all possible size-p subsets taken from an information set I. There is no point in choosing N larger than this number since otherwise all possible combinations of p elements out of I could be deterministically tested. A sensible choice for N and N' is $N = N' = \binom{k}{p} \Big/ \sqrt{\binom{2p}{p}}$.

8 Parameters

The iterations of Stern's algorithm for $\mathbf{F}_q$ with the speedups described in Section 4 are not independent. The number of iterations has to be estimated with a Markov chain computation. We adapted the Markov chain implementation from [4] to look for parameter ranges for McEliece-cryptosystem setups using codes over arbitrary fields $\mathbf{F}_q$. Moreover we took the parameters proposed in [1] and [13], respectively, and investigated their security against our attack. The results as well as the code can be found at `http://www.win.tue.nl/~cpeters/isdfq.html`.

Codes for 128-bit security. Our experiments show that an $[n,k]$-code over $\mathbf{F}_{31}$ with $n = 961$, $k = 771$, and $w = 48$ introduced errors achieves 128-bit security against the attack presented in Section 3 with improvements described in Section 4. Any Goppa code being the subfield subcode of a code in $\mathbf{F}_{31^2}$ with a degree-95 Goppa polynomial can be used. A successful attack needs about $2^{96.815}$ iterations with about $2^{32.207}$ bit operations per iteration. A good choice of parameters are $p = 2$, $\ell = 7$, $c = 12$, and $r = 1$. Using the algorithm in Section 6 costs about the same, namely $2^{129.0290}$ bit operations. In comparison to the classical disjoint split of the information set one can afford to spend more time on Gaussian elimination and consider $c = 17$ new columns in each iteration. Increasing the standard choice $\binom{k}{p}/\sqrt{\binom{2p}{p}}$ of the number of subsets A and B by a factor of 1.1 to $N = N' = 133300$ yields the best result. The expected number of iterations is $2^{95.913}$, each taking about $2^{33.116}$ bit operations.

A public key for a $[961, 771]$ code over $\mathbf{F}_{31}$ would consist of $k(n-k)\log_2 31 = 725740$ bits.

For comparison: a $[2960, 2288]$ binary Goppa code where $w = 57$ errors are added by the sender also achieves 128-bit security, but its public key needs 1537536 bits to store.

Note on fixed-distance decoding. Note that one can decode 48 errors in a length-961 code with dimension 771 over $\mathbf{F}_{31}$ by increasing the dimension by 1 and looking for a word of weight 48 in an extended code of dimension 772. This turns out to be more than 30% slower than direct decoding of the original dimension-771 code.

At a first glance a single iteration is less costly despite the larger dimension since the additions for $\mathbf{y}$ are not performed. However, the number of iterations increases significantly which makes the minimum-weight-word search less efficient. Increasing the dimension by 1 decreases the probability of the first round to succeed. If the iterations of the algorithms were independent one could easily see that the expected number of iterations increases. The same effect occurs with depending iterations: consider the Markov process described in Section 4 and observe that the success chance β of moving from state $2p$ to state "Done" decreases, resulting in a longer chain and thus more iterations.

Acknowledgments. The author would like to thank Dan Bernstein, Tanja Lange, and Henk van Tilborg for fruitful discussions, helpful suggestions and detailed comments.

References

1. Berger, T.P., Cayrel, P.-L., Gaborit, P., Otmani, A.: Reducing key length of the McEliece cryptosystem. In: Preneel, B. (ed.) Progress in Cryptology – AFRICACRYPT 2009. LNCS, vol. 5580, pp. 77–97. Springer, Heidelberg (2009)
2. Berger, T.P., Loidreau, P.: How to mask the structure of codes for a cryptographic use. Designs, Codes and Cryptography 35(1), 63–79 (2005)
3. Berlekamp, E.R., McEliece, R.J., van Tilborg, H.C.A.: On the inherent intractability of certain coding problems. IEEE Transactions on Information Theory 24, 384–386 (1978)
4. Bernstein, D.J., Lange, T., Peters, C.: Attacking and defending the McEliece cryptosystem. In: Buchmann, J., Ding, J. (eds.) PQCrypto 2008. LNCS, vol. 5299, pp. 31–46. Springer, Heidelberg (2008)
5. Bernstein, D.J., Lange, T., Peters, C., van Tilborg, H.C.A.: Explicit bounds for generic decoding algorithms for code-based cryptography. In: Pre-Proceedings of WCC 2009, pp. 168–180 (2009)
6. Canteaut, A., Chabaud, F.: A new algorithm for finding minimum-weight words in a linear code: application to McEliece's cryptosystem and to narrow-sense BCH codes of length 511. IEEE Transactions on Information Theory 44(1), 367–378 (1998)
7. Finiasz, M., Sendrier, N.: Security bounds for the design of code-based cryptosystems. In: Matsui, M. (ed.) ASIACRYPT 2009. LNCS, vol. 5912, pp. 88–105. Springer, Heidelberg (2009)
8. Hallgren, S., Vollmer, U.: Quantum computing. In: Bernstein, D.J., Buchmann, J., Dahmen, E. (eds.) Post-Quantum Cryptography, pp. 15–34. Springer, Berlin (2009)
9. Janwa, H., Moreno, O.: McEliece public key cryptosystems using algebraic-geometric codes. Designs, Codes and Cryptography 8(3), 293–307 (1996)
10. Lee, P.J., Brickell, E.F.: An observation on the security of McEliece's public-key cryptosystem. In: Günther, C.G. (ed.) EUROCRYPT 1988. LNCS, vol. 330, pp. 275–280. Springer, Heidelberg (1988)
11. Leon, J.S.: A probabilistic algorithm for computing minimum weights of large error-correcting codes. IEEE Transactions on Information Theory 34(5), 1354–1359 (1988)
12. McEliece, R.J.: A public-key cryptosystem based on algebraic coding theory. Jet Propulsion Laboratory DSN Progress Report 42–44 (1978), `http://ipnpr.jpl.nasa.gov/progress_report2/42-44/44N.PDF`

13. Misoczki, R., Barreto, P.S.L.M.: Compact McEliece keys from Goppa codes. In: Jacobson Jr., M.J., Rijmen, V., Safavi-Naini, R. (eds.) SAC 2009. LNCS, vol. 5867, pp. 376–392. Springer, Heidelberg (2009)
14. Overbeck, R., Sendrier, N.: Code-based cryptography. In: Bernstein, D.J., Buchmann, J., Dahmen, E. (eds.) Post-Quantum Cryptography, pp. 95–145. Springer, Berlin (2009)
15. Prange, E.: The use of information sets in decoding cyclic codes. IRE Transactions on Information Theory 8(5), 5–9 (1962)
16. Stern, J.: A method for finding codewords of small weight. In: Wolfmann, J., Cohen, G. (eds.) Coding Theory 1988. LNCS, vol. 388, pp. 106–113. Springer, Heidelberg (1989)

A Timing Attack against the Secret Permutation in the McEliece PKC

Falko Strenzke[1,2,⋆]

[1] FlexSecure GmbH, Germany
strenzke@flexsecure.de
[2] Cryptography and Computeralgebra, Department of Computer Science, Technische Universität Darmstadt, Germany

Abstract. In this work we present a novel timing attack against the McEliece public key cryptosystem (PKC). In contrast to former works investigating timing attacks that aim at recovering the message, we devise how to exploit a vulnerability in the Patterson algorithm that allows the attacker to gather information about the secret permutation through a timing side channel. This information can be used to dramatically reduce the cost of a brute force attack against the secret key. We also describe the results obtained from a proof of concept implementation of the attack and give an appropriate countermeasure.

Keywords: side channel attack, timing attack, post quantum cryptography, code-based cryptography.

1 Introduction

The McEliece PKC [1] so far has not experienced any use in real world applications. This is due basically to the enormous key sizes compared to other cryptosystems based on the integer factorization problem or the discrete logarithm problem [2,3,4,5]. But since these systems, that are widely used in public key infrastructures, are vulnerable to quantum computer attacks [6,7,8], schemes that are believed to be secure in the presence of quantum computers, like the McEliece PKC, are of certain interest concerning implementation issues.

One very important implementation aspect is side channel security. A side channel is given when a physical observable quantity that is measured during the operation of a cryptographic device, allows an attacker to gain information about a secret that is involved in the cryptographic operation. The usual observables used in this respect are the duration of the operation (timing attacks [9]), or the power consumption as a function over the time (power analysis attacks[10]).

So far, timing attacks against the decryption operation of the McEliece PKC targeting the plaintext have been developed [11,12]. But to the best of our knowledge, no timing attack targeting the McEliece private key has yet been published. In this work, we give the theoretical derivation of a side channel vulnerability

⋆ A part of the work of F. Strenzke was done at[2].

N. Sendrier (Ed.): PQCrypto 2010, LNCS 6061, pp. 95–107, 2010.

present in any implementation using the Patterson Algorithm [13] in the error correction phase of the decryption operation if no appropriate countermeasures are realized.

The buildup of this paper is as follows. In Section 2, we describe the McEliece PKC, where the focus lays on those aspects that are relevant for the understanding of the remainder of this paper. Then, in Section 3, we identify the novel timing side channel in the decryption routine. Section 4 explains how this side channel can be exploited by devising an attack against the permutation that is part of the McEliece private key. Consequently, Section 5 explains an appropriate countermeasure that closes the timing side channel. Section 6 describes our proof of concept implementation of the attack and gives experimental results. After that, we discuss difficulties and possible strategies for real life attacks in Section 7. Specifically, we show how an attacker can implement a maximum likelihood strategy and consider the threat resulting from a power analysis attack that exploits the same information leakage as our attack. In Section 8, we address topics closely related to the subject of this paper. Finally, we give the conclusion and an outlook in Section 9.

2 Preliminaries

In this work, we give a brief description of the McEliece PKC, and stress those features of the decryption algorithm, that are necessary to understand the timing attack presented in this paper. A more detailed description and security considerations can be found e.g. in [14].

Goppa Codes. Goppa codes [15] are a class of linear error correcting codes. The McEliece PKC makes use of irreducible binary Goppa codes, so we will restrict ourselves to this subclass.

Definition 1. *Let the polynomial $g(Y) = \sum_{i=0}^{t} g_i Y^i \in \mathbb{F}_{2^m}[Y]$ be monic and irreducible over $\mathbb{F}_{2^m}[Y]$, and let m, t be positive integers. Then $g(Y)$ is called a* Goppa polynomial *(for an irreducible binary Goppa code).*

Then an irreducible binary Goppa code is defined as $\Gamma(g(Y)) = \{\boldsymbol{c} \in \mathbb{F}_2^n | S_{\boldsymbol{c}}(Y) := \sum_{i=0}^{n-1} \frac{c_i}{Y-\gamma_i} = 0 \bmod g(Y)\}$, where $n = 2^m$, $S_{\boldsymbol{c}}(Y)$ is the syndrome of $\boldsymbol{c}$, the γ_i, $i = 0, \ldots, n-1$ are pairwise distinct elements of $\mathbb{F}_{2^m}$, and c_i are the entries of the vector $\boldsymbol{c}$.

The code defined in such way has length n, dimension $k = n - mt$ and can correct up to t errors. Note that in general, there is a freedom in choosing the ordering of the elements γ_i, $i = 0, \ldots, n-1$. Each such ordering will yield a different code. In this work, we choose lexicographical ordering for the γ_i.

As for any error correcting code, for a Goppa code there exists a generator matrix G and a parity check matrix H [16]. Given these matrices, a message $\boldsymbol{m}$ can be encoded into a codeword $\boldsymbol{c}$ of the code by computing $\boldsymbol{z} = \boldsymbol{m}G$, and the syndrome of a (potentially distorted) codeword can be computed as $\boldsymbol{s} = \boldsymbol{z}H$. Here, we do not give the formulas for the computation of these matrices as they are of no importance for the understanding of the attack developed in this work. The interested reader, however, is referred to [16].

Overview of the McEliece PKC. In this section we give a brief overview of the McEliece PKC, where we closely follow the one given in [17].

The McEliece *secret key* consists of the Goppa polynomial $g(Y)$ of degree t defining the secret code Γ, an $n \times n$ permutation matrix P and a non-singular $k \times k$ matrix S over $\mathbb{F}_2$. The *public key* is given by the public $n \times k$ generator matrix $G_p = SG_sP$ over $\mathbb{F}_2$, where G_s is a generator matrix of the secret code Γ. The *encryption* operation allows messages $\boldsymbol{m} \in \mathbb{F}_2^k$. A random vector $\boldsymbol{e} \in \mathbb{F}_2^n$ with hamming weight $\mathrm{wt}(\boldsymbol{e}) = t$ has to be created. Then the ciphertext is computed as $\boldsymbol{z} = \boldsymbol{m}G_p + \boldsymbol{e}$.

McEliece *decryption* is performed in the following way: First, compute $\boldsymbol{z}' = \boldsymbol{z}P^{-1} = \boldsymbol{m}SG_s + \boldsymbol{e}P^{-1}$. The right hand side of this equation demonstrates that applying error correction using the secret code Γ will recover the permuted error vector $\boldsymbol{e}' = \boldsymbol{e}P^{-1}$, since $\boldsymbol{m}SG_s$ is a code word of Γ. The error correction procedure is detailed in Section 2.

If the matrix S is chosen in such way that the public generator matrix is in reduced row echelon form, i.e. $G_p = [\mathbb{I}|G_2]$, then, in the decryption operation, $\boldsymbol{m}$ can be recovered by extracting the first k bits of $\boldsymbol{m}SG_s$. This would be a security problem if the McEliece PKC was used as proposed in [1]. But since the system has been proven to be insecure against adaptive chosen ciphertext attacks, a so called CCA2-Conversion [18,19] has to be applied in any case. Consequently, using the reduced row echelon form is not a problem [20]. In this case, the matrix S does not have to be part of the private key. This choice for the matrix S will be assumed for the remainder of the paper. In this work however, we describe the McEliece PKC without such a CCA2-Conversion, as this is of no relevance for the side channel attack devised in this work. This will be addressed in Section 8.

Appropriate choices for the security parameters of the scheme, n and t, would e.g. be $n = 2048$ and $t = 50$ for about 100 bit security [17].

The Decryption Operation in the McEliece PKC. As mentioned above, the first step in the decryption operation is computing $\boldsymbol{z}' = \boldsymbol{z}P^{-1}$. Then, the syndrome associated with this ciphertext has to be computed. This can be done using a parity check matrix H corresponding to the secret code Γ. Algorithm 1 depicts the top level McEliece decryption. It makes use of the error correction algorithm, given by the Patterson Algorithm [13], shown in Algorithm 2. Please note that in Step 1 of this algorithm, the multiplication with the coefficient vector is used to turn the syndrome vector into the syndrome polynomial $S(Y)$. The Patterson Algorithm, in turn, uses an algorithm for finding roots in polynomials over $\mathbb{F}_{2^m}$ (root_find()), and the Extended Euclidean Algorithm (XGCD) for polynomials with a break condition based on the degree of the remainder, given in Algorithm 3. The root finding can e.g. be implemented as an exhaustive search on $\mathbb{F}_{2^m}$. Please note that all polynomials appearing in the algorithms have coeffients in $\mathbb{F}_{2^m}$.

In the following, we turn to those details, that are relevant for the side channel issues we are going to address in Section 3. Please note that the error locator polynomial $\sigma(Y)$, which is determined in Step 4 of Algorithm 2, has the following form[1]:

$$\sigma(Y) = \sigma_t \prod_{j \in \mathcal{E}'} (Y - \gamma_j) = \sum_{i=0}^{t} \sigma_i Y^i. \tag{1}$$

where $\mathcal{E}'$ is the set of those indexes i, for which $e'_i = 1$, i.e. those elements of $\mathbb{F}_{2^m}$ that correspond to the error positions in the permuted error vector. The determination of the error vector in Step 6 of Algorithm 2 makes use of this property. Accordingly, $\deg(\sigma(Y)) = \mathrm{wt}(\boldsymbol{e})$ if $\mathrm{wt}(\boldsymbol{e}) \leqslant t$ holds.

Algorithm 1. The McEliece Decryption Operation

Require: the McEliece ciphertext z
Ensure: the message m
1: $\boldsymbol{z}' \leftarrow \boldsymbol{z}P^{-1}$
2: $\boldsymbol{e}' \leftarrow \mathrm{err\_corr}(\boldsymbol{z}', g(Y))$
3: $\boldsymbol{e} \leftarrow \boldsymbol{e}'P$
4: $\boldsymbol{m}' \leftarrow \boldsymbol{z} + \boldsymbol{e}$
5: $\boldsymbol{m} \leftarrow$the first k bits of $\boldsymbol{m}'$
6: return $\boldsymbol{m}$

Algorithm 2. The McEliece error correction with the Patterson Algorithm ($\mathrm{err\_corr}(\boldsymbol{z}', g(Y))$)

Require: the permuted ciphertext $\boldsymbol{z}'$, the secret Goppa polynomial $g(Y)$
Ensure: the permuted error vector $\boldsymbol{e}'$
1: $S(Y) \leftarrow \boldsymbol{z}' H^\top (Y^{t-1}, \cdots, Y, 1)^\top$
2: $\tau(Y) \leftarrow \sqrt{S^{-1}(Y) + Y} \bmod g(Y)$
3: $(\alpha(Y), \beta(Y)) \leftarrow \mathrm{XGCD}(\tau(Y), g(Y))$
4: $\sigma(Y) \leftarrow \alpha^2(Y) + Y\beta^2(Y)$
5: $\mathcal{E}' = \{E_0, \ldots, E_{t-1}\} \leftarrow \mathrm{rootfind}(\sigma(Y))$
// if γ_i is a root, then $\mathcal{E}'$ contains i
6: $\boldsymbol{e}' \leftarrow \boldsymbol{v} \in \mathbb{F}_2^n$ with $v_i = 1$ if and only if $i \in \mathcal{E}'$
7: **return** $\boldsymbol{e}'$

3 Identification of the Side Channel

In this section we will detail a timing side channel which allows for the construction of an attack against the permutation that is part of the private key, that will be given in Section 4.

While the attack presented in [11] is based on manipulations of valid ciphertexts, to which the underlying message shall be recovered, we focus on a different approach in this work. Specifically, that is the ability of the attacker to construct ciphertexts himself, having full control over the number of errors and the error pattern introduced during the encryption phase.

In the following, we investigate the effect of ciphertexts that were constructed by producing a correct code word in the public code by multiplying the message vector with the public matrix as described in Section 2, and then adding an error

[1] Usually, the error locator polynomial is defined to be monic, i.e $\sigma_t = 1$. But as a matter of fact the error locator polynomial generated in Step 4 of Algorithm 2 generally is not monic.

vector $\boldsymbol{e}$ with hamming weight $w < t$, thus violating the scheme. Specifically, we will turn to the case $w = 4$. In Section 8, we also consider the applicability of other values of w, but in the timing attack we develop in this work we only make use of $w = 4$, since it is the only one offering a plain timing side channel present in a straightforward implementation.

Algorithm 3. The Extended Euclidean Algorithm (XGCD($\tau(Y)$, $g(Y)$))

Require: the polynomial $\tau(Y)$ and the secret Goppa polynomial $g(Y)$, with $\deg(\tau(Y)) < \deg(g(Y))$
Ensure: two polynomials $\alpha(Y)$, $\beta(Y)$ satisfying $\alpha(Y) = \beta(Y)\tau(Y) \bmod g(Y)$ and $\deg(\alpha) \leqslant \lfloor \deg(g(Y))/2 \rfloor$

1: $d \leftarrow \lfloor \deg(g(Y))/2 \rfloor = \lfloor t/2 \rfloor$
2: $\beta_{-1} \leftarrow 0$
3: $\beta_0 \leftarrow 1$
4: $r_{-1} \leftarrow g(Y)$
5: $r_0 \leftarrow \tau(Y)$
6: $i \leftarrow 0$
7: **while** $\deg(r_i(Y)) > d$ **do**
8: $\quad i \leftarrow i + 1$
9: $\quad (q_i(Y), r_i(Y)) \leftarrow r_{i-2}(Y)/r_{i-1}(Y)$ // polynomial division with quotient q_i and remainder r_i
10: $\quad \beta_i(Y) \leftarrow \beta_{i-2}(Y) + q_i(Y)\beta_{i-1}(Y)$
11: **end while**
12: $\alpha(Y) \leftarrow r_i(Y)$
13: $\beta(Y) \leftarrow \beta_i(Y)$
14: **return** $(\alpha(Y), \beta(Y))$

For $w = 4$ we certainly have $\deg(\sigma(Y)) = 4$. This implies $\deg(\alpha(Y)) = 2$ and $\deg(\beta(Y)) \leqslant 1$. This freedom in the degree of $\beta(Y)$ results from the following two facts: First of all $w = 4$ is even, thus it is $\alpha(Y)$ that provides the leading coefficient of $\sigma(Y)$ (the summand polynomial providing the leading coefficient of $\sigma(Y)$ clearly never has any freedom in its degree for a given value of w). Furthermore, in contrast to the case of $w = 2$, here $\deg(\alpha(Y))$ is high enough to allow for more than just one value of $\deg(\beta(Y))$ (the only restriction on the summand polynomial not providing the leading coefficient self-evidently is that its degree must be just as small as not to provide the leading coefficient). This leads to two possible control flows in the decryption operation for $w = 4$: one iteration in the XGCD (Algorithm 3, the loop starting at Step 7), and zero iterations in the XGCD. Also, these two cases imply two different forms of the resulting error locator polynomial $\sigma(Y)$. These two possible forms of $\sigma(Y)$ are as follows, where N denotes the number of iterations in the XGCD. *The case* $N = 1$*:* looking at Step 4 of Algorithm 2 we find that $\sigma_3 \neq 0$, since here $\beta(Y) = q_1(Y)$. *The case* $N = 0$*:* here, clearly we have $\sigma_3 = 0$ due to $\beta(Y) = 1$. Experiments show that $N = 0$ appears with probability $\approx 2^{-m}$ if random ciphertexts with $w = 4$ are being decrypted. This clearly fits the interpretation, that the coefficient σ_3 is chosen randomly and equally distributed from $\mathbb{F}_{2^m}$ for a random ciphertext with the given properties. This is not essentially true, from the considerations given later in Section 7 we will see that the probability for $N = 0$ is in fact $1/(2^m - 3)$ instead of $1/2^m$.

This observation shows a side channel with a new quality compared to the one given in [11] : The error locator polynomial is related to the secret code, thus the distinction between $N = 0$ and $N = 1$ must be analyzed with respect to its potential of revealing information about the private key. This is done, with success, in Section 4.

It must be pointed out, however, that based on the implementation, there might be other sources of timing differences in the decryption algorithm, e.g. when inverting the syndrome polynomial $S(Y)$ modulo $g(Y)$ in Step 2 of Algorithm 2. Such an interference does not prevent the side channel, but it might imply difficulties that call for a more sophisticated statistical approach in the attack.

4 Construction of the Attack

In Section 3 it was found that if an attacker creates ciphertexts using error vectors of hamming weight $w = 4$, the decryption process can yield two different control flows. Specifically, in one case, N, the number of iterations in the XGCD, will be zero, in the other we have $N = 1$. A different number of iterations in the XGCD naturally leads to different timings, thus a timing side channel exists that allows to determine N.

As already denoted in Section 3, the side channel observable N is directly connected to the coefficient σ_3 of the error locator polynomial. In Step 3 of Algorithm 1 we can see that after the error vector has been determined, the secret permutation is applied to it when computing $\boldsymbol{e} = \boldsymbol{e}'P$. Clearly, the attacker knows $\boldsymbol{e}$, since he controlled the encryption operation. Let us denote the set of the indexes of the four positions having value 1 in an instance of $\boldsymbol{e}$ as $\mathcal{E} = \{f_1, f_2, f_3, f_4\}$.

In order to make the attack clear we want to introduce a new equation for the error locator polynomial in which the permutation is incorporated so that this polynomial is linked to the unpermuted error vector $\boldsymbol{e}$ instead of $\boldsymbol{e}'$. Thus we rewrite Equation (1) as

$$\sigma(Y) = \sigma_4 \prod_{j \in \mathcal{E}} (Y - \gamma_{P_j}), \tag{2}$$

where P_j refers to the notation of the permutation P as a vector: when $\boldsymbol{e} = \boldsymbol{e}'P$, then we can equivalently write $e_i = e'_{P_i}$ for the entries of the vector $\boldsymbol{e}$.

From this we find that we can write the coefficient of interest, σ_3, as a function of the error positions, namely $\sigma_3(f_1, f_2, f_3, f_4) = \sigma_4 \left(\gamma_{P_{f_1}} + \gamma_{P_{f_2}} + \gamma_{P_{f_3}} + \gamma_{P_{f_4}}\right)$, by simply writing out Equation (2).

The basic idea of the attack now is to build a list of linear equations describing the secret permutation. The attacker achieves this by generating random ciphertexts having error weight $w = 4$. He lets the decryption device decrypt these, and measures the timing. Every time he concludes from the timing that

$N = 0$, he adds one equation of the form $\sigma_3(f_1, f_2, f_3, f_4) = 0$ to his list, where the f_i stand for his actual choice of the four error positions. Please note that in Equation 2 the leading coefficient $\sigma_4 \neq 0$, so that we can omit the multiplication by σ_4 in the equations in our list.

After a certain number of equations has been gathered, the attacker will run a Gaussian elimination algorithm on his equation system. Note that due to the fact that $\gamma_j \in \mathbb{F}_{2^m}$, the equation system can be represented by an $l \times n$ binary matrix, where n is the length of the code used in the McEliece PKC and l is the number of equations in the list.

Depending on the defect of the matrix, a number of entries of the permutation have to be guessed in order to solve the system.

5 Countermeasure

The attack can easily be defeated by checking and, when required, manipulating the degree of $\tau(Y)$. This is due to the fact that $N = 0$ implies $\deg(\tau(Y)) \leqslant d = \lfloor t/2 \rfloor$, causing the break condition of the loop in Step 7 of Algorithm 3 to be fulfilled before the first iteration. The check that has to be performed is the test whether $\deg(\tau(Y)) < d$, this must be done after Step 2 of Algorithm 2. If that is the case, then $\tau(Y)$ is manipulated in such way that $\deg(\tau(Y)) = t - 1$. In the following, we will show that this is both sufficient to defeat the attack described in Section 4 and has no effect on the error correction for regular ciphertexts.

It defeats the attack, since it enforces the entering of the XGCD loop for all but one value of the degree of $\tau(Y)$. Entering the loop is sufficient if the countermeasures proposed in [11] are implemented, since then the maximum number of iterations (that would occur for $w = t$) are executed in the XGCD. The only uncovered case is $\deg(\tau(Y)) = d$. But this means for our attack that for $N = 0$ we would have $\deg(\sigma(Y)) = 2\deg(\alpha(Y)) = 2\deg(\tau(Y)) = 2d$. This would only work for $w = 4$ when $d = 2$ and thus $t = 4$ or $t = 5$ which is clearly not a realistic choice for this system parameter. Thus, for the cases relevant for our attack, the possibility $N = 0$ is taken away, removing the side channel observable. Furthermore, in Section 8, it is shown that other values of w can not be used to construct an analogous attack.

The countermeasure will never lead to erroneous decryption, since the inequality $\deg(\tau(Y)) < d$ is never fulfilled for the regular case $w = t$. For *even* values of the system parameter t this is evident since otherwise $\deg(\sigma(Y)) = 2\deg(\tau(Y)) < 2d = t$. For *odd* values of t we find that if it were that $\deg(\tau(Y)) < d$, we obviously would have $\deg(\beta(Y)) = 0$ leading to $\deg((\sigma(Y)) = 1 \neq t$, since here $\deg(\alpha(Y)) \leqslant \deg(\beta(Y))$.

Activating the countermeasure for higher values of $\deg(\tau(Y))$, e.g. already for $\deg(\tau(Y)) \leqslant d$ would cause the decryption routine to potentially produce errors for regular ciphertexts, as an error locator polynomial $\sigma(Y) = \alpha^2(Y) + \sigma_1 Y$ is valid[2] for even values of the system parameter t.

---

[2] It should be pointed out that this case is extremely unlikely and will not be observed for realistic values of the parameters t and m.

The manipulation of $\tau(Y)$ certainly has to be performed without introducing a timing difference. Please note that for the manipulation of the respective coefficients of $\tau(Y)$, one should not use truly random values, but rather fixed ones, or even better, use values that are pseudo-randomly derived from the ciphertext. Using truly random coefficients is a problem, since then the attacker might be able to determine that the decryption operation for a certain ciphertext is not deterministic. He might use another side channel instead of the timing of the operation, e.g. a power analysis attack could be mounted to this purpose. He would then try to find out whether the indeterministic countermeasure is activated for a specific ciphertext by repeatedly triggering the decryption of the same ciphertext and computing the variance of certain measured quantities, e.g. the power consumption at specific points in time. This is already pointed out in [11]. Furthermore, if the usage of fixed values allows an attacker to detect the appearance of these values e.g. through a power analysis attack, he could also conclude that the countermeasure was activated and conduct the same attack using this new side channel.

6 Implementation of the Attack and Results

The attack was implemented as a proof of concept. In this course, we did not use real timings, because such measurements are not very exact on modern high end CPUs found in today's general purpose computers. Also, the focus of this work lays on the exploration of the theoretic aspects of the underlying side channel. Thus, we added an iteration counter for the number of iterations in the XGCD and made this counter available to the attack routine. Please note that on devices like smart cards, the identification of the iteration count through an actual timing must be assumed to be rather easy. As already pointed out, the attack is founded on collecting linear equations about the entries of the permutation P_i. Experimental results showed that there seems to be a maximal rank of the equation system that can be achieved for a certain parameter set. In Table 1 the maximal ranks for those parameter sets we investigated are given. For the lowest parameter set a complete scan using all possible error vectors

Table 1. Maximal ranks of the equation system obtainable in the attack. The values in the third column are given for single runs and show certain variances, whereas the maximal ranks are firm.

parameters (n;t)	**maximal rank**	**number of ciphertexts to reach max. rank**
(64;5)	57	3,660
(256;10)	247	98,417
(512;20)	502	436,213
(1024;27)	1013	2,163,499
(2048;50)	2036	7,848,229

with wt $(e) = 4$ has been conducted, for the other parameter sets we used sets of at least five times the number of ciphertexts that were needed to achieve the maximal rank for this parameter set, the latter is given in column 3 of Table 1. For a particular attack to be executed, one needs to define a break rank, which in the optimal case is the maximal achievable rank for a given parameter set.

The McEliece implementation we attacked is based on the algorithms given in Section 2, written in the C programming language and run on a Linux machine. Any further details concerning the implementation and platform are unimportant since we do not measure real timings but count the iterations in the XGCD algorithm, as already pointed out.

In the following we give the description of the attack routine. It is used against a McEliece PKC which is described by the parameters $n = 2^m$ and $t = \deg(g(Y))$. The attack was executed for all the parameter sets given in Table 1.

First Step of the Attack. In the first step, the attack routine creates ciphertexts using random messages and random error vectors with wt $(e) = 4$. It then lets the decryption routine decrypt the ciphertext. By checking the iteration counter mentioned above the routine assesses whether zero or one iterations occurred in the XGCD. If one iteration occurred, nothing is done, if zero iterations occurred, the error vector is added as a new row of a matrix over $\mathbb{F}_2$ having n columns. Every time a row is added a Gauss-Jordan elimination is run on this equation system and the rank is determined. Once the break rank is reached, the first step of the attack is completed.

Second Step of the Attack. For the second step to be executed in a real attack, one would need a means of finding the correct Goppa polynomial $g(Y)$ used in the secret code, in order to recover the whole secret key. In this work, we do not give such an algorithm. What is done in the proof of concept implementation of the attack is to use real entries of the permutation for those variables P_i that have to be guessed in order to solve the system. Ending up with the correct permutation thus proves the correctness of the equations that were collected. The number of permutation entries that still has to be guessed given an equation system with rank r is determined by its defect, i.e. by $D = n - r$. This means for instance in the case of $n = 1024$ that $D = 11$. The number of overall guesses for these entries is found as $\prod_{i=0}^{10}(n - i)$, which is in the realm of 10^{33} for $n = 1024$. But clearly in a real attack one would implement additional consistency checks that are executed whenever a variable is determined by guessing or solving an equation: no element of the permutation may appear more than once.

7 Possible Approaches for a Real Life Attack

In this section we give two possible improvements of the attack, the first being useful if noisy timings are used and and the second one showing how a power analysis attack could be used to retrieve the same information.

"n-3" Scans. In real attacks, the attacker is confronted with the problem of receiving only noisy measurements. This means for our attack that the decision whether $N = 0$ or $N = 1$, based on a timing measurement might be very difficult or impossible for a single timing. But it is possible for the attacker to conduct measurements on certain sets containing $n-3$ error vectors, where he knows that exactly one of the vectors in the set causes $N = 0$. This is due to the following observation.

For every error vector of hamming weight $w = 4$, we have $\sigma_3(a,b,c,d) = \gamma_a + \gamma_b + \gamma_c + \gamma_d$ where a, b, c, d are all different values out of $\{0, \ldots, n-1\}$. Now take, w. l. o. g, the sum of three of these elements, $\gamma_a + \gamma_b + \gamma_c$. We now assume that there always exists some γ_d different from the former three elements, such that $\sigma_3(a,b,c,d) = 0$. We prove it by showing that assuming the opposite statement leads to a contradiction. Specifically, the non-existence of such a γ_d implies that the additive inverse of $\gamma_a + \gamma_b + \gamma_c$ is one out of the set $\{\gamma_a, \gamma_b, \gamma_c\}$. Since in a finite field of characteristic 2, each element is its own additive inverse, this in turn would imply $\gamma_a + \gamma_b + \gamma_c = \gamma_a$, w. l. o. g. But then we would have $\gamma_b = \gamma_c$, which is the contradiction we sought. This also implies that the probability for $N = 0$ for a ciphertext with a random error pattern with $w = 4$ is $1/(n-3)$.

Thus the attacker can proceed as follows: he fixes an error pattern of hamming weight $w = 3$ and produces the $n-3$ vectors that can be reached by adding one more error position and uses them to create $n-3$ ciphertexts and measures the corresponding decryption times. He can now use a maximum-likelihood strategy to determine the one timing which is corresponding to $N = 0$ iterations in the XGCD. He can selectively repeat measurements to increase the certainty of his decision if the amount of noise suggests this.

Starting Point for a Power Analysis Attack. From Algorithm 3 and the considerations given in Section 3, it is clear that in the case of $N = 0$ we have $\alpha(Y) = \tau(Y)$, and thus $\deg(\tau(Y)) = 2$ in Step 2 of Algorithm 2. On the other hand, if $N = 1$, then we know that $\deg(\tau(Y)) = t - 1$, because $\deg(\beta(Y)) = \deg(q_1(Y)) = 1$ is the only possibility according to Algorithm 3.

This means, that in Step 2 of Algorithm 2, a large number of coefficients turns out to be zero when the square root is computed. Since the hamming weight of registers respectively the number of the changed bits in a register are usual targets of a power analysis attack [21], one could expect that an unsecured implementation makes it possible to distinguish between the cases $N = 0$ and $N = 1$.

8 Related Topics

In the following, we turn our attention to the interplay of the attack devised in Section 4 with countermeasures against known timing attacks and integrity tests that might be employed in the decryption operation. Furthermore we will see why error vectors with a hamming weight other than four generally are not suitable to build an attack analogous to ours.

Known Timing Side Channels and Countermeasures. Both [11] and [12] examine a timing attack against the McEliece decryption operation. There, however, the secret that is targeted by the attack is the message. If the countermeasure proposed in [11] is incorporated in an implementation, but not the countermeasure described in Section 5, then the attack presented in this work becomes even easier. This is because the countermeasure from [11] tremendously bloats the timing difference that is exploited in the attack. Specifically, it will not alter the case of $N = 0$ on one hand, but will enforce the maximum number of iterations (that would occur for $w = t$) instead of $N = 1$ on the other hand. This is a direct consequence of the fact that this countermeasure so to say resides inside the XGCD loop, and will be skipped if that loop is skipped.

Integrity Tests during the Decryption Operation. No conceivable integrity test can prevent the side channel attack. In this context, by an integrity test we mean e.g. a CCA2-conversion [19,18]. Such a conversion ensures that if an attacker manipulates an existing ciphertext of the combined CCA2-McEliece scheme, the decryption device will detect such a manipulation and refuse to output the decrypted message. But since in the attack presented in this work, the attacker himself prepares the combined ciphertext, this integrity test will pass.

What remains to be considered is that the ciphertexts used in the attack violate the McEliece scheme by using error vectors with a hamming weight lower than t. This, of course, can easily be detected by the decryption device, specifically, in Step 4 of Algorithm 2, as in this case, as is pointed out in Section 2, the degree of the error locator polynomial $\sigma(Y)$ deviates from the intended value t. But this does not help to prevent the side channel attack. The XGCD has already been executed, the timing difference is already given, thus by simply letting the device return an error message the timing difference resulting from the two control flows for $N = 0$ and $N = 1$ would still be available to the attacker.

The Potential of Attacks with $\mathrm{wt}(\boldsymbol{e}) > 4$. For ciphertexts that are created by using error vectors with $w = \mathrm{wt}(\boldsymbol{e}) < 4$, there are no alternative control flows given the McEliece decryption is implemented as described in Section 2. This is easily verified when evaluating Algorithm 3 for these cases. What remains is to examine the potential of employing $w > 4$. First of all, using odd values of w can not lead to a side channel like the one we base our attack on, since in that case $\deg(\beta(Y))$ is always determined by w.

Given this, we first turn our attention to $w = 6$. There, we encounter three possibilities for the control flow: $N = 0$, $N = 1$, and $N = 2$. Analyzing Algorithm 3, we draw the following conclusions.

The case $N = 0$ is not very suitable to build an attack, as the probability for $\sigma_5 = 0$ and simultaneously $\sigma_3 = 0$ must be assumed to be in the realm of 2^{-2m}. Furthermore, no approach to build a maximum likelihood strategy as described for $w = 4$ in Section 7 is obvious.

Regarding $N = 1$, we find that the form of $\sigma(Y)$ is still ambiguous, as there are two qualitatively different causes for this control flow: *First*, we could have $\deg(\tau(Y)) = \deg(g(Y)) - 1$ and thus $\deg(q_1(Y)) = 1$. This leads to $\sigma_5 = 0$ since

$\beta(Y) = q_1(Y)$. *Second,* it can happen that $\deg(\tau(Y)) = \deg(g(Y)) - 2$ leading to $\deg(q_1(Y)) = 2$, leaving us with $\sigma_5 \neq 0$.

The case $N = 2$, however, is again the very general case were $q_1(Y)$ and $q_2(Y)$ both have degree one, and thus $\beta(Y) = 1 + q_1(Y)q_2(Y)$ has degree two.

It is obvious that the variety of causes for a certain value of N gets even bigger for larger (even) values of w, rendering them unsuitable to build an attack on. However, if an attacker is able to distinguish these "causes", e.g. by using power analysis, clearly, an attack would be possible.

9 Conclusion and Outlook

In this work, we have we have devised a timing attack which is generally applicable against any unsecured implementation of the McEliece scheme using the Patterson Algorithm for error correction. In contrast to other known timing side channels of the scheme (see Section 8), this vulnerability allows to gather information about the secret permutation that is part of the private key. However, it seems not to be possible to reduce the defect of the equation system that is build up in the course of the attack below a certain value that seems to be fixed for a certain parameter set. Thus, considerable effort remains if one aims at recovering the full permutation for a realistic parameter set. Since in the case of power analysis attacks, also given the countermeasure we developed to secure against the timing attack, a certain a amount of side channel information about the permutation might be available, it would be interesting to know exactly how costly a brute force attack on the secret key remains, given a certain knowledge about the permutation.

Furthermore, it would also be helpful to have a generic countermeasure, that randomizes the process of error correction, which is so vulnerable, because the number of errors [11,12] and, as shown in this work, special properties of the error locator polynomial, are fairly exposed to side channel attacks. Today, such a countermeasure has not been developed.

References

1. McEliece, R.J.: A public key cryptosystem based on algebraic coding theory. DSN progress report 42–44, 114–116 (1978)
2. Hankerson, D., Menezes, A., Vanstone, S.: Guide to Elliptic Curve Cryptography (2004) ISBN 978-0387952734
3. Miller, V.: Use of Elliptic Curves in Cryptography. In: Williams, H.C. (ed.) CRYPTO 1985. LNCS, vol. 218, pp. 417–426. Springer, Heidelberg (1986)
4. Rivest, R., Shamir, A., Adleman, L.: A method for obtaining digital signatures and public-key cryptosystems. Communications of the ACM 21(2), 120–126 (1978)
5. Diffie, W., Hellman, M.: New directions in cryptography. IEEE Transactions on Information Theory 22(6), 644–654 (1976)
6. Shor, P.W.: Algorithms for quantum computation: discrete logarithms and factoring. In: Proceedings of 35th Annual Symposium on Foundation of Computer Science (1994)

7. Peter, W.: Shor: Polynomial time algorithms for prime factorization and discrete logarithms on a quantum computer. SIAM Journal on Computing 26(5), 1484–1509 (1997)
8. Proos, J., Zalka, C.: Shor's discrete logarithm quantum algorithm for elliptic curves, Technical Report quant-ph/0301141, arXiv (2006)
9. Kocher, P.: Timing Attacks on Implementations of Diffie-Hellman, RSA, DSS, and Other Systems. In: Proceedings of the 16th Annual International Cryptology Conference on Advances in Cryptology, pp. 104–113 (1996)
10. Kocher, P.: Differential Power Analysis. In: Wiener, M. (ed.) CRYPTO 1999. LNCS, vol. 1666, pp. 388–397. Springer, Heidelberg (1999)
11. Shoufan, A., Strenzke, F., Molter, H.G., Stöttinger, M.: A Timing Attack Against Patterson Algorithm in the McEliece PKC (2009); To be published in ICISC 2009 (2009)
12. Strenzke, F., Tews, E., Molter, H.G., Overbeck, R., Shoufan, A.: Side Channels in the McEliece PKC. In: Buchmann, J., Ding, J. (eds.) PQCrypto 2008. LNCS, vol. 5299, pp. 216–229. Springer, Heidelberg (2008)
13. Patterson, N.: Algebraic decoding of Goppa codes. IEEE Trans. Info. Theory 21, 203–207 (1975)
14. Engelbert, D., Overbeck, R., Schmidt, A.: A Summary of McEliece-Type Cryptosystems and their Security. Journal of Mathematical Cryptology (2006)
15. Goppa, V.D.: A new class of linear correcting codes. Problems of Information Transmission 6, 207–212 (1970)
16. MacWilliams, F.J., Sloane, N.J.A.: The theory of error correcting codes. North-Holland, Amsterdam (1997)
17. Bernstein, D.J., Lange, T., Peters, C.: Attacking and defending the McEliece cryptosystem. In: Buchmann, J., Ding, J. (eds.) PQCrypto 2008. LNCS, vol. 5299, pp. 31–46. Springer, Heidelberg (2008)
18. Kobara, K., Imai, H.: Semantically secure McEliece public-key cryptosystems - conversions for McEliece PKC. In: Practice and Theory in Public Key Cryptography - PKC '01 Proceedings (2001)
19. Pointcheval, D.: Chosen-chipertext security for any one-way cryptosystem. In: Imai, H., Zheng, Y. (eds.) PKC 2000. LNCS, vol. 1751, pp. 129–146. Springer, Heidelberg (2000)
20. Biswas, B., Sendrier, N.: McEliece Cryptosystem Implementation: Theory and Practice. In: Buchmann, J., Ding, J. (eds.) PQCrypto 2008. LNCS, vol. 5299, pp. 47–62. Springer, Heidelberg (2008)
21. Mangard, S., Oswald, E., Popp, T.: Power Analysis Attacks: Revealing the Secrets of Smard Cards. Springer, Heidelberg (2007)

Practical Power Analysis Attacks on Software Implementations of McEliece

Stefan Heyse, Amir Moradi, and Christof Paar

Horst Görtz Institute for IT Security, Ruhr University Bochum, Germany
{heyse,moradi,cpaar}@crypto.rub.de

Abstract. The McEliece public-key cryptosystem is based on the fact that decoding unknown linear binary codes is an NP-complete problem. The interest on implementing post-quantum cryptographic algorithms, e.g. McEliece, on microprocessor-based platforms has been extremely raised due to the increasing storage space of these platforms. Therefore, their vulnerability and robustness against physical attacks, e.g., state-of-the-art power analysis attacks, must be investigated. In this work, we address mainly two power analysis attacks on various implementations of McEliece on an 8-bit AVR microprocessor. To the best of our knowledge, this is the first time that such side-channel attacks are practically evaluated.

1 Introduction

1.1 Motivation

Mainly all modern security systems rely on public-key cryptography. Most commonly used are RSA, ECC and Diffie-Hellman (DH) based schemes. They are well understood and withstand many types of attacks for years. However, these cryptosystems rely on two primitive security assumptions, namely the factoring problem (FP) and the discrete logarithm problem (DLP). A breakthrough in one of the currently known attacks (e.g, *Number Field Sieve* or *Index Calculus*) or newly introduced successful build of a quantum computer can make all of them useless.

Fortunately, there are alternative public-key primitives, like hash-based, lattice-based, MQ-methods and coding-based schemes. During the last years, much research effort has been put into determining strengths and weaknesses of these systems. They were implemented on different platforms, e.g., x86- and x64-based CPUs, GPUs, FPGAs and small embedded systems employing microcontrollers.

The oldest scheme, which is based on coding theory, has been presented by Robert J. McEliece in 1978. In its original form it withstands all the attacks. The most recent and effective attack reported during the last 30 years reduces the security of a system from 80- to 60-bit [2]. It has been implemented on several platforms including CPU [3], GPU [13], FPGA [8,28], and 8-bit microcontrollers [8]. To make this system a real alternative to the existing schemes,

N. Sendrier (Ed.): PQCrypto 2010, LNCS 6061, pp. 108–125, 2010.

or to let it be a candidate for the post-quantum era, all possible attacks have to be evaluated.

Since the first introduction of DPA in 1999 [15], it has become an alternative approach for extracting secret key of cryptographic devices by exploiting side-channel leakages despite robustness of the corresponding algorithms to cryptanalyzing methods. During the last ten years it has been showed by many articles (cf., e.g., the CHES workshop proceedings since 1999) that side-channel attacks must be considered as a potential risk for security related devices. The practical attacks mounted on a real-world and widespread security applications, e.g., [9], also strengthen the importance of side-channel attacks.

Though there are a few works on vulnerability and robustness of implementation of public-key algorithms to side-channel attacks (e.g., [7,20]), most of the published articles in the scientific literatures on this field concentrated on the state-of-the-art Differential Power Analysis (DPA) attacks on symmetric block ciphers, e.g., [21,25,30]. In addition to classical DPA approaches (like [5,11,15,19]) combination of cryptanalytic schemes and side-channel leakages led to innovative attacks, e.g., a couple of collision side-channel attacks [4,24,26] and algebraic side-channel attacks [23].

1.2 Related Works and Our Contribution

There are not many articles regarding the evaluation of side-channel attacks on post-quantum algorithms. The lattice based NTRUencrypt has been investigated in [29] and [34]. Hash trees look more like a protocol than to a cryptographic primitive, and they stand or fall with the underlying hash function. For MQ-based algorithms, we know no research inquiry. Only coding-based cryptography got some attention during the last two years.

Side-channel attacks on PC implementations of the McEliece scheme are already addressed in [32] and [12] where the authors mounted a timing attack. By means of this attack, the adversary would be able to decrypt only the attacked message. Though the attack is promising, the adversary needs to repeat the attack for every later ciphertext by having physical access to the target device. Further, recently another timing attack on McEliece has been published in [27] that shows the interest of the research community to side-channel attack on McEliece implementations.

Resistance of McEliece against fault injection attacks has been investigated in [6]. The authors stated that due to the error correction capability of this type of cryptosystem, it is heavily resistant against fault injection attacks because the faults are part of the algorithm and are simply corrected (maybe to a wrong message, but no secret information is revealed).

An algebraic side-channel attack on AES presented in [23] is able to recover the secret key of a microcontroller-based implementation by means of profiling and a single mean trace supposing that the attacker knows the execution path and can recover the Hamming weight (HW) of the operand of the selected instructions. Though this attack is even efficient to overcome arithmetic masking schemes supposing the same adversary model, solving the algebraic system equations encounters many problems by wrong HW predictions. Our proposed attacks are partially based on the same idea, i.e., examining the secret hypotheses considering the predicted HW of the processed data.

In contrary to the side-channel attacks proposed on the McEliece implementations so far, we have implemented and practically evaluated all steps of our proposed attacks. The target implementations which are considered in this work are based on the article recently published in CHES 2009 [8]. Since there is not a unique way to implement the McEliece decryption scheme by a microcontroller, we define four different implementation profiles to realize the decryption algorithm, and for each of which we propose an attack to recover the secret key. Generally our proposed attacks can be divided into two phases:

- collecting side-channel observations for chosen ciphertexts and generating a candidate list for each target secret element of the cipher and
- examining the candidates to check which hypotheses match to the public parameters of the cipher.

By means of our proposed attacks we are able to recover the permutation matrix and the parity check matrix if each one is performed solely. On the other hand if both matrices are combined in the target implementation, we are also able to recover the combined (permutation and parity check) matrix. Each of these attacks leads to breaking the decryption scheme and recovering the secret key. It should be noted that contrary to the attack presented in [23] our supposed adversary model does not need to profile the side-channel leakage of the target device, and our proposed attacks are more insensitive to wrong HW predictions than that of presented in [23].

1.3 Organization

In the next section, a short introduction to McEliece cryptosystem is given. Then, in Section 3 the implementation profiles which are considered in our attacks as the target implementation are defined. Section 4 briefly reviews the concept of power analysis attacks. In Section 5 first our supposed adversary model is introduced. Then, we explain how to use side-channel observations to directly recover a secret (e.g., the permutation matrix) or to partially predict a part of a secret (e.g., the parity check matrix). Afterwards, we show how to break the system using the revealed/predicted information. Further, we discuss possible countermeasures to defeat our proposed attacks in Section 6. Finally, Section 7 concludes our research.

2 McEliece in a Flash

This section gives a short overview on the original McEliece cryptosystem, and introduces the used Goppa codes. We stay superficial, and explain only what is necessary to understand the attacks described afterwards.

Algorithm 1. McEliece Message Encryption

Require: $m, K_{pub} = (\hat{G}, t)$
Ensure: Ciphertext c
Encode the message m as a binary string of length k
$c' \leftarrow m \cdot \hat{G}$
Generate a random n-bit error vector z containing at most t ones
$c = c' + z$
return c

Algorithm 2. McEliece Message Decryption

Require: $c, K_{sec} = (P^{-1}, G, S^{-1})$
Ensure: Plaintext m
$\hat{c} \leftarrow c \cdot P^{-1}$
Use a decoding algorithm for the code C to decode $\hat{c}$ to $\hat{m} = m \cdot S$
$m \leftarrow \hat{m} \cdot S^{-1}$
return m

2.1 Background on the McEliece Cryptosystem

The McEliece scheme is a public-key cryptosystem based on linear error-correcting codes proposed by Robert J. McEliece in 1978 [18]. The secret key is an efficient decoding algorithm of an error-correcting code with dimension k, length n and error correcting capability t. To create a public key, McEliece defines a random $k \times k$-dimensional scrambling matrix S and $n \times n$-dimensional permutation matrix P disguising the structure of the code by computing the product $\hat{G} = S \times G \times P$, where G is the generator matrix of the code. Using the public key $K_{pub} = (\hat{G}, t)$ and private key $K_{sec} = (P^{-1}, G, S^{-1})$, encryption and decryption algorithms can be given by Algorithm 1 and Algorithm 2 respectively.

Note that Algorithm 1 only consists of a simple matrix multiplication with the input message and then distributes t random errors on the resulting code word.

Decoding the ciphertext c for decryption as shown in Algorithm 2 is the most time-consuming process and requires several more complex operations in binary extension fields. In Section 2.2 we briefly introduce the required steps for decoding codewords.

2.2 Classical Goppa Codes

This section reviews the underlying code-based part of McEliece without the cryptographic portion. To encode a message m into a codeword c, the message m should be represented as a binary string of length k and be multiplied by the $k \times n$ generator matrix G of the code. Decoding a codeword $\underline{r}$ at the receiver side with a (possibly) additive error vector $\underline{e}$ is much more complex than a simple matrix vector multiplication for encoding. The most widely used decoding scheme for Goppa codes is the Patterson algorithm [22].

Here we only give a short introduction and define the necessary abbreviations.

Theorem 1. *[33] Let $g(z)$ be an irreducible polynomial of degree t over $GF(2^m)$. Then the set*

$$\Gamma(g(z), GF(2^m)) = \{(c_\alpha)_{\alpha \in GF(2^m)} \in \{0,1\}^n \mid \sum_{\alpha \in GF(2^m)} \frac{c_\alpha}{z-\alpha} \equiv 0 \bmod g(z)\} \tag{1}$$

defines a binary Goppa code C of length $n = 2^m$, dimension $k \geq n - mt$ and minimum distance $d \geq 2t+1$. The set of the α_i is called the support $\mathcal{L}$ of the code.

This code is capable of correcting up to t errors [1] and can be described as a $k \times n$ generator matrix G such that $C = \{mG : m \in GF_2^k\}$. This matrix is systematic, if it is in the form $(I_k \| Q)$, where I_k denotes the $k \times k$ identity matrix and Q is a $k \times (n-k)$ matrix. Then $H = (Q^T \| I_{n-k})$ is a parity-check matrix of C with $C = \{c \in GF_2^n : cH^T = 0\}$.

Since $\underline{r} = \underline{c} + \underline{e} \equiv \underline{e} \bmod g(z)$ holds, the syndrome $Syn(z)$ of a received codeword can be obtained from Equation (1) by

$$Syn(z) = \sum_{\alpha \in GF(2^m)} \frac{r_\alpha}{z-\alpha} \equiv \sum_{\alpha \in GF(2^m)} \frac{e_\alpha}{z-\alpha} \bmod g(z) \tag{2}$$

To finally recover $\underline{e}$, we need to solve the key equation $\sigma(z) \cdot Syn(z) \equiv \omega(z) \bmod g(z)$, where $\sigma(z)$ denotes a corresponding error-locator polynomial and $\omega(z)$ denotes an error-weight polynomial.

The roots of $\sigma(z)$ denote the positions of error bits. If $\sigma(\alpha_i) \equiv 0 \bmod g(z)$ where α_i is the corresponding bit of a generator in $GF(2^m)$, there was an error in the position i of the received codeword that can be corrected by bit-flipping.

This decoding process, as required in Step 2 of Algorithm 2 for message decryption, is finally summarized in Algorithm 3 in the appendix.

Instead of writing inverted polynomials to the columns parity check matrix H, there exist an alternative representation for the parity check matrix, which is important for the attack in Section 5.3.

From Equation (2) we can derive the parity check matrix H as

$$H = \begin{Bmatrix} \frac{g_t}{g(\alpha_0)} & \frac{g_t}{g(\alpha_1)} & \cdots & \frac{g_t}{g(\alpha_{n-1})} \\ \frac{g_{t-1}+g_t\cdot\alpha_0}{g(\alpha_0)} & \frac{g_{t-1}+g_t\cdot\alpha_0}{g(\alpha_1)} & \cdots & \frac{g_{t-1}+g_t\cdot\alpha_0}{g(\alpha_{n-1})} \\ \vdots & \ddots & & \vdots \\ \frac{g_1+g_2\cdot\alpha_0+\cdots+g_t\cdot\alpha_0^{s-1}}{g(\alpha_0)} & \frac{g_1+g_2\cdot\alpha_0+\cdots+g_t\cdot\alpha_0^{s-1}}{g(\alpha_1)} & \cdots & \frac{g_1+g_2\cdot\alpha_0+\cdots+g_t\cdot\alpha_0^{s-1}}{g(\alpha_{n-1})} \end{Bmatrix} \tag{3}$$

This can be split into

$$H = \begin{Bmatrix} g_t & 0 & \cdots & 0 \\ g_{s-1} & g_t & \cdots & 0 \\ \vdots & & \ddots & \vdots \\ g_1 & g_2 & \cdots & g_t \end{Bmatrix} * \begin{Bmatrix} \frac{1}{g(\alpha_0)} & \frac{1}{g(\alpha_1)} & \cdots & \frac{1}{g(\alpha_{n-1})} \\ \frac{\alpha_0}{g(\alpha_0)} & \frac{\alpha_1}{g(\alpha_1)} & \cdots & \frac{\alpha_{n-1}}{g(\alpha_{n-1})} \\ \vdots & & \ddots & \vdots \\ \frac{\alpha_0^{s-1}}{g(\alpha_0)} & \frac{\alpha_1^{s-1}}{g(\alpha_1)} & \cdots & \frac{\alpha_{n-1}^{s-1}}{g(\alpha_{n-1})} \end{Bmatrix}, \tag{4}$$

where the first part has a non-zero determinant, and following the second part $\hat{H}$ is equivalent to the parity check matrix, which has a simpler structure. By applying the Gaussian algorithm to the second matrix $\hat{H}$ one can bring it to systematic form $(I_k \mid \underline{H})$, where I_k is the $k \times k$ identity matrix. Note that whenever a column swap is performed, a swap on the corresponding elements of the support $\mathcal{L}$ is also performed. From the systematic parity check matrix $(I_k \mid \underline{H})$, now the systematic generator matrix G can be derived as $(I_{n-k} \mid \underline{H}^{\mathrm{T}})$.

In the context of McEliece decryption, reverting the permutation can be merged into the parity check matrix by permuting the support $\mathcal{L}$. Using $\mathcal{L}_P = P^{-1} * \mathcal{L}$ to generate H leads to a parity check matrix that computes the correct syndrome for a permuted codeword.

In the following we always refer to a binary irreducible Goppa code with $m = 11$ and $t = 27$. This is a symmetric equivalent security of 80 bits and leads to $n = 2048$ and $k = 1751$ [2].

3 Practical Aspects

The combination of the McEliece decryption Algorithm 2 and the Goppa decoding Algorithm 3 allows a wide range of different implementations. For our proposed attacks, the most interesting point is the specific implementation of step 1 of Algorithm 2 and step 1 of Algorithm 3 and whether they are merged together or not. According to these points we define four so-called implementation profiles:

Profile I. performs the permutation of the ciphertext and computes the columns of H as they are needed by either using the extended euclidean algorithm (EEA) or the structure given in Equation (3) or (4).

Profile II. also performs the permutation, but uses the precomputed parity check matrix H.

Profile III. does not really perform the permutation, but directly uses a permuted parity check matrix. As stated in Section 2.2, we can use $\mathcal{L}_P = P^{-1} * \mathcal{L}$ to compute the syndrome of the unpermuted ciphertext. This profile computes the permuted columns as needed.

Profile IV. does the same as profile III, but uses a precomputed and permuted parity check matrix.

4 Introduction to Power Analysis Attacks

Power analysis attacks exploit the fact that the execution of a cryptographic algorithm on a physical device leaks information about the processed data and/or executed operations through instantaneous power consumption [15]. Measuring and evaluating the power consumption of a cryptographic device allows exploiting information-dependent leakage combined with the knowledge about the plaintext or ciphertext in order to extract, e.g., a secret key. Since intermediate result of the computations are serially processed (especially in 8-,16-, or 32-bit architectures, e.g., general-purpose microcontrollers) a divide-and-conquer strategy becomes possible, i.e., the secret key could be recovered byte by byte.

A Simple Power Analysis (SPA) attack, as introduced in [15], relies on visual inspection of power traces, e.g., measured from an embedded microcontroller of a smartcard. The aim of an SPA is to reveal details about the execution of the program flow of a software implementation, like the detection of conditional branches depending on secret information. Recovering an RSA private key bit-by-bit by an SPA on square-and-multiply algorithm [15] and revealing a KeeLoq secret key by SPA on software implementation of the decryption algorithm [14] are amongst the powerful practical examples of SPA on real-world applications. Contrary to SPA, Differential Power Analysis (DPA) utilizes statistical methods and evaluates several power traces. A DPA requires no knowledge about the concrete implementation of the cipher and can hence be applied to most of unprotected black box implementations. According to intermediate values depending on key hypotheses the traces are correlated to estimated power values, and then correlation coefficients indicate the most probable hypothesis amongst all partially guessed key hypotheses [5]. In order to perform a correlation-based DPA, the power consumption of the device under attack must be guessed; the power model should be defined according to the characteristics of the attacked device, e.g., Hamming weight (HW) of the processed data for a microcontroller because of the existence of a precharged/predischarged bus in microcontrollers architecture. In case of a bad quality of the acquired power consumption, e.g., due to a noisy environment, bad measurement setup or cheap equipment, averaging can be applied by decrypting(encrypting) the same ciphertext(plaintext) repeatedly and calculating the mean of the corresponding traces to decrease the noise floor.

5 Our Proposed Attacks

In this section, we first specify the assumptions we have considered for a side-channel adversary in our proposed attacks. Afterwards, we review the side-channel vulnerabilities and information leakages which our specified adversary can recover considering the target microcontroller (AVR ATmega256). Taking the implementation profiles (defined in Section 3) into account different power analysis attacks are proposed in Section 5.2 to recover some secrets of the decryption algorithm. Finally, in Section 5.3 we discuss how to use the secrets recovered by means of the side-channel attacks to break the decryption scheme and reveal the system private key.

5.1 Adversary Model

In our proposed attacks we consider an adversary model:
The adversary knows what is public like $\hat{G}, t$. Also he knows the implementation platform (e.g., type of the microcontroller used), the implementation profile, i.e, complete source code of the decryption scheme (of course excluding memory

contents, precomputed values, and secret key materials). Also, he is able to select different ciphertexts and measure the power consumption during the decryption operation.

5.2 Possible Power Analysis Vulnerabilities

In order to investigate the vulnerability of the target implementation platform to power analysis attacks a measurement setup by means of an AVR ATmega256 microcontroller which is clocked by a 16MHz oscillator is developed. Power consumption of the target device is measured using a LeCroy WP715Zi 1.5GHz oscilloscope at a sampling rate of 10GS/s and by means of a differential probe which captures voltage drop of a 10Ω resistor at VDD (5V) path.

To check the dependency of power traces on operations, different instructions including arithmetic, load, and save operations are taken into account, and power consumption for each one for different operands are collected. In contrary to 8051-based or PIC microcontrollers, which need 16, 8, or 4 clock cycles to execute an operation, an AVR ATmega256 executes the instructions in 1 or 2 clock cycles[1]. Therefore, the power consumption pattern of different instructions are not so different from each other. As Figure 1 shows, though the instructions are not certainly recognizable, load instructions are detectable amongst others. As a result the adversary may be able to detect the execution paths by comparing the power traces. Note that as mentioned in Section 4 if the adversary is able to repeat the measurement for a certain input, averaging helps to reduce the noise and hence improve the execution path detection procedure.

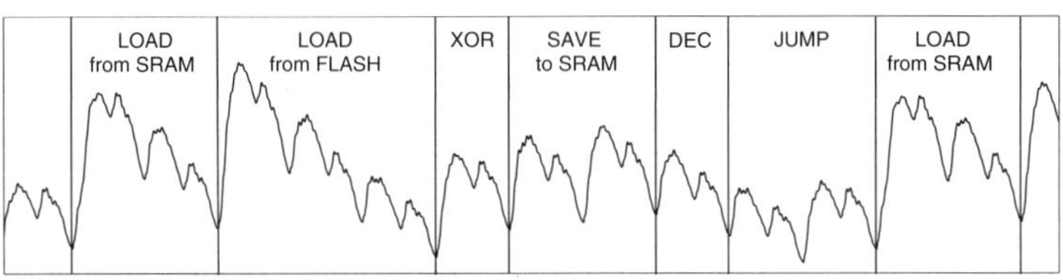

Fig. 1. A power consumption trace for different instructions

On the other hand, considering a fixed execution path, operand of instructions play a significant role in variety of power consumption values. As mentioned before, since the microcontrollers usually precharge/predischarge the bus lines, HW of the operands or HW of the results are proportional to power values. Figure 2 shows the dependency of power traces on the operands for XOR, LOAD, and SAVE instructions. Note that XOR instruction takes place on two registers, LOAD instruction loads an SRAM location to a specified register, and SAVE stores the content of a register back to the SRAM. According to Figure 2(c), HW of operands of SAVE instruction are more distinguishable in comparison to that of XOR and LOAD instructions. Therefore, according to the defined adversary

[1] Most of the arithmetic instructions in 1 clock cycle.

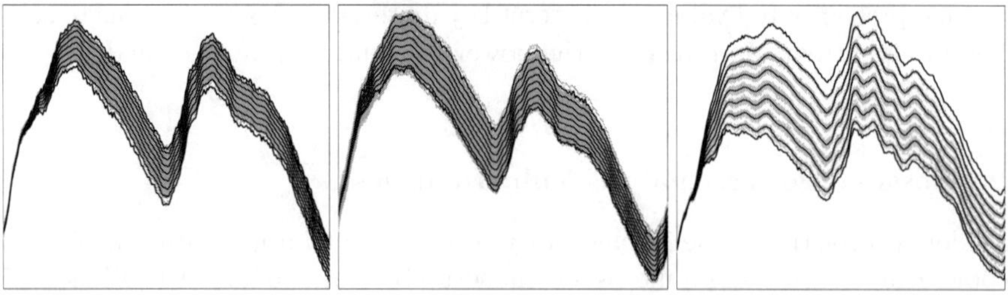

(a) (b) (c)

Fig. 2. Power consumption traces for different operands of (a) XOR, (b) LOAD, and SAVE instructions (all traces in gray and the averaged based on HWs in black)

model we suppose that the adversary considers only the leakage of the SAVE instructions. Now the question is "*How precisely the adversary can detect HW of the values stored by a SAVE instruction*?" It should be noted that a similar question has been answered in the case of a PIC microcontroller in [23] where the adversary (which fits to our defined adversary model in addition to profiling ability) has to profile the power traces in order to correctly detect the HWs. The same procedure can be performed on our implementation platform. However, in our defined adversary model the device under attack can be controlled by the attacker in order to repeat measurements as many as needed for the same input (ciphertext). Therefore, without profiling the attacker might be able to reach the correct HWs by means of averaging and probability distribution tests[2]. In contrary to an algebraic side-channel attack which needs all correct HW of the target bytes to perform a successful key recovery attack [23], as we describe later in Section 5.3 our proposed attack is still able to recover the secrets if the attacker guesses the HWs within a window around the correct HWs. Figure 3 presents success rate of HW detection for different scenarios. In the figure, the number of traces for the same target byte which are used in averaging is indicated by "avg". Further, "window" shows the size of a window which is defined around the correct HWs. As shown by Figure 3, to detect the correct HWs the adversary needs to repeat the measurements around 10 times, but defining a window by the size of 1 (i.e., correct HWs ± 1) leads to the success rate of 100% considering only one measurement.

Differential Power Analysis. First, one may think that the best side-channel attack on implementation of McEliece decryption scheme would be a DPA to reveal the secret key. However, the input (ciphertext) is processed in a bitwise fashion, and in contrary to symmetric block ciphers the secret key does not contribute as a parameter of a computation. Moreover, power traces for different ciphertexts would not be aligned to each other based on the computations,

[2] Probability distribution test here means to compare the probability distribution of the power values to the distribution of HW of random data in order to find the best match especially when highest (HW=8) or/and lowest (HW=0) is missing in measurements.

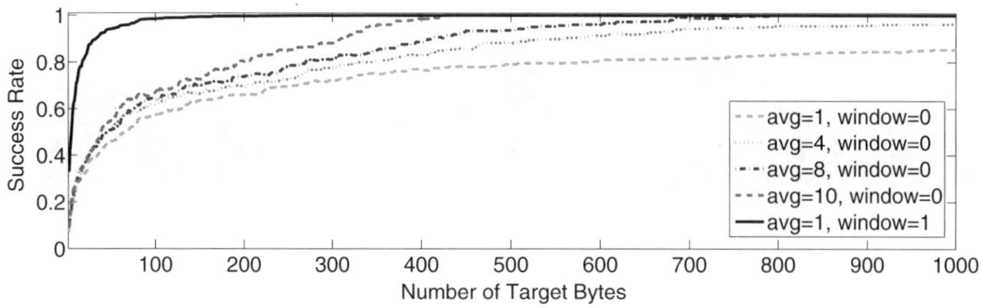

Fig. 3. Success rate of HW detection using the leakage of a SAVE instruction for different averaging and windowing parameters

and execution time of decryption also varies for different ciphertexts. As a consequence, it is not possible to perform a classical DPA attack on our target implementations.

SPA on Permutation Matrix. Considering implementation profiles I and II (defined in Section 3) the first secret information which is used in decryption process is permutation matrix P. After permuting the ciphertext it is multiplied by matrix H^T. Since the multiplication of $\hat{c}$ and H^T can be efficiently realized by summing up those rows of H for which corresponding bit of $\hat{c}$ is "1" and skip all "0" bits, running time of multiplication depends on the number of "1"s (let say HW) of $\hat{c}$. As mentioned before the side-channel adversary would be able to detect the execution paths. If so, he can recover the content of $\hat{c}$ bit-by-bit by examining whether the summation is performed or not. However, HW of $\hat{c}$ is the same as HW of c, and only the bit locations are permuted. To recover the permutation matrix, the adversary can consider only the ciphertexts with HW=1 (2048 different ciphertexts in this case), and for each ciphertext finds the instant of time when the summation is performed (according to $\hat{c}$ bits). Sorting the time instants allows recovery whole of the permutation matrix. Figure 4 shows two power traces of start of decryption for two different ciphertexts. Obviously start of the summation is recognizable by visual inspection, but a general scheme (which is supposed to work independent of the implementation platform) would be similar to the scheme presented in [14]. That is, an arbitrary part of a trace can be considered as the reference pattern, and computing the cross correlation of the reference pattern and other power traces (for other ciphertexts with HW=1) reveals the positions in time when the summation takes place. Figure 5 presents two correlation vectors for the corresponding power traces of Figure 4. Note that to reduce the noise effect we have repeated the measurements and took the average over 10 traces for each ciphertext. Using this scheme for all ciphertexts with HW=1, permutation matrix is completely recovered.

SPA on Parity Check Matrix. When implementation profiles III and IV are used, the permutation is not solely performed and hence the attack described above is not applicable. Therefore, the adversary has to take the multiplication

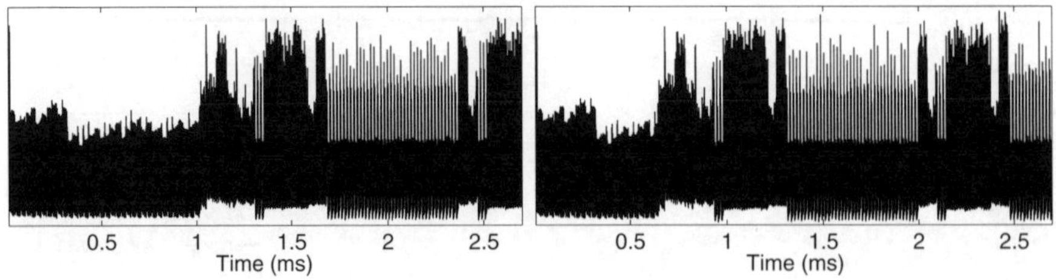

Fig. 4. Power traces of ciphertext (left) 0x0...01 and (right) 0x0...02

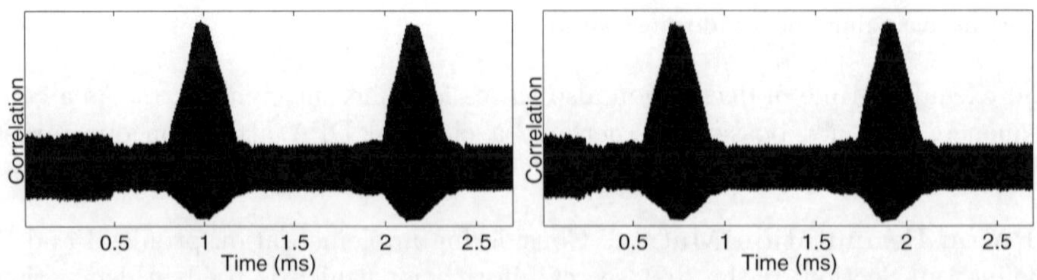

Fig. 5. Correlation vectors for ciphertexts (left) 0x0...01 and (right) 0x0...02

process into account. Since in this case, execution path of multiplication does not depend on any secret, recovering the conditional branches (which only depend on ciphertext bits) would not help the attacker revealing the secrets. As a consequence the adversary has to try revealing the content of the parity check matrix H. To do so, as described before he may reach (or guess) HW of the processed (or saved) data. Similarly to the last scheme the attacker can chose all ciphertexts with HW=1 and guess the HW of elements of each column of matrix H separately. Since 27 11-bit elements of each column of H are saved efficiently in a byte-wise fashion in 38-byte chunks[3], and the adversary can only guess the HW of each byte, he can not certainly guess the HW of each 11-bit element of H. Therefore, the number of candidates for the HW of each 11-bit element is increased. As the result of this procedure, the adversary will have a set of candidates for each 11-bit element of parity matrix H at row i and column j as follows:

$$\hat{H}_{i,j} = \left\{ h \in \{0,1\}^{11} \mid \text{HW}(h) \;=\; \text{the guessed HW by SPA } \pm \text{window} \right\}.$$

SPA on Goppa Polynomial. If the attacker can follow the execution path after the matrix multiplication, he would be able to measure the power consumption during the computation of the syndrome polynomial inversion (step 2 of Algorithm 3). Since at the start of this computation the Goppa polynomial is loaded, e.g., from a nonvolatile memory to SRAM, similarly to the scheme

[3] Each 11-bit can be saved in 2 bytes, but it wastes the memory and also simplifies the attack procedure by dividing the HW of an 11-bit value to the HW of two 8- and 3-bit parts.

explained above the adversary can predict HW of the transfered values, and hence make a list of candidates for each 11-bit element of the Goppa polynomial.

5.3 Gains of Power Analysis Vulnerabilities

This section discusses how to use the so far gathered information to perform a key recovery attack.

Attack I: Knowing the permutation matrix. Given the permutation matrix P (which is recovered by means of an SPA), we are able to completely break the systemwith one additional assumption. We need to know the original support $\mathcal{L}$. In [10], Section $3.1 it is stated that $\mathcal{L}$ can be published without loss in security. Using the public key $\hat{G} = S * G * P$, we can easily recover $S * G$. Multiplication by a message with only a single "1" at position i gives us row $S[i]$ because G is considered to be in the systematic form. Therefore, by $(n - k)$ multiplications we can extract the scrambling matrix S and consequently G as well.

Now it is possible to recover the Goppa polynomial. According to Equation (1) we know that for a valid codeword (i.e., error free) the corresponding syndrome modulo $g(z)$ equals to zero. It means that the gcd of two different syndromes, which can now be computed by Equation (2) using $G' = S * G$ and the original support $\mathcal{L}$, equals $g(z)$ with high probability. In our experiments, it never took more than one gcd-computation to recover the correct Goppa polynomial.

From this point on, we have extracted all parameters of the McEliece system, and hence are able to decrypt every ciphertext. In order to verify the revealed secrets, we executed the key generation algorithm with the extracted parameters and retrieved exactly the same secret key as in the original setup.

Attack II: knowing parity check matrix. Without knowing the original support $\mathcal{L}$, the attack described above is not applicable; moreover, in implementation profiles III and IV it is not possible to solely recover the permutation matrix. To overcome this problem we utilize the possible candidate lists $\hat{H}_{i,j}$ derived by an SPA attack. According to the structure of the parity check matrix H in Equation (3), every column is totally defined by elements α, $g(\alpha)$ and the coefficients of $g(z)$. We use this structure and the candidate lists in an exhaustive search. For every column $H[i]$ we randomly choose α_i and $g(\alpha_i)$ over all possible elements. These two elements are fixed for the entire column. Now we go recursively into the rows of column i. At every recursion level j we have to choose a random value for g_{t-j} and compute the actual value of $H[i][j]$ according to Equation (3). Only if this value is in the candidate list $\hat{H}_{i,j}$, we recursively call the search function for $H[i][j+1]$. If a test fails, we remove the currently selected element for g_{t-j} from the possible list and choose a new one. When the list gets empty, we return to one recursion level higher and try by a new element. Thereby we only go deeper into the search algorithm if our currently selected elements produce the values which are found in the corresponding candidate list.

If the algorithm reaches $row[t+1]$, with $t = 27$ in our case, we have selected candidates for α_i, $g(\alpha_i)$, and all coefficients of the Goppa polynomial $g(z)$. Now we can check backwards whether $g(z)$ evaluates to $g(\alpha_i)$ at α_i. If so, we have found a candidate for the Goppa polynomial and for the first support element.

While the above described algorithm continues to search new elements, we can validate the current one. By choosing another column $H[i]$ and one of the remaining $n-1$ support elements, we can test in t trials whether the given value exists in the corresponding candidate list. On success we additionally found another support element. Repeating this step $n-1$ times reveals the order of the support $\mathcal{L}$ and verifies the Goppa polynomial. Column four in Table 1 shows the average number of false αs, that pass the first searched column for the right Goppa polynomial. However, these candidates are quickly sorted out by checking them against another column of H. For all remaining pairs $(\mathcal{L}, g(z))$ it is simply tested whether it is possible to decode an erroneous codeword.

Because a single column of H is sufficient for the first part of the attack, we could speed it up by selecting the column with the lowest number of candidates for the 27 positions. Depending on the actual matrix the number of candidates for a complete column varies between 1 000 and 25 000. It turns out that most often the column constructed by $\alpha = 0$ has the lowest number of candidates. So in a first try we always examine the column with lowest number of candidates with $\alpha = 0$ before iterating over other possibilities.

Also every information that one might know can speed up the attack. If, for example, it is known that a sparse Goppa polynomial is chosen, we can first test coefficient $g_i = 0$ before proceeding to other choices. For testing we generate a McEliece key from a sparse Goppa polynomial where only 4 coefficients are not zero. Table 1 shows the results for that key.

Even if the permutation matrix P is merged into the computation of H (implementation profiles III and IV) this attack reveals a permuted support $\mathcal{L}_P$, which generates a parity check matrix capable of decoding the original ciphertext c. As a result, although merging P and H is reasonable from a performance point of view, this eases our proposed attack.

Attack III: Improving Attack II. Considering the fact mentioned at the end of Section 5.2 knowing some information about the coefficients of $g(z)$ dramatically reduces the number of elements to be tested on every recursion level. The use of additional information, here the HW of coefficients of $g(z)$, significantly speeds up the attack, as shown in Table 2.

As mentioned in the previous section, Table 1 shows the results for a sparse Goppa polynomial. These result were achieved using a workstation PC equipped by two Xeon E5345 CPUs and 16 GByte RAM and gcc-4.4 together with OpenMP-3.0. The results for a full random Goppa polynomial are given in Table 2.

In this table a window size of X means that we do not use the information about the Goppa polynomial. Instead, we iterate over all possibilities. $\#g(z)$ denotes the number of Goppa polynomials found until the correct one is hit, and $\#\ \alpha$ indicates how many wrong elements fulfil even the first validation round. The column *CPU Time* is the time for a single CPU core.

Table 1. Runtime of the Search Algorithm for sparse Goppa polynomial

Window Size H	Window Size $g(z)$	$\#g(z)$	$\#\ \alpha$	CPU Time
0	X	$> 10^6$	112	115 hours
1	X	$> 2^{32}$	$> 2^{32}$	150 years
0	0	3610	68	< 1 sec
1	0	112527	98	10 sec
0	1	793898	54	186 min
1	1	$> 10^6$	112	71 days

Table 2. Runtime of the Search Algorithm for full random Goppa polynomial

Window Size H	Window Size $g(z)$	$\#g(z)$	$\#\ \alpha$	CPU Time
0	X	$> 10^6$	52	90 hours
1	X	$> 2^{32}$	$> 2^{32}$	*impossible*
0	0	4300	50	69 min
1	0	101230	37	21 hours
0	1	$> 2^{32}$	$> 2^{32}$	26 days
1	1	$> 2^{32}$	$> 2^{32}$	5 years

Note that the values in the second and last row of each table are only estimates. They are based on the progress of the search in around 2 weeks and on the knowledge of the right values. The *impossible* means, that there was only little progress and the estimate varied by hundreds of years.

Also it should be investigated whether the additional information from the side-channel attacks can improve one of the already known attacks, e.g., [2,16,17,31]. The information gathered by means of side-channels ought to be useful since it downsizes the number of possibilities.

6 Countermeasures

Since the multiplication of the permuted ciphertext and parity check matrix H^T is efficiently implementing by summing up (XORing) some H rows which have "1" as the corresponding permuted ciphertext, the order of checking/XORing H rows can be changed arbitrarily. Since we have supposed that the attacker (partially) knows the program code, any fix change on the execution path, e.g., changing the order of summing up the H rows would not help to counteract our first attack (SPA on permutation matrix explained in Section 5.2). However, one can change the order of checking/XORing randomly for every ciphertext, and hence the execution path for a ciphertext in different instances of time will be different. Therefore, the adversary (which is not able to detect the random value and the selected order of computation) can not recover the permutation matrix. Note that as mentioned before if the permutation is not merely performed (e.g., in implementation profiles III and IV) our first attack is inherently defeated.

Defeating our second attack (SPA on parity check matrix explained in Section 5.2) is not as easy as that of the first attack. One may consider changing randomly the order of checking the H rows, which is described above, as a countermeasure against the second attack as well. According to the attack scenario the adversary examines the power traces for the ciphertexts with HW=1; then, by means of pattern matching techniques he would be able to detect at which instance of time the desired XOR operations (on the corresponding row of H) is performed. As a result, randomly changing the order to computations does not help to defeat the second attack. An alternative would be to randomly execute dummy instructions[4]. Though it leads to increasing the run time which is an important parameter for post quantum cryptosystems especially for software implementations, it extremely hardens our proposed attacks. A boolean masking scheme may also provide robustness against our attacks. A simple way would be to randomly fill the memory location which stores the result of XORing H rows before start of the multiplication (between the permuted ciphertext and the parity check matrix), and XORing the final results by the same start value. This avoids predicting HW of H elements if the attacker considers only the leakage of the SAVE instructions. However, if he can use the leakage of LOAD instructions (those which load H rows), this scheme does not help to counteract the attacks. One can make a randomly generated mask matrix as big as H, and save the masked matrix. Since in order to avoid the effect of the masking after multiplication it is needed to repeat the same procedure (multiplication) using the mask matrix, this scheme doubles the run time (for multiplication) and the area (for saving the mask matrix) as well though it definitely prevents our proposed attacks. As a result designing a masking scheme which is adopted to the limitations of our implementation platform is considered as a future work.

7 Conclusions

In this paper, we presented the first practical power analysis attacks on different implementations of the McEliece public-key scheme which use an 8-bit general-purpose AVR microprocessor to realize the cipher decryption. Since we believe that with growing memory of embedded systems and future optimizations McEliece can be developed as a quantum computer-resistant replacement for RSA and ECC, vulnerability and robustness of McEliece implementations in the presence of side-channel attacks should be addressed before its widespreading into pervasive applications and devices which are under control of the side-channel adversaries. Further, to defeat the described vulnerabilities we introduced and discussed possible countermeasures which seem not to be perfect because of their high time and memory overheads. As a result, designing a suitable countermeasure which fits to the available resources of low-cost general-purpose microprocessors and provides a reasonable level of security against side-channel attacks is considered as a future work. This work shows clearly that

[4] In our implementation platform it can be done by a random timer interrupt which runs a random amount of dummy instructions.

every part of the secret key materials namely the support $\mathcal{L}$, the Goppa polynomial $g(z)$, the permutation P and every (precomputed) part of the parity check matrix H have to be well protected.

References

1. Berlekamp, E.R.: Goppa Codes. IEEE Trans. on Information Theory 19(3), 590–592 (1973)
2. Bernstein, D.J., Lange, T., Peters, C.: Attacking and Defending the McEliece Cryptosystem. In: Buchmann, J., Ding, J. (eds.) PQCrypto 2008. LNCS, vol. 5299, pp. 31–46. Springer, Heidelberg (2008), http://eprint.iacr.org/2008/318
3. Biswas, B., Sendrier, N.: McEliece Cryptosystem Implementation: Theory and Practice. In: Buchmann, J., Ding, J. (eds.) PQCrypto 2008. LNCS, vol. 5299, pp. 47–62. Springer, Heidelberg (2008)
4. Bogdanov, A., Kizhvatov, I., Pyshkin, A.: Algebraic Methods in Side-Channel Collision Attacks and Practical Collision Detection. In: Chowdhury, D.R., Rijmen, V., Das, A. (eds.) INDOCRYPT 2008. LNCS, vol. 5365, pp. 251–265. Springer, Heidelberg (2008)
5. Brier, E., Clavier, C., Olivier, F.: Correlation Power Analysis with a Leakage Model. In: Joye, M., Quisquater, J.-J. (eds.) CHES 2004. LNCS, vol. 3156, pp. 16–29. Springer, Heidelberg (2004)
6. Cayrel, P.-L., Dusart, P.: Fault Injection's Sensitivity of the McEliece PKC (2009), http://www.cayrel.net/IMG/pdf/Fault_injection_s_sensitivity_of_the_McEliece_PKC.pdf
7. den Boer, B., Lemke, K., Wicke, G.: A DPA Attack against the Modular Reduction within a CRT Implementation of RSA. In: Kaliski Jr., B.S., Koç, Ç.K., Paar, C. (eds.) CHES 2002. LNCS, vol. 2523, pp. 228–243. Springer, Heidelberg (2003)
8. Eisenbarth, T., Güneysu, T., Heyse, S., Paar, C.: MicroEliece: McEliece for Embedded Devices. In: Clavier, C., Gaj, K. (eds.) CHES 2009. LNCS, vol. 5747, pp. 49–64. Springer, Heidelberg (2009)
9. Eisenbarth, T., Kasper, T., Moradi, A., Paar, C., Salmasizadeh, M., Shalmani, M.T.M.: On the Power of Power Analysis in the Real World: A Complete Break of the KeeLoq Code Hopping Scheme. In: Wagner, D. (ed.) CRYPTO 2008. LNCS, vol. 5157, pp. 203–220. Springer, Heidelberg (2008)
10. Engelbert, D., Overbeck, R., Schmidt, A.: A Summary of McEliece-Type Cryptosystems and their Security. Journal of Mathematical Cryptology 1(2), 151–199 (2006), http://eprint.iacr.org/2006/162
11. Gierlichs, B., Batina, L., Tuyls, P., Preneel, B.: Mutual Information Analysis. In: Oswald, E., Rohatgi, P. (eds.) CHES 2008. LNCS, vol. 5154, pp. 426–442. Springer, Heidelberg (2008)
12. Hoerder, S.: Explicit Computational Aspects of McEliece Encryption Scheme. Master's thesis, Ruhr University Bochum, Germany (2009)
13. Howenga, T.: Efficient Implementation of the McEliece Cryptosystem on Graphics Processing Units. Master's thesis, Ruhr-University Bochum, Germany (2009)
14. Kasper, M., Kasper, T., Moradi, A., Paar, C.: Breaking KeeLoq in a Flash. In: Preneel, B. (ed.) AFRICACRYPT 2009. LNCS, vol. 5580, pp. 403–420. Springer, Heidelberg (2009)

15. Kocher, P.C., Jaffe, J., Jun, B.: Differential Power Analysis. In: Wiener, M. (ed.) CRYPTO 1999. LNCS, vol. 1666, pp. 388–397. Springer, Heidelberg (1999)
16. Lee, P.J., Brickell, E.F.: An Observation on the Security of McEliece's Public-Key Cryptosystem. In: Günther, C.G. (ed.) EUROCRYPT 1988. LNCS, vol. 330, pp. 275–280. Springer, Heidelberg (1988)
17. Leon, J.S.: A Probabilistic Algorithm for Computing Minimum Weights of Large Error-Correcting Codes. IEEE Transactions on Information Theory 34(5), 1354–1359 (1988)
18. McEliece, R.J.: A Public-Key Cryptosystem Based On Algebraic Coding Theory. Deep Space Network Progress Report 44, 114–116 (1978)
19. Messerges, T.S.: Using Second-Order Power Analysis to Attack DPA Resistant Software. In: Paar, C., Koç, Ç.K. (eds.) CHES 2000. LNCS, vol. 1965, pp. 238–251. Springer, Heidelberg (2000)
20. Oswald, E.: Enhancing Simple Power-Analysis Attacks on Elliptic Curve Cryptosystems. In: Kaliski Jr., B.S., Koç, Ç.K., Paar, C. (eds.) CHES 2002. LNCS, vol. 2523, pp. 82–97. Springer, Heidelberg (2003)
21. Oswald, E., Mangard, S., Herbst, C., Tillich, S.: Practical Second-Order DPA Attacks for Masked Smart Card Implementations of Block Ciphers. In: Pointcheval, D. (ed.) CT-RSA 2006. LNCS, vol. 3860, pp. 192–207. Springer, Heidelberg (2006)
22. Patterson, N.: The Algebraic Decoding of Goppa Codes. IEEE Transactions on Information Theory 21, 203–207 (1975)
23. Renauld, M., Standaert, F.-X., Veyrat-Charvillon, N.: Algebraic Side-Channel Attacks on the AES: Why Time also Matters in DPA. In: Clavier, C., Gaj, K. (eds.) CHES 2009. LNCS, vol. 5747, pp. 97–111. Springer, Heidelberg (2009)
24. Schramm, K., Leander, G., Felke, P., Paar, C.: A Collision-Attack on AES: Combining Side Channel- and Differential-Attack. In: Joye, M., Quisquater, J.-J. (eds.) CHES 2004. LNCS, vol. 3156, pp. 163–175. Springer, Heidelberg (2004)
25. Schramm, K., Paar, C.: Higher Order Masking of the AES. In: Pointcheval, D. (ed.) CT-RSA 2006. LNCS, vol. 3860, pp. 208–225. Springer, Heidelberg (2006)
26. Schramm, K., Wollinger, T.J., Paar, C.: A New Class of Collision Attacks and Its Application to DES. In: Johansson, T. (ed.) FSE 2003. LNCS, vol. 2887, pp. 206–222. Springer, Heidelberg (2003)
27. Shoufan, A., Strenzke, F., Molter, H.G., Stoettinger, M.: A Timing Attack Against Patterson Algorithm in the McEliece PKC. In: International Conference on Information Security and Cryptology - ICISC 2009. LNCS, Springer, Heidelberg (2009) (to appear)
28. Shoufan, A., Wink, T., Molter, G., Huss, S., Strentzke, F.: A Novel Processor Architecture for McEliece Cryptosystem and FPGA Platforms. In: Application-specific Systems, Architectures and Processors - ASAP 2009, pp. 98–105. IEEE Computer Society, Los Alamitos (2009)
29. Silverman, J.H., Whyte, W.: Timing Attacks on NTRUEncrypt Via Variation in the Number of Hash Calls. In: Abe, M. (ed.) CT-RSA 2007. LNCS, vol. 4377, pp. 208–224. Springer, Heidelberg (2007)
30. Standaert, F.-X., Örs, S.B., Quisquater, J.-J., Preneel, B.: Power Analysis Attacks Against FPGA Implementations of the DES. In: Becker, J., Platzner, M., Vernalde, S. (eds.) FPL 2004. LNCS, vol. 3203, pp. 84–94. Springer, Heidelberg (2004)

31. Stern, J.: A Method for Finding Codewords of Small Weight. In: Wolfmann, J., Cohen, G. (eds.) Coding Theory 1988. LNCS, vol. 388, pp. 106–113. Springer, Heidelberg (1989)
32. Strenzke, F., Tews, E., Molter, H.G., Overbeck, R., Shoufan, A.: Side Channels in the McEliece PKC. In: Buchmann, J., Ding, J. (eds.) PQCrypto 2008. LNCS, vol. 5299, pp. 216–229. Springer, Heidelberg (2008)
33. van Tilborg, H.C.: Fundamentals of Cryptology. Kluwer Academic Publishers, Dordrecht (2000)
34. Vizev, N.V.: Side Channel Attacks on NTRUEncrypt. Bachelor's thesis, Technical University of Darmstadt, Germany (2007), `http://www.cdc.informatik.tu-darmstadt.de/reports/reports/Nikolay_Vizev.bachelor.pdf`

Appendix

Algorithm 3. Decoding Goppa Codes

Require: Received codeword r with up to t errors, inverse generator matrix iG
Ensure: Recovered message $\hat{m}$

Compute syndrome $Syn(z)$ for codeword r
$T(z) \leftarrow Syn(z)^{-1} \mod g(z)$
if $T(z) = z$ **then**
  $\sigma(z) \leftarrow z$
else
  $R(z) \leftarrow \sqrt{T(z) + z}$
  Compute $a(z)$ and $b(z)$ with $a(z) \equiv b(z) \cdot R(z) \mod g(z)$
  $\sigma(z) \leftarrow a(z)^2 + z \cdot b(z)^2$
end if
Determine roots of $\sigma(z)$ and correct errors in r which results in $\hat{r}$
$\hat{m} \leftarrow \hat{r} \cdot iG$ {Map r_{cor} to $\hat{m}$}
return $\hat{m}$

Key Exchange and Encryption Schemes Based on Non-commutative Skew Polynomials

Delphine Boucher[1], Philippe Gaborit[2], Willi Geiselmann[3], Olivier Ruatta[2], and Felix Ulmer[1]

[1] Université de Rennes 1,
IRMAR, CNRS, UMR 6625,
Université européenne de Bretagne
[2] Université de Limoges, CNRS, XLIM-DMI,
123, Av. Albert Thomas
87060 Limoges Cedex, France
[3] Karlsruhe Institut of Technology (KIT)
Am Fasanengarten 5
76131 Karsruhe, Germany

Abstract. In this paper we introduce a new key exchange algorithm (Diffie-Hellman like) based on so called (non-commutative) skew polynomials. The algorithm performs only polynomial multiplications in a special small field and is very efficient. The security of the scheme can be interpretated in terms of solving binary quadratic equations or exhaustive search of a set obtained through linear equations. We give an evaluation of the security in terms of precise experimental heuristics and usual bounds based on Groebner basis solvers. We also derive an El Gamal like encryption protocol. We propose parameters which give 3600 bits exchanged for the key exchange protocol and a size of key of 3600 bits for the encryption protocol, with a complexity of roughly 2^{23} binary operations for performing each protocol. Overall this new approach based on skew polynomials, seems very promising, as a good tradeoff between size of keys and efficiency.

1 Introduction

The Diffie-Hellman protocol introduced in 1976 was a milestone in modern cryptography. The key part of the protocol lies in the commutativity of the exponentiation. Although the protocol is widely used nowadays, it has two drawbacks. First it is rather costly in the sense that both parts have to do a general exponentiation with a cubic complexity in the size of the key. Although for common non recurrent use, it is not so important, there are cases in which one has to proceed such a key exchange continuously, so that eventually it becomes a real stake. The second drawback is that, like all protocols based on number theory, it is broken if one day a putative quantum computer comes to exist.

Hence it makes sense to first find a secure faster key exchange protocol as well as non number theory based protocols.

N. Sendrier (Ed.): PQCrypto 2010, LNCS 6061, pp. 126–141, 2010.

In this paper we propose such a protocol. Our protocol also uses a commutativity property of particular objects, the so called skew polynomials. More precisely we start from special non commutative polynomials, from which we construct a commutative subset (but not in the center). In some ways our approach can be related to the approach of braid cryptography, but without the problem of the random braid generator, which was the cause of many efficient attacks on braid cryptography.

Overall we obtain a very efficient protocol both in terms of complexity and size of key. The security of our protocol is related to problems of multivariate cryptography, but has the advantage of having only a small key size in comparison with classical multivariate cryptography.

Skew polynomials are defined as follows. Let $\mathbb{K} = \mathbb{F}_q$ be a finite field and let $\theta \in \mathbf{Aut}(\mathbb{K})$, we define a ring structure on the set

$$\mathbb{K}[X, \theta] = \{a_n X^n + \cdots + a_1 X + a_0 | n \in \mathbb{N} \text{ and } a_i \in \mathbb{K}, \forall i \in \{0, \ldots, n\}\}.$$

The addition of polynomials is the usual one and the multiplication is obtained using the rule $Xa = \theta(a)X$. We still denote $\mathbb{K}[X, \theta]$ the resulting ring. If $\theta = \mathbf{Id}$ we obtain the classical polynomial ring $\mathbb{K}[X]$. If θ is not the identity, then the ring $\mathbb{K}[X, \theta]$ is not commutative, which implies that there exist a and $b \in \mathbb{K}[X, \theta]$ such that $ab \neq ba$ since there exists $a \in \mathbb{K}$ such that $\theta(a) \neq a$ and so $Xa = \theta(a)X \neq aX$. Those rings are well known and were introduced in [10] in 1933. Over a finite field, they are the most general polynomial rings with a commutative field of coefficients, where the degree of a product of two elements is the sum of the degrees of the elements. The ring $\mathbb{K}[X, \theta]$ is a left and right Euclidean ring, whose left and right ideals are principal ([10,9]). Left and right gcd and lcm exist in $\mathbb{K}[X, \theta]$ and can be computed using the left and right Euclidean algorithm [3]. However, the ring $\mathbb{K}[X, \theta]$ is not a unique factorization domain. The main properties of $\mathbb{K}[X, \theta]$ used here are discussed in a section below. The non unicity of factorization and the non-commutativity allow us to give a sketch of the proposed protocol.

The paper is organized as follows, Section 2 recalls main facts about skew polynomials, Section 3 proposes new algorithms: a Diffie-Hellman like key exchange and a related El Gamal like encryption scheme. In section 4 we discuss a general setting for the security of the scheme, Section 5 looks at specific attacks and at last Section 6 gives parameters for our scheme.

2 Background on Skew Polynomials Ring

2.1 Definition and Basic Properties

Let $\mathbb{K} = \mathbb{F}_q$ be a finite field and let θ be an automorphism of $\mathbb{K}$. Let us define:

$$\mathbb{K}[X, \theta] = \{a_n X^n + \cdots + a_1 X + a_0 | a_i \in \mathbb{K}, \forall i \in \{0, \ldots, n\} \text{ and } n \in \mathbb{N}\}$$

This set has a ring structure. The addition is defined as usually and the product is such that $X^n a = \theta^n(a) X^n$ for all $n \in \mathbb{N}$. If $P = \sum_{i=0}^{n} a_i X^i$ and $Q = \sum_{j=0}^{n} b_j X^j$, we have:

$$PQ = \sum_{k=0}^{n+m} \sum_{i+j=k} a_i \theta^i(b_j) X^k.$$

The ring is non-commutative as soon as $\theta \neq \mathbf{Id}$ since if $\theta \neq \mathbf{Id}$ there exists $a \in \mathbb{K}$ such that $\theta(a) \neq a$ and then $Xa = \theta(a)X \neq aX$.

Example 1. For instance, take $\mathbb{K} = \mathbb{F}_4$ and $\theta : a \to a^2$, the Frobenius automorphism.

The ring $\mathbb{K}[X, \theta]$ is both left and right Euclidean (there is an Euclidean division on the left and another on the right). Here right division means that for $f, g \in \mathbb{K}[X, \theta]$ which are non zero, there exist unique polynomials $Q_r, R_r \in \mathbb{K}[X, \theta]$ such that

$$f = Q_r \cdot g + R_r.$$

If $R_r = 0$ then g is a right divisor of f in $\mathbb{K}[X, \theta]$. The definition of left divisor in $\mathbb{K}[X, \theta]$ is similar, using the left Euclidean division. In the ring $\mathbb{K}[X, \theta]$ left and right gcd and lcm exist and can be computed using the left and right Euclidean algorithm ([3]).

Example 2. We denote α a generator of the multiplicative group of $\mathbb{F}_4$ and $\theta : a \to a^2$, the Frobenius automorphism. The left and right division of $X + \alpha$ by $\alpha X + 1$ are

$$\begin{aligned} X + \alpha &= \alpha^2 \, (\alpha X + 1) \, + \, 1 \\ &= (\alpha X + 1) \, \alpha \, + \, 0 \end{aligned}$$

An effect of the non-commutativity of such a ring is the non-uniqueness of a factorization in form of products of irreducible factors. Two skew polynomials P and Q are similar, noted $P \sim Q$, if the left (or right) $\mathbb{K}[X, \theta]$ modules $\mathbb{K}[X, \theta]/(P)$ and $\mathbb{K}[X, \theta]/(Q)$ are isomorphic.

Theorem 1. *(cf. [8]) If $P \in \mathbb{K}[X, \theta]$ has two decompositions into irreducible factors*

$$P = P_1 P_2 \cdots P_n = \tilde{P}_1 \tilde{P}_2 \cdots \tilde{P}_m,$$

then $n = m$ and there exists a permutation $\sigma \in S_n$ such that P_i and $\tilde{P}_{\sigma(i)}$ are similar.

Example 3. Taking again $\mathbb{K} = \mathbb{F}_4 = \mathbb{F}_2[\alpha]$ and $\theta : a \to a^2$, then $X^4 - 1$ admits 15 distinct decompositions as products of irreducible polynomials.

$$\begin{aligned}
X^4 - 1 &= (X+\alpha^2)(X+\alpha)(X+\alpha)(X+\alpha^2)\\
&= (X+\alpha^2)(X+\alpha)(X+\alpha^2)(X+\alpha)\\
&= (X+1)(X+1)(X+\alpha^2)(X+\alpha)\\
&= (X+1)(X+1)(X+\alpha)(X+\alpha^2)\\
&= (X+\alpha^2)(X+1)(X+1)(X+\alpha)\\
&= (X+1)(X+\alpha^2)(X+\alpha)(X+1)\\
&= (X+\alpha^2)(X+\alpha)(X+1)(X+1)\\
&= (X+1)(X+\alpha)(X+\alpha^2)(X+1)\\
&= (X+\alpha)(X+\alpha^2)(X+1)(X+1)\\
&= (X+\alpha)(X+\alpha)(X+\alpha^2)(X+\alpha^2)\\
&= (X+\alpha)(X+1)(X+1)(X+\alpha^2)\\
&= (X+\alpha)(X+\alpha^2)(X+\alpha^2)(X+\alpha)\\
&= (X+\alpha^2)(X+\alpha^2)(X+\alpha)(X+\alpha)\\
&= (X+1)(X+1)(X+1)(X+1)\\
&= (X+\alpha)(X+\alpha^2)(X+\alpha)(X+\alpha^2)
\end{aligned}$$

The polynomial $X^6 - 1$ has 90 distinct decompositions and $X^8 - 1$ has 543 distinct decompositions.

Most of the polynomials do not commute in $\mathbb{K}[X,\theta]$. According to ([9], Theorem II.12), the monic polynomials who generate two sided ideals of $\mathbb{K}[X,\theta]$are of the form $(b_0 + b_1X^m + b_2X^{2m} + \ldots + X^{s\cdot m})X^t$, where m is the order of θ and $b_i \in (\mathbb{K})^\theta$ the fixed field of θ. The center of $\mathbb{K}[X,\theta]$ is $\mathbb{K}^\theta[X^m]$. A polynomial in the center is said to be central, it commutes with all polynomials of $\mathbb{K}[X,\theta]$. However, there are sets of polynomials which are not central and which commute together.

Example 4. Taking $\mathbb{K} = \mathbb{F}_4$ and $\theta : a \to a^2$ again, the center of $\mathbb{F}_4[X,\theta]$ is $\mathbb{F}_2[X^2]$. The three polynomials $Q_1 = X + \alpha, Q_2 = X^2 + X + \alpha^2$ and $Q_3 = X^3 + \alpha^2X^2 + 1$ commute without being central since:

$$\begin{aligned}
Q_1Q_2 = Q_2Q_1 &= X^3 + \alpha^2X^2 + 1\\
Q_1Q_3 = Q_3Q_1 &= X^4 + X^2 + X + \alpha\\
Q_2Q_3 = Q_3Q_1 &= X^5 + \alpha X^4 + X^3 + \alpha^2X^2 + X + \alpha^2.
\end{aligned}$$

All the properties mentioned here will be used in order to design the protocol described in this paper.

2.2 Difficult Problem for Skew Polynomials

The non commutativity of skew polynomials make some computational problems like factorization more difficult. However the difficulty of the factorization is not at the same level as for integer factorization. As we saw in examples, the difficulty of the factorization of skew polynomials is linked to the large number of distinct possible factorizations.

The number of factorizations grows with the number of polynomials, since the more polynomials commute the more the effect of non-commutativity is developed, as it is expressed in the previous examples.

Given the product $p = p_1 ... p_r$ of a set of small polynomials it is difficult to recover *precisely* the set $\{p_1, ..., p_r\}$, in fact there is an algorithm to find a factorization of p ([7]), but only one in a set of *a priori* exponential size.

We will describe more formally the different problems in Section 4.

3 The Cryptosystems

3.1 A Diffie Helmann Like Key Exchange

We want that A and B construct and exchange a secret key using a Diffie Helmann like cryptosystem.

We construct first a set $\mathcal{S}$ of polynomials in $\mathbb{K}[X, \theta]$ which commute each other without commuting with all polynomials (i.e. without being central). We hence get that for any polynomials L_1 and L_2 in $\mathcal{S}$, $L_1 L_2 = L_2 L_1$, meanwhile for any other polynomial Q not in $\mathcal{S}$, we have in general (in fact almost always) that $L_1 Q \neq Q L_1$. Notice such a set $\mathcal{S}$ has not any particular structure and is obtained simply by random search, we will see in Section 6 an example of such a set. The idea of protocol consists in taking advantage that in some cases, when polynomials are well chosen, it is possible that they commute. Let us consider A and B who want to exchange a common secret. We consider a situation such that A and B can take advantage of the commutativity but an observer C cannot. It can be obtained in the following way: A chooses two polynomials L_A and R_A in $\mathcal{S}$ and computes $L_A Q R_A$ using a random polynomial Q (*a priori* not in $\mathcal{S}$), B proceeds in the same way with L_B and R_B and the same polynomial Q. The idea of the protocol is then that knowing $L_A Q R_A$ and Q, it is difficult to recover L_A and R_A, since even if L_A and R_A commute, the fact that Q is between them makes their commutativity ineffective for an observer. Now if B knows only $L_A Q R_A$, he can multiply the two sides of this polynomial and take advantage of the commutativity. We then obtain the following Diffie-Hellman like secret sharing protocol:

◇ DH-like protocol with skew polynomials

1. A and B publicly agree on a set of commutative polynomials $\mathcal{S}$, a security parameter d and a public polynomial Q of degree d (constructed with random factors of small degree (*ie* between 6 and 10)).
2. A (resp. B) chooses two polynomials L_A and R_A (resp. L_B and R_B) of degree d in $\mathcal{S}$ (constructed as products of 8 to 15 polynomials obtained as sums of products of elements of $\mathcal{S}$) and sends the polynomial $P_A = L_A Q R_A$ to B (resp. B sends $P_B = L_B Q R_B$ to A).
3. A (resp. B) computes the common secret shared polynomial $P = L_A P_B R_B$ (resp. $P = L_B P_A R_B$)

Proof of protocol: By recovering P_B, A can compute $L_A P_B R_A = L_A L_B Q R_B R_A$. Since L_A and L_B are constructed as products of sums of products of polynomials of $\mathcal{S}$ which commute, L_A and L_B commute together (resp. R_A and R_B) and one obtains $L_A P R_A = L_B L_A Q R_A R_B = L_B P_A R_B$ and hence by computing $L_B P_A R_B$, B recovers the same secret shared polynomial. □

Remark 1: The set $\mathcal{S}$ has not to be computed each time of course, it can be computed once and made publicly known. The set typically contains more than 90 elements of degree 8 or 9 (see Appendix), so that it can be used as often as necessary.

Remark 2: The particular structure of L_A, L_B, R_A and R_B is chosen in order to assure a tradeoff between the combinatorial complexity to recover their structure (choice of sum of products of elements of $\mathcal{S}$) and the overall effect of the non-commutativity which increases when the number of factors increases (choice of 8 to 10 factors for L_A, L_B, R_A and R_B). The two configurations we want to avoid are: only one factor in these polynomials which limits the effect of non-commutativity or a product of polynomial directly in $\mathcal{S}$, which can be tested one by one.

3.2 A El-Gamal Like Public Key Encryption Scheme

It is well known that it is possible to derive an encryption protocol from a Diffie-Hellman like protocol, the idea is to fix, as public key, one of the sent data in the Diffie-Hellman protocol. It is then possible for the person who wants to encrypt to compute a common secret which is used to compute a common data used as mask in a one-time pad protocol. The protocol is described in the following.

◇ **El-Gamal like protocol with skew polynomials**

1. **Precomputation step and public data** As for the key exchange protocol, one considers that a special set $\mathcal{S}$ of commutative polynomials is known, we also consider as known a hash function h of output size n.
2. **Key generation** A chooses two polynomials L_A and R_A of degree d in $\mathcal{S}$ and a random polynomial Q of degree d as for the Key exchange protocol, then A computes $P_A = L_A Q R_A$. The **secret key** is the set $\{L_A, R_A\}$, the **public key** is the triple $\{\mathcal{S}, P_A, Q\}$.
3. **Encryption** B obtains the public key of A, cuts it into pieces of length n and chooses two polynomials L_B and R_B of degree d in S. The encrypted message is the set $\{c, P\}$, with $c = m \oplus h(L_B P_A R_B)$, and $P = L_B Q R_B$.
4. Decryption A receives the encrypted message $\{c, P\}$, and computes $m = c \oplus h(L_A P R_A)$.

Proof of the encryption protocol: By recovering P, B can reconstruct $L_A P R_A = L_A L_B Q R_B R_A$, since L_A and L_B commute (resp. R_A and R_B), one obtains $L_A P R_A = L_B L_A Q R_A R_B = L_B P_A R_B$ and hence $c \oplus h(L_A P R_A) = m \oplus h(L_B P_A R_B) \oplus h(L_A P R_A) = m$. □

Remark: The protocol is not constructed to be very efficient, since only n bits are encrypted at each step, when in fact the entropy of the system could probably assure more. Meanwhile since public key protocols are used essentially for identification or key exchange, in practice it is enough.

3.3 Size of Parameters and Complexity of the Schemes

The scheme is very fast since only polynomial products are performed, moreover the size of the public keys and private keys remain reasonable.

Size of keys

- Key exchange protocol: both sides exchange a polynomial of degree $3d$ over $\mathbb{F}_4$ hence $6d$ bits.
- Encryption protocol:

Private key: polynomials L_A and R_A: $6d$ bits.

Public key: P_A: $6d$ bits

Remark: One may also consider sending the set S (even though it is public data), it is composed of roughly 100 polynomials of degree 8 or 9, hence 1800 more bits.

Complexity

- Key exchange protocol: the first step consists in the creation of the polynomials L_A and R_A and the creation of the polynomial $P_A = L_AQR_A$. The second part is the most important and has a complexity in $d \cdot d + 2d \cdot d$ multiplications in $\mathbb{F}_4$, hence an overall complexity in $3d^2$ multiplications. The second step is the computation of the shared polynomial $L_AP_BR_A$, since P_B has degree $3d$, the complexity of this step is $d \cdot 3d + 4d \cdot d = 7d^2$ multiplications in $\mathbb{F}_4$.
- Encryption protocol: the complexity is the same as for the Key exchange protocol except that both steps are done simultanously, hence $10d^2$ multiplications in F_4.

We will see in the last section that parameters can be chosen of order 600, which makes an overall complexity of our schemes of roughly 2^{23} binary operations, which is very fast in comparison to other existing algorithms. Moreover the size of parameters remains reasonable with only of few thousands bits.

4 General Setting for the Security of the Scheme

4.1 General Setting and Definition of Our "Difficult Problem"

Our method relies on the following problem:

◇ **Simple factorization over skew ring**

1. **Data** A skew polynomial F
2. **Output** Find skew polynomials $f_1, f_2, .., f_k$ such that $F = f_1 \cdots f_k$.

There exists an algorithm which computes a right factor in polynomial time ([7]). But, since there exists in general a very large number of possible factorizations, finding a factorization is not enough to break our method. The number of factorizations grows combinatorially with the number of possible factors. The difficulty of our problem is based on finding a particular factorization in a very huge set of factorizations. This problem, although not proven NP-hard seems very hard to solve based on the combinatorial growths of possible factorizations.

Now our problem to recover directly the public key is a little more constrained and can be formulated in the following way:

◇ **Key factorization**

1. **Data** A skew polynomial K product of three polynomials, i.e. $K = LQR$, the skew polynomial Q and a subset $\mathcal{S} \subset \mathbb{F}_4[X, \theta]$ of polynomials commuting together and such that L and R can be obtained with sum and product from elements of $\mathcal{S}$.
2. **Output** Recover $\tilde{L}$ and $\tilde{R}$ such that they commute with all element of $\mathcal{S}$ and $K = \tilde{L}Q\tilde{R}$.

We only have to find L or R in order to solve this problem, since the solution can then be obtained by performing divisions. In the following subsections, we propose different approaches to solve this problem. Those approaches are all based on a solution of the following equation:

$$P = LQR, . \tag{1}$$

We propose a structural approach, using the fact that computing a right factor can be done in polynomial time. Our second approach consists in deriving a set of quadratic polynomial equations with the coefficients of L and R as unknown. It is well known (see [6]) that solving quadratic polynomial systems is NP-complete. We are not able to show that the instance proposed here is NP-complete, but we give experimental results that show that the problem is difficult. We also propose a randomized algorithm reducing the resolution of (1) to a linear system. We study the complexity of the proposed attacks in order to propose parameters for our method.

As for the discrete logarithm, it is possible to define by analogy with the computational Diffie-Hellman the following problem:

◇ **Computational key recovering**

1. **Data** Two skew polynomials K_A and K_B, each is a product of three polynomials, i.e. $K_A = L_A Q R_A$ and $K_B = L_B Q R_B$, the skew polynomial Q and a subset $\mathcal{S} \subset \mathbb{F}_4[X, \theta]$ of polynomials commuting together and such that L_A, L_B, R_A and R_B can be obtained with sum and product from elements of $\mathcal{S}$.
2. **Output** Compute $K = L_A L_B Q R_B R_A$.

We do not have any proposition to solve this problem without solving the key factorization problem. In order to evaluate the complexity of our attacks, we will need some basic results on complexity of algebraic system solved over $\mathbb{F}_2$. This is the object of the following subsection.

4.2 Multivariate Interpretation of the Skew Factorization Problem

The problem of solving systems of multivariate polynomial equations is NP-complete and it has been shown that this problem remains NP-complete is the equations of the sytems are quadratic over $\mathbb{F}_2$ ([4,6]). Here a first attack leads to the resolution of a polynomial system over $\mathbb{F}_4[x_1, \ldots, x_n]/(x_1^4 - x_1, \ldots, x_n^4 - x_n)$. We denote $P = \sum p_i X^i$, $Q = \sum q_i X^i$ and d_Q the degree of Q. The polynomials L and R are unknown polynomials but we will assume that we know their degrees d_L and d_R. We will see them as polynomials in $\mathbb{F}_4[l_0, \ldots, l_{d_L-1}, r_0, \ldots, r_{d_R-1}]$ $[X, \theta]$. The equation (1) is equivalent to the polynomial system:

$$p_i = \sum_{j=max(0,i-d_Q-d_R)}^{min(d_L,i)} \sum_{k=max(0,i-d_R-j)}^{min(d_Q,i-j)} l_j q_k^{2^j} r_{i-j-k}^{2^{j+k}}, \; i = 0, \ldots, d_Q + d_L + d_R - 1$$

in the multivariate *commutative* polynomial ring $\mathbb{F}_4[l_0, \ldots, r_0, \ldots]/(l_0^4 - l_0, \ldots, r_0^4 - r_0, \ldots)$. Considering the equations for $i = d_Q + d_L + d_R - 1, \ldots, d_Q + d_R$, we get a triangular linear system with unknown $l_0, l_1, \ldots, l_{d_L-1}$, so the equation (1) can be reduced to a polynomial system with $d_Q + d_R$ equations and d_R unknowns in $\mathbb{F}_4[r_0, \ldots, r_{d_R-1}]/(r_0^4 - r_0, \ldots, r_{d_R-1}^4 - r_{d_R-1})$

4.3 Some Bounds for over Constrained Polynomial Systems Solving

Here, we consider algorithms using Gröbner bases to solve polynomial systems. All the bounds are extracted from [2]. The number of arithmetic operations needed to compute a Gröbner basis is controlled by a degree, called regularity degree and denoted D_{deg}. Here the complexity is given for the F5-matrical algorithm (see [5]) which is the best known algorithm for Gröbner. For a system over $\mathbb{F}_2$ with αn equations in n variables (α is a scalar), which is semi-regular and for $n \to \infty$, we have:

$$D_{deg} \sim (-\alpha + \frac{1}{2} + \frac{1}{2}\sqrt{\alpha^2 - 10\alpha - 1 + 2(\alpha+2)\sqrt{\alpha(\alpha+2)}})n$$

The complexity is exponential of this degree. Not all the systems are semi-regular. But it is conjectured and often checked experimentally that the probability to be semi-regular for an over constrained system tends to 1 as n growth. There are easier cases, but also worse cases (doubly exponential). The fact that the complexity of a generic problem is not the worst is generally explained by the fact that over constrained systems have few solutions. Some particular bounds can be computed if the systems have very few solutions (typically 1 solution). But, we will see that our method gives rise to systems with more solutions and that systems are not too over constrained.

Following directly the previous bounds leads to an overestimated security of our scheme, since we are not in a completely random case.

In the following section we consider specific attacks taking account of the particular structure of our scheme and try to do better than the generic bounds using a specific exploitation of data.

5 Specific Attacks

In this section we look at three natural specific attacks in order to obtain a security order for our scheme. The first attack is related to the direct structure of the factorization problem and can be considered as a structural attack, it tries to recover directly the correct factorization without considering unknowns. The second attack is based on a quadratic interpretation from our problem and shows that at some point it seems difficult to do better than direct solvers. The third attack, based on linear algebra, leads to a solution of our system. This attack tries to recover a special set of unknowns through a complete search. Eventually the first two attacks seems to be quickly ineffective when the security parameter d increase beyond a few hundred. The last attack based on a linear interpretation seems to be the most effective and we evaluate its complexity.

5.1 Structural Attack Using Factorization

To solve the equation (1), we can proceed as follows, assuming that we know the degree d_R of R :

1. Using the bifactorization algorithm of Giesbrecht ([7]), find a right factor $\tilde{R}$ of P of degree d_R.
2. Compute the quotient $\tilde{P}$ in the right division of P by $\tilde{R}$ and perform the right division of $\tilde{P}$ by Q. If the remainder is not zero then go back to 1.
3. Denote $\tilde{L}$ the quotient of the (exact) right division of $\tilde{P}$ by Q. If $\tilde{L}Q\tilde{R} = P$, then $(\tilde{L}, \tilde{R})$ is a solution to the equation (1), else return to 1.

The first step can be done in polynomial time, however, the algorithm of [7] enables to find only one right factor and there may be an exponential number of such factors. So L and R have to be chosen so that the number of the factorizations of LQR becomes exponentially big.

Note also that the equation (1) may have many solutions, so at step 3 of the algorithm, we are not sure to get the right L and the right R. One could check at least if the two polynomials commute. We can improve this attack in several ways. At step 1, each time we compute a right factor, to check that it is a right factor of the correct type. The problem of checking that the computed factor as the right type can be a difficult problem depending on the way the factors are chosen.

One can try to compute factors and hope that the method will give a suitable pair $(\tilde{L}, \tilde{R})$. But the ratio of acceptable pair is very low. The good right factors can be obtained only by commutation of factors of R . The number of factors in K is higher (at least by a factor 2) and the set of possible commutations between factors of K growth exponentially. One can check that this factor is not one coming from a factor of Q, but even this does not improve this approach. Hence these attacks seems largely unpractical in our setting.

5.2 Attacks Using Vector Spaces and Quadratic Equations/Linear

To get a better understanding of the structure of possible secret keys, we use a different way to represent the set of all possible secret keys Q, R. Let

$$V := \{C \in \mathbb{F}_4[X,\theta]4 \mid \deg(C) \le d, S \cdot C = C \cdot S \;\forall S \in \mathcal{S}\}$$

be the set of all polynomials of maximum degree d that commute with all elements of $\mathcal{S}$. It is straight forward to check that V is an $\mathbb{F}_2$ vector space (note: not necessarily an $\mathbb{F}_4$ vector space). Let $b_1, \ldots, b_c$ be a basis of V, then each secret key L (resp. R) can be represented as an $\mathbb{F}_2$ linear combination of these basis elements (as long as the maximum degree d of elements in V is not smaller than $\max\{\deg(L), \deg(R)\}$). The basis can be selected as the central polynomials x^{2j} with $0 \le j \le \lfloor d/2 \rfloor$ and polynomials of odd degree; there are at most two polynomials of identical degree. Thus the dimension c of V is bounded by $d + d/2$, in all examples we tried, c was slightly smaller than d.

Using V, we can represent the secret keys L, R of Equation 1 as $\mathbb{F}_2$ linear combinations of basis elements with $2 \cdot c$ variables, and write the equation as

$$\sum_{i=1}^{c} \lambda_i b_i \cdot Q \cdot \sum_{i=1}^{c} \tilde{\lambda}_i b_i = L \cdot Q \cdot R = P,$$

where $\lambda_i, \tilde{\lambda}_i$ are unknowns over $\mathbb{F}_2$.

With known P, Q, comparing the coefficients of Equation 1 gives us $\deg(P)$ quadratic equations in $2 \cdot c$ variables (with coefficients in $\mathbb{F}_4$) for the unknown L, R. Only solutions in $\mathbb{F}_2$ are allowed here, therefore we can split each equation into two equations over $\mathbb{F}_2$ (say "the part not in $\mathbb{F}_2$" and "the part in $\mathbb{F}_2$") and end up with a system of $2 \cdot \deg(P)$ equations over $\mathbb{F}_2$ in $2 \cdot c$ unknowns.

The number of variables and the number of equations increases linearly in the "size of the key exchange" (the degree of the secret keys and the degree of the polynomial transmitted). This should make this attack infeasible for larger parameters, at least if some additional structure in the system of equations can not be used to reduce the growth in the complexity significantly. One obvious structure in the system of equations is: there are equations with few unknowns, the ones coming from the highest degrees of x. Therefore there is a reasonable chance to get solutions for some variables by solving only a few equations (and ignoring the rest).

This worked quite well in all the examples we tried; this technique produced e.g. some 2000 solutions for some 20 unknowns. When selecting one of theses solutions and substituting the 20 "known" variables in all equations, we got (e.g. by calculating a Gröbner basis truncated at degree 2) a reasonable amount of linear equations for the remaining (several hundred) unknowns, or could show reasonably fast, that the partial solution (of the selected 20 variables) does not continue to a full solution. Substituting the linear equations again in the original system resulted in a system of equations that could be solved completely by Gröbner bases, if the parameters were not too big. Systems with about 380 unknowns and about 1050 equations ($\deg(L) \approx \deg(R) \approx 190$, $\deg(Q) \approx 150$) could be solved in around 20 h of CPU time on a 2.6 GHz Opteron 252 with 16 GB of memory. Systems with about 500 unknowns and about 1400 equations ($\deg(L) \approx \deg(R) \approx 250$, $\deg(Q) \approx 200$) could be solved in around 60 h of CPU time on the same machine. For all systems of this size, we found something between 3 and 10 different solutions.

For slightly larger systems, $\deg(L) \approx \deg(R) \approx 350$, $\deg(Q) \approx 250$ the attack did not work any more: already in the second step, falsifying a partial solution required much more equations and worked in fewer cases. In the many cases that survived, only few linear equations were found, so that it was impossible to go on to the next step. At this level, all our strategies of selecting equations and term orderings reached the point, where the expected exponential growth in the complexity made it infeasible to find a solution of the full system.

We expect that other strategies might come a bit further, but they probably will reach a point where the very large number of variables (> 700) does not allow to take enough advantage of the structure of the system and thus is left with the complexity of calculating a Gröbner basis of a system of "randomly" selected quadratic equations.

5.3 An Attack Using Linear Algebra

In a second attack using the vector space structure, we reduce Equation 1 modulo some central polynomial f with $\deg(f) > \deg(Q \cdot R)$. Now let us assume L is invertible modulo f, then we write the equation as:

$$Q \cdot R = L^{-1} \cdot P \pmod{f}$$

where R, L^{-1} are unknown. The calculation mod f will add solutions that do not correspond with "real solutions", but the original solution will remain in the solution space of the equation.

The one factor R can be represented as a linear combination of the basis elements $b_1, \ldots, b_c$ of V as before, and L^{-1} can be handled in a similar way: Let $\overline{V}$ be the $\mathbb{F}_2$ vector space that commutes with all $v^{-1} \mod f$ for all $v \in V$ that are invertible mod f. Let $\bar{b}_1, \ldots, \bar{b}_{\bar{c}}$ be a basis of $\overline{V}$. The dimension $\bar{c}$ is bounded by $2/3 \cdot \deg(f)$ with the same argument as before.

When representing the unknown R, L^{-1} as linear combinations of basis elements with unknown coefficients, the key equation now becomes $\sum_{i=1}^{c} \lambda_i Q \cdot b_i + \sum_{i=1}^{\bar{c}} \bar{\lambda}_i \bar{b}_i \cdot P = 0$, where the products $\bar{b}_i \cdot P$ are calculated mod f.

This gives a system of linear equations over $\mathbb{F}_4$, where we are only interested in solutions over $\mathbb{F}_2$. Solving the systems results in a high dimensional solution space W. The real solutions are included in W, but nearly all of the solutions for L^{-1} have no inverse element in V. These are the solutions added through the reduction mod f. To find a **valid** solution, we are left to search through all elements of W e.g. for R, and check if R is a right divisor of P. Therefore the dimension of W is a suitable measure for the complexity of this attack, and, in contrast to the previous section, can easily be calculated.

The dimension of W increases with increasing degrees of Q, L, R as expected. There are some variations in the dimension of W for different tuples of (Q, L, R) of identical degrees, and different degrees of f, but the range is not too large.

The following 5-tuples give the degrees of L, Q, R, the degree of factors of L and Q and the range of dimensions of W that occurred in our examples: $(200, 200, 200, 18, 30)$, $(300, 300, 300, 23, 25–30)$, $(400, 400, 400, 50, 53–60)$, $(500, 500, 500, 65, 71–103)$, $(600, 600, 600, 75, 82–116)$.

6 Parameters

6.1 Construction of a Set $\mathcal{S}$ of Commuting Elements

Constructing a set $\mathcal{S}$ of polynomials which commute together without being in the center is not an easy task, but it can be obtained by a brute force approach. In practice we give ourselves a set of polynomials G, a polynomial $g_0 = g \in G$ and $\mathcal{S} = \{g_0\}$. Then for $i \geq 1$ we take a polynomial h in G, if h commutes with $g_0, \ldots, g_{i-1}$ then $g_i := h$, $\mathcal{S} := \mathcal{S} \cup \{h\}$ and $G := G - \{h\}$, else we take another h and we repeat until $G = \{g_0\}$.

We recall that in our algorithm the computation of the set $\mathcal{S}$ is done only once and made public, so that the long computation is done only once and for all.

In the following we give two examples of such sets which can be used with our algorithm, the sets have 96 polynomials which commute over $\mathbb{F}_4[X, \theta]$ where θ is the Frobenius automorphism. For each of these examples G was the set of irreducible polynomials of degree 8 and 9:

6.2 Set of Parameters

The security analysis of Section 5, leads to the conclusion that in order to resist to attacks one has to get a security parameter d of size greater than 600 to obtain a security in 2^{80}. In that case the number of bits exchanged is 3600 in the key exchange protocol and the public key has size 3600 for the encryption protocol and the number of binary operations is roughly 2^{23}. Overall is compares very well with other existing schemes.

7 Conclusion

In this paper we propose a new approach for key exchange protocol by introducing skew polynomials. Our system can be naturally interpretated in term of quadratic equations. A closer look at possible attacks lead to a better class of attack but still with an heuristic exponential complexity on which we based our security. Overall the approach we propose seems very promising by achieving seemingly a good tradeoff between speed, size of parameters, size of keys and security.

References

1. Bosma, W., Cannon, J., Playoust, C.: The magma algebra system i: The user language. Journal of Symbolic Computation 24, 235–265 (1997)
2. Turrel-Bardet, M.: Etude des systèmes algébriques surdéterminés. Applications aux codes correcteurs et la cryptographie., Ph.D. Thesis, Université de Paris VI, Pierre et Marie Curie (2004)
3. Bronstein, M., Petkovsek, M.: On Ore Rings, Linear Operators and Factorisation. Programming and Computer Software 20, 27–44 (1994)
4. Courtois, N., Klimov, A., Patarin, J., Shamir, A.: Efficient Algorithms for Solving Overdefined Systems of Multivariate Polynomil Equations. In: Preneel, B. (ed.) EUROCRYPT 2000. LNCS, vol. 1807, pp. 392–407. Springer, Heidelberg (2000)
5. Faugère, J.-C.: A new efficient algorithm for computing Grobner bases without reduction to zero (f5). In: Mora, T. (ed.) ISSAC 2002, pp. 75–83 (2002)
6. Fraenkel, A.S., Yesha, Y.: Complexity of problems in games, graphs and algebraic equations. Discrete Applied Mathematics 1, 15–30 (1979)
7. Giesbrecht, M.: Factoring in skew-polynomial rings over finite fields. J. Symbolic Comput. 26(4), 463–486 (1998)
8. Jacobson, N.: The theory of rings. Publication of the AMS (1943)
9. McDonald, B.R.: Finite Rings with Identity. Marcel Dekker Inc., New York (1974)
10. Ore, O.: Theory of non-commutative polynomials. Ann. of Math. 34 (1933)

Appendix

In the following we give two examples of sets $\mathcal{S}$ with more than 90 polynomials of degree 8 or 9

$\{X^8+X^6+X^5+X^3+\alpha, X^9+X^8+X^7+X^6+X^5+\alpha\,X^4+X^3+X^2+\alpha, X^9+X^8+X^7+X^6+X^5+\alpha^2\,X^4+X^3+\alpha, X^8+X^7+X^5+\alpha\,X^2+1, X^8+X^6+X^5+X^3+\alpha^2, X^8+X^7+X^6+X^4+X^3+\alpha^2\,X^2+\alpha^2, X^9+X^6+\alpha\,X^4+X^3+\alpha\,X^2+\alpha, X^9+X^6+\alpha\,X^4+X^3+\alpha^2\,X^2+\alpha, X^9+X^6+\alpha^2\,X^4+X^3+\alpha\,X^2+\alpha, X^9+X^8+X^7+X^5+\alpha^2\,X^4+X^3+X^2+\alpha, X^9+X^8+X^7+X^5+\alpha\,X^4+X^3+\alpha, X^8+X^5+X^3+X^2+\alpha, X^8+X^7+X^3+\alpha\,X^2+\alpha, X^8+X^7+X^5+\alpha^2\,X^2+1, X^9+\alpha\,X^4+X^3+\alpha^2\,X^2+\alpha, X^8+X^5+X^3+X^2+\alpha^2, X^9+\alpha^2\,X^4+X^3+\alpha\,X^2+\alpha, X^9+\alpha^2\,X^4+X^3+\alpha^2\,X^2+\alpha, X^9+X^6+X^5+\alpha\,X^4+\alpha^2\,X^2+1, X^9+X^6+X^5+\alpha^2\,X^4+\alpha\,X^2+1, X^8+X^6+X^5+X^4+X^3+\alpha, X^9+X^8+X^6+\alpha\,X^4+X^3+\alpha\,X^2+\alpha, X^9+X^8+X^6+\alpha\,X^4+X^3+\alpha^2\,X^2+\alpha, X^8+X^7+X^5+X^4+\alpha\,X^2+1, X^9+X^8+X^6+$

$\alpha^2 X^4+X^3+\alpha^2 X^2+\alpha, X^9+X^5+\alpha X^4+\alpha X^2+1, X^8+X^6+X^5+X^4+X^3+$
$\alpha^2, X^9+X^7+X^6+X^5+\alpha X^4+X^3+X^2+\alpha^2, X^9+X^5+\alpha^2 X^4+\alpha^2 X^2+1, X^8+$
$X^7+X^3+\alpha^2 X^2+\alpha^2, X^9+X^7+X^6+X^5+\alpha^2 X^4+X^3+\alpha^2, X^9+X^8+\alpha X^4+$
$X^3+\alpha X^2+\alpha, X^8+X^5+X^4+X^3+X^2+\alpha, X^9+X^8+\alpha^2 X^4+X^3+\alpha X^2+$
$\alpha, X^9+X^8+X^6+X^5+\alpha X^4+\alpha X^2+1, X^9+X^8+\alpha^2 X^4+X^3+\alpha^2 X^2+\alpha, X^9+$
$X^8+X^6+X^5+\alpha^2 X^4+\alpha^2 X^2+1, X^8+X^7+X^5+X^4+\alpha^2 X^2+1, X^9+X^7+X^5+$
$\alpha^2 X^4+X^3+X^2+\alpha^2, X^9+X^7+X^5+\alpha X^4+X^3+\alpha^2, X^8+X^5+X^4+X^3+X^2+$
$\alpha^2, X^9+X^7+X^6+\alpha X^4+X^2+1, X^9+X^7+X^6+\alpha^2 X^4+X^2+1, X^9+X^7+X^6+$
$\alpha X^4+1, X^8+X^7+X^4+X^3+\alpha X^2+\alpha^2, X^9+X^7+X^6+\alpha^2 X^4+1, X^9+X^8+$
$X^5+\alpha X^4+\alpha^2 X^2+1, X^9+X^8+X^5+\alpha^2 X^4+\alpha X^2+1, X^8+X^5+X^3+\alpha, X^9+$
$X^8+X^7+X^6+X^5+\alpha^2 X^4+X^3+X^2+\alpha^2, X^9+X^8+X^7+X^6+X^5+\alpha X^4+X^3+$
$\alpha^2, X^8+X^7+X^4+X^3+\alpha^2 X^2+\alpha, X^9+X^7+\alpha X^4+X^2+1, X^8+X^7+X^6+X^5+$
$\alpha X^2+1, X^9+X^7+\alpha^2 X^4+X^2+1, X^9+X^7+\alpha X^4+1, X^8+X^5+X^3+\alpha^2, X^9+$
$X^7+\alpha^2 X^4+1, X^9+X^8+X^7+X^5+\alpha X^4+X^3+X^2+\alpha^2, X^9+X^6+\alpha X^4+X^3+$
$\alpha^2 X^2+\alpha^2, X^9+X^6+\alpha^2 X^4+X^3+\alpha X^2+\alpha^2, X^9+X^6+\alpha^2 X^4+X^3+\alpha^2 X^2+$
$\alpha^2, X^8+X^6+X^5+X^3+X^2+\alpha, X^9+X^8+X^7+X^6+\alpha X^4+X^2+1, X^9+X^8+$
$X^7+X^5+\alpha^2 X^4+X^3+\alpha^2, X^9+X^8+X^7+X^6+\alpha^2 X^4+X^2+1, X^9+X^8+X^7+$
$X^6+\alpha X^4+1, X^8+X^7+X^6+X^5+\alpha^2 X^2+1, X^9+X^8+X^7+X^6+\alpha^2 X^4+1, X^8+$
$X^6+X^5+X^3+X^2+\alpha^2, X^9+\alpha X^4+X^3+\alpha X^2+\alpha^2, X^9+\alpha X^4+X^3+\alpha^2 X^2+$
$\alpha^2, X^9+\alpha^2 X^4+X^3+\alpha X^2+\alpha^2, X^8+X^7+X^6+X^3+\alpha X^2+\alpha^2, X^9+X^8+X^7+$
$\alpha X^4+X^2+1, X^9+X^8+X^7+\alpha^2 X^4+X^2+1, X^9+X^8+X^7+\alpha X^4+1, X^8+X^5+$
$X^4+X^3+\alpha, X^9+X^8+X^7+\alpha^2 X^4+1, X^8+X^7+X^6+X^3+\alpha^2 X^2+\alpha, X^9+X^8+$
$X^6+\alpha X^4+X^3+\alpha X^2+\alpha^2, X^8+X^7+X^6+X^5+X^4+\alpha X^2+1, X^9+X^8+X^6+$
$\alpha^2 X^4+X^3+\alpha X^2+\alpha^2, X^9+X^8+X^6+\alpha^2 X^4+X^3+\alpha^2 X^2+\alpha^2, X^8+X^5+X^4+$
$X^3+\alpha^2, X^9+X^7+X^6+X^5+\alpha^2 X^4+X^3+X^2+\alpha, X^9+X^7+X^6+X^5+\alpha X^4+$
$X^3+\alpha, X^8+X^6+X^5+X^4+X^3+X^2+\alpha, X^9+X^8+\alpha X^4+X^3+\alpha X^2+\alpha^2, X^9+$
$X^8+\alpha X^4+X^3+\alpha^2 X^2+\alpha^2, X^8+X^7+X^6+X^4+X^3+\alpha X^2+\alpha, X^9+X^8+$
$\alpha^2 X^4+X^3+\alpha^2 X^2+\alpha^2, X^9+X^7+X^5+\alpha X^4+X^3+X^2+\alpha, X^8+X^7+X^6+X^5+$
$X^4+\alpha^2 X^2+1, X^8+X^6+X^5+X^4+X^3+X^2+\alpha^2, X^9+X^7+X^5+\alpha^2 X^4+X^3+\alpha\}$

$\{X^9+X^8+\alpha X^6+\alpha^2 X^4+\alpha X^2+X+\alpha^2, X^9+X^7+\alpha X^6+X^5+X^4+\alpha X^2+X+$
$\alpha, X^8+X^7+X^5+\alpha^2 X^4+1, X^9+X^7+\alpha^2 X^6+X^5+X^4+\alpha^2 X^2+X+\alpha, X^9+X^7+$
$\alpha X^6+X^5+\alpha^2 X^2+X+\alpha, X^8+X^7+X^6+\alpha X^4+X^3+\alpha X^2+1, X^8+X^7+\alpha^2 X^4+$
$\alpha^2 X^2+X+\alpha^2, X^9+\alpha X^6+X^5+\alpha X^4+X^3+X^2+X+\alpha, X^8+X^7+X^6+\alpha X^4+$
$\alpha X^2+X+\alpha, X^9+X^8+X^7+\alpha^2 X^6+X^3+X+\alpha^2, X^8+X^3+X^2+X+\alpha, X^9+$
$\alpha X^6+X^5+\alpha^2 X^4+X^3+X+\alpha, X^9+X^8+X^7+\alpha X^6+X^5+X^4+\alpha X^2+X+$
$\alpha, X^9+\alpha^2 X^6+X^5+\alpha^2 X^4+X^3+X^2+X+\alpha, X^8+X^7+X^6+X^5+\alpha^2 X^4+X^3+$
$X^2+X+\alpha^2, X^9+\alpha^2 X^6+X^5+\alpha^2 X^4+X^3+X+\alpha, X^9+X^8+X^7+\alpha^2 X^6+X^5+$
$X^4+\alpha X^2+X+\alpha, X^9+X^8+X^7+\alpha^2 X^6+X^5+X^4+\alpha^2 X^2+X+\alpha, X^9+\alpha X^6+$
$X^5+\alpha X^4+1, X^8+X^3+X^2+X+\alpha^2, X^9+X^8+X^7+\alpha^2 X^6+X^5+\alpha X^2+X+$
$\alpha, X^9+\alpha^2 X^6+X^5+\alpha^2 X^4+1, X^9+X^7+\alpha X^6+X^5+X^4+X^3+\alpha^2 X^2+1, X^9+$
$\alpha^2 X^6+\alpha X^4+\alpha X^2+X+\alpha, X^8+X^7+X^6+X^5+\alpha X^4+X^3+X+\alpha^2, X^9+X^8+$
$\alpha X^6+X^5+\alpha X^4+X^3+X^2+X+\alpha, X^9+X^7+\alpha^2 X^6+X^5+X^4+X^3+\alpha X^2+$
$1, X^9+\alpha^2 X^6+\alpha^2 X^4+\alpha^2 X^2+X+\alpha, X^9+X^8+\alpha X^6+X^5+\alpha^2 X^4+X^3+X+$
$\alpha, X^9+X^8+\alpha^2 X^6+X^5+\alpha^2 X^4+X^3+X^2+X+\alpha, X^9+X^8+\alpha X^6+X^5+\alpha X^4+$

$X^2+1, X^8+X^7+X^5+\alpha X^4+X^2+1, X^8+X^7+X^6+\alpha^2 X^4+X^3+\alpha^2 X^2+1, X^9+$
$X^8+\alpha^2 X^6+X^5+\alpha^2 X^4+X^2+1, X^9+X^7+\alpha X^6+X^4+1, X^9+X^7+\alpha^2 X^6+$
$X^4+1, X^9+X^8+X^7+\alpha X^6+X^5+X^4+X^3+\alpha X^2+1, X^9+X^7+\alpha X^6+X^5+$
$X^4+\alpha X^2+X+\alpha^2, X^8+X^7+X^6+X^5+\alpha^2 X^4+X^3+X+\alpha, X^9+X^8+\alpha^2 X^6+$
$\alpha X^4+\alpha^2 X^2+X+\alpha, X^9+X^8+X^7+\alpha^2 X^6+X^5+X^4+X^3+\alpha^2 X^2+1, X^9+$
$X^7+\alpha^2 X^6+X^5+X^4+\alpha^2 X^2+X+\alpha^2, X^8+X^3+X+\alpha, X^9+X^7+\alpha^2 X^6+X^5+$
$\alpha X^2+X+\alpha^2, X^8+X^7+X^6+\alpha^2 X^4+\alpha^2 X^2+X+\alpha^2, X^9+\alpha X^6+\alpha X^4+X^3+$
$\alpha^2 X^2+1, X^9+X^8+X^7+\alpha X^6+X^4+X^2+1, X^8+X^3+X+\alpha^2, X^9+X^8+X^7+$
$\alpha X^6+X^3+X+\alpha, X^9+\alpha^2 X^6+\alpha^2 X^4+X^3+\alpha X^2+1, X^9+\alpha X^6+X^5+\alpha X^4+$
$X^3+X^2+X+\alpha^2, X^9+X^8+X^7+\alpha^2 X^6+X^4+X^2+1, X^8+X^7+X^5+\alpha^2 X^4+$
$X^2+1, X^8+X^7+\alpha X^4+\alpha X^2+X+\alpha, X^8+X^6+X^5+X^3+\alpha X^2+1, X^9+\alpha X^6+$
$X^5+\alpha X^4+X^3+X+\alpha^2, X^9+X^8+X^7+\alpha X^6+X^5+X^4+\alpha X^2+X+\alpha^2, X^9+$
$X^8+X^7+\alpha X^6+1, X^9+\alpha^2 X^6+X^5+\alpha^2 X^4+X^3+X^2+X+\alpha^2, X^8+X^7+\alpha X^4+$
$X^3+\alpha^2 X^2+1, X^9+X^8+X^7+\alpha X^6+X^5+X^4+\alpha^2 X^2+X+\alpha^2, X^9+\alpha^2 X^6+$
$X^5+\alpha X^4+X^3+X+\alpha^2, X^9+X^8+X^7+\alpha^2 X^6+1, X^9+X^8+X^7+\alpha^2 X^6+X^5+$
$X^4+\alpha^2 X^2+X+\alpha^2, X^9+X^8+X^7+\alpha X^6+X^5+\alpha^2 X^2+X+\alpha^2, X^8+X^7+X^5+$
$\alpha X^4+1, X^8+X^6+X^5+X^3+\alpha^2 X^2+1, X^9+\alpha X^6+\alpha X^4+\alpha X^2+X+\alpha^2, X^8+$
$X^6+X^5+\alpha X^2+X+\alpha^2, X^9+\alpha X^6+\alpha^2 X^4+\alpha^2 X^2+X+\alpha^2, X^8+X^7+\alpha^2 X^4+$
$X^3+\alpha X^2+1, X^9+X^8+\alpha X^6+X^5+\alpha X^4+X^3+X^2+X+\alpha^2, X^8+X^6+X^5+$
$\alpha^2 X^2+X+\alpha, X^8+X^7+X^6+X^5+\alpha X^4+X^3+X^2+X+\alpha, X^9+X^8+\alpha^2 X^6+$
$X^5+\alpha^2 X^4+X^3+X^2+X+\alpha^2, X^9+X^8+\alpha^2 X^6+X^5+\alpha X^4+X^3+X+\alpha^2\}$

Designing a Rank Metric Based McEliece Cryptosystem

Pierre Loidreau

DGA and IRMAR, Université de Rennes 1
Pierre.Loidreau@univ-rennes1.fr

Abstract. In this paper we describe the rank metric based McEliece type cryptosystems which where first introduced by Gabidulin, Paramonov and Tretjakov in the 90's. Then we explain the principle of Overbeck's attack is so efficient on these types of systems. Finally we show how to choose the parameters so that the public-key size remain relatively small (typically less than 20 000 bits), with a good security against structural and decoding attacks.

1 Introduction

Code based public-key cryptosystem form an interesting alternative to public-key cryptosystems based on coding theory. Their principle was first stated by McEliece in the early days of public-key cryptography, [20]. These systems have some nice properties such as

- they are very fast in encryption and decryption compared to number theory based systems,
- there are no algorithms working on quantum computers that would enable to decrease the complexity of the attacks contrarily to number theory based cryptosystems,
- the related complexity problem have been widely investigated since Shannon's seminal paper more than 60 years ago.

The main drawback which made them unpractical in the 70's and 80's is that the public-key size is too large to be implemented on limited resource devices, typically several hundreds of thousands of bits. Therefore one of the great challenges designing of code based cryptosystems is to find a way to reduce the public-key size, sufficiently to be implemented on cheap devices.

Since 20 years several proposals were made in that sense. Basically two directions have been considered. The first one consists of exploiting the algebraic structure of families of codes to diminish the key-size. For instance using of Goppa codes with a non-trivial automorphism group as the family of codes, [18], hiding the structure of codes by taking subcodes of generalised Reed-Solomon codes [5], and more recently the using quasi-cyclic codes [14], or dyadic Goppa codes [21]. However attacks against some of these systems show that the structure of the codes introduces structural weaknesses in the public-key [17,3,23].

N. Sendrier (Ed.): PQCrypto 2010, LNCS 6061, pp. 142–152, 2010.

The second direction which is the heart of this paper consists of using rank metric rather than Hamming metric, a metric in which the decoding problems have the reputation to be more complex. This idea was first used by Gabidulin, Paramonov and Tretjakov in 1991, who proposed a public-key cryptosystem based on a family of codes published by Gabidulin correcting rank errors, [13]. In the seminal paper, they proposed to use public-keys as low as 5 000 bits. During the 90's, different modifications of the system were published, see [5,12,25,26,4] especially after the design of structural attacks by Gibson [15,16] which lead to increasing the key size, however these kind of systems survived until Overbeck designed a somehow devastating attack exploiting fully the structure of the underlying family of codes, [30].

Until now the question was to know if cryptosystems based on rank metric can be made resistant to Overbeck's attack or not, by keeping a public-key size reasonably small compared to the counterpart in Hamming metric. A first step in the analysis of the problem consists in fully understanding the principle on which is based Overbeck's attack, that is to know, the relative stability of the codes under the action of the Frobenius automorphism of the codes. In a second step, we establish results and relations between parameters so that the attack does not work.

In a first part we recall some essential properties of rank metric and of Gabidulin codes. In a second part we design an attack on the system. This attack uses the same structural flaw as Overbeck's attack, and has the same working domain. From the study of the working domain of the attack, a conceiver can deduce parameters to secure the cryptosystem.

2 Background on Rank Metric and Gabidulin Codes

In this section we briefly recall the definition of rank metric and Gabidulin codes, which form the heart of rank metric based cryptosystems. We will use only fields of characteristic 2 but all these results can be extended to fields of any prime characteristic.

2.1 Rank Metric

Let $GF(2^m)$ be the finite field with 2^m elements and let $(\beta_1, \ldots, \beta_m)$ be a basis of $GF(2^m)$ over $GF(2)$.

Définition 1 ([9])
Let $\mathbf{x} = (x_1, \ldots, x_n) \in GF(2^m)^n$. *The rank of* $\mathbf{x}$ *in* $GF(2)$ *is the rank of the matrix* $\mathbf{X} = (x_{ij})$, *where* $x_j = \sum_{i=1}^{m} x_{ij}\beta_i$. *It is written* $\mathrm{Rg}(\mathbf{x})$.

The rank of a vector is a norm, independent of the chosen basis $(\beta_1, \ldots, \beta_m)$, and if $\mathcal{C}$ is a linear code, the minimum rank distance of $\mathcal{C}$ is naturally defined by

$$d \stackrel{def}{=} \min_{c \in \mathcal{C}^*}(\mathrm{Rg}(\mathbf{c}))$$

Let $\mathcal{C}$ be a code, $\mathbf{y}$ be a vector and t be an integer, the complexity problem **Bounded decoding** for codes in rank metric can be defined as:

Bounded decoding$(\mathbf{y}, \mathcal{C}, t)$
Find if exists $\mathbf{c} \in \mathcal{C}$ *and* $\mathbf{e} \in GF(2^m)^n$ *with* $\mathrm{Rg}(\mathbf{e}) \leq t$ *such that* $\mathbf{y} = \mathbf{c} + \mathbf{e}$.

If d denotes the minimum rank distance of $\mathcal{C}$, k its dimension, and in the case where $t \leq (d-1)/2$, this problem has either one or zero solution. In the case where there is exactly one solution, the best algorithms to find the solution are probabilistic algorithms due to Ourivski and Johannson and have average work factor, which are based on the principle of finding codewords of the smallest rank in a linear code, [27]:

- Basis enumeration algorithm: $W_{\text{bases}} \approx (k+t)^3 2^{(t-1)(m-t)+2}$.
- Coordinate enumeration algorithm: $W_{\text{coord}} \approx (k+t)^3 t^3 2^{(t-1)(k+1)}$.

If we consider the same problem on the same parameters but in Hamming metric, solving the problem is considerably less difficult, [7,1]. This is the reason why McEliece types rank metric based cryptosystems can theoretically employ public-keys of much smaller size than for Hamming metric based cryptosystems.

2.2 Gabidulin Codes

Let $\mathbf{g} = (g_1, \ldots, g_n) \in GF(2^m)$ linearly independent over $GF(2)$. Let

$$\mathbf{G} = \begin{pmatrix} g_1 & \cdots & g_n \\ \vdots & \ddots & \vdots \\ g_1^{[k-1]} & \cdots & g_n^{[k-1]} \end{pmatrix}, \tag{1}$$

where $[i] \stackrel{def}{=} 2^i$ is the ith power of the Frobenius automorphism of $GF(2^m)/GF(2)$.

Définition 2 ([9])
The Gabidulin code $Gab_k(\mathbf{g})$ *over* $GF(2^m)$ *of dimension* k *and generator vector* $\mathbf{g}$ *is the code generated by* $\mathbf{G}$.

The error-correcting capability of $Gab_k(\mathbf{g})$ is $\lfloor (n-k)/2 \rfloor$. There are very efficient decoding algorithms for Gabidulin codes up to the rank error correcting capability [9,10,32,31,19].

3 McEliece Type Cryptosystems Based on Rank Metric

In this section we first describe the original GPT cryptosystem, published in 1991, by Gabidulin, Paramonov and Tretjakov, [13]. Other versions where later published like the one by Ourivski and Gabidulin, using a right scrambler which is a linear isometry of rank metric [25]. It is immediate to see that this version is a generalisation of the initial proposition. Therefore we will only present this version of the cryptosystem.

3.1 The Original System

Parameters

- The field $GF(2^m)$
- An integer t_1

Key generation. The *private key* is composed with

- $\mathbf{S}$, a $k \times k$ non-singular matrix with coefficients in $GF(2^m)$.
- $\mathbf{G}$, a $k \times n$ matrix over $GF(2^m)$ generating a Gabidulin code of generator vector $\mathbf{g} = (g_1, \dots, g_n)$ under the canonical form given in (1). Hence we can correct up to rank $t = \lfloor (n-k)/2 \rfloor$ errors.
- $\mathbf{Z}$, a $k \times t_1$ matrix with coefficients in $GF(2^m)$.
- $\mathbf{T}$, a $(n+t_1) \times (n+t_1)$ non-singular matrix with coefficients in $GF(2)$. The matrix $\mathbf{T}$ is a *linear isometry* of rank metric [2].

The public-key is thus the $k \times (n+t_1)$ matrix

$$\mathbf{G}_{\text{pub}} = \mathbf{S}(\mathbf{G} \mid \underbrace{\mathbf{Z}}_{t_1\ cols})\mathbf{T} \tag{2}$$

The encryption procedure is exactly the same as for the original McEliece cryptosystem:

Encryption. Let $\mathbf{x} \in GF(2^m)^k$ be the information vector that must be encrypted. The ciphertext $\mathbf{y}$ is

$$\mathbf{y} = \mathbf{x}\mathbf{G}_{\text{pub}} + \mathbf{e}$$

where $\mathbf{e}$ is a vector of rank $\leq t = \lfloor (n-k)/2 \rfloor$ The decryption procedure is:

Decryption. Let $\mathbf{y}$ be the received ciphertext, we have

$$\mathbf{y} = \mathbf{x}\mathbf{G}_{\text{pub}} + \mathbf{e},$$

where $\text{Rg}(\mathbf{e}) \leq t$. Then the receiver computes

$$\mathbf{y}\mathbf{T}^{-1} = \mathbf{x}(\mathbf{G} \mid \mathbf{Z}) + \mathbf{e}\mathbf{T}^{-1},$$

and removes the last t_1 positions of $\mathbf{y}\mathbf{T}^{-1}$. Finally he decodes in the Gabidulin code of generator matrix $\mathbf{G}$.

The security of the cryptosystem relies on the following two assumptions:

- The code generated by $\mathbf{G}_{\text{pub}}$ behaves randomly.
- Solving **Bounded decoding**$(\mathbf{y}, \mathcal{C}, t)$, where $\mathcal{C}$ is a random code of length n, dimension k over $GF(2^m)$ is difficult

As shown in section 2.1, the second assumption is satisfied provided the parameters are sufficiently large. The first assumption however is more problematic, since the previous cryptosystems based on scrambled Gabidulin codes have until now been severely attacked.

3.2 Structural Attacks

One of the main problem in designing rank metric based cryptosystems is that there is only known family of codes with a fast decoding algorithm, the family of Gabidulin codes. Therefore all rank metric based cryptosystems have to rely on codes derived from Gabidulin codes (scrambled codes, subfield subcode for instance). Moreover, it is impossible to use Gabidulin codes without scrambling the structure as it was shown by Gabidulin (case where $t_1 = 0$). Namely in that case there exists an attack recovering a decoder for the public-code in polynomial time. This attack is an analog of Sidel'nikov-Shestakov attack in the case where Generalised Reed-Solomon codes are used in the Hamming metric based McEliece cryptosystem.

Moreover, different attacks have shown that the scrambling matrix $\mathbf{Z}$ had to be very carefully chosen. The first person to attack structurally the initial parameters was Gibson [15,16], who exploited some properties of Gabidulin codes. After these attacks some new parameters, as well as modifications of the system were proposed to render Gibson attacks inefficient, [12,25]. More recently Overbeck used Gibson's attacks as black boxes against the new versions of the system, [29]. But the most powerful attack until now using fully the structure of the codes was still proposed by Overbeck who cryptanalysed almost all versions of McEliece type cryptosystems based Gabidulin codes, [28,30]. To prevent the attack from succeeding, the parameters should be so much increased that the interest of rank metric systems decreases compared to Hamming based systems.

The success of this approach is that Overbeck fully exploits the large structure of Gabidulin codes, that is that the intersection of a k–dimensional Gabidulin code and the Gabidulin code on which the Frobenius automorphism acts is a $k-1$–dimensional Gabidulin code, namely it:

$$Gab_k(\mathbf{g}) \cap Gab_k(\mathbf{g})^{[1]} = Gab_{k-1}(\mathbf{g}^{[1]})$$

To show how to design cryptosystems which are resistant to Overbeck's attacks, and still with very reasonable key sizes, we first need to present an attack whose efficiency is comparable to that of Overbeck's. The heart of the attack is described in proposition 1, which is not in Overbeck's work.

The public key is given by the matrix $\mathbf{G}_{\text{pub}}$ from equation (2). Let us recall that $\mathbf{G}^{[i]}$ is the matrix derived from $\mathbf{G}$, by elevating each component to the ith power of the Frobenius automorphism, that is to the power 2^i.

If all the components of $\mathbf{G}_{\text{pub}}$ are elevated to the powers $[1], [2], \ldots, [n-k-1]$, we obtain

$$\underbrace{\begin{pmatrix} \mathbf{G}_{\text{pub}} \\ \mathbf{G}_{\text{pub}}^{[1]} \\ \vdots \\ \mathbf{G}_{\text{pub}}^{[n-k-1]} \end{pmatrix}}_{\mathcal{G}_{\text{pub}}} = \underbrace{\begin{pmatrix} \mathbf{S} & 0 & \cdots & 0 \\ 0 & \mathbf{S}^{[1]} & \ddots & 0 \\ \vdots & 0 & \ddots & \vdots \\ 0 & \cdots & & \mathbf{S}^{[n-k-1]} \end{pmatrix}}_{\mathcal{S}} \underbrace{\left(\begin{array}{c|c} \mathbf{G} & \mathbf{Z} \\ \mathbf{G}^{[1]} & \mathbf{Z}^{[1]} \\ \vdots & \vdots \\ \mathbf{G}^{[n-k-1]} & \mathbf{Z}^{[n-k-1]} \end{array}\right)}_{(\mathcal{G} \mid \mathcal{Z})} \mathbf{T}, \tag{3}$$

where

- $\mathcal{G}_{\text{pub}}$ is a $k(n-k) \times n$ matrix of rank $n-1$, thanks to the properties of Gabidulin codes.
- Since $\mathbf{S}$ is non-singular, so is $\mathcal{S}$.
- Since $\mathbf{T}$ has coefficients in the base field $GF(2)$, for all i, $\mathbf{T}^{[i]} = \mathbf{T}$, and $\mathbf{T}$ has rank $n + t_1$.
- $\mathcal{Z}$ is a $k(n-k) \times t_1$ matrix of rank $s \le \min(k(n-k), t_1)$.

Since we want to optimise the public-key size in the design of the system it is reasonable to suppose that t_1 is much less than $k(n-k)$. In that case, if $\mathbf{Z}$ is chosen randomly, then $\mathcal{Z}$ has very probably rank t_1. This implies that $\mathcal{G}_{\text{pub}}$ is very probably of rank $n + t_1 - 1$. Hence its right kernel has rank 1. This leads to the following proposition which shows that in the cases where the right kernel is one dimensional, a decoder form the public-code can be recovered in polynomial-time.

Proposition 1
If the right kernel $\ker_r(\mathcal{G}_{\text{pub}})$ *of* $\mathcal{G}_{\text{pub}}$ *has dimension* 1, *then*

- *There exists a vector* $\mathbf{h}$ *of rank* n *over* $GF(2)$ *such that*

$$\ker(\mathcal{G}_{\text{pub}}) = \{ \ \mathbf{T}^{-1}(\alpha\mathbf{h} \mid \mathbf{0})^T \mid \alpha \in GF(2^m)\}.$$

- *Let* $\mathbf{y} \in \ker(\mathcal{G}_{\text{pub}})$, *then every matrix* $\mathbf{Q}$ *of size* $(n+t_1) \times (n+t_1)$ *and with coefficients in* $GF(2)$ *such that* $\mathbf{Qy} = (\mathbf{x} \mid \mathbf{0})^T$, *is non-singular and satisfies*

$$\mathbf{TQ}^{-1} = \begin{pmatrix} \mathbf{A} & \mathbf{B} \\ \mathbf{0} & \mathbf{D} \end{pmatrix},$$

where $\mathbf{A}$ *is an* $n \times n$ *non-singular matrix, and* $\mathbf{D}$ *is an* $t_1 \times t_1$ *non-singular matrix. Such a matrix* $\mathbf{Q}$ *can be determined in polynomial-time.*

Proof

- Since the right kernel of $\mathcal{G}_{\text{pub}}$ has dimension 1 the kernel of $(\mathcal{G} \mid \mathcal{Z})$ is of the form $(\alpha\mathbf{h} \mid \mathbf{0})$ where $\mathbf{h}$ generates the right kernel of $\mathcal{G}$. But $\mathcal{G}$ generates a $n-1$–dimensional Gabidulin code whose *dual* is a 1–dimensional Gabidulin code with generator vector $\mathbf{h}$. This implies in particular that $\mathbf{h}$ has rank n over $GF(2)$.

– Let $\mathbf{y} \in \ker(\mathcal{G}_{\text{pub}})$. From the structure of the kernel describe in the preceding item, we have $\mathbf{y} = \mathbf{T}^{-1}(\alpha\mathbf{h} \mid \mathbf{0})^T$. Suppose we have determined a binary non-singular matrix $\mathbf{Q}$ such that

$$\mathbf{Q}\mathbf{y} = (\mathbf{x} \mid \mathbf{0})^T = \mathbf{Q}\mathbf{T}^{-1}(\alpha\mathbf{h} \mid \mathbf{0})^T.$$

If we split $\mathbf{Q}\mathbf{T}^{-1}$ into four blocks such that

$$\mathbf{Q}\mathbf{T}^{-1} = \begin{pmatrix} \mathbf{A}' & \mathbf{B}' \\ \mathbf{C}' & \mathbf{D}' \end{pmatrix},$$

then we have $\mathbf{C}'\mathbf{h}^T = \mathbf{0}$. Therefore for all $i = 1, \dots t_1$, $\mathbf{c}_i\mathbf{h}^T = 0$ where $\mathbf{c}_i$ is the ith row of $\mathbf{C}'$. Since the components of $\mathbf{C}'$ are in $GF(2)$ and since $\mathbf{h}$ has rank n over $GF(2)$, we have that $\alpha\mathbf{h}$ has also rank n over $GF(q)$ and for all $i = 1, \dots, t_1$ we have $\mathbf{c}_i = \mathbf{0}$. Moreover, since $\mathbf{Q}$ is non-singular, the inverse $(\mathbf{Q}\mathbf{T}^{-1})^{-1} = \mathbf{T}\mathbf{Q}^{-1}$ is also upper-triangular by blocks.

Given $\mathbf{y} \in \ker(\mathcal{G}_{\text{pub}})$ we determine a non-singular matrix $\mathbf{Q}$ by:

1. Solving the equation$\mathbf{Q}_2\mathbf{y}^T = \mathbf{0}$ where $\mathbf{Q}_2$ is a $t_1 \times (n + t_1)$ matrix of rank t_1.
2. Determining a matrix $\mathbf{Q}_1$ such that

$$\mathbf{Q} \stackrel{def}{=} \begin{pmatrix} \mathbf{Q}_1 \\ \mathbf{Q}_2 \end{pmatrix},$$

is invertible

Since $\mathbf{y}$ has rank n over $GF(2)$ the matrix $\mathbf{Y}$ obtained by expanding the components of $\mathbf{y}$ over a basis of $GF(2^m)/GF(2)$ has size $m \times (n + t_1)$ and rank n. Hence the right kernel of $\mathbf{Y}$ has dimension t_1. Finding $\mathbf{Q}_2$ consists thus in finding a bases of the right kernel of $\mathbf{Y}$, since we have to solve $\mathbf{Y}\mathbf{Q}_2^T = 0$. This can be done in polynomial time. ■

Now whenever the right kernel $\ker_r(\mathcal{G}_{\text{pub}})$ has rank 1, by applying the previous proposition, we can find a matrix $\mathbf{Q}$ satisfying

$$\mathbf{G}_{\text{pub}}\mathbf{Q}^{-1} = \mathbf{S}(\mathbf{G}\mathbf{A} \mid \mathbf{Z}').$$

Since $\mathbf{A}$ is non-singular and has components in the base field $GF(2)$, the matrix $\mathbf{G}' = \mathbf{G}\mathbf{A}$ generates $Gab_k(\mathbf{g}\mathbf{A})$. If we denote by $\mathbf{G}_1$ the n first columns of $\mathbf{G}_{\text{pub}}\mathbf{Q}^{-1}$, the attacker has to solve the equation

$$\mathbf{G}_1 = \mathbf{S}\mathbf{G}',$$

that is $\mathbf{G}_1$ is a randomly chosen generator matrix of $Gab_k(\mathbf{g}\mathbf{A})$. This can be done in polynomial time [11]. The matrix $\mathbf{S}$ thus determined is unique.

We have just proved the following proposition

Proposition 2
If the right kernel of $\mathcal{G}_{\text{pub}}$ *given by the equation* (3) *has dimension* 1, *an attacker can recover in polynomial-time matrices* $\mathbf{Q}, \mathbf{S}$ *and* $\mathbf{Z}$ *such that*

$$\mathbf{G}_{\text{pub}}\mathbf{Q}^{-1} = \mathbf{S}(\mathbf{G}' \mid \mathbf{Z}'),$$

where

- $\mathbf{Q}$ *is a* $(n+t_1) \times (n+t_1)$ *matrix with coefficients in* $GF(2)$,
- $\mathbf{S}$ *is a* $k \times k$ *non-singular matrix*
- $\mathbf{G}'$ *generates a* k*-dimensional Gabidulin code,*
- $\mathbf{Z}'$ *is a* $k \times t_1$ *matrix.*

4 Which Parameters for a Rank Metric Based Cryptosystem

From previous section, the parameters of the system must be chosen so that the dimension of the right kernel of $\mathcal{G}_{pub}$ is greater than 1, and even sufficiently large to avoid enumeration so that an attacker fall by chance on a vector of the dual of the Gabidulin code by selecting a vector randomly in the kernel.

The following corollary gives us information to choose the parameters of the system so that we cannot apply the previous attack.

4.1 Design Criteria

Corollary 1. *Let* $\mathbf{G}_{\text{pub}} = \mathbf{S}(\mathbf{G} \mid \mathbf{Z})\mathbf{T}$ *of size* $k \times (n+t_1)$. *If there is an integer* ℓ *such that*

$$1 \le \text{Rg}(\mathbf{Z}) \le \frac{t_1 - \ell}{n-k},$$

then the dimension of $\ker_r(\mathcal{G}_{\text{pub}})$ *is greater or equal to* $1+\ell$.

Proof
If $s = \text{Rg}(\mathbf{Z})$, then $\text{Rg}(\mathcal{Z}) \le s(n-k)$. Hence $\text{Rg}(\mathcal{G}_{\text{pub}}) \le s(n-k) + n - 1$. Then if $s(n-k) \le t_1 - \ell$, the right kernel of $\mathcal{G}_{\text{pub}}$ has dimension $\ge 1+\ell$. ∎

Therefore to prevent attacks based on the principle described in previous section, it suffices to choose $\ell \ge 1$ and the distortion matrix $\mathbf{Z}$ such that

$$\text{Rg}(\mathbf{Z}) \le \frac{t_1 - \ell}{n-k},$$

which implies $t_1 > (n-k)$.

Now here are the criteria that have to be taken into account in the design of the cryptosystem:

- First note that the dimension of $\ker_r(\mathcal{G}_{pub})$ must be large enough to avoid enumerations since the vector $\mathbf{h}$ discussed in proposition 1
- Second, the best decoding attack has to be of sufficient complexity. We take as references the complexities given in section 2.1
- Third we try to obtain the smallest possible size for these systems.

4.2 Proposition of Parameters

Suppose that we want to reach a security of 2^{80} binary operations for the system. In table 1 we propose two sets of parameters, involving a Gabidulin code correcting rank 6 errors over $GF(2^{24})^{24}$. We can easily show that the complexity of the decoding attacks is larger than 2^{80}

- In the first proposal $\ker_r(\mathcal{G}_{pub})$ has dimension 5 over $GF(2^{24})$
- In the second proposal $\ker_r(\mathcal{G}_{pub})$ has also dimension 4 over $GF(2^{24})$

This implies that an attack consisting in enumerating the right kernel and testing all vectors candidates for being $\mathbf{h}$ will take on average $(2^{120}-1)/(2^{24}-1) \approx 2^{96}$ tries.

The last column shows how it is possible to improve the transmission rate of the system by using a modification proposed in [4]. It increases the transmission rate by

$$\frac{(m+n-t)t-r}{m(n+t_1)},$$

where r is the number of selected random bits.

Table 1. Proposed parameters

$m=n$	k	s	t_1	Key size	Decoding	k/n	Improv. BeLoi2004
24	12	3	40	14 976bits	$> 2^{83}$	19%	30%
24	12	4	52	18 432bits	$> 2^{83}$	15,8%	24,3%

5 Conclusion and Perspectives

In this paper we have shown how to choose parameters be to design rank metric based cryptosystems. The resulting proposals are public-key cryptosystems with public-keys of very reasonable sizes compared to the original McEliece cryptosystem.

The performances of the systems in encryption and decryption have to be compared to Hamming metric based cryptosystems, but this is another story.

References

1. Barg, A.: Handbook of Coding Theory, ch. 7, vol. 1, pp. 649–754. North-Holland, Amsterdam (1998)
2. Berger, T.P.: Isometries for rank distance and permutation group of Gabidulin codes. IEEE Transactions on Information Theory 49(11), 3016–3019 (2003)
3. Berger, T.P., Cayrel, P.L., Gaborit, P., Otmani, A.: Reducing key-length of the McEliece cryptosystem. In: Preneel, B. (ed.) AFRICACRYPT 2009. LNCS, vol. 5580, pp. 77–97. Springer, Heidelberg (2009)

4. Berger, T.P., Loidreau, P.: Designing an efficient and secure public-key cryptosystem based on reducible rank codes. In: Canteaut, A., Viswanathan, K. (eds.) INDOCRYPT 2004. LNCS, vol. 3348, pp. 218–229. Springer, Heidelberg (2004)
5. Berger, T.P., Loidreau, P.: How to mask the structure of codes for a cryptographic use. Designs, Codes and Cryptography 35, 63–79 (2005)
6. Berlekamp, E.R., McEliece, R.J., van Tilborg, H.C.: On the inherent intractability of certain coding problems. IEEE Transactions on Information Theory 24(3) (May 1978)
7. Canteaut, A., Chabaud, F.: A new algorithm for finding minimum-weight words in a linear code: Application to McEliece's cryptosystem and to narrow-sense BCH codes of length 511. IEEE Transactions on Information Theory 44(1), 367–378 (1998)
8. Courtois, N., Finiasz, M., Sendrier, N.: How to achieve a McEliece-based signature scheme. In: Boyd, C. (ed.) ASIACRYPT 2001. LNCS, vol. 2248, pp. 151–174. Springer, Heidelberg (2001)
9. Gabidulin, E.M.: Theory of codes with maximal rank distance. Problems of Information Transmission 21, 1–12 (1985)
10. Gabidulin, E.M.: A fast matrix decoding algorithm for rank-error correcting codes. In: Cohen, G., Litsyn, S., Lobstein, A., Zémor, G. (eds.) Algebraic Coding 1991. LNCS, vol. 573, pp. 126–133. Springer, Heidelberg (1991)
11. Gabidulin, E.M.: Public-key cryptosystems based on linear codes over large alphabets: efficiency and weakness. In: Farrell, P.G. (ed.) Codes and Cyphers, Formara Limited, Southend-on-sea, Essex, pp. 17–31 (1995)
12. Gabidulin, E.M., Ourivski, A.V.: Modified GPT PKC with right scrambler. In: Augot, D., Carlet, C. (eds.) Proceedings of the 2nd International workshop on Coding and Cryptography, WCC 2001, pp. 233–242 (2001), ISBN Number: 2-761-1179-3
13. Gabidulin, E.M., Paramonov, A.V., Tretjakov, O.V.: Ideals over a non-commutative ring and their application in cryptology. In: Davies, D.W. (ed.) EUROCRYPT 1991. LNCS, vol. 547, pp. 482–489. Springer, Heidelberg (1991)
14. Gaborit, P.: Shorter keys for code based cryptography. In: Proceedings of WCC 2005 (2005)
15. Gibson, J.K.: Severely denting the Gabidulin version of the McEliece public-key cryptosystem. Designs, Codes and Cryptography 6, 37–45 (1995)
16. Gibson, J.K.: The security of the Gabidulin public-key cryptosystem. In: Maurer, U.M. (ed.) EUROCRYPT 1996. LNCS, vol. 1070, pp. 212–223. Springer, Heidelberg (1996)
17. Kobara, K., Imai, H.: On the one-wayness against chosen-plaintext attacks of the Loidreau's modified McEliece PKC. IEEE Transactions on Information Theory 49(12), 3160–3168 (2003)
18. Loidreau, P.: Strengthening McEliece public-key cryptosystem. In: Okamoto, T. (ed.) ASIACRYPT 2000. LNCS, vol. 1976, p. 585. Springer, Heidelberg (2000)
19. Loidreau, P.: A Welch-Berlekamp like algorithm for decoding Gabidulin codes. In: Ytrehus, Ø. (ed.) WCC 2005. LNCS, vol. 3969, pp. 36–45. Springer, Heidelberg (2006)
20. McEliece, R.J.: A public-key cryptosystem based on algebraic coding theory. Technical report, Jet Propulsion Lab. DSN Progress Report (1978)
21. Misoczki, R., Barreto, P.: Compact McEliece keys from goppa codes. In: Rijmen, V. (ed.) SAC 2009. LNCS, vol. 5867, pp. 376–392. Springer, Heidelberg (2009)
22. Niederreiter, H.: Knapsack-type cryptosystems and algebraic coding theory. Problems of Control and Information Theory 15(2), 159–166 (1986)

23. Otmani, A., Tillich, J.P., Dallot, L.: Cryptanalysis of two mceliece cryptosystems based on quasi-cyclic codes. Mathematics in Computer Science (to appear)
24. Ourivski, A.V.: Recovering a parent code for subcodes of maximal rank distance codes. In: Augot, D., Charpin, P., Kabatianski, G. (eds.) Proceedings of the 3rd International workshop on Coding and Cryptography, WCC 2003, pp. 357–363 (2003), ISBN Number: 2-7261-1205-6
25. Ourivski, A.V., Gabidulin, E.M.: Column scrambler for the GPT cryptosystem. Discrete Applied Mathematics 128(1), 207–221 (2003); Special issue of the second International Workshop on Coding and Cryptography (WCC 2001)
26. Ourivski, A.V., Gabidulin, E.M., Honary, B., Ammar, B.: Reducible rank codes and their applications to cryptography. IEEE Transactions on Information Theory 49(12), 3289–3293 (2003)
27. Ourivski, A.V., Johannson, T.: New technique for decoding codes in the rank metric and its cryptography applications. Problems of Information Transmission 38(3), 237–246 (2002)
28. Overbeck, R.: A new structural attack for GPT and variants. In: Dawson, E., Vaudenay, S. (eds.) Mycrypt 2005. LNCS, vol. 3715, pp. 50–63. Springer, Heidelberg (2005)
29. Overbeck, R.: Extending Gibson's attacks on the GPT cryptosystem. In: Ytrehus, Ø. (ed.) WCC 2005. LNCS, vol. 3969, pp. 178–188. Springer, Heidelberg (2006)
30. Overbeck, R.: Structural attacks for public-key cryptosystems based on gabidulin codes. Journal of Cryptology 21(2), 280–301 (2008)
31. Richter, G., Plass, S.: Fast decoding of rank-codes with rank errors and column erasures. In: 2004 IEEE International Symposium on Information Theory, ISIT 2004 (2004)
32. Roth, R.M.: Maximum-Rank array codes and their application to crisscross error correction. IEEE Transactions on Information Theory 37(2), 328–336 (1991)
33. Sendrier, N.: Cryptosystèmes à clé publique basés sur les codes correcteurs d'erreurs (2001)
34. Vardy, A.: The intractability of computing the minimum distance of a code. IEEE Transactions on Information Theory 43(6), 1757–1766 (1997)

Secure Variants of the Square Encryption Scheme

Crystal Lee Clough[1] and Jintai Ding[2,3]

[1] Nanyang Technological University, Singapore
clclough@ntu.edu.sg
[2] University of Cincinnati, Cincinnati, OH USA
[3] Southern Chinese University of Technology

Abstract. This paper discusses two encryption schemes to fix the Square scheme. Square+ uses the Plus modification of appending randomly chosen polynomials. Double-Layer Square uses a construction similar to some signature schemes, splitting the variables into two layers, one of which depends on the other.

1 Introduction

Multivariate public-key cryptosystems (MPKCs) are thought to be one of the options for cryptography in a post-quantum setting. Some secure MPKC encryption schmes exist but they are slow and unwieldy in comparison with multivariate signature schemes. There is room for improvement in the realm of MPKCs.

In this paper we will show some new encryption schemes based on Square. The original Square system was broken via a differential attack and we show two different ways to thwart this attack. Square+ is a minor reformulation which differs from Square only by the addition of a few extra polynomials. Double-Layer Square is a more structural renovation, using layers of variables much like the Rainbow and Square-Vinegar signature schemes [1,7]. We make the case that both of these new options are secure against known attacks.

This paper is organized as follows: in Section 2 we describe the Square and HFE cryptosystems and attacks on them, in Section 3 we describe and analyze Square+, in Section 4 we describe and analyze Double-Layer Square, and we conclude in Section 5.

2 Background

The Square system and the variants of it that we will introduce here can be seen as a natural evolution of a sequence of MPKC schemes. Though not the first in this vein[1], the HFE (Hidden Field Equations) system of Patarin is a good starting point for this discussion because it is very general and also extensively analyzed (e.g., [4,8,9,11,12,13,16]).

[1] For example, the C^* scheme of Matsumoto and Imai [14] predates HFE by about 8 years.

N. Sendrier (Ed.): PQCrypto 2010, LNCS 6061, pp. 153–164, 2010.

2.1 HFE

Let k a field of size q and K a degree-n extension of k, say $K \cong k[y]/\langle g(y) \rangle$ for some irreducible g. In the original versions of HFE, k is characteristic 2.

The construction exploits the relationship between the standard vector space k^n and the field K (they are isomorphic as vector spaces but K has additional structure). Plaintext and ciphertext are vectors in k^n and accordingly, the public key is a map $k^n \to k^n$. The private key is a detour through K, using a map of a specific form.

Definition 1. *An HFE polynomial with bound D over K is a univariate polynomial of the form*

$$G(X) = \sum_{q^i+q^j \leq D} \alpha_{ij} X^{q^i+q^j} + \sum_{q^j \leq D} \beta_j X^{q^j} + \gamma,$$

with α_{ij}, β_j, $\gamma \in K$.

The reason for using HFE polynomials is to guarantee that the components of the public key are quadratic. Explicitly, an HFE system is constructed as follows: the public key is

$$P = L_1 \circ \varphi \circ F \circ \varphi^{-1} \circ L_2, \text{ where}$$

- $L_1, L_2 \colon k^n \to k^n$ are invertible affine maps
- $\varphi \colon K \to k^n$ is the vector space isomorphism

$$a_1 + a_2 y + \cdots + a_n y^{n-1} \mapsto (a_1, \ldots, a_n)$$

- $F \colon K \to K$ is an HFE polynomial of some bound D.

See Figure 1. The private key is the decomposition of P. Since F is a univariate polynomial of bounded degree, preimages under F can be found, using Berlekamp's algorithm for example.

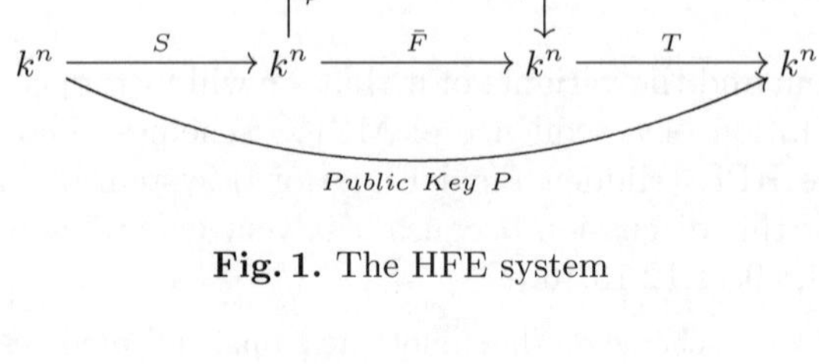

Fig. 1. The HFE system

Algebraic Attacks. The most straighforward way for an attacker holding a ciphertext $(y_1, \ldots, y_n) \in k^n$ and the public key P is to try to find the corresponding plaintext is to solve $P(x_1, \ldots, x_n) = (y_1, \ldots, y_n)$. This is a system of n quadratic equations in the n variables $x_1, \ldots, x_n$:

$$\begin{aligned} P_1(x_1, \ldots, x_n) - y_1 &= 0 \\ P_2(x_1, \ldots, x_n) - y_2 &= 0 \\ &\vdots \\ P_n(x_1, \ldots, x_n) - y_n &= 0. \end{aligned} \tag{1}$$

Breaking an MPKC by solving these equations directly is known as an algebraic attack. Since solutions to (1) are in the variety of the ideal $\langle P_1 - y_1, \ldots, P_n - y_n \rangle \subset k[x_1, \ldots, x_n]$, a Gröbner basis of this ideal is extremely helpful. For cases of cryptographic interest, the reduced Gröbner basis with respect to lex ordering will usually look like

$$\{f_1(x_n), f_2(x_{n-1}, x_n), \ldots, f_n(x_1, x_2, \ldots, x_n)\},$$

whose zero set can be found, via back-substitution, as easily as n univariate polynomial equations can be solved. One of the best algorithms to compute a Gröbner basis is the F_4 algorithm of Faugère [10].

In fact, using F_4 for find the Gröbner basis of the corresponding ideal seems to be the most effective way of algebraically attacking MPKCs[2] and are particularly effective against characteristic-2 HFE systems. Faugère used F_4 to break several instances of HFE [11], though it is important to note that these are characteristic-2 cases. It was later pointed out that the characteristic has a significant effect on the performance of F_4 , since an attacker can make use of the field equations $x^q - x = 0$ [8].

2.2 Square

Square was proposed in [3]. This attempt at a new MPKC was motivated by observations about the characteristic's effect on F_4 [8], and the then-apparent success in using odd-characteristic HFE as the foundation of a signature scheme [1]. All of the ideas of Square have been seen before; what makes this system novel is that these ideas are combined in a new way.

See Figure 2. Let k be a field of size q, and here we force $q \equiv 3 \mod 4$. Plaintexts will be vectors in k^n. Embed k^n into a larger space k^{n+l} via an injective affine map $L_1 \colon k^n \to k^{n+l}$. We choose n and l so that $n + l$ is odd.

Let K be a degree $n+l$ extension of k. Just as for HFE, we use a vector space isomorphism $\varphi \colon K \to k^{n+l}$ and an invertible affine map $L_2 \colon k^{n+l} \to k^{n+l}$. For the core map $K \to K$, we use

$$F(X) = X^2,$$

[2] Other polynomial solving algorithms exist, in particular the XL algorithm and its improvements [13,15], but at present they outperform F_4 only in contrived cases.

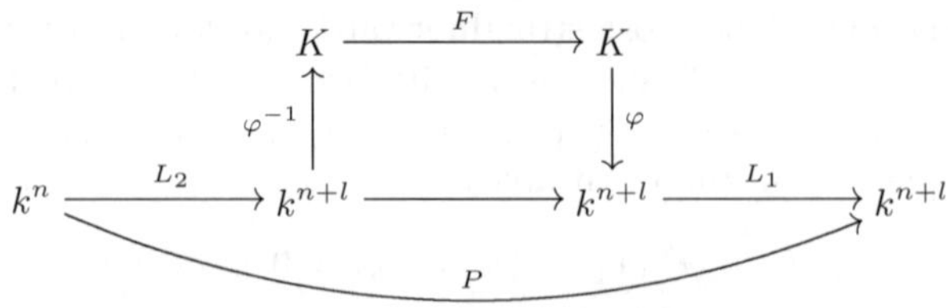

Fig. 2. The Square system

hence the name Square. From these we construct the public key

$$P = L_1 \circ \varphi \circ F \circ \varphi^{-1} \circ L_2.$$

P will be an $(n+l)$-tuple of quadratic polynomials in n variables. The Square setup is quite similar to that of HFE and the earlier C^* scheme of [14]; in fact one may think of it as an odd-characteristic, embedded HFE with $D = 2$ and a specifically chosen HFE polynomial.

The decryption process is the real selling point of Square. When $|K| \equiv 3 \mod 4$, we can find preimages under F using the square root formula

$$X = \pm Y^{\frac{q^{n+l}+1}{4}}. \tag{2}$$

This makes decryption fast, especially in comparison to traditional characteristic-2 HFE systems, whose core maps have very high degree.

An Attack on Square. Though Square was shown to be strong against algebraic attacks, it was broken by what may be categorized as a differential attack [2]. Recall that the discrete differential of a function f is

$$Df(A, X) = f(A+X) - f(A) - f(X) + f(0).$$

We will hereafter refer to the below as the "Square attack".

Let us work over K. To emphasize that L_1 and L_2 (and hence their lifts) are affine, let

$$\varphi^{-1} \circ L_1 \circ \varphi = \widehat{L}_1 + \hat{l}_1,$$
$$\varphi^{-1} \circ L_2 \circ \varphi' = \widehat{L}_2 + \hat{l}_2,$$

where $\varphi' : \mathbb{F}_{q^n} \to k^n$, $\widehat{L}_i$ linear and $\hat{l}_i \in K$. Also let

$$\widehat{P} = \varphi^{-1} \circ P \circ \varphi',$$

$$X = \varphi^{-1}(\overrightarrow{x}) \text{ and } Y = \varphi^{-1}(\overrightarrow{y}).$$

Using this notation,

$$\begin{aligned}\widehat{P}(X) &= \widehat{L}_1(\widehat{L}_2(X)^2) + \widehat{L}_1(\hat{l}_2 \cdot \widehat{L}_2(X)) + \hat{l}_1 \\ &= \text{quadratic} + \text{linear} + \text{constant}.\end{aligned}$$

By fixing some $A \in K$, we can view the differential $D\widehat{P}$ as a univariate function

$$D\widehat{P}_A(X) = D\widehat{P}(X, A) = \widehat{L}_1 \circ M_A \circ \widehat{L}_2(X),$$

where M_A denotes multiplication by a constant which depends on A $\{D\widehat{P}_A \colon A \in K\}$ are all linear maps and they form a vector space over K.

Now, every $D\widehat{P}_A$ is of the form $\widehat{L}_1 \circ M_A \circ \widehat{L}_2$ and the linear part of $\widehat{P}$, $\widehat{L}_1(\hat{l}_2 \cdot \widehat{L}_2(X))$, has a similar form. By picking a basis for these we obtain a set

$$\begin{aligned} \Delta &= \{D\widehat{P}_{A_1} \dots, D\widehat{P}_{A_n}\} \cup \{\widehat{L}_1(\hat{l}_2 \cdot \widehat{L}_2(X))\} \\ &= \{D_i = \widehat{L}_1 \circ M_{\lambda_i} \circ \widehat{L}_2; M_{\lambda_i}(X) = \lambda_i X, i = 1, \dots, n+1\} \end{aligned}$$

for some unknown $\lambda_1, \dots, \lambda_{n+1}$.

The maps of Δ are helpful because they can help us identify $\widehat{L}_1$. This is due to the fact that

$$(\widehat{L}_1 \circ M_\lambda \circ \widehat{L}_1^{-1})(\widehat{L}_1 \circ M_{\lambda_i} \circ \widehat{L}_2) = \widehat{L}_1 \circ M_{\lambda\lambda_i} \circ \widehat{L}_2. \tag{3}$$

We look for solutions L to the system of equations

$$L \circ D_i \in Span\{D_j \colon j > m\}, \quad i \leq m. \tag{4}$$

We are guaranteed by (3) that among the solutions will be some $\widehat{L}_1 \circ M_\lambda \circ \widehat{L}_1^{-1}$.

Once such an L is known, L_1 and L_2 can be recovered and Square is broken.

3 Square+

The Plus modification has been seen before, first by Patarin [17], but was considered useless and did not receive much attention. The real example of its use is to counter differential attacks of a system called Perturbed Matsumoto-Imai [6]. This motivated us to look at a Plus variant of Square.

The modification is simple: for any MPKC, a Plus variant can be constructed by appending some number p of randomly chosen quadratic polynomials to the public key before a final mixing process. Let us describe this specifically for the case of Square.

As usual, let k be a field of size q, where $q \equiv 3 \mod 4$. Plaintexts will be vectors in k^n, we will embed the space of plaintexts into k^{n+l}, and K is a field extension of degree $n+l$. Let $m = n+l+p$. As for Square, we make use of the following maps: the vector space isomorphism $\varphi\colon K \to k^{n+l}$, the core map $F\colon K \to K$ given by

$$F(X) = X^2,$$

and an injective affine map $L_2\colon k^n \to k^{n+l}$. We also use p quadratic polynomials in $n+l$ variables,

$$g_1, \dots, g_p \in k[x_1, \dots, x_{n+l}]$$

and an invertible affine map $L_1\colon k^m \to k^m$.

Since $\varphi \circ F \circ \varphi^{-1}$ is an $(n+l)$-tuple of quadratic polynomials, by appending $g_1, \ldots, g_p$ we can create a map $\overline{F}^+ : k^n \to k^m$. From this we construct the public key

$$P^+ = L_1 \circ \overline{F}^+ \circ L_2.$$

See Figure 3. P^+ will be an m-tuple of quadratic polynomials

$$P^+(x_1, \ldots, x_n) = \begin{pmatrix} P_1^+(x_1, \ldots, x_n) \\ P_2^+(x_1, \ldots, x_n) \\ \vdots \\ P_m^+(x_1, \ldots, x_n) \end{pmatrix}.$$

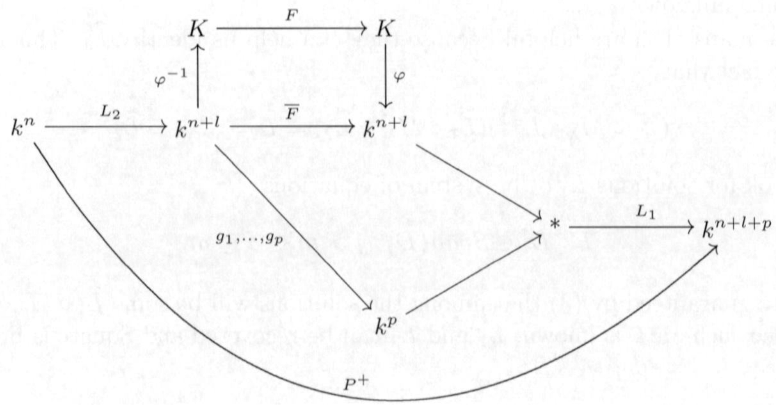

Fig. 3. Overview of the Square+ system. The * denotes concatenation.

Encryption with Square+. A plaintext $(s_1, \ldots, s_n) \in k^n$ in encrypted by computing

$$(c_1, \ldots, c_m) = P^+(s_1, \ldots, s_n).$$

Decryption with Square+. For a ciphertext $(c_1, \ldots, c_m) = P^+(s_1, \ldots, s_n) \in k^m$, decryption is performed as follows: first, let

$$(y_1, \ldots, y_m) = L_1^{-1}(c_1, \ldots, c_m)$$

and

$$Y = \varphi^{-1}(y_1, \ldots, y_{n+l}) \in K.$$

In other words, we "unmix" the random polynomials and discard them before moving the ciphertext to the big field. Then we solve $X^2 = Y$. Due to our choice of q and $n + l$, we can use the square root formula (2). This gives two solutions. Since L_2 is affine, in general only one of them will be in the image of $\varphi^{-1} \circ L_2$. The preimage of the solution will be $(s_1, \ldots, s_n)$. Note that with the Plus polynomials, we have a backup method of deciding between the two square roots. The addition of random polynomials all but ensures that only one of them will actually be a preimage of the ciphertext under P^+.

Security Analysis. The main question regarding the security of Square+ is, How do the Plus polynomials change the potency of attacks against Square? The answer is that some attacks become more successful, some are thwarted, and others are mostly unaffected.

When Square was proposed, justifications were made for its resilience to attacks reliant on invariant subspaces and/or properties of the bilinear forms associated to the public key [3]. The addition of random polynomial information will not increase the probability of linear algebraic properties of the core map. Of course, an attacker could find linear combinations of the public key polynomials and come across a large enough collection (around $n+l$) which are a combination of only the original Square public key components. The chance of an attacker doing so randomly is $q^{-p(n+l)}$ and at present there does not seem to be any way to find these combinations in a more effficient way. So, there is no reason that Plus polynomials will make these attacks suddenly dangerous.

On the other hand, providing more polynomial information about the plaintext-ciphertext relationship *will* make algebraic attacks predictably more effective. See Figures 4 and 5 for a summary of our experiments regarding algebraic attack times for some Square+ systems. Thus it is important to use a small p not only for practicality reasons but also security. Considering the results of our algebraic attack experiments and extrapolating the data, it seems that a Square+ scheme with $q = 31$, $n = 48$, $l = 3$, and $p = 5$ looks promising.

The reason for adding the Plus polynomials is to dodge the Square attack. Since we add quadratic polynomials, the "noise" they create affects the differentials. In particular, if we proceed as in the Square atttack - work in an extension

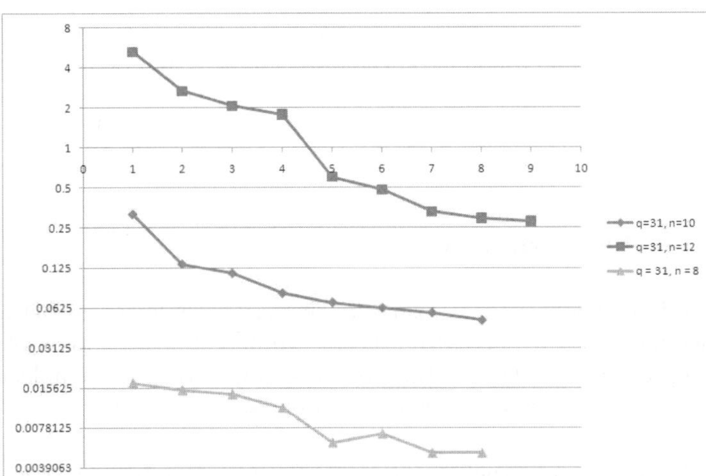

Fig. 4. Algebraic Attack times against Square+ vs p, for various q and n. The value of l is 3 for all tests.

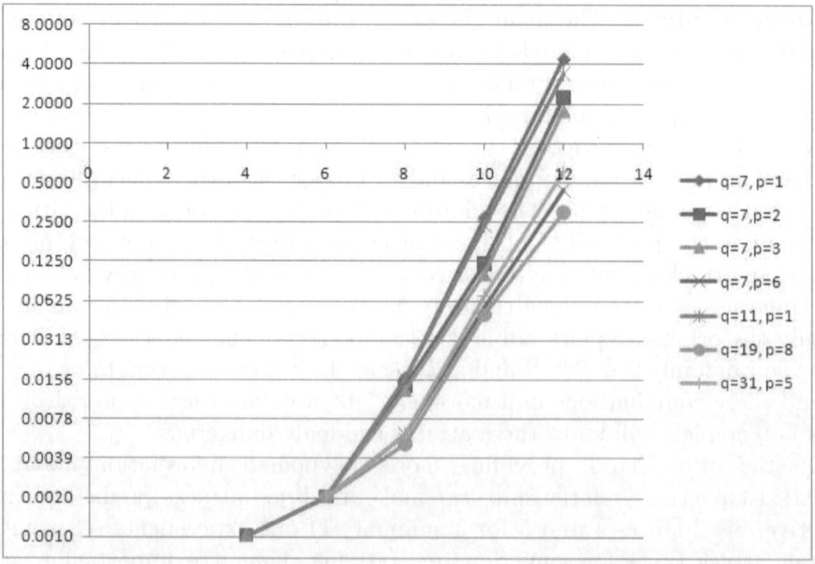

Fig. 5. Algebraic Attack times against Square+ vs n, for various q and p. The value of l is 3 for all tests.

field and fix one input of the differential as in (2.2), we see that

$$D\widehat{P}_A = \widehat{L}_1 \circ M_A \circ \widehat{L}_2 + L,$$

for some linear map L which comes from the randomly-chosen Plus polynomials and thus should also be random. So the differentials of teh Square+ public key cannot be used in the same way as in 3 to identify the secret transformation. Plus was effectively used to protect the Perturbed Matsumoto-Imai system from differential attack in [6].

4 Double-Layer Square

The Plus variant of Square uses "cosmetic" changes to the structure of the system to obstruct an attacker's access to the nice differential properties of Square. Another approach is to destroy the properties altogether by complicating the core map. This is the main idea behind Double-Layer Square.

Construction. The construction takes cues from the Rainbow signature scheme [7]. The variables are split into two "layers"; some of the input components determine the polynomial into which other components are fed. We will discuss below why an attacker should not be able to separate the layers.

Again $|k| = q \equiv 3 \mod 4$. Plaintexts are vectors in k^{2n}, n odd. Let $L_2 \colon k^{2n} \to k^{2n+l}$ be an affine transformation of rank $2n$.

Remark. Here, we would like to note that this map L_2 uses the idea of embedding proposed to enhance the security of Sflash in [5]. The application of this embedding is critical in ensuring the security of our new scheme.

The first layer: Let $K \cong k^{n+l}$ via vector space isomorphism φ and $F\colon K \to K$ be given by $F(X) = X^2$. The map

$$\overline{F} = \varphi \circ F \circ \varphi^{-1}$$

is an $(n+l)$-tuple of quadratic polynomials in $n+l$ variables.

The second layer: Let $K' \cong k^n$ via the vector space isomorphism φ'. Consider the map $G\colon k^{n+l} \times K' \to K'$ given by

$$G((x_1, \ldots, x_{n+l}), X) = \alpha X^2 + \beta(x_1, \ldots, x_{n+l})X + \gamma(x_1, \ldots, x_{n+l}),$$

where $\alpha \in K'$, β is affine and γ is quadratic[3]. The map

$$\overline{G} = \varphi' \circ G \circ (id \times \varphi'^{-1}),$$

is an n-tuple of quadratic polynomials in $2n+l$ variables.

Altogether by concatenating the first and second layers, we obtain a map $k^{2n+l} \to k^{2n+l}$ given by

$$\overline{F} * \overline{G} = \begin{pmatrix} \overline{F}_1(x_1, \ldots, x_{n+l}) \\ \overline{F}_2(x_1, \ldots, x_{n+l}) \\ \vdots \\ \overline{F}_{n+l}(x_1, \ldots, x_{n+l}) \\ \overline{G}_1(x_1, \ldots, x_{2n+l}) \\ \overline{G}_2(x_1, \ldots, x_{2n+l}) \\ \vdots \\ \overline{G}_n(x_1, \ldots, x_{2n+l}) \end{pmatrix}.$$

Using with the embedding L_2 and a final invertible transformation $L_1\colon k^{2n+l} \to k^{2n+l}$ we get a public key $P\colon k^{2n} \to k^{2n+l}$

$$P = L_1 \circ (\overline{F} * \overline{G}) \circ L_2.$$

Encryption. To encrypt a message $(m_1, \ldots, m_{2n}) \in k^{2n}$, simply compute

$$(c_1, \ldots, c_{2n+l}) = P(m_1, \ldots, m_{2n}).$$

---

[3] More precisely the maps β_i and γ are of the form

$$\beta_i(x_1, \ldots, x_{n+l}) = \sum_{1 \le j \le n+l} \xi_{ij} x_j + \nu_i,$$

$$\gamma(x_1, \ldots, x_{n+l}) = \sum_{1 \le j < l \le n+l} \eta_{jk} x_j x_k + \sum_{1 \le j \le n+l} \sigma_j x_j + \tau,$$

where ξ_{ij}, ν_i, η_{jl}, σ_j and τ are randomly chosen from K'.

Decryption. Given a ciphertext $(c_1, \ldots, c_{2n+l})$ we must first compute

$$(c'_1, \ldots, c'_{2n+l}) = L_1^{-1}(c_1, \ldots, c_{2n+l}) \in k^{2n+l}.$$

We know that $\overline{F}(x_1 \ldots, x_{n+l}) = (c'_1, \ldots, c'_{n+l})$. We can easily find preimages under $\overline{F}$ by going back to the "big field" K and using the square root formula in K:

$$\sqrt{Y} = \pm Y^{\frac{q^{n+l}+1}{4}} \tag{5}$$

Suppose $(z_1^{(1)}, \ldots, z_{n+l}^{(1)})$ and $(z_1^{(2)}, \ldots, z_{n+l}^{(2)})$ are the two preimages under $\overline{F}$. Now we find a preimage under $\overline{G}$ using each as vinegar variables. We solve

$$G((z_1^{(i)}, \ldots, z_{n+l}^{(i)}), X) = \varphi'^{-1}(c_{n+l+1}, \ldots, c_{2n+l}).$$

With the $z_j^{(i)}$s plugged in, this is just a univariate polynomial equation over K'. We can solve it either by Berlekamp's algorithm or via the quadratic formula, again using the square root formula (5).

Now there are up to four preimages of $\overline{F} * \overline{G}$. However, the correct preimage must lie in $L_2(k^n)$; in general only one will do so and that preimage is the plaintext. We work under the assumption that we are trying to decrypt an encrypted message, so at least one of the possibilities will lie in this space.

Remark 1. There is no reason why we cannot use more than two layers in this construction. However, each layer will increase by a factor of 2 the number of preimages to be checked in the final stage of the decryption process. Since two layers seem to be enough to stymie attacks, there is no reason to slow the decryption process with added layers.

Security Analysis. First we observe that algebraic attacks against Double-Layer Square systems perform about as well as against Square systems with the same number of variables. Thus we believe that Double-Layer Square is safe from algebraic attacks.

Many successful attacks on MPKCs exploit the simplicity of private maps when viewed as univariate polynomials, and this gives Double-Layer Square an advantage. The univariate polynomial which corresponds to $\overline{F} * \overline{G}$ is an HFE polynomial over a degree $2n + l$ extension, but in general it will have maximum degree $(2q^{n+l-1})$ and many terms. The Square attack relies on the differential property $DF(A, X) = 2AX$ which is not true for most HFE polynomials.

So, lifting to a large field and working with a univariate polynomial does not seem to help an attacker. Let us consider the differential of the core map as it is given. Let

$$(a_1, \ldots, a_{2n+l}), (x_1, \ldots, x_{2n+l}) \in k^{2n+l},$$

$$\boldsymbol{a} = (a_1, \ldots, a_{n+l}) \in k^{n+l},$$

$$A = \varphi^{-1}(\boldsymbol{a}) \in K,$$

$$A' = \varphi^{-1'}(a_{n+l+1}, \ldots, a_{2n+l}) \in K'.$$

(Analogous $\boldsymbol{x}$, X and X'.) Then the differentials are

$$DF(A, X) = 2AX \tag{6}$$

$$DG((\boldsymbol{a}, A'), (\boldsymbol{x}, X')) = 2\alpha A'X"' + \beta(\boldsymbol{a})X' + \beta(\boldsymbol{x})A' + D\gamma(\boldsymbol{a}, \boldsymbol{x}). \tag{7}$$

It is true that DF is the same as for Square. However $\boldsymbol{a}$ and $\boldsymbol{x}$ appear in both (6) and (7), and γ is randomly chosen so we cannot expect $D\gamma$ to have any nice properties. Once $\overline{F}$ and $\overline{G}$ are mixed together by L_1, it seems highly unlikely that an attacker can untangle the two differentials to access the simpler one (6).

5 Conclusions

In this paper, we proposed two new encryption schemes based on the Square system. Square+ evades differential attacks by adding noise to the differentials by way of Plus polynomials; Double-Layer Square achieves the same end by using a more complicated core map structure. We explained the new constructions and gave arguments and evidence suggesting that both are secure options.

Acknowledgments. The authors would like to thank Dr. John Baena Giraldo for his help designing the experiments. Thanks also go to the Singapore MoE Tier 2 grant T208B2206, the NSF, NSF China and the Charles Phelps Taft Foundation.

References

1. Baena, J., Clough, C., Ding, J.: Square-Vinegar Signature Scheme. In: Buchmann, J., Ding, J. (eds.) PQCrypto 2008. LNCS, vol. 5299, pp. 17–30. Springer, Heidelberg (2008)
2. Billet, O., Gilles, M.-R.: Cryptanalysis of the Square Cryptosystems. In: Matsui, M. (ed.) ASIACRYPT 2009. LNCS, vol. 5912, pp. 451–468. Springer, Heidelberg (2009)
3. Clough, C., Baena, J., Ding, J., Yang, B.-Y., Chen, M.: Square, a new multivariate encryption scheme. In: Fischlin, M. (ed.) CT-RSA 2009. LNCS, vol. 5473, pp. 252–264. Springer, Heidelberg (2009)
4. Courtois, N.: The security of hidden field equations (HFE). In: Naccache, D. (ed.) CT-RSA 2001. LNCS, vol. 2020, pp. 266–281. Springer, Heidelberg (2001)
5. Ding, J., Dubois, V., Yang, B.-Y., Owen Chen, C.-H., Cheng Could, C.-M.: Could SFLASH be Repaired? In: Aceto, L., Damgård, I., Goldberg, L.A., Halldórsson, M.M., Ingólfsdóttir, A., Walukiewicz, I. (eds.) ICALP 2008, Part II. LNCS, vol. 5126, pp. 691–701. Springer, Heidelberg (2008)
6. Ding, J., Gower, J.E., et al.: Inoculating Multivariate Schemes against differential attacks. In: Yung, M., Dodis, Y., Kiayias, A., Malkin, T.G. (eds.) PKC 2006. LNCS, vol. 3958, pp. 290–301. Springer, Heidelberg (2006)
7. Ding, J., Schmidt, D.: Rainbow, a new multivariable polynomial signature scheme. In: Ioannidis, J., Keromytis, A.D., Yung, M. (eds.) ACNS 2005. LNCS, vol. 3531, pp. 164–175. Springer, Heidelberg (2005)

8. Ding, J., Schmidt, D., Werner, F.: Algebraic attack on HFE revisited. In: Wu, T.-C., Lei, C.-L., Rijmen, V., Lee, D.-T. (eds.) ISC 2008. LNCS, vol. 5222, pp. 215–227. Springer, Heidelberg (2008)
9. Dubois, V., Granboulan, L., Stern, J.: An efficient provable distinguisher for HFE. In: Bugliesi, M., Preneel, B., Sassone, V., Wegener, I. (eds.) ICALP 2006. LNCS, vol. 4052, pp. 156–167. Springer, Heidelberg (2006)
10. Faugére, J.-C.: A new efficient algorithm for computing Gröbner bases (F_4). J. Pure Appl. Algebra 139(1-3), 61–88 (1999); Effective methods in algebraic geometry (Saint-Malo, 1998)
11. Faugère, J.-C., Joux, A.: Algebraic cryptanalysis of hidden field equation (HFE) cryptosystems using Gröbner bases. In: Boneh, D. (ed.) CRYPTO 2003. LNCS, vol. 2729, pp. 44–60. Springer, Heidelberg (2003)
12. Jiang, X., Ding, J., Hu, L.: Public Key Analysis-Kipnis-Shamir Attack on HFE Revisited. In: Pei, D., Yung, M., Lin, D., Wu, C. (eds.) Inscrypt 2007. LNCS, vol. 4990, pp. 399–411. Springer, Heidelberg (2008)
13. Kipnis, A., Shamir, A.: Cryptanalysis of the HFE public key cryptosystem by relinearization. In: Wiener, M. (ed.) CRYPTO 1999. LNCS, vol. 1666, pp. 19–30. Springer, Heidelberg (1999)
14. Matsumoto, T., Imai, H.: Public quadratic polynomial-tuples for efficient signature-verification and message-encryption. In: Günther, C.G. (ed.) EUROCRYPT 1988. LNCS, vol. 330, pp. 419–453. Springer, Heidelberg (1988)
15. Mohamed, M.S.E., Mohamed, W., Ding, J., Buchmann, J.: MXL2: Solving Polynomial Equations over GF (2) Using an Improved Mutant Strategy. In: Buchmann, J., Ding, J. (eds.) PQCrypto 2008. LNCS, vol. 5299, pp. 203–215. Springer, Heidelberg (2008)
16. Patarin, J.: Hidden Field Equations (HFE) and Isomorphisms of Polynomials (IP): Two new families of asymmetric algorithms. In: Maurer, U.M. (ed.) EUROCRYPT 1996. LNCS, vol. 1070, pp. 33–48. Springer, Heidelberg (1996)
17. Patarin, J., Goubin, L., Courtois, N.: C*-+ and HM: Variations around two schemes of T. Matsumoto and H. Imai. In: Ohta, K., Pei, D. (eds.) ASIACRYPT 1998. LNCS, vol. 1514, pp. 35–50. Springer, Heidelberg (1998)

Low-Reiter: Niederreiter Encryption Scheme for Embedded Microcontrollers

Stefan Heyse

Horst Görtz Institute for IT Security
Ruhr University Bochum
44780 Bochum, Germany
heyse@crypto.rub.de

Abstract. Most modern security systems rely on public-key schemes based either on the factorization or the discrete logarithm problem. Since both problems are known to be closely related, a major breakthrough in cryptanalysis affecting one of those problems could render a large set of cryptosystems completely useless. Coding based public-key schemes are based on the alternative security assumption that decoding unknown linear binary codes is NP-complete. There exist two basic schemes of this type, namely McEliece and the Niederreiter variant, whereas the security of both schemes are equivalent. The latter has the advantage of smaller public keys, but the disadvantage of a computationally expensive mapping, which slows down encryption and decryption.

In this work, we investigate the efficient implementation of the Niederreiter scheme on very constrained micro controllers. We adopt existing algorithms to the limited abilities of the target platform and finally compare the implementation to widely used schemes and also to other alternative public schemes.

1 Introduction

The advanced properties of public-key cryptosystems are required for many cryptographic issues, such as key establishment between parties and digital signatures. In this context, RSA, ElGamal, and later ECC have evolved as most popular choices and build the foundation for virtually all practical security protocols and implementations with requirements for public-key cryptography. However, these cryptosystems rely on two primitive security assumptions, namely the factoring problem (FP) and the discrete logarithm problem (DLP), which are also known to be closely related. With a significant breakthrough in cryptanalysis or a major improvement of the best known attacks on these problems (i.e., the *Number Field Sieve* or *Index Calculus*), a large number of recently employed cryptosystems may turn out to be insecure overnight. Already the existence of a quantum computer that can provide computations on a few thousand qubits would render FP and DLP-based cryptography useless. Though quantum computers of that dimension have not been reported to be built yet, we already want to encourage a larger *diversification* of cryptographic primitives in

N. Sendrier (Ed.): PQCrypto 2010, LNCS 6061, pp. 165–181, 2010.

future public-key systems. However, to be accepted as real alternatives to conventional systems like RSA and ECC, such security primitives need to support efficient implementations on recent computing platforms with a comparable level of security.

The first cryptosystem based on error correcting codes was proposed by Robert J. McEliece in 1978 [22]. The Niederreiter encryption scheme was derived from it in 1986 [24], but has the advantage of smaller keys (and it can be transformed into a signature scheme).

Both cryptosystems incorporate a linear error-correcting code (namely a Goppa code) which is hidden as a general linear code. For Goppa codes, fast decoding algorithms exist when the code is known, while decoding codewords without knowledge of the coding scheme is proven NP-complete [2]. Contrary to DLP and FP-based systems, this makes this scheme also suitable in the post-quantum era. Currently there is no know attack when appropriately chosen security parameters are used [5].

The vast majority[1] of today's computing platforms are embedded systems[33]. Only a few years ago, most of these devices could only provide a few hundred bytes of RAM and ROM which was a strong restriction for application (and security) designers. Thus, both schemes were regarded impracticable on such small and embedded systems due to the large size of the private and public keys. But nowadays, recent families of microcontrollers provide several hundreds of bytes of Flash-ROM. In particular, these memories can be used to store the keys of the Niederreiter cryptosystem.

In this work, we present an implementation of the Niederreiter encryption scheme on a popular 8-bit AVR micro controller, namely the ATxMega256, which is suitable for many embedded system applications. To the best of our knowledge, no implementation of the Niederreiter scheme has been proposed targeting 8 bit micro controllers. Unlike FP and DLP-based cryptosystems, operations on binary codes do not require computationally expensive multi-precision integer arithmetic which is beneficial for small computing platforms.

This paper is structured as follows: we start with a brief introduction of the Niederreiter scheme and shortly explain necessary operations on Goppa codes. In Section 4, we discuss requirements and strategies to implement Niederreiter on memory-constrained embedded devices. Section 5 describes our actual implementation on an AVR 8-bit microprocessor. Finally, we present our result in Section 6.

2 Previous Work

Although proposed already more than 30 years ago, coding based encryption schemes have never gained much attention due to their large keys and thus have not been implemented in many products. The most recent implementation of the McEliece scheme on PCs is due to Biswas and Sendrier [7] and presented

[1] Already in 2002, 98% of 32-bit microprocessors in world-wide production were integrated in embedded platforms.

a slightly modified version that achieves about 83 bit security (taking the attack in [5] into account). Comparing their implementation to other public key schemes, it turns out that McEliece encryption can even be faster than of RSA and NTRU [4]. In addition to those, only few further McEliece software implementations have been published up to now and they were all designed for 32 bit architectures [26,27]. The more recent implementation [27] is available only as uncommented C-source code and was nevertheless used for the open-source P2P software Freenet and Entropy [16].

The latest implementation of McEliece for embedded devices is [14]. It is very interesting to compare our work to this implementation, because it uses the same security parameters and nearly the same platform.

3 Background on the Niederreiter Cryptosystem

Because Niederreiter heavily relies on Goppa codes, we start with an introduction to this class of error correcting codes.

3.1 Classical Goppa Codes

Theorem 1. *[34] Let $G(z)$ be an irreducible polynomial of degree t over $GF(2^m)$. Then the set*

$$\Gamma(G(z), GF(2^m)) = \{(c_\alpha)_{\alpha \in GF(2^m)} \in \{0,1\}^n \mid \sum_{\alpha \in GF(2^m)} \frac{c_\alpha}{z-\alpha} \equiv 0 \bmod G(z)\} \tag{1}$$

defines a binary Goppa code C of length $n = 2^m$, dimension $k \geq n - mt$ and minimum distance $d \geq 2t + 1$. The set of the α_i is called the support$\mathcal{L}$ of the code.

There exist fast decoding algorithms with a runtime of $O(n \cdot t)$ operations (e.g [25,32]). For each irreducible polynomial $G(z)$ over $GF(2^m)$ of degree t exists a binary Goppa code of length $n = 2^m$ and dimension $k = n - mt$. This code is capable of correcting up to t errors [1] and can be described as a $k \times n$ generator matrix G such that $C = \{mG : m \in F_2^k\}$.

To encode a message m into a codeword c, represent the message m as a binary string of length k and multiply it with the $k \times n$ matrix G.

However, decoding such a codeword $r = c + e$ on the receiver's side with a (possibly) additive error vector e is far more complex. For decoding, we use Patterson's algorithm [25] with improvements from [31].

Since $r = c + e \equiv e \mod G(z)$ holds, the syndrome $Syn(z)$ of a received codeword can be obtained from Equation (1) by

$$Syn(z) = \sum_{\alpha \in GF(2^m)} \frac{r_\alpha}{z-\alpha} \equiv \sum_{\alpha \in GF(2^m)} \frac{e_\alpha}{z-\alpha} \mod G(z) \tag{2}$$

To finally recover $\underline{e}$, we need to solve the key equation $\sigma(z) \cdot Syn(z) \equiv \omega(z) \mod G(z)$, where $\sigma(z)$ denotes a corresponding error-locator polynomial and

$\omega(z)$ denotes an error-weight polynomial. Note that it can be shown that $\omega(z) = \sigma(z)'$ is the formal derivative of the error-locator and by splitting $\sigma(z)$ into even and odd polynomial parts $\sigma(z) = a(z)^2 + z \cdot b(z)^2$, we finally determine the following equation to determine error positions:

$$Syn(z)(a(z)^2 + z \cdot b(z)^2) \equiv b(z)^2 \mod G(z) \tag{3}$$

To solve Equation (3) for a given codeword $\underline{r}$, the following steps have to be performed:

1. Compute the syndrome $Syn(z)$ from the received codeword r according to Equation (2). This can be done by using the extended euclidean algorithm or by directly computing corresponding field elements. Another option is to precompute the parity check matrix and perform the matrix multiplication as simple table lookups.
2. Compute an inverse polynomial $T(z)$ with $T(z) \cdot Syn(z) \equiv 1 \mod G(z)$ (or provide a corresponding table). It follows that $(T(z) + z)b(z)^2 \equiv a(z)^2 \mod G(z)$.
3. There is a simple case if $T(z) = z \Rightarrow a(z) = 0$ s.t. $b(z)^2 \equiv z \cdot b(z)^2 \cdot Syn(z) \mod G(z) \Rightarrow 1 \equiv z \cdot Syn(z) \mod G(z)$ which directly leads to $\sigma(z) = z$. Contrary, if $T(z) \neq z$, compute a square root $R(z)$ for the given polynomial $R(z)^2 \equiv T(z) + z \mod G(z)$. Based on an observation by Huber [19] this can be done by a simple polynomial multiplication. We can then determine solutions $a(z), b(z)$ satisfying
$$a(z) = b(z) \cdot R(z) \mod G(z). \tag{4}$$
using the extended euclidean algorithm. The computation is stopped, when $a(z)$ reaches degree $\lfloor \frac{t}{2} \rfloor$. Finally, we use the identified $a(z), b(z)$ to construct the error-locator polynomial $\sigma(z) = a(z)^2 + z \cdot b(z)^2$.
4. The roots of $\sigma(z)$ denote the positions of error bits. If $\sigma(\alpha_i) \equiv 0 \mod G(z)$ with α_i being the corresponding bit of a generator in $GF(2^{11})$, there was an error at position i in the received codeword which can be corrected by bit-flipping. Searching the roots of polynomials of degree t over $GF(2^m)$ is very time consuming. Aside of plain evaluation in all support elements, the two most commonly used methods are the Chien search [9] and the Horner scheme [18]. We use the latter one, because is it slightly faster and the field elements can be searched independently. This property can be useful, while implementing side channel countermeasures. Another method proposed in [6], which is faster on PCs, turned out to be slower on microprocessor since we can not store the necessary precomputed values for a fast implementation.

This decoding process, as required in Step 2 of Algorithm 3 for message decryption, is finally summarized in Algorithm 1.

3.2 The Niederreiter Public Key Scheme

The Niederreiter scheme is a public key cryptosystem based on linear error-correcting codes. The secret key is the parity check matrix H of an error-correcting code with dimension k, length n and error correcting capability t.

Algorithm 1. Decoding Goppa Codes

Input: Received codeword r with up to t errors, inverse generator matrix iG
Output: Recovered message $\hat{m}$

```
Compute syndrome Syn(z) for codeword r
T(z) ← Syn(z)^{-1} mod G(z)
if T(z) = z then
    σ(z) ← z
else
    R(z) ← √(T(z) + z)
    Compute a(z) and b(z) with a(z) ≡ b(z) · R(z) mod G(z)
    σ(z) ← a(z)^2 + z · b(z)^2
end if
Determine roots of σ(z) and correct errors in r which results in r̂
m̂ ← r̂ · iG {Map r_cor to m̂}
return m̂
```

To create a public key, Niederreiter defined a random $n \times n$-dimensional permutation matrix P disguising the structure of the code by computing the product $\hat{H} = S \times H \times P$. Here, S is the $(n-k) \times (n-k)$ matrix, which brings $\hat{H}$ to systematic form. Using the public key $K_{pub} = (\hat{H}, t)$ and private key $K_{sec} = (P^{-1}, H, S^{-1})$, encryption and decryption algorithms can be given by Algorithm 2 and Algorithm 3, respectively.

Using our parameter set $(m = 11, t = 27)$ leads to a size of S of 374 KBytes, which is too large to be efficiently stored inside the microcontroller. We decide to use a PRNG to generate the columns of S at runtime, but then S is a random matrix and can not bring $\hat{H}$ to systematic form. But saving 374 KBytes for S by allowing $\hat{H}$ to be 74 Kbyte instead of 63 Kbyte makes it possible to store all secret information inside the flash of the AVR.

Algorithm 2. Niederreiter Message Encryption

Input: $m, K_{pub} = (\hat{H}, t)$
Output: Ciphertext c

```
Encode the message m as a binary string of length n and weight t called e
c = Ĥe^T
return c
```

Note that Algorithm 2 only consists of a simple matrix multiplication with the input message after it is transformed into a so called constant weight word. The algorithm for constant weight encoding (Bin2CW) is given in Section 3.4.

Decoding the ciphertext c for decryption as shown in Algorithm 3 is the most time-consuming process and requires several more complex operations in binary extension fields. In Section 3.1 we briefly introduced the required steps for decoding codewords that we need to implement on embedded systems.

As mentioned in the introduction, the main caveat against coding based cryptosystems is the significant size of the public and private keys. Even the choice

Algorithm 3. Niederreiter Message Decryption

Input: $c, K_{sec} = (P, S, g(z), \mathcal{L})$
Output: message m
1: $c' \leftarrow S^{-1}c$
2: decode c' to error vector $e' = Pe^T$
3: $e \leftarrow P^{-1}e'$
4: Decode the error vector e to the binary message m
5: **return** m

of a minimal set of security parameters ($m = 10, n = 1024, t = 38, k \geq 644$) according to [23] already translates to a size of 47,5 kByte for the public key and at least 52 kByte for the private key (without any optimizations). However, this setup only provides the comparable security of a 60 bit symmetric cipher. For appropriate 80 bit security, even larger keys, for example the parameters $m = 11, n = 2048, t = 27, k \geq 1751$, are required (more details in Section 3.3).

An effective approach for secret key protection is the use of secure on-chip key memories that would require (with appropriate security features such as prohibited memory readback) invasive attacks on the chip to reveal the key. However, secure storage of key bits usually prove costly in hardware so that effective strategies are required to reduce the size of the private key to keep costs low. Addressing this issue, we use the in [14] introduced technique of on-the-fly generation of the large scrambling matrix S^{-1} instead of storing it in memory as in previous implementations. We build the PRNG around the hardware accelerated DES engine of the ATxMega.

3.3 Security Parameters

All security parameters for cryptosystems are chosen in a way to provide sufficient protection against the best known attack (whereas the notion of "sufficient" is determined by the requirements of an application). A recent paper [5] by Bernstein *et al.* presents a state-of-the-art attack of McEliece.

This attack reduces the binary work factor to break the original McEliece scheme with a (1024, 524) Goppa code and $t = 50$ to $2^{60.55}$ bit operations. According to [5], Table 1 summarizes the security parameters for specific security levels. Some suggestions include the use of a list decoding algorithm [3] for binary Goppa codes, which allows to correct more errors than the Patterson algorithm.

Table 1. Security of Niederreiter Depending on Parameters

Security Level	**Parameters** (n, k, t), errors added	**Size** K_{pub} in KBits	**Size** K_{sec} $(G(z), P, S)$ in KBits
Short-term (60 bit)	(1024, 644, 38), 38	644	(0.38, 10, 405)
Mid-term I (80 bit)	(2048, 1751, 27), 27	3,502	(0.30, 22, 2994)
Mid-term II (128 bit)	(2690, 2280, 56), 57	1537536	(0.30, 22, 2994)
Long-term (256 bit)	(6624, 5129, 115), 117	33,178	(1.47, 104, 25690)

3.4 Constant Weight Encoding

Before encrypting a message, it has to be encoded into an error vector. This means transforming the message into a bit vector of length n and maximum weight t. There exist a lot of encoding algorithms, e.g. [15,11,28]. We use the recursive algorithm in [29], with some minor changes to speed up the encoding with only negligible losses in efficiency. The original encoding algorithm (Bin2CW) is given in Algorithm 4. It returns a t-tuple of integers, which indicate the distance of two ones in the vector.

Read(B,i) is a function, that reads the next i bits from the string B and returns them as Integer. *decodefd* and *best_d* are two somewhat complex functions, which determine depending on the actual value of n and t, how many message bits should be encoded into the next string of zeros. Note that during the recursions *decodefd*, n and t are constantly decreased until the algorithm terminates. *Decodefd* is given in Algorithm 8 in the appendix.

To calculate the value d, the author gives the following formula:

$$d \approx \frac{ln(2)}{t} \cdot (n - \frac{t-1}{t}) \tag{5}$$

He also states that the algorithm will terminate for other values of d and u, with only negligible efficiency loss, as long as the difference to the optimal value is not large. See [29] for a brief explanation on these steps.

Our primary goal in optimizing this algorithm was to avoid multiplication with a float ($ln(2)$) and the division by t. These operations are very time consuming on AVR micro controllers. We decided to merge *decodefd* and *best_d*, and additionally fix the choice of the optimal d to powers of two by a table lookup.

By running the original encoding algorithm several times with random input strings, we detected the most likely behaviour of n and t during the recursion and also the minimal amount of bits that can be encoded into an error vector

Algorithm 4. Bin2CW

Input: n, t, δ, binary stream B
Output: t-tuple of Integers

if $t = 0$ **then**
    return
else if $n \leq t$ **then**
    return δ, Bin2CW$(n-1, t-1, 0, B)$
else
    $d \leftarrow$best_d(n, t)
    if read$(B, 1) = 1$ **then**
        return Bin2CW$(n-d, t, \delta+d, B)$
    else
        $i \leftarrow decodefd(d, B)$
        return $\delta + i$, Bin2CW$(n-i-1, t-1, 0, B)$
    end if
end if

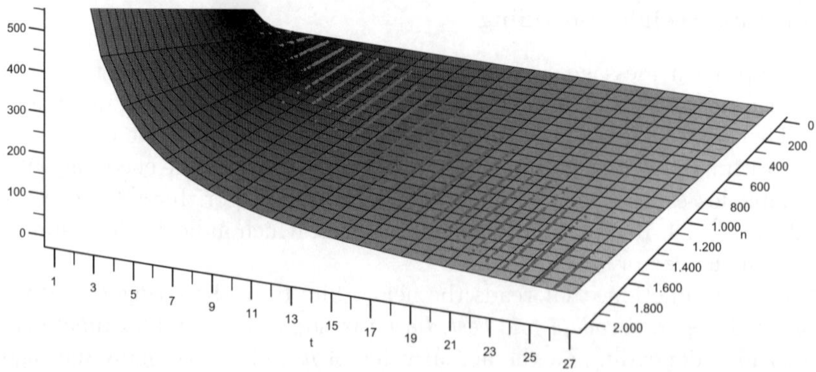

Fig. 1. Run of bestD(n,t)

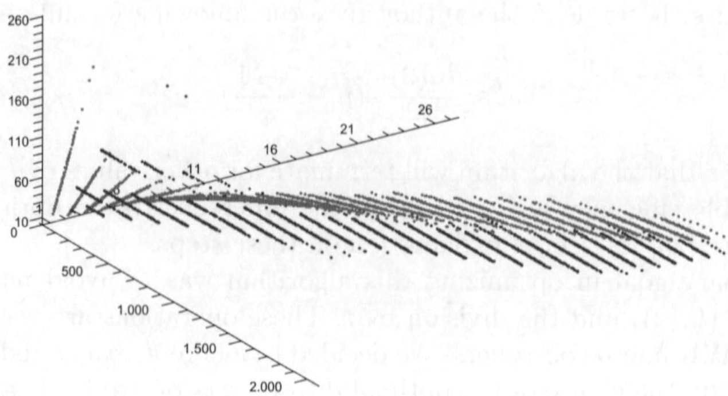

Fig. 2. Run of table based bestD(n,t)

of length t. Figure 1 depicts the behaviour of d over several runs of the original encoding algorithm for random input strings. Afterwards, we precomputed a table containing 4096 elements, each representing the power of two of d, which is in fact u. Thus, d can be computed as $(1 << u)$. The index to this table is the concatenation of the upper seven bits of n and all five bits of t in binary representation. Ignoring the lower five bits of n keeps the difference to the original value d small, because only for small t and large n, which never happens according to Figure 1, these bits have a large impact on d. This reduces the size of the lookup table to only 4 KByte. There is a lot of freedom in further reducing the size of this table, if one accepts a lower efficiency, e.g. by encoding only 128 bits into an error vector. Figure 2 shows the original d in red and the table based in blue. It shows that our algorithm is close to the original behaviour. The complete optimized encoding algorithm is given in Algorithm 5.

The decoding algorithm was adapted in a similar way, and is given in Algorithm 6. The counterpart to *decodefd* is *encodefd* and is given in Algorithm 7 in the appendix for completeness. For practical purposes, we finally fix the size of

Algorithm 5. Bin2CWsmall

Input: n, t, δ, binary stream B
Output: t-tuple of Integers

```
if t = 0 then
    return
else if n ≤ t then
    return δ,Bin2CWsmall(n − 1, t − 1, 0, B)
else
    u ← uTable[(n&0xFFE0) + t]
    d ← (1 << u)
    if read(B, 1) = 1 then
        return Bin2CWsmall(n − d, t, δ + d, B)
    else
        i ← read(B, u)
        return δ + i Bin2CWsmall(n − i − 1, t − 1, 0, B)
    end if
end if
```

Algorithm 6. CW2Binsmall

Input: n, t, δ, t-tuple $(\delta_1, ..., \delta_t)$ of Integers
Output: binary stream B

```
if t = 0 or n ≤ t then
    return
end if
u ← uTable[(n&0xFFE0) + t]
d ← (1 << u)
if δ1 ≥ d then
    Write(1, B), CW2Binsmall(n − d, t, (δ1 − d, ..., δt))
else
    Write(0|δ1, B), CW2Binsmall(n − δ1 − 1, t − 1, (δ2, ..., δt))
end if
```

a message to 192 bits, which can in every case encoded into an appropriate error vector.

4 Design Criteria for Embedded Systems

In this section, we discuss our assumptions, requirements and restrictions which are required when implementing the Niederreiter cryptosystem on small, embedded systems. Target platform for our investigation is an 8-bit AVR microprocessor, namely the ATXMega256A1.

4.1 Requirements and Assumptions

For many embedded systems such as prepaid phones or micropayment systems, the short life cycle or comparably low value of the enclosed product often does not demand for long-term security. Hence, mid-term security parameters for public-key cryptosystems providing a comparable security to 64-80 key bits of symmetric ciphers are often regarded sufficient (and help reducing system costs). Hence, our implementations are designed for security parameters that correspond to an 80 bit key size of a symmetric cipher. A second important design requirement is the processing and storage of the private key solely *on-chip*, ensuring that all secrets are never used outside the device. With appropriate countermeasures to prevent data extraction from on-chip memories, an attacker can then recover the private key only by sophisticated invasive attacks. For this purpose, AVR μCs provide a lock-bit feature to enable write and read/write protection of the Flash memory [10]. The lock-bits are used to set protection levels on the different flash sections. They are used to block read and/or write access of the code. Lock bits can be written by an external programmer and from the application software to set a more strict protection level, but not to set a less strict protection level. Chip erase is the only way to erase the lock bits. The lock bits are erased after the rest of the flash memory is erased. An unprogrammed fuse or lock bit will have the value one, while a programmed flash or lock bit will have the value zero. Both fuses and lock bits are reprogrammable like the Flash Program memory.

Analyzing Niederreiter encryption and decryption algorithms (cf. Section 3.1), the following arithmetic components are required supporting computations in $GF(2^m)$: a multiplier, a squaring unit, calculation of square roots, and an inverter. Furthermore, a binary matrix multiplier for encryption and a permutation element for step 2 in Algorithm 2 are needed. Many arithmetic operations in Niederreiter can be replaced by table lookups to significantly accelerate computations at the cost of additional memory.

The susceptibility of the Niederreiter cryptosystem to side channel attacks has not extensively been studied, yet. However, embedded systems can always be subject to passive attacks such as timing analysis [20] and power/EM analysis [21]. In [30], a successful timing attack on the Patterson algorithm was demonstrated. The attack does not recover the key, but reveals the error vector z and hence allows for efficient decryption of the message c. Our implementations are not susceptible to this attack due to unconditional instruction execution, e.g., our implementation will not terminate after a certain number of errors have been corrected. This leads to a constant runtime of the root searching part and prevents the above mentioned attack. Differential EM/power attacks and timing attacks are impeded by the permutation and scrambling operations (P and S) obfuscating all internal states, and finally, the large key size. Yet template-like attacks [8] might be feasible if no further protection is applied.

5 Implementation on AVR Microprocessors

In this section, we discuss our implementation of the Niederreiter cryptosystem for 8-bit AVR microcontrollers, a popular family of 8-bit RISC microcontrollers (μC) used in embedded systems. The Atmel AVR processors operate at clock frequencies of up to 32 MHz, provide few kBytes of SRAM, up to hundreds of kBytes of Flash program memory, and additional EEPROM or mask ROM. For our design, we chose an ATxMega256A1 μC due to its 16 kBytes of SRAM and the integrated crypto accelerator engine for DES and AES [10]. The crypto accelerator is particularly useful for a fast implementation of a CPRNG that generates the scrambling matrix S^{-1} on-the-fly. Arithmetic operations in the underlying field $GF(2^{11})$ can be performed efficiently with a combination of polynomial and exponential representations. We store the coefficients of a value $a \in GF(2^{11})$ in memory using a polynomial basis with natural order. Given an $a = a_{10}\alpha^{10} + a_9\alpha^9 + a_8\alpha^8 + \cdots + a_0\alpha^0$, the coefficient $a_i \in GF(2)$ is determined by bit i of an unsigned 16 bit integer where bit 0 denotes the least significant bit. In this representation, addition is fast just by performing an exclusive-or operation on 2×2 registers. For more complex operations, such as multiplication, squaring, inversion and root extraction, an exponential representation is more suitable. Since every element except zero in $GF(2^{11})$ can be written as a power of some primitive element α, all elements in the finite field can also be represented by α^i with $i \in \mathbb{Z}_{2^m-1}$. Multiplication and squaring can then be performed by adding the exponents of the factors over $\mathbb{Z}_{2^m-1}$ such as

$$c = a \cdot b = \alpha^i \cdot \alpha^j = \alpha^{i+j} \mid a, b \in GF(2^{11}), 0 \leq i, j \leq 2^m - 2. \tag{6}$$

If one of the elements equals zero, obviously the result is zero. The inverse of a value $d \in GF(2^{11})$ in exponential representation $d = \alpha^i$ can be obtained from a single subtraction in the exponent $d^{-1} = \alpha^{2^{11}-1-i}$ with a subsequent table-lookup. Root extraction, i.e., given a value $a = \alpha^i$ to determine $r = a^{i/2}$ is simple, when i is even and can be performed by a simple right shift on index i. For odd values of i, $m - 1 = 10$ left shifts followed by a reduction with $2^{11} - 1$ determine the square root.

To allow for efficient conversion between the two representations, we employ two precomputed tables (so called *log* and *antilog* tables) that enable fast conversion between polynomial and exponential representation. Each table consists of 2048 11-bit values that are stored as a pair of two bytes in the program memory. Hence, each lookup table consumes 4 kBytes of Flash memory. Due to frequent access, we copy the tables into the faster SRAM at startup time. Accessing the table directly from Flash memory significantly reduces performance, but allows migration to a (slightly) cheaper device with only 4 kBytes of SRAM. For multiplication, squaring, inversion, and root extraction, the operands are transformed on-the-fly to exponential representation and reverted to the polynomial basis after finishing the operation.

5.1 Generation and Storage of Matrices

All matrices as shown in Table 2 are precomputed and stored in Flash memory of the μC . We store the permutation matrix P^{-1} as an array of 2048 16-bit unsigned integers containing 11-bit indices. Matrix $\hat{H}$ is written in transposed form to simplify multiplications (i.e., all columns are stored as consecutive words in memory for straightforward index calculations). Additionally, arrays for the support of the code and the Goppa polynomial reside in Flash memory as well.

Table 2 shows the requirements of precomputed tables separated by actual size and required size in memory including the necessary 16-bit address alignment and/or padding.

Table 2. Sizes of tables and values in memory including overhead for address alignment

Use	Name	Actual Size	Size in Memory
Encryption	Public Key $\hat{H}$	74,032 byte	74,032 byte
Decryption	Private Key S^{-1} (IV only)	8 byte	8 byte
Decryption	Private Key P^{-1} array	2,816 byte	4,096 byte
Decoding	Goppa polynomial	309 bits	56 byte
Decoding	ω-polynomial	297 bits	54 byte
Decoding	Log table	22,528 bits	4,096 byte
Decoding	Antilog table	22,528 bits	4,096 byte

Step 1 of Algorithm 3 can be implemented as the addition of a row from S^{-1} if the corresponding cipher bit is 1. But if this bit is 0, we also have to trigger the PRNG to get them generate the right next rows. To avoid this step, which consist of five times DES (16 clock cycles each) per row, we construct a key scheduling algorithm. This algorithm depends on the actual row of S and the IV.Using this algorithm every row can be generated independently and the PRNG can skip zero bits in the ciphertext.

5.2 System and Compiler Limitations

Due to the large demand for memory for $\hat{H}$, we need to take care of some peculiarities in the memory management of the AVR microcontroller. Since originally AVR microcontrollers supported only a small amount of internal memory, the AVR uses 16 bit pointers to access its Flash memory. Additionally, each Flash cell comprises 16 bits of data, but the μC itself can only handle 8 bits. Hence, one bit of this address pointer must be reserved to select the corresponding byte in the retrieved word, reducing the maximal address range to 64 KByte (or 32K 16 bit words). To address memory segments beyond 64K, additional RAMP-registers need to be used. Additionally, the used avr-gcc compiler internally treats pointers as signed 16 bit integer halving the addressable memory space again. For this reason, the public matrix $\hat{H}$ need to be split into multiple parts resulting in an additional overhead in the program code.

6 Results

We now present the results of our Niederreiter implementations providing 80 bit security ($n = 2048, k = 1751, t = 27$) for the AVR 8-bit microcontroller. We report performance figures for the ATxMega256A1 obtained from the avr-gcc compiler v4.3.2. The code size for combined encryption and decryption on the AVR μC is 172.9 kB, including all tables.

Table 3 summarizes the clock cycles needed for every part of the de- and encryption routines. When looking at Figure 3, it is obvious that searching the roots of $\sigma(z)$ is the most time consuming step of the decryption algorithm. Even an optimized implementation in assembly language reduced the runtime only marginally.

Table 3. Performance of Niederreiter implementation with $n = 2048, k = 1751, t = 27$ on the AVR ATxMega256 μC

	Aspect	**ATxMega256 μC**
Encrypt.	Maximum frequency	32 MHz
	CW encode $e = encode(m)$	21,540 cycles
	Encrypt $c = e \cdot \hat{H}$	29,707 cycles
Decryption	Maximum frequency	32 MHz
	Undo scrambling $c \cdot S^{-1}$	198,946 cycles
	convert to polynomial	15,785 cycles
	Compute $T = Syn(z)^{-1}$	492,656 cycles
	Compute $\sqrt{T+z}$	107,569 cycles
	Solve Equation (4) with EEA	170,121 cycles
	Search roots	4,693,080 cycles
	CW decode	71,987 cycles

The public-key cryptosystems RSA-1024 and ECC-P160 are assumed[2] to roughly achieve a similar margin of 80 bit symmetric security [13]. We finally compare our results to published implementations of these systems that target similar platforms (i.e., AVR ATMega μC). Note that the figures for ECC are obtained from the ECDSA signature scheme.

Embedded implementations of other alternative public key encryption schemes are very rare. The proprietary encryption scheme NTRUEncrypt has received some attention. An embedded software implementation of the related NTRUSign performs one signature on an ATMega128L clocked at 7,37 MHz in 619 ms [12]. However, comparable performance figures of NTRU encryption and decryption for the AVR platform are not available. As mentioned in the introduction, we also compare our work with the implementation from [14]. This gives a direct comparison between two algorithms, offering the same security level and being based on the same underlying problem. Note that both microcontroller used only differ in the amount of Flash memory. Available SRAM, instruction set and frequency are exactly the same.

[2] According to [13], RSA-1248 actually corresponds to 80 bit symmetric security. However, no implementation results for embedded systems are available for this key size.

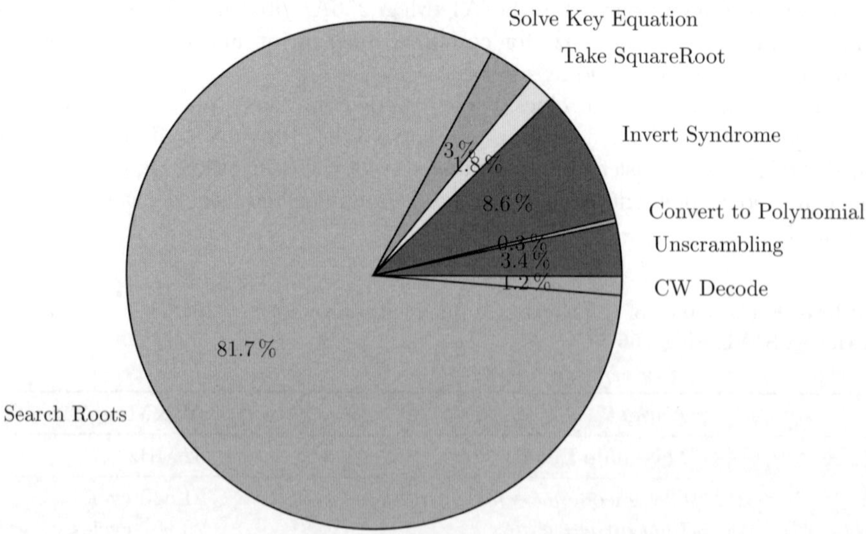

Fig. 3. Timing of Decryption

Note that all throughput figures are based on the number of plaintext bits processed by each system and do not take any message expansion in the ciphertext into account.

The main speed up of Niederreiter encryption compared to McEliece comes from the smaller public key. Another advantage is the lower Hamming weight of the message after it is transformed to the constant weight word. These properties lead to less data to be processed and thus a higher performance, which is increased by a factor of 112. The decryption could not be improved in the same order of magnitude. The main reason is the very expensive root searching

Table 4. Comparison of our Niederreiter implementation with single-core ECC and RSA implementations and McEliece for 80 bit security

	Method	Platform	Time ms/op	Throughput bits/sec
8-bit μC	Niederreiter encryption	ATxMega256@32MHz	1.6	119,890
	Niederreiter decryption	ATxMega256@32MHz	180	1,062
	McEliece encryption	ATxMega192@32MHz	450	3,889
	McEliece decryption	ATxMega192@32MHz	618	2,835
	ECC-P160 (SECG) [17]	ATMega128@8MHz	810/203[1]	197/788[1]
	RSA-1024 $2^{16}+1$ [17]	ATMega128@8MHz	430/108[1]	2,381/9,524[1]
	RSA-1024 random [17]	ATMega128@8MHz	10,990/2,748[1]	93/373[1]

[1] For a fair comparison with our implementation running at 32MHz, timings at lower frequencies were scaled accordingly.

algorithm, which is necessary in both schemes. Decryption benefits from the fact that the syndrome computation is already done by the sender of the ciphertext. The additional constant weight decoding can be neglected.

7 Conclusions

In this paper, we described the first implementations of the Niederreiter public-key scheme for embedded systems using an AVR μC . Our performance results for Niederreiter providing 80 bit security on these system exceed all other systems in terms of operations per second, except RSA with a small exponent. Especially the encryption routine outperforms them all and with its convenient block size of 192 bits it fits best for key transportation.

In direct comparison with McEliece, the Niederreiter scheme performs very well. Note, that the McEliece scheme needs 1751 plaintext bits at our security level, so that is it often not the best choice to encrypt small blocks, even if the throughput in encryption is nearly by a factor of three larger.

However, although our implementations still leave room for further optimizations, our results already show better performance than every other system, except RSA encrypt. Thus, we believe with growing memories in embedded systems, ongoing research and further optimizations, Niederreiter has almost evolved to a suitable and quantum computer-resistant alternative to RSA and ECC that have been extensively studied for years.

The next step, which is already in progress, is to investigate possible side channels. There seems to be a lot starting points due to the very structured algorithms and know relations from input to intermediate values.

References

1. Berlekamp, E.R.: Goppa Codes. IEEE Trans. on Information Theory 19(3), 590–592 (1973)
2. Berlekamp, E.R., McEliece, R.J., van Tilborg, H.C.A.: On the inherent intractability of certain coding problems. IEEE Trans. Information Theory 24(3), 384–386 (1978)
3. Bernstein, D.J.: List decoding for binary codes. Technical report, University of Illinois at Chicago (2008), `http://cr.yp.to/codes/goppalist-20081107.pdf`
4. Bernstein, D.J., Lange, T.: ebacs: Ecrypt benchmarking of cryptographic systems (February 17, 2009), `http://bench.cr.yp.to`
5. Bernstein, D.J., Lange, T., Peters, C.: Attacking and Defending the McEliece Cryptosystem. In: Buchmann, J., Ding, J. (eds.) PQCrypto 2008. LNCS, vol. 5299, pp. 31–46. Springer, Heidelberg (2008), `http://eprint.iacr.org/2008/318`
6. Biswas, B., Herbert, V.: Efficient Root Finding of Polynomials over Fields of Characteristic 2. In: WEWoRC 2009. LNCS. Springer, Heidelberg (2009) (to appear)
7. Biswas, B., Sendrier, N.: Mceliece crypto-system: A reference implementation, `http://www-rocq.inria.fr/secret/CBCrypto/index.php?pg=hymes`
8. Chari, S., Rao, J.R., Rohatgi, P.: Template Attacks. In: Kaliski Jr., B.S., Koç, Ç.K., Paar, C. (eds.) CHES 2002. LNCS, vol. 2523, pp. 13–28. Springer, Heidelberg (2003)

9. Chien, R.T.: Cyclic decoding procedure for the bose-chaudhuri-hocquenghem codes. IEEE Trans. Information Theory IT-10(10), 357–363 (1964)
10. Corp, A.: 8-bit xmega a microcontroller. User Guide (February 2009), http://www.atmel.com/dyn/resources/prod_documents/doc8077.pdf
11. Cover, T.: Enumerative source encoding 19(1), 73–77 (1973)
12. Driessen, B., Poschmann, A., Paar, C.: Comparison of Innovative Signature Algorithms for WSNs. In: Proceedings of ACM WiSec 2008. ACM, New York (2008)
13. ECRYPT. Yearly report on algorithms and keysizes (2007-2008). Technical report, D.SPA.28 Rev. 1.1 (July 2008), http://www.ecrypt.eu.org/documents/D.SPA.10-1.1.pdf
14. Eisenbarth, T., Gneysu, T., Heyse, S., Paar, C.: MicroEliece: McEliece for Embedded Devices. In: Clavier, C., Gaj, K. (eds.) CHES 2009. LNCS, vol. 5747, pp. 49–64. Springer, Heidelberg (2009)
15. Fischer, J.-B., Stern, J.: An Efficient Pseudo-Random Generator Provably As Secure As Syndrome Decoding. In: Maurer, U.M. (ed.) EUROCRYPT 1996. LNCS, vol. 1070, pp. 245–255. Springer, Heidelberg (1996)
16. Freenet and Entropy. Open-source p2p network applications (2009), s http://freenetproject.org, http://entropy.stop1984.com
17. Gura, N., Patel, A., Wander, A., Eberle, H., Shantz, S.C.: Comparing elliptic curve cryptography and rsa on 8-bit cpus. In: Joye, M., Quisquater, J.-J. (eds.) CHES 2004. LNCS, vol. 3156, pp. 119–132. Springer, Heidelberg (2004)
18. Horner, W.G.: A new method of solving numerical equations of all orders, by continuous approximation. Philosophical Transactions of the Royal Society of London, 308–335 (1819)
19. Huber, K.: Note on decoding binary goppa codes. Electronics Letters 32, 102–103 (1996)
20. Kocher, P.C.: Timing Attacks On Implementations of Diffie-Hellman, RSA, DSS, and Other Systems. In: Koblitz, N. (ed.) CRYPTO 1996. LNCS, vol. 1109, pp. 104–113. Springer, Heidelberg (1996)
21. Mangard, S., Oswald, E., Popp, T.: Power Analysis Attacks: Revealing the Secrets of Smartcards. Springer, Heidelberg (2007)
22. McEliece, R.J.: A public-key cryptosystem based on algebraic coding theory. Deep Space Network Progress Report 44, 114–116 (1978)
23. Menezes, A.J., van Oorschot, P.C., Vanstone, S.A.: Handbook of Applied Cryptography. CRC Press, New York (1996)
24. Niederreiter, H.: Knapsack-type cryptosystems and algebraic coding theory. Problems of Control and Information Theory 15, 159–166 (1986)
25. Patterson, N.: The Algebraic Decoding of Goppa Codes. IEEE Transactions on Information Theory 21, 203–207 (1975)
26. Preneel, B., Bosselaers, A., Govaerts, R., Vandewalle, J.: A Software Implementation of the McEliece Public-Key Cryptosystem. In: Proceedings of the 13th Symposium on Information Theory in the Benelux, Werkgemeenschap voor Informatie en Communicatietheorie, pp. 119–126. Springer, Heidelberg (1992)
27. Prometheus. Implementation of McEliece Cryptosystem for 32-bit microprocessors, c-source (2009), http://www.eccpage.com/goppacode.c
28. Sendrier, N.: Efficient generation of binary words of given weight. In: Boyd, C. (ed.) Cryptography and Coding 1995. LNCS, vol. 1025, pp. 184–187. Springer, Heidelberg (1995)
29. Sendrier, N.: Encoding information into constant weight words. In: Proc. International Symposium on Information Theory ISIT 2005, September 4-9, pp. 435–438 (2005)

30. Strenzke, F., Tews, E., Molter, H., Overbeck, R., Shoufan, A.: Side Channels in the McEliece PKC. In: Buchmann, J., Ding, J. (eds.) PQCrypto 2008. LNCS, vol. 5299, pp. 216–229. Springer, Heidelberg (2008)
31. Sugiyama, Y., Kasahara, M., Hirasawa, S., Namekawa, T.: A Method for Solving Key Equation for Decoding Goppa Codes. IEEE Transactions on Information and Control 27, 87–99 (1975)
32. Sugiyama, Y., Kasahara, M., Hirasawa, S., Namekawa, T.: An erasures-and-errors decoding algorithm for goppa codes (corresp.). IEEE Transactions on Information Theory 22, 238–241 (1976)
33. Turley, J.: The two percent solution (December 2002), `http://www.embedded.com/story/OEG20021217S0039`
34. van Tilborg, H.C.: Fundamentals of Cryptology. Kluwer Academic Publishers, Dordrecht (2000)

Appendix

Algorithm 7. encodefd

Input: d, binary stream B
Output: a binary string

$u \leftarrow \lceil log_2(d) \rceil$
if $\delta \leq 2^u - d$ **then**
    $u \leftarrow u - 1$
else
    $\delta \leftarrow delta + 2^u - d$
end if
return $base_2(\delta, u)$

Algorithm 8. decodefd

Input: d, binary stream B
Output: a binary string

$u \leftarrow \lceil log_2(d) \rceil$
$\delta \leftarrow read(B, u - 1)$
if $\delta \geq 2^u - d$ **then**
    $\delta \leftarrow 2 * delta + read(B, 1) - 2^u + d$
end if
return δ

Strongly Unforgeable Signatures and Hierarchical Identity-Based Signatures from Lattices without Random Oracles

Markus Rückert*

Cryptography and Computeralgebra
Department of Computer Science
TU Darmstadt
markus.rueckert@cased.de

Abstract. We propose a variant of the "bonsai tree" signature scheme, a lattice-based *existentially unforgeable* signature scheme in the standard model. Our construction offers the same efficiency as the "bonsai tree" scheme but supports the stronger notion of *strong unforgeability*. Strong unforgeability demands that the adversary is unable to produce a new message-signature pair $(\mathfrak{m}, \mathfrak{s})$, even if he or she is allowed to see a different signature $\mathfrak{s}'$ for $\mathfrak{m}$.

In particular, we provide the first treeless signature scheme that supports strong unforgeability for the post-quantum era in the standard model. Moreover, we show how to *directly* implement identity-based, and even hierarchical identity-based, signatures (IBS) in the same strong security model without random oracles. An additional advantage of this direct approach over the usual generic conversion of hierarchical identity-based encryption to IBS is that we can exploit the efficiency of ideal lattices without significantly harming security.

We equip all constructions with strong security proofs based on mild worst-case assumptions on lattices and we also propose concrete security parameters.

Keywords: Post-quantum cryptography, lattice cryptography, digital signatures, identity-based cryptography, standard model.

1 Introduction

Digital signature schemes are the cornerstone of e-business, e-government, software security, and many more applications. Their importance is likely to grow in the future as more and more everyday tasks and processes are computerized. With identity-based signature schemes (IBS), motivated by Shamir [34], one can get rid of public-key infrastructures. The public key is replaced with a unique identifier string, such as an e-mail address, and the secret key is "extracted" by a trusted party for this identifier. In hierarchical identity-based signatures

* This work was supported by CASED (www.cased.de).

N. Sendrier (Ed.): PQCrypto 2010, LNCS 6061, pp. 182–200, 2010.

(HIBS), this concept is generalized so that each party can act as a key extraction authority for its subordinates.

There are two classes of signature schemes. The first comprises *tree-based* and stateful Merkle signature schemes [29] with a limited signature capacity. Such schemes can be solely based on the security of hash functions. The drawback is that they require an inefficient key generation phase, where all signatures need to be prepared in advance. Furthermore, its statefulness poses a synchronization problem as soon as more than one computer, or process thread, is supposed to issue signatures with the same secret key.

The second class contains *treeless* constructions that are typically more efficient and allow for an unlimited number of signatures without a complex setup phase. Currently, we mainly use schemes that fall into the second category because they are easier to handle. Most of them rely on the hardness of factoring or computing discrete logarithms.

Alternatives for the post-quantum era can be based on the hardness of the decoding problem in error correcting codes, on the hardness of solving nonlinear multivariate equation systems, or on the hardness of lattice problems. Refer to [7] for an overview of each field. Basically, all three alternatives rely on the hardness of certain *average-case* problems and, at first, it is unclear how to generate hard instances of these problems. More precisely, we always need to know a "hard" distribution of keys that admits efficient key generation. Unlike with multivariate or code-based cryptography, lattice-based constructions have a "trust anchor" in the form of Ajtai's worst-case to average-case reduction [2] that is not found anywhere else in cryptography. It states that solving a certain average-case problem, which is relevant in cryptography, implies a solution to a related worst-case problem. Although this may sound purely theoretical, it is of great practical value as keys that are chosen uniformly at random already provide *worst-case* security guarantees. The hardness of this underlying worst-case problem is also plausible as the best known algorithm to solve the relevant lattice problems requires exponential time [3].

Another advantage of lattice-based cryptography over the alternatives is that there is a whole range of provably secure signature schemes. In the random oracle model there are schemes due to Gentry, Peikert, and Vaikuntanathan [16]; Stehlé, Steinfeld, Tanaka, and Xagawa [35]; and Lyubashevsky [26]. As for the standard model, there are the works of Lyubashevsky and Micciancio [27] (tree-based); and Cash, Hofheinz, Kiltz, and Peikert [12].

However, there is a gap in this range because none of the above schemes is *stateless*, provably secure in the *standard model*, and *strongly unforgeable*. Strong unforgeability under chosen message attacks (SU-CMA) is stronger than existential unforgeability (EU-CMA) in the sense that the adversary is not artificially restricted by the security model. In EU-CMA, the adversary is forced to output a signature for a *fresh message* $\mathfrak{m}^*$ after seeing signature for messages $\mathfrak{m}_i \neq \mathfrak{m}^*$of his or her choice. The SU-CMA adversary is also allowed to output a *fresh signature* for one of the $\mathfrak{m}_i$.

Strong unforgeability is interesting in both, theory and practice. Consider generic tranformations from CPA to CCA2 security in the standard model, e.g., Dolev, Dwork, and Naor [13] or Boneh, Canetti, Halevi, and Katz [9]. They typically involve a strongly unforgeable signature scheme to make the ciphertext authentic and non-malleable. An EU-CMA signature of the CPA ciphertext may already provide some security against CCA1 adversaries but a CCA2 attack would certainly still succeed. Another reason is the construction of ID-based blind signatures due to Galindo, Herranz, and Kiltz [14].

As a practical example, consider an access control protocol where you may delegate certain rights to another party by signing a description for these rights with a signature $\mathfrak{s}$. You want to be able to revoke them at any time in the future via an online revocation system. The rights are revoked as soon as the online system has $\mathfrak{s}$ in its database. If the signature scheme is only EU-CMA secure, the delegee can construct another signature $\mathfrak{s}^*$ for the same set of rights and present this token instead of $\mathfrak{s}$ — the revocation mechanism breaks down.

Notice that there are generic transformations from EU-CMA to SU-CMA. They typically only apply to a certain small subclass of signature schemes, e.g., Boneh-Shen-Waters [10]. Recently, Bellare and Shoup [6] proposed an unrestricted transformation. However, all lose efficiency compared to the underlying EU-CMA scheme because they require multiple signing steps.

Similarly, HIBS can be constructed from any signature scheme, e.g., via the certification approach [17] by Gentry and Silverberg or via Append-Only Signatures due to Kiltz, Mityagin, Panjwani, and Raghavan [20]. Here, the key extraction authority basically emulates a public-key infrastructure: It generates a new public key for each identity and issues a certificate, binding the key to the identity. In consequence, the resulting identity-based signatures grow by the size of one public key, which will not be practical in our case.

Our Contribution. Table 1 compares our result with the current state-of-the-art for lattice signatures, including the typical improvements with ideal lattices [32,30]. All previously known SU-CMA schemes are either stateful, causing, e.g., synchronization problems, or they require random oracles. Using random oracles is discouraged by the works of Canetti, Goldreich, and Halevi [11], as well as by the more practical work of Leurent and Nguyen [24]. The only known scheme that directly provides SU-CMA security in the standard model is stateful and has a large secret key.[1] Our construction in Section 4.1 offers the same complexity as [12]. In our case, signing involves a simple additional linear algebra step that can be pre-computed. Thus, we achieve a stronger security notion without additional cost.

The situation is quite similar for HIBS. With the exception of Libert and Quisquater [25], previous results deal only with existentially unforgeable HIBS. They typically provide hierarchical identity-based encryption (HIBE) and then apply a generic conversion, e.g., [21], to obtain an HIBS. Both, HIBE and HIBS,

[1] Trade-offs are possible but the key generation complexity is $n^{\mathcal{O}(1)}$, typically for a large polynomial.

Table 1. Comparison of the properties of current lattice-based signature schemes

Scheme	Stateless	Standard model	SU-CMA	Public key	Secret Key	Signature
[16] with [35]	*Yes*	No	*Yes*	$\tilde{\mathcal{O}}(n)$	$\tilde{\mathcal{O}}(n^2)$	$\tilde{\mathcal{O}}(n)$
[26]	*Yes*	No	*Yes*	$\tilde{\mathcal{O}}(n)$	$\mathcal{O}(n)$	$\tilde{\mathcal{O}}(n)$
[12]	*Yes*	*Yes*	No	$\tilde{\mathcal{O}}(n)$	$\tilde{\mathcal{O}}(n^2)$	$\tilde{\mathcal{O}}(n)$
[27] with [29]	No	*Yes*	*Yes*	$\mathcal{O}(n)$	$n^{\mathcal{O}(1)}$	$\tilde{\mathcal{O}}(n)$
Section 4.1	*Yes*	*Yes*	*Yes*	$\tilde{\mathcal{O}}(n)$	$\tilde{\mathcal{O}}(n^2)$	$\tilde{\mathcal{O}}(n)$

can be classified as selective-ID or adaptive-ID secure. Selective-ID security forces the adversary to name its target identity before seeing the public key. In the adaptive case, it may output a forgery for any identity. So far, lattice-based IBE schemes either support selective-ID security [12,1] in the standard model or they support adaptive-ID security [16] in the random oracle model. In contrast to our constructions, using the HIBE to HIBS conversion with the above HIBE schemes requires a subexponential time quantum reduction in the security proof when using efficient ideal lattices [35].

Note that using the generic construction [17] in conjunction with our SU-CMA signature scheme (Section 4) would work and the result would be a strongly-unforgeable HIBS. However, the resulting signature size would be completely impractical.

Hence, in addition to the first stateless standard-model SU-CMA signature scheme from lattices in Section 4.1, we provide the first direct lattice-based constructions for adaptive-ID secure and strongly unforgeably HIBS in the random oracle model in Section 3.2 and for strongly unforgeable HIBS in the standard model in Section 4.2. Our constructions in Section 4 rely on Chameleon hash functions [23]. The security proofs involve a generic transformation to SU-CMA from a slightly weaker notion, which was not explicitly known before (cf. Section 2). Due to space restrictions, some of the proofs had to be moved to the full version [33].

Our Modifications to [12]. For those familiar with [12], we give a brief overview of the changes that are necessary to achieve SU-CMA security. In [12], signatures are short vectors $\mathfrak{s}$ that satisfy $\mathbf{A}\mathfrak{s} \equiv \mathbf{0} \pmod{q}$, i.e., they are in the q-ary lattice $\Lambda_q^\perp(\mathbf{A})$. An adversary may succeed in breaking SU-CMA security of this scheme by simply asking for a signature $\mathfrak{s}$ for a message $\mathfrak{m}$ and then return $(\mathfrak{m}, -\mathfrak{s})$ as its forgery. Such an answer is useless in the reduction because the simulator had to know a trapdoor for $\Lambda_q^\perp(\mathbf{A})$ beforehand.

Instead, we let the signature algorithm sample short vectors from a random coset $\{\mathbf{x} : \mathbf{A}\mathbf{x} \equiv \mathbf{y} \pmod{q}\}$. The appraoch is similar to [16] but with a fixed $\mathbf{y}$ that is part of the public key. In the simulation, we can prepare $\mathbf{y}$ such that we know a corresponding signature $\mathfrak{s}$ that is used to simulate the signature oracle. Now, the adversary against SU-CMA security needs to output a different short vector $\mathfrak{s}^*$ from the same coset. This, however enables the simulation to find a short vector $\mathfrak{s} - \mathfrak{s}^*$ in $\Lambda_q^\perp(\mathbf{A})$ and solve the underlying problem.

2 Preliminaries

The security parameter is n. The statement $x \leftarrow_{\$} X$ means x is chosen uniformly at random from X. With $x \sim \Delta(X)$, we denote that x is chosen according to a distribution Δ over X. The concatenation of strings, vectors, and matrix columns is done via $\circ$. Furthermore, $x \sqsubset y$ means x is a prefix of y and $\varnothing$ is the empty string. Lower-case boldface identifies vectors and upper-case boldface denotes a matrix. For a given matrix $\mathbf{X} \in \mathbb{R}^{m \times m}$, we write $\tilde{\mathbf{X}}$ for its Gram-Schmidt orthogonalization.

2.1 Security Models

Throughout the paper we stick to the following notation. The length of identities is κ, the message length is λ, and ℓ is the hierarchy depth, meaning that there are $\ell+1$ levels in the hierarchy tree. With $\{x_i\}_1^m$ we denote the set $\{x_1, \ldots, x_m\}$. The subsequent paragraphs deal with the specification of strongly unforgeable signature schemes $\mathsf{DSig} = (\mathsf{Kg}, \mathsf{Sign}, \mathsf{Vf})$ and hierarchical identity-based signature schemes $\mathsf{HIBS} = (\mathsf{Kg}, \mathsf{Extract}, \mathsf{Sign}, \mathsf{Vf})$.

Signature Schemes. We follow the standard specification for digital signature schemes: $\mathsf{Kg}(1^n)$ outputs a private signing key sk and a public verification key pk; $\mathsf{Sign}(\mathsf{sk}, \mathfrak{m})$ outputs a signature $\mathfrak{s}$ under sk for the message $\mathfrak{m}$; $\mathsf{Vf}(\mathsf{pk}, \mathfrak{s}, \mathfrak{m})$ outputs 1 iff $\mathfrak{s}$ is a valid signature on $\mathfrak{m}$ under pk.

Most schemes are proven to be existentially unforgeable under chosen message attacks (EU-CMA), but we will consider the stronger notion of strongly unforgeability under chosen message attacks (SU-CMA) as described in the following experiment, where $\mathcal{H}$ is a family of random oracles.

Experiment $\mathsf{Exp}^{\mathsf{SU\text{-}CMA}}_{\mathcal{A},\mathsf{DSig}}(n)$
 $\mathsf{H} \leftarrow \mathcal{H}(1^n)$; $(\mathsf{sk}, \mathsf{pk}) \leftarrow \mathsf{Kg}(1^n)$
 $(\mathfrak{m}^*, \mathfrak{s}^*) \leftarrow \mathcal{A}^{\mathsf{Sign}(\mathsf{sk},\cdot),\mathsf{H}(\cdot)}(\mathsf{pk})$
 Let $(\mathfrak{m}_i, \mathfrak{s}_i)$ be the answer returned by $\mathsf{Sign}(\mathsf{sk}, \cdot)$ on input $\mathfrak{m}_i$, for $i = 1, \ldots, k$.
 Return 1 iff $\mathsf{Vf}(\mathsf{pk}, \mathfrak{m}^*, \mathfrak{s}^*) = 1$ and $(\mathfrak{m}^*, \mathfrak{s}^*) \notin \{(\mathfrak{m}_1, \mathfrak{s}_1), \ldots, (\mathfrak{m}_k, \mathfrak{s}_k)\}$.

DSig is $(t, q_{\mathsf{S}}, q_{\mathsf{H}}, \epsilon)$-strongly unforgeable if there is no t-time adversary that succeeds with probability $\geq \epsilon$ after making $\leq q_{\mathsf{S}}$ signature oracle queries and $\leq q_{\mathsf{H}}$ random oracle queries. In the standard model, we leave out H and q_{H}.

The difference to the EU-CMA model is that the adversary in the SU-CMA model even wins if it outputs a new signature for a message that it already knows a signature for. In the EU-CMA model, the adversary is forced to output a forgery for a "fresh" message. Instead of directly providing SU-CMA security in our main constructions in Section 4, we use the weaker notion of strong unforgeability against static message attacks (SU-SMA). Here, the adversary submits all messages $\mathfrak{m}_1, \ldots, \mathfrak{m}_{q_{\mathsf{S}}}$ before seeing the public key and the corresponding signatures. Then, we use a generic transformation to achieve full security.

HIBS Schemes. The specification for HIBS schemes is a straightforward generalization of that for digital signature schemes. The main difference is that there are no per-signer verification keys but rather a shared verification key for the entire system. Moreover, the signer's public key is easily computable from a unique user identification string ID over a binary alphabet. The corresponding secret signing key is "extracted" by a trusted authority using a master secret key. The hierarchy is modeled by letting identities be a concatenation of per-level identifiers with decreasing rank, i.e., $\mathsf{ID} = \mathsf{ID}_0 \circ \mathsf{ID}_1 \circ \mathsf{ID}_2$ describes an identity on level 2 with parent identity $\mathsf{ID}_0 \circ \mathsf{ID}_1$, whose parent identity is the master identity ID_0.

More formally: $\mathsf{Kg}(1^n)$ outputs a master private key msk and a master public key mpk. The master identity is the empty string $\varnothing$; $\mathsf{Extract}(\mathsf{sk}_{\mathsf{ID}^\star}, \mathsf{ID})$ outputs a secret signing key sk for ID if $\mathsf{ID}^\star \sqsubset \mathsf{ID}$, otherwise $\perp$; $\mathsf{Sign}(\mathsf{sk}_{\mathsf{ID}}, \mathsf{ID}, \mathfrak{m})$ outputs a signature $\mathfrak{s}$ under $\mathsf{sk}_{\mathsf{ID}}$ for $\mathfrak{m}$; $\mathsf{Vf}(\mathsf{mpk}, \mathsf{ID}, \mathfrak{s}, \mathfrak{m})$ outputs 1 iff $\mathfrak{s}$ is a valid signature on $\mathfrak{m}$ for the given identity and master public key.

The security models for HIBS and ordinary signatures are tightly related with the exception that one has to deal with the additional key extraction mechanism. We consider two variants, selective-ID security (similar to selective-secure HIBE [8]) and the stronger notion of adaptive-ID security. In both models, the adversary can query a key extraction oracle E, a signature oracle, and an optional random oracle. The experiment $\mathsf{Exp}_{\mathcal{A},\mathsf{HIBS}}^{\mathsf{SU\text{-}CMA\text{-}SelectiveID}}$ describes selective-ID security, where the adversary has to fix an identity ID^* before seeing the master public key. He is then forced to output a forgery for ID^*. The adversary gets secret keys for all identities that are not a prefix of ID^*. Furthermore, it can query a signature oracle $\mathsf{S}(\mathsf{ID}, \mathfrak{m})$ with arbitrary identities and messages.

Experiment $\mathsf{Exp}_{\mathcal{A},\mathsf{HIBS}}^{\mathsf{SU\text{-}CMA\text{-}SelectiveID}}(n)$
 $\mathsf{H} \leftarrow \mathcal{H}(1^n)$; $(\mathsf{ID}^*, state) \leftarrow \mathcal{A}(1^n)$; $(\mathsf{msk}, \mathsf{mpk}) \leftarrow \mathsf{Kg}(1^n)$
 $(\mathfrak{m}^*, \mathfrak{s}^*) \leftarrow \mathcal{A}^{\mathsf{E}(\mathsf{msk},\cdot)\setminus\{\cdot \sqsubset \mathsf{ID}^*\},\mathsf{S}(\cdot,\cdot),\mathsf{H}(\cdot)}(\mathsf{mpk}, state)$
 Let $\{(\mathsf{ID}_i, \mathfrak{m}_i, \mathfrak{s}_i)\}_1^k$ be the query-answer tuples for S.
 Return 1 iff $\mathsf{Vf}(\mathsf{mpk}, \mathsf{ID}^*, \mathfrak{s}^*, \mathfrak{m}^*) = 1$ and $(\mathsf{ID}^*, \mathfrak{m}^*, \mathfrak{s}^*) \notin \{(\mathsf{ID}_i, \mathfrak{m}_i, \mathfrak{s}_i)\}_1^k$.

In the stronger model of adaptive-ID security, the adversary can output a forgery for any identity, for which he has never queried a prefix to the extraction oracle before.

Experiment $\mathsf{Exp}_{\mathcal{A},\mathsf{HIBS}}^{\mathsf{SU\text{-}CMA\text{-}AdaptiveID}}(n)$
 $\mathsf{H} \leftarrow \mathcal{H}(1^n)$; $(\mathsf{msk}, \mathsf{mpk}) \leftarrow \mathsf{Kg}(1^n)$
 $(\mathsf{ID}^*, \mathfrak{m}^*, \mathfrak{s}^*) \leftarrow \mathcal{A}^{\mathsf{E}(\mathsf{msk},\cdot),\mathsf{S}(\cdot,\cdot),\mathsf{H}(\cdot)}(\mathsf{mpk})$
 Let $\{(\mathsf{ID}_i, \mathfrak{m}_i, \mathfrak{s}_i)\}_1^k$ be the query-answer tuples of S;
 Let $\{\mathsf{ID}_j\}_1^l$ be the query-answer pairs of E.
 Return 1 iff $\mathsf{Vf}(\mathsf{mpk}, \mathsf{ID}^*, \mathfrak{s}^*, \mathfrak{m}^*) = 1$
  and $(\mathsf{ID}^*, \mathfrak{m}^*, \mathfrak{s}^*) \notin \{(\mathsf{ID}_i, \mathfrak{m}_i, \mathfrak{s}_i)\}_1^k$
  and $\{\mathsf{ID}_j\}_1^l \ni \mathsf{ID}_j \not\sqsubset \mathsf{ID}^*$.

HIBS is $(t, q_{\mathsf{E}}, q_{\mathsf{S}}, q_{\mathsf{H}}, \epsilon)$-strongly unforgeable under chosen message and selective (adaptive) identity attacks if there is no t-time adversary that succeeds with probability $\geq \epsilon$ after making $\leq q_{\mathsf{E}}$ extraction queries, $\leq q_{\mathsf{S}}$ signature oracle queries, and $\leq q_{\mathsf{H}}$ random oracle queries in the respective experiment. Again, we leave out H and q_{H} in the standard model.

In Section 4, we will provide instantiations secure against static message attacks (SMA) and then use the following transformation to achieve CMA security.

From SMA to CMA. Krawczyk and Rabin [23] proposed Chameleon hashes to be hash functions with a trapdoor and the following properties. 1) The function $\mathsf{C} : D \times E \to R$ is chosen from a family $\mathcal{C}$ of Chameleon hashes along with a secret trapdoor t. 2) In order to sample from the distribution $(d, e, \mathsf{C}(d)) \in D \times E \times R$, we can do one of two things. Either we run C on the given document d and a randomness $e \sim \Delta(E)$ (efficiently sampleable), or we apply an inversion algorithm $e \leftarrow \mathsf{C}_t^{-1}(r, d)$ on a given image $r \in R$ and a target document $d \in D$. Thus, we obtain a randomness e such that $\mathsf{C}(d) = (e, r)$. It is important that the resulting distributions are within negligible statistical distance. Note that whenever we need the Chameleon hash to map to a certain range $\neq R$, we can compose it with an arbitrary collision resistant hash function. As for their realization, Krawczyk and Rabin claim in [22] that Chameleon hash functions exist if there are claw-free trapdoor permutations. Interestingly, they can be easily implemented with the lattice-based trapdoor function in [16] as observed in [12].

A helpful fact about Chameleon hash functions is that if they exist, then there is a generic transformation from EU-SMA to EU-CMA signatures. This was known since [23] and it is proven in [19]. We show that the transformation also works for *SU*-SMA to *SU*-CMA in the full version [33]. Observe that it is also applicable to selective-ID secure HIBS schemes as it only affects the way the signature oracle is simulated for the challenge identity.

Lemma 1. *SU-SMA implies SU-CMA if Chameleon hash functions exist.*

2.2 Lattices

In this work, we deal only with full-rank q-ary lattices, i.e., lattices that represent the kernel of the linear map $\mathbf{x} \mapsto \mathbf{A}\mathbf{x} \bmod q$ for a prime modulus q and a matrix $\mathbf{A} \in \mathbb{Z}_q^{n \times m}$. These lattices are denoted with $\Lambda_q^{\perp}(\mathbf{A}) := \{\mathbf{v} \in \mathbb{Z}^m : \mathbf{A}\mathbf{v} \equiv \mathbf{0} \pmod{q}\}$. As with all lattices of dimension $m \geq 2$, they have infinitely many bases. A basis of $\Lambda_q^{\perp}(\mathbf{A})$ is a matrix $\mathbf{B} \in \mathbb{Z}^{m \times m}$, such that $\Lambda(\mathbf{B}) := \{\mathbf{B}\mathbf{x} : \mathbf{x} \in \mathbb{Z}^m\}$ is equal to $\Lambda_q^{\perp}(\mathbf{A})$. The quantity $\det(\Lambda) = |\det(\mathbf{B})|$ (for any basis) is a lattice constant. The main computational problem in q-ary lattices is the "short integer solution" problem SIS. It is parameterized with positive integers $n, m = \mathsf{poly}(n), q = \mathsf{poly}(n)$, and a real norm bound ν and it is formulated as an average-case problem: Given a uniformly random $\mathbf{A} \in \mathbb{Z}_q^{n \times m}$, find a non-zero $\mathbf{v} \in \Lambda_q^{\perp}(\mathbf{A})$ with $\|\mathbf{v}\|_2 \leq \nu$. Ajtai showed in [2] that this problem is at least as hard as finding short vectors in *all* lattices of dimension n, i.e., solving a related worst-case problem. A recent improvement to this reduction can be formulated as follows.

Theorem 1 (Worst-case to Average-case Reduction [16] (informal)). *If there is a polynomial time algorithm that breaks* $\mathsf{SIS}(n, m, q, \nu)$ *for* $q \geq \nu\,\omega(\sqrt{n\log(n)})$, $\nu = \mathsf{poly}(n)$ *with non-negligible probability, then there is a polynomial time algorithm that finds short non-zero vectors, which are only a* $\gamma \geq \nu\widetilde{O}(\sqrt{n})$ *factor longer than the shortest vector, in* all *lattices of dimension* n.

In cryptography, we typically hand over $\mathbf{A}$, or a "bad" basis with long vectors, as the public key and keep a "good" (short) basis as our secret. The length of a basis is $\|\mathbf{B}\| := \max_{i=1,\dots,m} \|\mathbf{b}_i\|_2$. This principle goes back to Ajtai. The most recent improvement for generating such a matrix $\mathbf{A}$ together with a particularly short trapdoor $\mathbf{T}$ for SIS is due to Alwen and Peikert [5].

2.3 Bonsai Trees

The notion of "bonsai trees" on lattices is introduced in [12] in analogy to arboriculture. An arborist always starts with a certain amount of *undirected*, i.e., random, natural growth that he cannot control. Then, he applies his tools and starts cultivating individual branches to achieve the desired looks via *directed* growth. The arborist is successful if the resulting tree still looks sufficiently natural to the observer. Once cultivated, a branch can easily be *extended* to form more directed growth without too much additional care. Instead of extending directed growth, the arborist can also generate a *randomized* offstrings, which can be given to another arborist that can easily cultivate them by *extending* growth. The offsprings hide the first arborist's work and the employed techniques. We formalize these concepts in the context of lattices. A (binary) bonsai tree is generated out of a root $\mathbf{A}^\star$ and branches $\mathbf{A}_i^{(b)} \in \mathbb{Z}_q^{n\times m_i}$, $b \in \{0,1\}, i \leq k \leq \mathsf{poly}(n)$, that are statistically close to uniform. The entire tree is the set $\{\mathbf{A}^\star \circ \mathbf{A}_1^{(x_1)} \circ \dots \circ \mathbf{A}_k^{(x_k)} : \mathbf{x} \in \{0,1\}^{\leq k}\}$.

Proposition 1 (Directed Growth). *Let* $\delta > 0$ *be any fixed real constant and let* $q \geq 3$ *be odd. There is a polynomial time algorithm* $\mathsf{ExtLattice}(\mathbf{A}_1, m_2)$ *that, given uniformly random* $\mathbf{A} \in \mathbb{Z}_q^{n\times m_1}$ *for any* $m_1 \geq (1+\delta)n\log_2(q)$ *and* $\mathsf{poly}(n)$*-bounded* $m_2 \geq (4+2\delta)n\log_2(q)$*, outputs* $(\mathbf{A}_2 \in \mathbb{Z}_q^{n\times m_2}, \mathbf{S} \in \mathbb{Z}^{m\times m})$*, where* $m = m_1 + m_2$*, such that* $\mathbf{A} = \mathbf{A}_1 \circ \mathbf{A}_2$ *is within negligible statistical distance of uniform;* $\mathbf{S}$ *is a basis of* $\Lambda_q^\perp(\mathbf{A}_1 \circ \mathbf{A}_2)$*;* $\|\mathbf{S}\| \leq L = Cn\log_2(q)$ *with overwhelming probability; and* $\left\|\tilde{\mathbf{S}}\right\| \leq \tilde{L} = 1 + C\sqrt{(1+\delta)n\log_2(n)} \leq 1 + C\sqrt{m_1}$ *with overwhelming probability.*

The proposition reflects the most recent result on lattice trapdoors from [4]. In the following, we will use $C = 20$, $\delta = 1$ for simplicity and assume that $\mathbf{A}_2$ is uniformly random instead of within negligible statistical distance from uniform. The resulting key sizes can be optimized by taking δ close to 0 instead. This results in a less uniform distribution of $\mathbf{A}_2$ but it is still within distance $m_2 q^{-\delta n/2}$ from uniform. The interpretation in terms of arboriculture is generating "directed growth" out of "undirected growth" because one starts with some random growth $\mathbf{A}_1$ and cultivates a branch $\mathbf{A}_1 \circ \mathbf{A}_2$ along with a trapdoor $\mathbf{T}$, which is the arborist's journal or a trace of his work. However, the observer cannot distinguish undirected growth from directed growth.

An important observation is that knowing a trapdoor for $\mathbf{A} \in \mathbb{Z}_q^{n \times m}$ implies knowing a trapdoor for all $\mathbf{A}' \in \mathbb{Z}_q^{n \times m'}$, $m' \geq m$, when $\mathbf{A} \sqsubset \mathbf{A}'$. This is because one can apply the trapdoor in dimension m and then pad the resulting vector with zeros to solve SIS in dimension m'.

Proposition 2 (Extending Control). *There is polynomial time algorithm* $\mathsf{ExtBasis}(\mathbf{S}_1, \mathbf{A} = \mathbf{A}_1 \circ \mathbf{A}_2)$ *that takes a basis* $\mathbf{S}$ *of* $\Lambda_q^{\perp}(\mathbf{A}_1)$ *and a matrix* $\mathbf{A}$ *with* $\mathbb{Z}_q^{n \times m_1} \ni \mathbf{A}_1 \sqsubset \mathbf{A} \in \mathbb{Z}_q^{n \times (m_1 + m_2)}$ *as input. If* $m_1 \geq 2n \log_2(q)$, *it outputs a basis* $\mathbf{S}$ *for* $\Lambda_q^{\perp}(\mathbf{A})$ *with* $\left\|\tilde{\mathbf{S}}\right\| = \left\|\tilde{\mathbf{S}}_1\right\|$.

Whenever trapdoor delegation is required, one cannot simply use extending control and hand over the resulting basis as it leaks information about the original trapdoor. Here, we can use tree propagation to obtain a *randomized* offspring with a new, random trapdoor.

Proposition 3 (Randomizing Control). *On input a basis* $\mathbf{S}$ *of the lattice* $\Lambda_q^{\perp}(\mathbf{A})$ *of dimension* m *and a Gaussian parameter* $s \geq \left\|\tilde{\mathbf{S}}\right\| \omega(\sqrt{\log(n)})$, *the polynomial time algorithm* $\mathsf{RandBasis}(\mathbf{S}, s)$ *outputs a basis* $\mathbf{S}'$ *of* $\Lambda_q^{\perp}(\mathbf{A})$ *with* $\left\|\tilde{\mathbf{S}}'\right\| \leq s\sqrt{m}$. *The basis is independent of* $\mathbf{S}$ *in the sense that for any two bases* $\mathbf{S}_0, \mathbf{S}_1$ *of* $\Lambda_q^{\perp}(\mathbf{A})$ *and* $s \geq \max\{\left\|\tilde{\mathbf{S}}_0\right\|, \left\|\tilde{\mathbf{S}}_1\right\|\}\omega(\sqrt{\log(n)})$, $\mathsf{RandBasis}(\mathbf{S}_0, s)$ *is within negligible statistical distance of* $\mathsf{RandBasis}(\mathbf{S}_1, s)$.

Estimating Secure Parameters. We could use the worst-case to average-case reduction for selecting secure parameters but that might be too conservative as the reduction is quite loose with respect to the ratio $m/n = \Omega(\log(n))$. The observations of Gama and Nguyen in [15] may be more realistic. They assume that lattice reduction algorithms find short lattice vectors $\mathbf{v}$ in lattices Λ of dimension d with $\|\mathbf{v}\|_2 \leq \delta^d \det(\Lambda)^{1/d}$ for some $\delta > 0$. This value δ is supposed to "summarize" the capability of the employed lattice reduction algorithm. Nguyen and Gama analyze random lattices from a certain distribution and find that reaching $\delta < 1.01$ in high dimensions is hard.

Since the distribution of lattices in the SIS problem is different, their conjecture is not directly applicable. Furthermore, Micciancio and Regev describe an attack that works best in a sub-lattice of the usual q-ary lattice $\Lambda_q^{\perp}(\mathbf{A})$. Assuming an adversary with capability δ^*, they show that for given parameters n and q, the best strategy of for the adversary is to attack a sub-lattice of dimension $d^* = \sqrt{n \log(q) / \log(\delta^*)}$. In this dimension, the adversary finds vectors of Euclidean length $\nu^* = \min\{q, 2^{2\sqrt{n \log(q) \log(\delta^*)}}\}$ [31]. For our parameter choices, we will always assume that the adversary is capable of reaching $\delta^* = 1.01$, but no less. All schemes in Sections 3 and 4 are based on the hardness of SIS in q-ary lattices of dimension m for a particular norm bound ν. Given this norm bound and δ^*, we need to establish that $\nu^* \gg \nu$, e.g., with a factor of 10 between both sides. The implicit assumption is that lattice basis reduction algorithms behave the same on random q-ary sub-lattices. Whether this heuristic is completely sound, is still unknown.

3 Warm-Up — Constructions with Random Oracles

In this section, we recall strongly unforgeable GPV signatures as introduced in [16]. Then, we show how to use GPV together with the Bonsai-tree concept to build strongly unforgeable hierarchical identity-based signatures in the random oracle model. The proposed scheme is also secure under adaptive-identity queries.

3.1 Strongly Unforgeable Signatures

Lattice-based strongly unforgeable signatures were first proposed by Gentry, Peikert, and Vaikuntanathan in [16]. They introduce a family of preimage sampleable functions $\mathsf{GPV} = (\mathsf{TrapGen}, \mathsf{Eval}, \mathsf{SamplePre})$ on lattices. Its parameters $q, m, \tilde{L}, s = \omega(\sqrt{\log(n)})\tilde{L}$ only depend on the security parameter n as in Proposition 1. We define the sets $D_d := \{\mathbf{x} \in \mathbb{Z}^m \setminus \{\mathbf{0}\} : \|\mathbf{x}\|_2 \leq d\}$ and $R := \mathbb{Z}_q^n$.

The algorithm $\mathsf{TrapGen}(1^n)$ outputs a public description $\mathbf{A} \in \mathbb{Z}_q^{n\times m}$ together with a secret trapdoor $\mathbf{T} \in \mathbb{Z}^{m\times m}$, $\left\|\tilde{\mathbf{T}}\right\| \leq \tilde{L}$. Evaluation of the function $f_{\mathbf{A}} : \mathbb{Z}_q^m \to R$ is performed by $\mathsf{Eval}(\mathbf{A}, \mathbf{x}) = \mathbf{A}\mathbf{x} \bmod q$. Finally, the inversion algorithm $\mathsf{SamplePre}(\mathbf{T}, s, \mathbf{y})$ samples from the set of preimages $\{\mathbf{x} \in D_{s\sqrt{m}} : f_{\mathbf{A}}(\mathbf{x}) = \mathbf{y}\}$. Preimages have a conditional min-entropy of $\omega(\log(n))$ and follow a certain Gaussian distribution that can be efficiently sampled with $\mathsf{SampleDom}$, even without the trapdoor. By construction, the function compresses the input and therefore admits collisions. Finding collisions in D_d, however, is at least as hard as solving $\mathsf{SIS}(n, q, m, 2d)$.

Now, we can define $\mathsf{DSig}^{\mathsf{GPV}}$ accordingly. Let $\mathcal{H}$ be a family of random oracles $\mathsf{H} : \{0,1\}^* \to R = \mathbb{Z}_q^n$. The key generator simply forwards the output of $\mathsf{TrapGen}$. Signing a message $\mathfrak{m}$ involves choosing $r \leftarrow_\$ \{0,1\}^n$, computing $\mathbf{y} \leftarrow \mathsf{H}(\mathfrak{m}, r)$, and calling $\mathfrak{s} \leftarrow \mathsf{SamplePre}(\mathbf{T}, s, \mathbf{y})$. A signature $(\mathfrak{s}, r)$ for $\mathfrak{m}$ verifies if $\mathfrak{s} \in D_{s\sqrt{m}}$ and $f_{\mathbf{A}}(\mathfrak{s}) = \mathsf{H}(\mathfrak{m}, r)$.

Security. Notice that the signature oracle can be efficiently simulated without the trapdoor by standard random oracle techniques. A forgery $(\mathfrak{m}^*, \mathfrak{s}^*, r^*)$ in the SU-CMA experiment implies a collision $(\mathfrak{s}^*, \mathfrak{s}_i)$ with $f_{\mathbf{A}}(\mathfrak{s}_i) = f_{\mathbf{A}}(\mathfrak{s}^*) = \mathsf{H}(\mathfrak{m}^*, r^*)$, where $\mathfrak{s}_i$ was chosen during the random oracle simulation. By the conditional min-entropy, we know that $\mathfrak{s}_i \neq \mathfrak{s}^*$ with probability $1 - n^{-\omega(1)}$. Let $T_{\mathsf{TrapGen}}(n)$, $T_{\mathsf{SampleDom}}(n)$, and $T_{\mathsf{Eval}}(n)$ be the cost functions for trapdoor generation, sampling, and trapdoor evaluation. In addition, let $T_{\mathsf{List}}(n)$ be the cost function for list processing in the simulation of the random oracle.

Theorem 2 (Strong Unforgeability [16]). *For the above choice of parameters, $\mathsf{DSig}^{\mathsf{GPV}}$ is $(t, q_{\mathsf{S}}, q_{\mathsf{H}}, \epsilon)$-strongly unforgeable in the random oracle model if $\mathsf{SIS}(n, m, q, 2s\sqrt{m})$ is $(t + q_{\mathsf{S}}T_{\mathsf{List}} + q_{\mathsf{H}}(T_{\mathsf{SampleDom}}(n) + T_{\mathsf{Eval}}(n) + T_{\mathsf{List}}(n)), (\epsilon - q_{\mathsf{S}}^2/2^n)(1 - n^{-\omega(1)}))$-hard.*

Via Theorem 1, a corollary states that a successful attacker can find the shortest vector in all lattices of dimension n up to an approximation factor $\gamma \geq \tilde{L}\widetilde{\mathcal{O}}(n) = \widetilde{\mathcal{O}}(n\sqrt{n})$.

Secure Parameters. We estimate secure paramters for $\mathsf{DSig}^{\mathsf{GPV}}$ as described in Section 2. For a given security parameter n, we choose the remaining parameters according to Proposition 1 and a prime $q \approx n^{4.5}$. For $n \geq 197$, we obtain the required hardness of the underlying SIS problem.

3.2 Strongly Unforgeable Hierarchical ID-Based Signatures

Using the signature scheme from the previous section, we can can directly apply the Bonsai-tree concept to obtain a hierarchical identity-based signature scheme $\mathsf{HIBS}^{\mathsf{GPV}}$ in the random oracle model. The idea is that, based on a given ID, the secret key extraction algorithm $\mathsf{Extract}$ first uses $\mathsf{ExtBasis}$ to extend the matrix $\mathbf{A}^\star$ to $\mathbf{A}_{\mathsf{ID}}$ and the secret master key $\mathbf{T}^\star$ to $\mathbf{T}_{\mathsf{ID}}$ such that $\mathbf{A}_{\mathsf{ID}}\mathbf{T}_{\mathsf{ID}} \equiv \mathbf{0}$. Then, in order to protect the master key, it uses $\mathsf{RandBasis}$ and outputs a randomized trapdoor $\mathbf{S}_{\mathsf{ID}}$. The individual signers use $\mathsf{DSig}^{\mathsf{GPV}}$ and we have an identity-based signature scheme that is strongly unforgeable. This concept can be transfered to the hierarchical setting, where every signer may act as a key extraction entity. Note that the number of levels in the hierarchy affects the tightness of the security proof as these randomized trapdoors are slightly worse than the master trapdoor.

We assume that all identities on all levels have length κ. The maximum number of levels, including the master-key, is $\ell+1$. We denote the basis length on level k with $\tilde{L}_k$ and the corresponding Gaussian parameter with $s_k = \omega(\sqrt{\log(n)})\tilde{L}_k$.

Master-key Generation. Let $q, \tilde{L}, m_1, m_2$ be chosen according to Proposition 1 and let $d = \tilde{L}\omega(\sqrt{\log(n)})^{\ell+1}\sqrt{m_1 + (\ell\kappa+1)m_2}^{\,\ell+1}$. These parameters may be excluded from the public key as they are the same for all users. Generate a description $\mathbf{A}^\star \in \mathbb{Z}_q^{n\times m_1+m_2}$ of the master lattice $\Lambda_q^\perp(\mathbf{A}^\star)$ together with a trapdoor $\mathbf{S}^\star$ such that $\left\|\tilde{\mathbf{S}}\right\| \leq \tilde{L}$ with $\mathsf{ExtLattice}$. Then, choose random matrices $\langle\mathbf{A}\rangle := \left\{(\mathbf{A}_i^{(0)}, \mathbf{A}_i^{(1)})\right\}_1^{\ell\kappa}$ from $\mathbb{Z}_q^{n\times m_2}$. The secret is $\mathbf{S}^\star$ and the public key is $(\mathbf{A}^\star, \langle\mathbf{A}\rangle)$.

Key Extraction. On input $\mathbf{S}^\star_{\mathsf{ID}^\star}$, ID with $\mathsf{ID} = \mathsf{ID}^\star \circ \mathsf{ID}'$, $|\mathsf{ID}| = l \leq \ell\kappa$, $\mathsf{ID}' = \mathsf{ID}'_1, \ldots, \mathsf{ID}'_\kappa \in \{0,1\}^\kappa$ recursively define the matrix $\mathbf{A}_{\mathsf{ID}} := \mathbf{A}_{\mathsf{ID}^\star} \circ \mathbf{A}_{l+1}^{(\mathsf{ID}'_1)} \circ \cdots \circ \mathbf{A}_{l+\kappa}^{(\mathsf{ID}'_\kappa)}$ with $\mathbf{A}_\varnothing := \mathbf{A}^\star$, and call $\mathbf{T}_{\mathsf{ID}} \leftarrow \mathsf{ExtBasis}(\mathbf{S}^\star_{\mathsf{ID}^\star}, \mathbf{A}_{\mathsf{ID}})$. Then, let $s = \left\|\tilde{\mathbf{T}}_{\mathsf{ID}}\right\| \omega(\sqrt{\log(n)})$ and output the randomized basis $\mathbf{S}_{\mathsf{ID}} \leftarrow \mathsf{RandBasis}(\mathbf{S}_{\mathsf{ID}}, s)$ with $\left\|\tilde{\mathbf{S}}_{\mathsf{ID}}\right\| \leq s\sqrt{\dim(\mathbf{S}_{\mathsf{ID}})}$. For inappropriate inputs, return $\perp$.

Signing. On input a message $\mathfrak{m} \in \{0,1\}^*$ and the trapdoor $\mathbf{S}_{\mathsf{ID}}$, the signer with identity ID on level k chooses $r \leftarrow_\$ \{0,1\}^n$ and computes $\mathfrak{s} \leftarrow \mathsf{SamplePre}(\mathbf{S}_{\mathsf{ID}}, s_k, \mathsf{H}(\mathfrak{m}, r, \mathsf{ID}))$. It outputs $(\mathfrak{s}, r)$.

Verification. On input $(\mathbf{A}^\star, \langle\mathbf{A}\rangle)$, an identity ID, a signature $(\mathfrak{s}, r)$, and a message $\mathfrak{m}$, the algorithm outputs 1 if and only if $\mathfrak{s} \in D_d$ and $f_{\mathbf{A}_{\mathsf{ID}}}(\mathfrak{s}) = \mathsf{H}(\mathfrak{m}, r, \mathsf{ID})$.

Recall that $\mathsf{SamplePre}$ outputs a vector of length at most $s\sqrt{m}$ with $s = \omega(\sqrt{\log(n)})\tilde{L}$ when called with a trapdoor of length at most $\tilde{L}$ in dimension m. The maximum dimension in the scheme is $m_1 + (\ell\kappa + 1)m_2$ on level ℓ. The maximum basis length on level i is $\tilde{L}_i = s_{i-1}\sqrt{m_1 + (\ell\kappa + 1)m_2}$ with $\tilde{L}_0 := \tilde{L}$. The Gaussian parameter for presampling on level i is $s_i = \omega(\sqrt{\log(n)})\tilde{L}_i$ with $s_0 = s$. This recurrence yields $\tilde{L}_\ell = \tilde{L}\omega(\sqrt{\log(n)})^\ell \sqrt{m_1 + (\ell\kappa + 1)m_2}^\ell$. Signing with such a basis yields signatures of Euclidean length at most $\omega(\sqrt{\log(n)})\tilde{L}_\ell \sqrt{m_1 + (\ell\kappa + 1)m_2} = d$. Thus, such signatures are accepted by the verifier. The security guarantees scale with the depth of the hierarchy as the norm bound becomes looser for increasing ℓ.

Security. We prove that $\mathsf{HIBS}^{\mathsf{GPV}}$ is secure under selective identity attacks. The second theorem shows that it is even secure under *adaptive* identity attacks, but with a looser reduction. The latter reduction, however, is not as loose as the generic method of guessing the right identity with probability $2^{-\kappa}$ [8]. Let $T_{\mathsf{func}}(x)$ be the cost function for function func and let $T_{\mathsf{List}}(n)$ be the cost function for list processing for simulating a random oracle.

Theorem 3 (Selective Security). $\mathsf{HIBS}^{\mathsf{GPV}}$ *is* $(t, q_{\mathsf{S}}, q_{\mathsf{H}}, \epsilon)$*-strongly unforgeable under selective identity attacks in the random oracle model if* SIS *is* $(t + 2T_{\mathsf{ExtLattice}} + q_{\mathsf{E}}T_{\mathsf{Extract}} + (q_{\mathsf{H}} + q_{\mathsf{S}})T_{\mathsf{H}}, (1 - n^{-\omega(1)})(\epsilon - q_{\mathsf{S}}^2/2^n))$*-hard with norm bound* $\nu = 2\tilde{L}\omega(\sqrt{\log(n)})^{\ell+1}\sqrt{m_1 + (\ell\kappa + 1)m_2}^{\ell+1}$.

Notice the the GPV signature scheme can be efficiently simulated by a standard random oracle technique. Moreoever, the adversary will make $\leq q_{\mathsf{E}}$ extraction queries that need to be answered. We prepare for this by “knowing” a trapdoor for a prefix of all but the challenge identity. Upon an extraction query, this trapdoor can be extended to a trapdoor for the requested identity. The external challenge, the input $\mathbf{A}$ from the SIS problem, is embedded in the public key of the challenge identity. Via random oracle techniques, the reduction knows a valid signature for the output message of the adversary. However, the adversary outputs a different signature with probability $1 - n^{-\omega(1)}$ by the conditional min-entropy of the set of possible signature. The proof is in the full version [33].

Theorem 4 (Adaptive Security). $\mathsf{HIBS}^{\mathsf{GPV}}$ *can be made* $(t, q_{\mathsf{S}}, q_{\mathsf{H}}, q_{\mathsf{G}}, \epsilon)$*-strongly unforgeable under* adaptive *identity attacks in the random oracle model if it is* $(t, q_{\mathsf{S}}, q_{\mathsf{H}}, q_{\mathsf{G}}, \epsilon/q_{\mathsf{G}})$*-strongly unforgeable under* selective *identity attacks.*

Here, we only give the idea of the conversion. We need to change the way the identities are mapped to the branches of the Bonsai tree. Instead of directly using the binary representation of ID or its hash value, we apply a random oracle G to the individual substrings of length κ first. Thus, every ID is mapped to a random position in the tree. Assume that the adversary makes q_{G} queries to this random oracle, we can prepare a randomly selected path in the tree with "undirected growth" and program the random oracle to map one of the q_{G} queries to this path. Therefore, the success probability of the reduction degrades with a factor $1/q_{\mathsf{G}}$ instead of the generic $1/2^{\kappa}$.

The worst-case to average-case reduction guarantees security if finding shortest vectors up to an approximation factor $\gamma \geq 2d\widetilde{\mathcal{O}}(\sqrt{n}) = \widetilde{\mathcal{O}}(\sqrt{n}^{\ell+3})$ is hard in the worst case in dimension n.

Secure Parameters. We assume identites of length $\kappa = 40$ bits, which should be sufficient in practical scenarios. The parameter q is crucial as it greatly influences the hardness of SIS and the worst-case to average-case reduction only holds for large enough q. The scheme's efficiency greatly depends on the number $\ell + 1$ of layers in the hierarchy. For larger ℓ, we are forced to increase q. Possible secure choices for (ℓ, n, q) are $(1, 467, n^6)$, $(2, 692, n^8)$, $(3, 1011, n^9)$, or $(4, 1258, n^{11})$.

4 Constructions without Random Oracles

In the following, we propose our main constructions. We start with a strongly unforgeable signature scheme and then propose a strongly unforgeable hierarchical identity-based signature scheme that is secure under selective identity attacks. Both constructions are secure in the standard model.

In the following, we let $\mathsf{H} : \{0,1\}^* \to \{0,1\}^{\lambda}$ be a collision-resistant hash function that maps into the message space. Finding collisions in polynomial time is only possible with probability $\leq c$.

4.1 Strongly Unforgeable Signatures

We propose a variant of the EU-CMA signature scheme [12]. The authors first create an EU-SMA secure signature scheme in the standard model and then apply a generic conversion from EU-SMA to EU-CMA, using a Chameleon hash function. We follow this line of thought and construct a signature scheme that is even secure in the SU-CMA sense. We achieve this by computing the signatures in a different way, compared to [12] scheme. In their scheme, there is a matrix $\mathbf{A}_{\mathfrak{m}}$ and a corresponding lattice $\Lambda_q^{\perp}(\mathbf{A}_{\mathfrak{m}})$ for which the signer can derive a trapdoor. The matrix $\mathbf{A}_{\mathfrak{m}}$ is formed as in Section 3.2. The signatures in their work are short lattice vectors in $\Lambda_q^{\perp}(\mathbf{A}_{\mathfrak{m}})$, i.e., short vectors $\mathfrak{s} \neq \mathbf{0}$ such that $\mathbf{A}_{\mathfrak{m}}\mathfrak{s} \equiv \mathbf{0}$. In our scheme, we fix a random $\mathbf{y} \in \mathbb{Z}_q^n$ and let the signer solve $\mathbf{A}_{\mathfrak{m}}\mathfrak{s} \equiv \mathbf{y}$ instead. The overhead is a simple linear algebra step (cf. [16]) that can done once during key generation. Surprisingly, this slight change enables us to prove *strong* unforgeability. It is important to note that, unlike in [12], we need to be able to answer all signature queries in the security proof, i.e., even for the message $\mathfrak{m}^*$ that the adversary outputs a forgery for.

First of all, we demonstrate that the scheme in [12] is not strongly unforgeable by showing an attack that only works in the SU-SMA model and not in EU-SMA. The adversary in the SU-SMA experiment queries its signature oracle with a random message $\mathfrak{m}^*$ and receives a signature $\mathfrak{s}$ such that $\mathfrak{s} \in D(s\sqrt{m})$ and $\mathbf{A}_{\mathfrak{m}}\mathfrak{s} \equiv \mathbf{0}$. The adversary simply returns the valid forgery $\mathfrak{s}^* \leftarrow -\mathfrak{s}$.

We specify $\mathsf{DSig}^{\mathsf{su\text{-}sma}}$, where one may interpret the randomness-message pair as an identity.

Key Generation. Let $q, \tilde{L}, m_1, m_2$ be chosen according to Proposition 1 and let $s = \tilde{L}\omega(\sqrt{\log(n)})$ and $d = s\sqrt{m_1 + (\lambda+1)m_2}$. These parameters may be excluded from the public key as they are the same for all users. Use $\mathsf{ExtLattice}$ to generate a description $\mathbf{A}^\star \in \mathbb{Z}_q^{n \times m_1 + m_2}$ of the master lattice $\Lambda_q^\perp(\mathbf{A}^\star)$ together with a trapdoor $\mathbf{S}^\star$ such that $\left\|\tilde{\mathbf{S}}\right\| \leq \tilde{L}$. Furthermore, generate a set $\langle \mathbf{B} \rangle := \left\{(\mathbf{B}_i^{(0)}, \mathbf{B}_i^{(1)})\right\}_1^\lambda$ random matrices in $\mathbb{Z}_q^{n \times m_2}$. Finally, choose $\mathbf{y} \leftarrow_\$ \mathbb{Z}_q^n$ and output the secret key $\mathbf{S}^\star$ and the public key $(\mathbf{A}^\star, \langle \mathbf{B} \rangle, \mathbf{y})$.

Signing. On input a message $\mathfrak{m} \in \{0,1\}^*$ and the secret trapdoor $\mathbf{S}^\star$, the signer with identity chooses $r \leftarrow_\$ \{0,1\}^n$ and computes $h \leftarrow \mathsf{H}(\mathfrak{m}, r)$, $\mathfrak{s} \leftarrow \mathsf{SamplePre}(\mathbf{S}_h, s, \mathbf{y})$. The trapdoor $\mathbf{S}_h$ is formed via $\mathsf{ExtBasis}(\mathbf{S}^\star, \mathbf{A}_h)$, where $\mathbf{A}_h := \mathbf{A}^\star \circ \mathbf{B}_1^{(h_1)} \circ \cdots \circ \mathbf{B}_\lambda^{(h_\lambda)}$. It outputs $(\mathfrak{s}, r)$.

Verification. On input $(\mathbf{A}^\star, \langle \mathbf{B} \rangle, \mathbf{y})$, a signature $(\mathfrak{s}, r)$, and a message $\mathfrak{m}$, the algorithm outputs 1 if and only if $\mathfrak{s} \in D_d$ and $\mathbf{A}_{\mathsf{H}(\mathfrak{m},r)}(\mathfrak{s}) = \mathbf{y}$.

The scheme is complete because all signatures are generated using a basis of length $\tilde{L}$ and with the Gaussian parameter $s = \omega(\sqrt{\log(n)})\tilde{L}$. The total dimension is $m = m_1 + (\lambda+1)m_2$. Thus, $\mathsf{SamplePre}$ outputs signatures of length at most $s\sqrt{m_1 + (\lambda+1)m_2} = d$ that are accepted by Vf. In order to get the full (SU-CMA) scheme, we wrap the message with a Chameleon hash function.

Security. We prove that $\mathsf{DSig}^{\mathsf{su\text{-}sma}}$ is SU-SMA secure and then apply the black-box conversion in Lemma 1. Let $T_{\mathsf{func}}(n)$ be the cost function for the function func and let $T_{\mathsf{List}}(n)$ be the cost function for list processing, which is explained in the analysis below.

Theorem 5 (Strong Unforgeability). $\mathsf{DSig}^{\mathsf{su\text{-}sma}}$ *is* (t, ϵ) *strongly unforgeable under static message attacks (SU-SMA) if* SIS *with* $\nu = 2\tilde{L}\omega(\sqrt{\log(n)})$ $\sqrt{m_1 + (\lambda+1)m_2}$ *is* $(t + \lambda q_{\mathsf{S}} T_{\mathsf{List}} + T_{\mathsf{ExtLattice}} + q_{\mathsf{S}}(T_{\mathsf{SamplePre}} + T_{\mathsf{ExtBasis}}), 1/2(1 - n^{-\omega(1)})(\epsilon - q_{\mathsf{S}}^2/2^n - c)/(\lambda q_{\mathsf{S}}))$*-hard.*

The idea is to separate the adversaries into two classes. One works in the EU-SMA sense and the other exploits the additional freedom of the SU-SMA setting. The reduction guesses the type of adversary before handing over the public key. If it expects an EU-SMA forger, the reduction knows $\mathbf{x}$ with $\mathbf{A}^\star\mathbf{x} \equiv \mathbf{y}$ and forces the forger to solve an inhomogeneous SIS, for which the reduction does not know the trapdoor. Together with $\mathbf{x}$, it can solve the corresponding SIS with overwhelming probability. For the SU-SMA forger, the reduction has to guess the index i^* of the signature query that will be recycled in the forgery with probability $1/q_{\mathsf{S}}$. There, it plants an $\mathbf{x}$ with $\mathbf{A}_{\mathsf{H}(\mathfrak{m}_{i^*}, r_{i^*})}\mathbf{x} \equiv \mathbf{y}$. Again, with the adversary's help, the reduction solves SIS with overwhelming probability, while being able to answer a single signature query for $\mathfrak{m}_{i^*}$ with $\mathbf{x}$. The key extraction queries are answered as described in Section 3.2. The full proof is in the full version [33]

Therefore, $\mathsf{DSig}^{\mathsf{su\text{-}sma}}$ is secure if finding shortest vectors in dimension n, within factors $\gamma \geq \widetilde{\mathcal{O}}(n\sqrt{n})$, is hard in the worst case. Via Lemma 1, we immediately get similar results for SU-CMA.

Secure Parameters. The underlying problem is SIS with $\nu = 2\omega(\sqrt{\log(n)})\tilde{L}\sqrt{m_1 + (\lambda+1)m_2}$. Let $\lambda = 160$ and consider $\log(n) = \omega(\sqrt{\log(n)})$. As before, q is chosen such that the worst-case to average-case reduction holds ($q \approx n^5$). Now, for $n \geq 247$, we obtain the required complexity of SIS.

4.2 Strongly Unforgeable Hierarchical ID-Based Signatures

By adding more layers to the hierarchy in Section 4.1, we construct a hierarchical identity-based signature scheme $\mathsf{HIBS}^{\mathsf{su\text{-}sma}}$ that is strongly unforgeable. The identities are handled as in Section 3.2 but then we use an additional Bonsai tree to sign.

The length of each sub-identity on each level is κ, the number of levels is ℓ, and messages have λ bits. $\tilde{L}_k$ is the basis length on level k. The corresponding Gaussian parameter is $s_k := \omega(\sqrt{\log(n)})\tilde{L}_k$.

Master-key Generation. Let $q, \tilde{L}, m_1, m_2$ be chosen according to Proposition 1 and let $d = \tilde{L}\omega(\sqrt{\log(n)})^{\ell+1}\sqrt{m_1 + (\ell\kappa + \lambda + 1)m_2}^{\ell+1}$. These parameters may be excluded from the public key as they are the same for all users. Use $\mathsf{ExtLattice}$ to generate a description $\mathbf{A}^\star \in \mathbb{Z}_q^{n \times m_1 + m_2}$ of the master lattice $\Lambda_q^\perp(\mathbf{A}^\star)$ together with a trapdoor $\mathbf{S}^\star$ such that $\left\|\tilde{\mathbf{T}}\right\| \leq \tilde{L}$. Furthermore, generate the sets $\langle \mathbf{A} \rangle := \left\{(\mathbf{A}_i^{(0)}, \mathbf{A}_i^{(1)})\right\}_1^{\ell\kappa}$, $\langle \mathbf{B} \rangle := \left\{(\mathbf{B}_i^{(0)}, \mathbf{B}_i^{(1)})\right\}_1^{\lambda}$ of random matrices in $\mathbb{Z}_q^{n \times m_2}$. Finally, choose $\mathbf{y} \leftarrow_\$ \mathbb{Z}_q^n$ and output the secret key $\mathbf{S}^\star$ and the public key $(\mathbf{A}^\star, \langle \mathbf{A} \rangle, \langle \mathbf{B} \rangle, \mathbf{y})$.

Key Extraction. On input $\mathbf{S}^\star_{\mathsf{ID}^\star}$, ID with $\mathsf{ID} = \mathsf{ID}^\star \circ \mathsf{ID}'$, $|\mathsf{ID}| = l \leq \ell\kappa$, $\mathsf{ID}' = \mathsf{ID}'_1, \ldots, \mathsf{ID}'_\kappa \in \{0,1\}^\kappa$ recursively define the matrix $\mathbf{A}_{\mathsf{ID}} := \mathbf{A}_{\mathsf{ID}^\star} \circ \mathbf{A}_{l+1}^{(\mathsf{ID}'_1)} \circ \cdots \circ \mathbf{A}_{l+\kappa}^{(\mathsf{ID}'_\kappa)}$ with $\mathbf{A}_\varnothing := \mathbf{A}^\star$, and call $\mathbf{T}_{\mathsf{ID}} \leftarrow \mathsf{ExtBasis}(\mathbf{S}^\star_{\mathsf{ID}^\star}, \mathbf{A}_{\mathsf{ID}})$. Then, let $s = \left\|\tilde{\mathbf{T}}\right\| \omega(\sqrt{\log(n)})$ and output the randomized basis $\mathbf{S}_{\mathsf{ID}} \leftarrow \mathsf{RandBasis}(\mathbf{T}_{\mathsf{ID}}, s)$ with $\left\|\tilde{\mathbf{S}}_{\mathsf{ID}}\right\| \leq s\sqrt{\dim(\mathbf{T}_{\mathsf{ID}})}$. For inappropriate inputs, return $\perp$.

Signing. On input a message $\mathfrak{m} \in \{0,1\}^*$ and a secret trapdoor $\mathbf{S}_{\mathsf{ID}}$, the signer with identity ID on level k chooses $r \leftarrow_\$ \{0,1\}^n$ and computes $\mu \leftarrow \mathsf{H}(\mathfrak{m}, r)$. Now μ is used to form $\mathbf{A}_{\mathsf{ID}\circ\mu} := \mathbf{A}_{\mathsf{ID}} \circ \mathbf{B}_1^{(\mu_1)} \circ \cdots \circ \mathbf{B}_\lambda^{(\mu_\lambda)}$. Then, the signer extends its secret basis by calling $\mathbf{S}_{\mathsf{ID}\circ\mu} \leftarrow \mathsf{ExtBasis}(\mathbf{S}_{\mathsf{ID}}, \mathbf{A}_{\mathsf{ID}\circ\mu})$. Finally, it outputs $\mathfrak{s} \leftarrow \mathsf{SamplePre}(\mathbf{S}_{\mathsf{ID}\circ\mu}, s_k, \mathbf{y})$ and r.

Verification. On input $(\mathbf{A}^\star, \langle \mathbf{A} \rangle, \langle \mathbf{B} \rangle, \mathbf{y})$, a signature $(\mathfrak{s}, r)$, and a message $\mathfrak{m}$, the algorithm outputs 1 if and only if $\mathfrak{s} \in D_d$ and $\mathbf{A}_{\mathsf{ID}\circ\mathsf{H}(\mathfrak{m},r)}(\mathfrak{s}) = \mathbf{y}$.

Notice that the scheme is complete by a similar argument as in Section 3.2. The maximum trapdoor length (level ℓ) is $\tilde{L}_\ell = \tilde{L}\omega(\sqrt{\log(n)})^\ell \sqrt{m_1 + (\ell\kappa + \lambda + 1)m_2}^\ell$.

This basis is extended once before signing, which is length-preserving. Then, signing is done via SamplePre that outputs a vector of length at most $\omega(\sqrt{\log(n)})\tilde{L}_\ell \sqrt{m_1 + (\ell\kappa + \lambda + 1)m_2} \leq d$. Thus, the verification algorithm accepts.

Unforgeability. We prove that $\mathsf{HIBS}^{\text{su-sma}}$ is SU-SMA secure under a selective-identity attack. Then, we can apply the transform in Lemma 1 to make it SU-CMA secure. For the transformation to be identity-based as well, the Chameleon hash function needs to be published as part of mpk.

Theorem 6 (Selective Security). *$\mathsf{HIBS}^{\text{su-sma}}$ is $(t, q_\mathsf{S}, \epsilon)$ SU-SMA secure under selective identity attacks if* SIS *is $(t + 3T_{\mathsf{ExtLattice}} + q_\mathsf{E}T_{\mathsf{Extract}} + \lambda q_\mathsf{S}T_{\mathsf{List}} + q_\mathsf{S}(T_{\mathsf{SamplePre}} + T_{\mathsf{ExtBasis}}), 1/2(1 - n^{-\omega(1)})(\epsilon - q_\mathsf{S}^2/2^n - c)/(\lambda q_\mathsf{S}))$-hard with norm bound $\nu = 2\tilde{L}\omega(\sqrt{\log(n)})^{\ell+1}\sqrt{m_1 + (\ell\kappa + \lambda + 1)m_2}^{\ell+1}$.*

Proof (Sketch). We assume that there is a successful adversary $\mathcal{A}$ against unforgeability of $\mathsf{HIBS}^{\text{su-sma}}$ and construct a reduction $\mathcal{B}$ that solves SIS. The setup is as in Theorem 3 in order to be able to simulate the key extraction queries for all identities that are not a prefix of the challenge identity I. However, the input $\mathbf{A}$ of the reduction needs to be wider, namely in $\mathbb{Z}_q^{m_1+(\ell\kappa+\lambda+1)m_2}$ in order to simulate the static signature queries for identity I. Signature queries for identities $I' \neq I$ can be simulated with a known trapdoor. The overhead of the reduction is $2T_{\mathsf{ExtLattice}} + q_\mathsf{E}T_{\mathsf{Extract}}$ for setting up and running the extraction oracle. The overhead for signing is $\lambda q_\mathsf{S}T_{\mathsf{List}} + T_{\mathsf{ExtLattice}} + q_\mathsf{S}(T_{\mathsf{SamplePre}} + T_{\mathsf{ExtBasis}})$. As in Theorem 5, the reduction sets $\mathbf{y}$ such that it knows a preimage $\mathbf{x}$ either for EU-SMA or for SU-SMA forgers. In both cases, the reduction solves SIS. The probability that the adversary outputs a signature that yields a solution to SIS is as in Theorem 5 because we use the same signature scheme here and we can prepare for all extraction queries.

The full proof is a combination of the techniques that are used in Theorems 3 and 5. □

In consequence, $\mathsf{HIBS}^{\text{su-sma}}$ is secure as long as finding shortest lattice vectors up to approximation factors $\gamma \geq 2d\widetilde{O}(\sqrt{n}) = \widetilde{O}(n\sqrt{n}^{\ell+3})$ is hard in the worst case in dimension n.

Secure Parameters. We let $\kappa = 40$ and $\lambda = 160$ and estimate secure parameters for $\ell = 1, 2, 3, 4$, i.e., for $2, 3, 4, 5$ levels. For (ℓ, n, q), we obtain $(1, 478, n^7)$, $(2, 730, n^9)$, $(3, 1082, n^{10})$, or $(4, 1362, n^{12})$.

5 Conclusions

We have shown three results. As a warm-up, we have constructed an adaptive-ID secure, strongly unforgeable hierarchical identity-based signature scheme in the random oracle model. Then, we have shown the first lattice-based strongly unforgeable signature scheme without Merkle trees [29] in the standard model. And, finally, we provide the first strongly unforgeable hierarchical identity-based signatures scheme in the standard model from lattices. For each construction, we have proposed a set of secure parameters based on today's knowledge about lattice reduction algorithms. Another benefit is that all of our constructions can be transferred to ideal lattices that admit short keys and efficient operations. Moreover, we can use mild, worst-case hardness assumptions in lattices as the basis of security in all constructions.

Acknowledgments

The author would like to thank Benoît Libert for a helpful discussion on HIBS. He also thanks Pierre-Louis Cayrel and Dominique Schröder for reviewing parts of this work. Furthermore, the author thanks the anonymous reviewers of PQC 2010 for their constructive comments. The author is indebted to one of the reviewers, who suggested a simplification for demonstrating that the scheme in [12] is not SU-CMA secure. This part of Section 4 is now much easier to understand.

References

1. Agrawal, S., Boyen, X.: Identity-based encryption from lattices in the standard model (July 2009) (manuscript), http://www.cs.stanford.edu/~xb/ab09/
2. Ajtai, M.: Generating hard instances of lattice problems (extended abstract). In: STOC, pp. 99–108. ACM, New York (1996)
3. Ajtai, M., Kumar, R., Sivakumar, D.: A sieve algorithm for the shortest lattice vector problem. In: STOC, pp. 601–610. ACM, New York (2001)
4. Alwen, J., Peikert, C.: Generating shorter bases for hard random lattices. Cryptology ePrint Archive, Report 2008/521 (2008), http://eprint.iacr.org/
5. Alwen, J., Peikert, C.: Generating shorter bases for hard random lattices. In: Albers, S., Marion, J.-Y. (eds.) STACS. Dagstuhl Seminar Proceedings, vol. 09001, pp. 75–86. Schloss Dagstuhl - Leibniz-Zentrum fuer Informatik, Germany Internationales Begegnungs- und Forschungszentrum fuer Informatik (IBFI), Schloss Dagstuhl, Germany (2009)
6. Bellare, M., Shoup, S.: Two-tier signatures, strongly unforgeable signatures, and fiat-shamir without random oracles. In: Okamoto, T., Wang, X. (eds.) PKC 2007. LNCS, vol. 4450, pp. 201–216. Springer, Heidelberg (2007)
7. Bernstein, D.J., Buchmann, J.A., Dahmen, E. (eds.): Post-Quantum Cryptography. Springer, Heidelberg (2008)
8. Boneh, D., Boyen, X.: Efficient selective-id secure identity-based encryption without random oracles. In: Cachin, C., Camenisch, J.L. (eds.) EUROCRYPT 2004. LNCS, vol. 3027, pp. 223–238. Springer, Heidelberg (2004)
9. Boneh, D., Canetti, R., Halevi, S., Katz, J.: Chosen-ciphertext security from identity-based encryption. SIAM J. Comput. 36(5), 1301–1328 (2007)
10. Boneh, D., Shen, E., Waters, B.: Strongly unforgeable signatures based on computational diffie-hellman. In: Yung, M., Dodis, Y., Kiayias, A., Malkin, T.G. (eds.) PKC 2006. LNCS, vol. 3958, pp. 229–240. Springer, Heidelberg (2006)

11. Canetti, R., Goldreich, O., Halevi, S.: The random oracle methodology, revisited. J. ACM 51(4), 557–594 (2004)
12. Cash, D., Hofheinz, D., Kiltz, E., Peikert, C.: Bonsai trees, or how to delegate a lattice basis. In: EUROCRYPT 2010 (to appear, 2010)
13. Dolev, D., Dwork, C., Naor, M.: Nonmalleable cryptography. SIAM J. Comput. 30(2), 391–437 (2000)
14. Galindo, D., Herranz, J., Kiltz, E.: On the generic construction of identity-based signatures with additional properties. In: Lai, X., Chen, K. (eds.) ASIACRYPT 2006. LNCS, vol. 4284, pp. 178–193. Springer, Heidelberg (2006)
15. Gama, N., Nguyen, P.Q.: Predicting lattice reduction. In: Smart, N.P. (ed.) EUROCRYPT 2008. LNCS, vol. 4965, pp. 31–51. Springer, Heidelberg (2008)
16. Gentry, C., Peikert, C., Vaikuntanathan, V.: Trapdoors for hard lattices and new cryptographic constructions. In: Ladner, R.E., Dwork, C. (eds.) STOC, pp. 197–206. ACM, New York (2008)
17. Gentry, C., Silverberg, A.: Hierarchical id-based cryptography. In: Zheng, Y. (ed.) ASIACRYPT 2002. LNCS, vol. 2501, pp. 548–566. Springer, Heidelberg (2002)
18. Halevi, S. (ed.): CRYPTO 2009. LNCS, vol. 5677. Springer, Heidelberg (2009)
19. Hohenberger, S., Waters, B.: Short and stateless signatures from the rsa assumption. In: Halevi (ed.) [18], pp. 654–670.
20. Kiltz, E., Mityagin, A., Panjwani, S., Raghavan, B.: Append-only signatures. In: Caires, L., Italiano, G.F., Monteiro, L., Palamidessi, C., Yung, M. (eds.) ICALP 2005. LNCS, vol. 3580, pp. 434–445. Springer, Heidelberg (2005)
21. Kiltz, E., Neven, G.: Identity-based signatures. In: Joye, M., Neven, G. (eds.) Cryptology and Information Security Series, vol. 2, pp. 31–44. IOS Press, Amsterdam (2008)
22. Krawczyk, H., Rabin, T.: Chameleon hashing and signatures. Cryptology ePrint Archive, Report 1998/010 (1998), `http://eprint.iacr.org/`
23. Krawczyk, H., Rabin, T.: Chameleon signatures. In: NDSS. The Internet Society (2000)
24. Leurent, G., Nguyen, P.Q.: How risky is the random-oracle model? In: Halevi (ed.) [18], pp. 445–464
25. Libert, B., Quisquater, J.-J.: The exact security of an identity based signature and its applications. Cryptology ePrint Archive, Report 2004/102 (2004), `http://eprint.iacr.org/`
26. Lyubashevsky, V.: Fiat-shamir with aborts: Applications to lattice and factoring-based signatures. In: Matsui (ed.) [28], pp. 598–616
27. Lyubashevsky, V., Micciancio, D.: Asymptotically efficient lattice-based digital signatures. In: Canetti, R. (ed.) TCC 2008. LNCS, vol. 4948, pp. 37–54. Springer, Heidelberg (2008)
28. Matsui, M. (ed.): ASIACRYPT 2009. LNCS, vol. 5912. Springer, Heidelberg (2009)
29. Merkle, R.C.: A certified digital signature. In: Brassard, G. (ed.) CRYPTO 1989. LNCS, vol. 435, pp. 218–238. Springer, Heidelberg (1990)
30. Micciancio, D.: Generalized compact knapsacks, cyclic lattices, and efficient one-way functions. Computational Complexity 16(4), 365–411 (2007); Prelim. in FOCS 2002 (2002)
31. Micciancio, D., Regev, O.: Lattice-based cryptography. In: Bernstein, et al. (eds.) [7], pp. 147–191
32. Peikert, C., Rosen, A.: Efficient collision-resistant hashing from worst-case assumptions on cyclic lattices. In: Halevi, S., Rabin, T. (eds.) TCC 2006. LNCS, vol. 3876, pp. 145–166. Springer, Heidelberg (2006)

33. Rückert, M.: Strongly unforgeable signatures and hierarchical identity-based signatures from lattices without random oracles. Cryptology ePrint Archive, Report 2010/070 (2010), `http://eprint.iacr.org/`
34. Shamir, A.: Identity-based cryptosystems and signature schemes. In: Blakely, G.R., Chaum, D. (eds.) CRYPTO 1984. LNCS, vol. 196, pp. 47–53. Springer, Heidelberg (1985)
35. Stehlé, D., Steinfeld, R., Tanaka, K., Xagawa, K.: Efficient public key encryption based on ideal lattices. In: Matsui (ed.) [28], pp. 617–635

Proposal of a Signature Scheme Based on STS Trapdoor

Shigeo Tsujii[1], Masahito Gotaishi[1], Kohtaro Tadaki[1,2], and Ryo Fujita[1]

[1] Research & Development Initiative, Chuo University
[2] JST CREST
1–13–27 Kasuga, Bunkyo-ku, Tokyo 112–8551, Japan

Abstract. A New digital signature scheme based on Stepwise Triangular Scheme (STS) is proposed. The proposed trapdoor has resolved the vulnerability of STS and secure against both Gröbner Bases and Rank Attacks. In addition, as a basic trapdoor, it is more efficient than the existing systems. With the efficient implementation, the Multivariate Public Key Cryptosystems (MPKC) signature public key has the signature longer than the message by less than 25 %, for example.

Keywords: public key cryptosystem, multivariate polynomial, multivariate public key cryptosystem, stepwise triangular scheme, digital signature.

1 Introduction

Various kinds of Multivariate Public Key Cryptosystem (MPKC) are actively developed worldwide. Like traditional cryptosystems such as RSA or ElGamal, MPKCs are used both for encryption and signature. Historically most of them are based on either of the two basic trapdoors:

(i) MI-HFE Trapdoor (Matsumoto, Imai, Patarin)
The development of the first MPKC in the world had been launched around 1983 by Matsumoto and Imai [24]. The new cryptosystem, which is widely known as "Matsumoto-Imai cryptosystem" (MI), was proposed in EUROCRYPT in 1988 [25]. MI was successfully cryptanalyzed by Patarin [27]. Patarin has extended the idea of MI further and proposed Hidden Field Equation (HFE) cryptosystem in 1996 [28]. Both MI and HFE are applied to signature schemes, resulting in SFLASH and QUARTZ [7,31]. Although SFLASH was accepted as one of the final selections for the NESSIE, it was cryptanalyzed by Shamir et al. [14] in 2007. QUARTZ was one of the candidates for short digital signatures of NESSIE, but it consumes so much memory that it is difficult to implement in a practical system.

(ii) STS Trapdoor (Tsujii, et al. Shamir, Kasahara, et al.)
STS trapdoor was proposed by the group in Tokyo Institute of Technology led by Tsujii in 1985 [33]. Its initial scheme, which was named "Sequential Solution Method" [34], was cryptanalyzed by Kaneko, et al. in 1987 [18].

N. Sendrier (Ed.): PQCrypto 2010, LNCS 6061, pp. 201–217, 2010.

Table 1. Taxonomy of MPKC

Basic Scheme	Encryption	Signature
MI-HFE	MI Scheme A or C^* [25]	SFLASH [7]
	Hidden Field Equation [28]	QUARTZ [31]
	ℓ-IC [11]	ℓ-IC$^-$ [11]
	Square [4]	Square-Vinegar [1]
STS [17,42]	Sequential Solution Method [34]	Birational Permutation [32,19]
	TTM [26]	TTS [3,43]
	RSE [20], RSSE [21]	Our Proposal
	Tractable Rational Map [39], MFE [41]	TRMS [40]
UOV	None	Unbalanced Oil and Vinegar [23], Rainbow [10]

Tsujii et al. proposed the improved version in 1989 [35]. While the above cryptosystems have been proposed in Japan for encryption, Shamir proposed the signature scheme based on the same trapdoor, with its linear polynomials hidden, in CRYPTO 1993 [32]. His signature was also cryptanalyzed by Coppersmith et al. [5], with the attack similar to the Rank Attack, which is described later in this paper. 1989 version of Tsujii's cryptosystem, which was translated to English by Tadaki, et al. and published on the Cryptology ePrint Archive [36] in 2004, was cryptanalyzed by Ding et al. in PQCrypto 2008 [12].

Afterwards Kasahara et al. actively published various schemes including RSE, generalizing the concept of Sequential Solution Method [20,21]. Moh et al. proposed their scheme utilizing the Sequential Solution Method [26,39,41]. When Wolf, et al. attacked Kasahara's scheme with Rank Attack, they specified the family of the cryptosystems which Kasahara's group proposed as "Stepwise Triangular System" (STS) [42]. Here the family of MPKCs based on the trapdoor of Sequential Solution Method is called "STS scheme" in this paper.

Although both MI-HFE and STS have been studied for long time, it would safely be said that the application of STS to signatures is not so thoroughly discussed yet [3,43,40,19] compared with the MI-HFE. On the other hand, one of the MPKCs exclusively for signature is UOV (Unbalanced Oil and Vinegar) scheme, which was proposed in 1999 and also well-known worldwide [29,23]. The current situation is illustrated in the Table 1.

We propose a new signature scheme based on STS. Random variables are included in each step according to the number of variables. All of the resulting polynomials have the same number of variables and therefore every public key polynomial has the same rank, regardless of the step (refer to Figure 4 and formula (1)). The resulting system would become secure against both Gröbner bases and Rank attack. We have presented the idea of applying the concept to encryption system [38][37]. Here we propose a signature scheme. As explained in the subsequent sections, the signature scheme which we propose here has the structure entirely different from STS, although it is based on STS scheme. Our scheme would be specified as another basic trapdoor for signatures.

2 Preliminaries

2.1 General Design of MPKC

In general, MPKCs are structured as shown in Figure 1 and Figure 2.

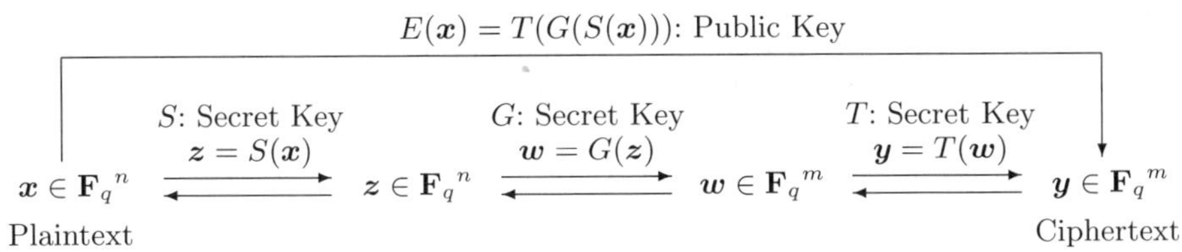

Fig. 1. Multivariate Public Key Cryptosystem (Encryption Scheme)

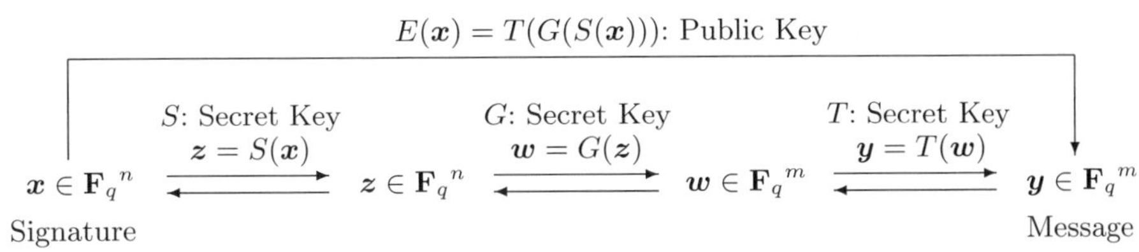

Fig. 2. Multivariate Public Key Cryptosystem (Signature Scheme)

Figure 1 shows the case of encryption, Figure 2 the signature. The plaintext variable vector is transformed to intermediate variable vector by the initial affine transformation S in the encryption scheme. On the other hand, in signature schemes, it is the message variable vector that is transformed. Subsequently, the central map part transforms the intermediate vector with the system of polynomials (usually quadratic) which has some trapdoor structure. Finally, intermediate polynomial vector is transformed by the affine transformation T to form the polynomial vector. The resulting polynomial vector is the public key.

2.2 Summary of STS Scheme and Its Security

Sequential Solution Method [34] is a cryptosystem for encryption. The equation system obtained by inverting the affine transformation is shown in Figure 3,

$$
\begin{aligned}
w_1 &= g_1(v_1, v_2, \dots, v_{k-1}, v_k) \\
w_2 &= g_2(v_1, v_2, \dots, v_{k-1}) \\
&\vdots \\
w_{k-1} &= g_{k-1}(v_1, v_2) \\
w_k &= g_k(v_1)
\end{aligned}
$$

Fig. 3. Non-linear Transformations in the Sequential Solution Method

where the last polynomial is univariate. And the number of variables increases as the sequential number of the polynomial decreases. When the i variables up to v_i are obtained by solving the n-th to $(n-i+1)$-th equation, the $(n-i)$-th equation becomes univariate by substituting the variables up to v_i with solution. The system is thus solved by solving the sequence of univariate equations one by one, as shown in Figure 3. Random Singular Simultaneous Equation (R(S)SE) cryptosystem [20][21] proposed by Kasahara et al. is a system where the equation is solved by solving each r-variate *determined* equation system, instead of the univariate equation. Kasahara et al. published various encryption system for the case of $r = 4$ and $r = 5$. In the case of $r = 4$, the legitimate receiver solves the 4-variate *determined* random equation in the L-th step. $(L-1)$-th step has 4 polynomials with 8 variables. Among them, 4 variables are obtained by solving the 4-variate *determined* system of equation in the L-th step. In this way, the overall system is solved by solving the subsystems of equation step by step. It should be noted that both RSSE, one of the variants of STS scheme, and MI are bijections, while the majority of MPKCs are not.
The STS Scheme has 2 vulnerabilities:

(i) Vulnerability to the Gröbner Bases Attack [6,15]
It is possible to solve multivariate algebraic equation systems by computing the Gröbner bases of the ideal generated by the public key. This is the Gröbner bases attack, which successfully cryptanalyzed various MPKCs including HFE [15]. According to the ideal theory, the affine transformation, which seems to effectively disguise the structure of the central map, does not influence the complexity of computing Gröbner bases. The structure of the STS polynomials in the central map is vulnerable to Gröbner bases algorithm and easily computed. According to our experiments, the time complexity of computing Gröbner bases of the STS scheme is roughly the same as MI scheme.

(ii) Vulnerability to the Rank Attack [17,42]
Since public key and central map polynomials of MPKCs are quadratic,
Since elements of the 1st layer have n variables, In the STS scheme where r is 4, the linear space spanned by the central map polynomials has 4 linearly independent polynomials with the rank less than 4. Likewise, it has 8 polynomials with the rank up to 8. If the public key is 100-variate *determined* polynomial system, the linear space spanned by the polynomials has 25 subspaces with the dimension 4.

The central map polynomial vector is hidden by the affine transformation T. However, it is possible to compute a transformation equivalent for the inverse transformation T^{-1}. If it is found, low-rank central equations, which are easy to solve, are computed from the public key [17,42]. Therefore it should be possible to compute the bases of the linear space equivalent for the central map vectors. Although the effectiveness of the Rank Attack should be discussed more in detail, we have to consider the countermeasure against Rank Attack in designing MPKCs. It has been pointed out that STS scheme is also vulnerable to Rank Attack.

3 Enhanced STS Scheme

3.1 The Key Idea

The vulnerability of the STS Scheme to Rank Attack is caused by the difference of rank among each step. On the other hand, all polynomials in the top steps of STS are random and with high rank. Therefore if two independent STS schemes are symmetrically combined together, this vulnerability would be corrected. One of the systems increases the number of variables by r from the initial r variables and the other decreases by r from the initial m. If a new central map is created by linearly combining the elements of each system in the same step, the rank of all elements in the central map becomes the same. Consequent cryptosystem should be secure both against Gröbner Bases and Rank Attack. The concept of the structure is illustrated in Figure 5.

The purpose of Figure 5 is to describe the essentials of our idea and therefore we prioritized the understandability over the preciseness, i.e. the definition and description of $\boldsymbol{u}, \boldsymbol{v}$ is not accurate. Precise definition of polynomials and variables are provided in the next subsection.

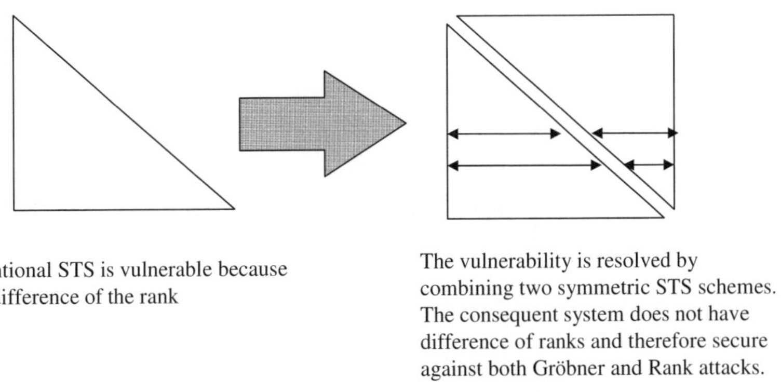

Fig. 4. Basic Idea of Enhanced STS

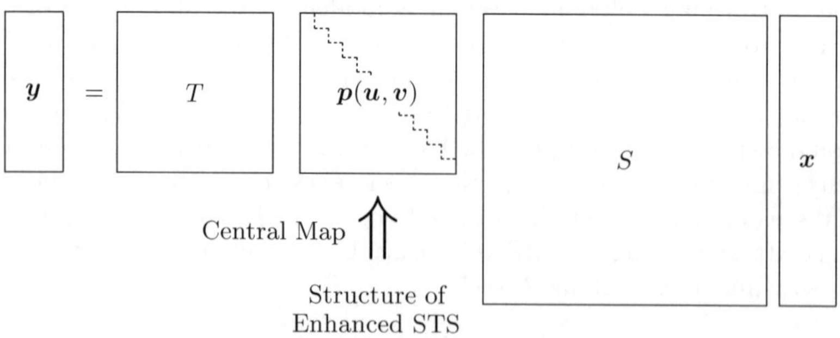

Fig. 5. Structure of Enhanced STS

3.2 Enhanced STS Trapdoor

Enhanced STS Signature Scheme is described as follows:
$\boldsymbol{u} := (u_1, \ldots, u_m)$ and $\boldsymbol{v} := (v_1, \ldots, v_{m-r})$ are sets of variables. The number of the steps L is equal to m/r, hence m must be divisible by r. Let the polynomial vectors $\boldsymbol{p} \in \boldsymbol{F}_q[\boldsymbol{u}, \boldsymbol{v}]^m$ be a polynomial vector described in the formula (1). The length of the variable $\boldsymbol{x}$ (signature length) is $n(= 2m - r)$. Polynomials in the step 1 of $\boldsymbol{p}$ include r variables $u_1, \ldots, u_r \in \boldsymbol{u}$ and all variables of $\boldsymbol{v}$, with the total number of variables m. The variables of $\boldsymbol{u}$ increase by r as the step proceeds, and so many variables of $\boldsymbol{v}$ decrease, thereby keeping the total number of variables included in each polynomial at m. Hence the polynomials in the last step $L := m/r$ have all variables of $\boldsymbol{u}$ and no variable of $\boldsymbol{v}$.

$$
\begin{array}{ll}
\text{Step } 1 & \left\{ \begin{array}{l} p_1(u_1, \ldots, u_r,\ v_1, \ldots, v_{m-r}) \\ \qquad\vdots \\ p_r(u_1, \ldots, u_r,\ v_1, \ldots, v_{m-r}) \end{array} \right. \\
 & \quad\vdots \\
\text{Step } i & \left\{ \begin{array}{l} p_{(i-1)r+1}(u_1, \ldots, u_{ir},\ v_{(i-1)r+1}, \ldots, v_{m-r}) \\ \qquad\vdots \\ p_{(i-1)r+r}(u_1, \ldots, u_{ir},\ v_{(i-1)r+1}, \ldots, v_{m-r}) \end{array} \right. \\
 & \quad\vdots \\
\text{Step } L-1 & \left\{ \begin{array}{l} p_{(L-2)r+1}(u_1, \ldots, u_{m-r}, v_{m-2r+1}, \ldots, v_{m-r}) \\ \qquad\vdots \\ p_{(L-2)r+r}(u_1, \ldots, u_{m-r}, v_{m-2r+1}, \ldots, v_{m-r}) \end{array} \right. \\
\text{Step } L & \left\{ \begin{array}{l} p_{(L-1)r+1}(u_1, \ldots, u_m) \\ \qquad\vdots \\ p_{(L-1)r+r}(u_1, \ldots, u_m) \end{array} \right.
\end{array}
\tag{1}
$$

All polynomials of $\boldsymbol{p}$ have the rank m, but when constant value $\boldsymbol{c} := (c_1, \dots, c_{m-r})$ are assigned to $\boldsymbol{v}$, the consequent polynomial vector $\boldsymbol{p}' = \boldsymbol{p}(\boldsymbol{u}, \boldsymbol{c})$ has STS structure (formula (2)).

$$
\begin{array}{ll}
\text{Step } 1 & \left\{ \begin{array}{l} p'_1(u_1, \dots, u_r) \\ \quad\vdots \\ p'_r(u_1, \dots, u_r) \end{array} \right. \\
 & \quad\vdots \\
\text{Step } i & \left\{ \begin{array}{l} p'_{(i-1)r+1}(u_1, \dots, u_{ir}) \\ \quad\vdots \\ p'_{(i-1)r+r}(u_1, \dots, u_{ir}) \end{array} \right. \\
 & \quad\vdots \\
\text{Step } L-1 & \left\{ \begin{array}{l} p'_{(L-2)r+1}(u_1, \dots, u_{m-r}) \\ \quad\vdots \\ p'_{(L-2)r+r}(u_1, \dots, u_{m-r}) \end{array} \right. \\
\text{Step } L & \left\{ \begin{array}{l} p'_{(L-1)r+1}(u_1, \dots, u_{m-r}, \dots, u_m) \\ \quad\vdots \\ p'_{(L-1)r+r}(u_1, \dots, u_{m-r}, \dots, u_m) \end{array} \right.
\end{array}
\tag{2}
$$

The central map of the Enhanced STS $\boldsymbol{w}$ is created by substituting $\boldsymbol{u}$ with $\boldsymbol{z}_1 := (z_1, \dots, z_m)$ and $\boldsymbol{v}$ with $\boldsymbol{z}_2 := (z_{m+1}, \dots, z_n)$ in the polynomial vector $\boldsymbol{p}$. The linear polynomial vector $\boldsymbol{z} := \boldsymbol{z}_1 || \boldsymbol{z}_2 = (z_1(\boldsymbol{x}), \dots, z_n(\boldsymbol{x}))$ is the image of the affine transformation $S(\boldsymbol{x})$.

$$
\boldsymbol{w} := \boldsymbol{p}(\boldsymbol{z}_1, \boldsymbol{z}_2) = \left(\begin{array}{c}
p_1(z_1, \dots, z_r,\ z_{m+1}, \dots, z_n) \\
\vdots \\
p_r(z_1, \dots, z_r,\ z_{m+1}, \dots, z_n) \\
\vdots \\
\vdots \\
p_{m-2r+1}(z_1, \dots, z_{m-r},\ z_{n-r+1}, \dots, z_n) \\
\vdots \\
p_{m-r}(z_1, \dots, z_{m-r},\ z_{n-r+1}, \dots, z_n) \\
p_{m-r+1}(z_1, \dots, z_m) \\
\vdots \\
p_m(z_1, \dots, z_m)
\end{array} \right)
\tag{3}
$$

Finally, the public key $\boldsymbol{y}$ is created by applying affine transformation T to the central map $\boldsymbol{w}$

$$
\boldsymbol{y} := T(\boldsymbol{w}) \tag{4}
$$

Public Key

- Polynomial Vector $\boldsymbol{y}$

Secret Key

- Central Map $\boldsymbol{w}$
- Affine Transformations S and T

3.3 Signature and Verification

The message $\boldsymbol{m} := (m_1, \ldots, m_m)$ is signed as follows:

Signature

(i) Apply the inverse affine transformation T^{-1} to the message $\boldsymbol{m}$.
(ii) Substitute each element of $\boldsymbol{v}$ with random number.
(iii) Since thus computed set of polynomials $p_1(u_1, \ldots, u_r), \ldots, p_m(u_1, \ldots, u_m)$ has the structure of m-variate STS, $\boldsymbol{u}$ is computed by decrypting the STS cryptosystem.
(iv) Value of $\boldsymbol{x}$ is computed by inverting the affine transformation S to the vector $\boldsymbol{u}||\boldsymbol{v}$. Thus obtained vector $(s_1, \ldots, s_n)$ is the signature of $\boldsymbol{m}$.

Verification
Signature verification is done by assigning the signature $(s_1, \ldots, s_n)$ to $\boldsymbol{x}$ of the public key and checking whether the value is equal to $\boldsymbol{m}$.

4 Discussion of the Security

Following attacks for MPKCs should be possible both to encryption and signature schemes:

(i) Gröbner Bases Attack [6,15]
(ii) Rank Attack [17,42]
(iii) Differential Attack [16,13,14]
(iv) Other attacks exploiting other Vulnerability of the Trapdoor

Security against these attacks is discussed.

4.1 Security against Gröbner Bases Attack

Besides the constraint on the rank of the two STS systems, quadratic polynomials in the central map are all random. Since coefficients are randomly determined, there is not a structural vulnerability for Gröbner Bases algorithm to exploit. Consequently, it is expected that the system is secure against Gröbner Bases Attack. The above assumption is validated by experiment by a computer.

Experiment. The above Enhanced STS Signature System is implemented in the script language of Magma, the computational algebra system. The public keys generated by the above program were tested the time complexity of Gröbner Bases Attack and compared with the random system of n-variate system with m polynomials.

Since the signature polynomials are underdetermined, usually Gröbner Bases Attacks are done after excess variables are eliminated. In this experiment random values were assigned to the variables $x_{m+1}, \ldots, x_n$. Thus obtained m-variate *determined* polynomial sets are the generators of the ideals.

Computing Environment

We perform the experiments using the computational algebra system Magma. Gröbner bases are computed by $F4$ algorithm implemented in Magma as the function `GroebnerBasis()`. The attack is repeated 10 times for each condition. All computer experiments are performed with the following environment:

(i) Computer: Japan Computing System (JCS) VC98220WSA-4U/T workstation, with CPU AMD Opteron 8220 (2.80 GHz) quadcore and 128 Gbyte Memory

(ii) Magma ver. 2.15-15 running on Red Hat Enterprise Linux Advanced Platform Standard. The computation time is counted by the function `Cputime()` of Magma.

Condition

The parameter r is fixed at 4 and the message length m is varied from 18 to 25. The signature length n is set $2m - r$. The public key is generated under the above condition.

Result is shown in Table 2 and Figure 6.

Table 2. F4 computation time vs. the size of the signed messages

	F4 Computation Time in Second	
Message Length	Enhanced STS	Random System
18	4.06	4.32
19	8.05	8.24
20	17.04	16.47
21	34.44	33.25
22	103.41	99.99
23	166.10	159.57
24	1038.48	1020.04
25	2159.80	2125.24

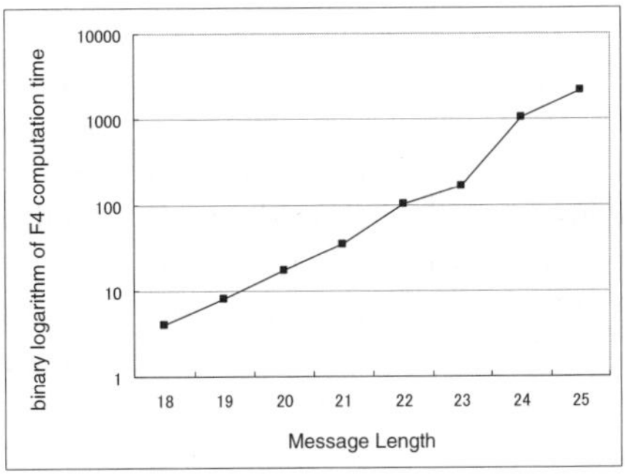

Fig. 6. Relationship between the size of the message and binary logarithm of F4 computation time

Not only the time complexity of computation increases exponentially as the message length increases, the F4 computing time is almost equal to the random system. Hence the signature system is expected to be sufficiently secure against Gröbner bases attack.

4.2 Security against Rank Attack

As discussed above, all polynomials in all steps of the central map have the same rank. Since there is not a difference of rank between each polynomial, the public key is entirely inoculate to Rank Attacks.

4.3 Security against Differential Attack

Differential Attack was designed to attack internally perturbed system such as PMI [8] and IPHFE [9], both of which are created by modifying existing trapdoors such as MI and HFE. Since our scheme does not depend on any trapdoors of MI or HFE, it is not applicable.

4.4 Attacks Exploiting Other Vulnerabilities of the Trapdoor

We are going to further investigate its security and discuss whether there is not any such vulnerability.

5 Efficiency of the Basic Trapdoor Scheme

Now the efficiency of the proposed system is discussed by comparing the size of the polynomial with existing schemes. The Oil and Vinegar system, which is classified as the only basic trapdoor for signature, requires the variables to be "Unbalanced." Hence the Vinegar variables must be longer than the Oil variables. Consequently the signature becomes far longer than the message. Although, as shown in the discussion of the security, the proposed system is sufficiently secure with the signature as short as a twice of the message. Therefore the implementation of the proposed scheme is expected to be more compact than the Unbalanced Oil and Vinegar. Besides, Oil and Vinegar scheme has the constraint that a product of two Oil variables does not exist. Nevertheless, the proposed scheme is not restricted in such a way.

Consequently, our scheme is closer to random polynomials than existing MPKCs and therefore it should be highly secure. Since the time complexity of attacks increases more steeply than existing systems, use of computing resources such as CPU and memory would be more efficient than the existing MPKC signature schemes.

6 Improvement in the Practical Implementation

The new idea of applying the STS cryptosystem to signature scheme is proposed. The structure of the central map was described above. Here we propose further improvement to employ in implementation. One is to shorten the signature (number of variables) and thereby making the public key more compact. Another one is an idea to further improve the security.

6.1 Further Improving the Efficiency of the Public Key

The advantage of the Enhanced STS over existing trapdoors has been described above. Although, the signature is still at least twice (precisely, $(2 - r/m)$ times) as long as the message. Now we propose to divide the overall polynomial system into several blocks. The central map $\boldsymbol{w}$ is divided into k blocks $B_1, \ldots, B_k$, each of which has $b := m/k$ polynomials. So $\boldsymbol{w} := B_1||B_2, \ldots, ||B_k := [\boldsymbol{p}_1(\boldsymbol{u}_1, \boldsymbol{v}_1), \ldots, \boldsymbol{p}_k(\boldsymbol{u}_k, \boldsymbol{v}_k)]^T$. Each block B_i has the structure of Enhanced STS, where the polynomial system $\boldsymbol{p}_i(\boldsymbol{u}_i, \boldsymbol{v}_i)$ becomes STS when random values are assigned

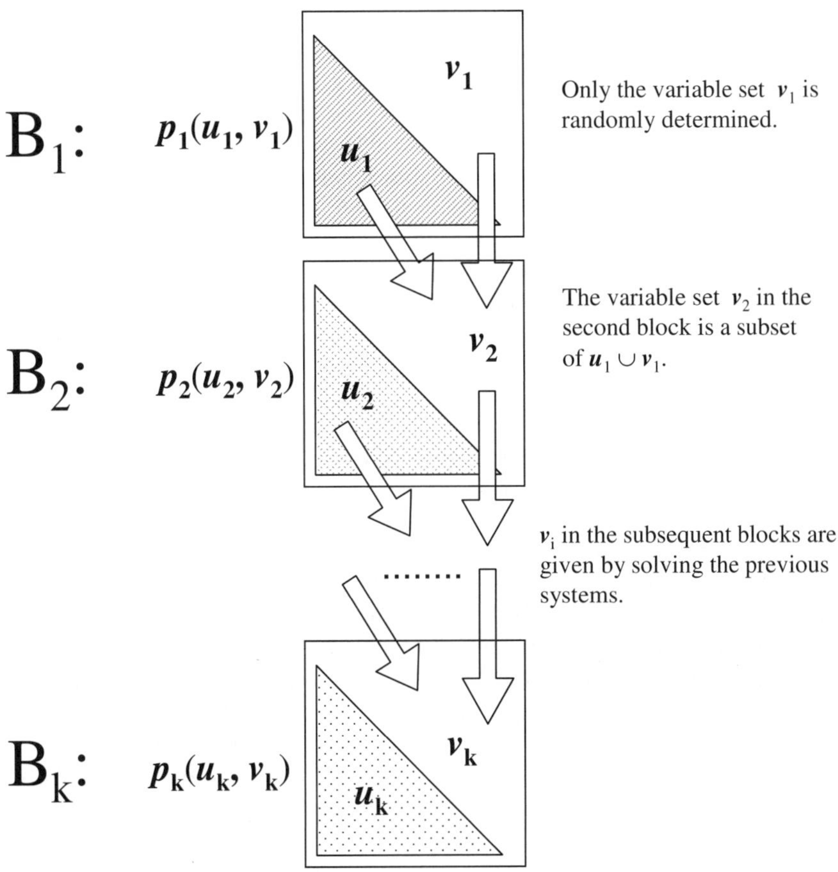

Fig. 7. Implementation of Enhanced STS and operation of signing

$\boldsymbol{u}_1||\boldsymbol{u}_2||\ldots||\boldsymbol{u}_k$. The variable set $\boldsymbol{u}_1$ and $\boldsymbol{v}_1$ are given initially and $\boldsymbol{v}_i$ $(2 \le i \le k)$ is defined such that the $(b-r)$ dimensional linear space spanned by $\boldsymbol{v}_i$ is contained in the one spanned by $\boldsymbol{u}_1 \cup \boldsymbol{v}_1 \cup \boldsymbol{u}_2 \ldots \boldsymbol{u}_{i-1} \cup \boldsymbol{v}_{i-1}$. As illustrated in Figure 7, the value of $\boldsymbol{v}_i$ is given by solving all systems $B_1, \ldots, B_{i-1}$. In this case the set of variables $\boldsymbol{u}_1 \cup \boldsymbol{u}_2 \ldots \cup \boldsymbol{u}_k \cup \boldsymbol{v}_1 \ldots \cup \boldsymbol{v}_k$ has the dimension $m + b - r$, i.e. the signature length exceeds the message length by $b - r$. Therefore the ratio of signature to message length is $1 + (b - r)/m$. Generally the system takes the above structure. A message is signed as follows.

Signing a Message

(i) Give random values to the variables $\boldsymbol{v}_1$.
(ii) Equation system B_1, which becomes STS, is solved to find the values of $\boldsymbol{u}_1$.
(iii) Since the value of $\boldsymbol{v}_1$ and $\boldsymbol{u}_1$ is found, $\boldsymbol{v}_2$ is known.
(iv) Step 2 to 3 are repeated until the last block.

The security of the combined signature system is assured as long as the basic trapdoor of Enhanced STS is structurally secure.

Example
If a system has the message length $m = 256$ and the STS step size $r = 4$, and divided into 4 blocks $(k = 4)$, each block has $m/k = 64$ polynomials. Each variable set $\boldsymbol{u}_i$ has 64 elements and $\boldsymbol{v}_i$ has 56. In this case the signature length is $256 + 64 - 4 = 316$, which is approximately 1.23 times as long as the message. Although characteristic of the finite field is 2 in the above discussion, we think that the base ring should be $GF(2^8)$. Other environmental factor should have to be considered in the actual implementation.

6.2 Security Improvement by Check Polynomial System

Vulnerability of Underdetermined MPKC signature scheme
Almost all MPKC signature schemes are underdetermined, in order to enable preimage of every message to exist. As well as it increases the public key size compared with the message length (number of equations), it might generate vulnerability for the attackers to exploit. If the signature public key has m polynomials with n variables defined on $GF(q)$, the equation system derived from the public key has q^{n-m} solutions as a rule of thumb. In the case of our Complementary STS signature, there can be more than q^{m-r} valid signatures. We propose here a further security improvement by appending extra polynomials.

It should be noted that most of the MPKC signature public keys have subsets of the variable set. Messages are signed by assigning value to the elements of one subset and solving the consequent equation. Therefore typically the structure of the subsets constitutes an important part of the secret key. In the case of Enhanced STS, variables are specified into subsets $\boldsymbol{u}$ and $\boldsymbol{v}$. Most of the attacks to MPKC signatures are done by finding the elements of the subsets, like done to the Balanced Oil and Vinegar [29]. In case an attack should be developed to distinguish the variables of $\boldsymbol{u}$ from the ones of $\boldsymbol{v}$, the signature scheme is in serious jeopardy.

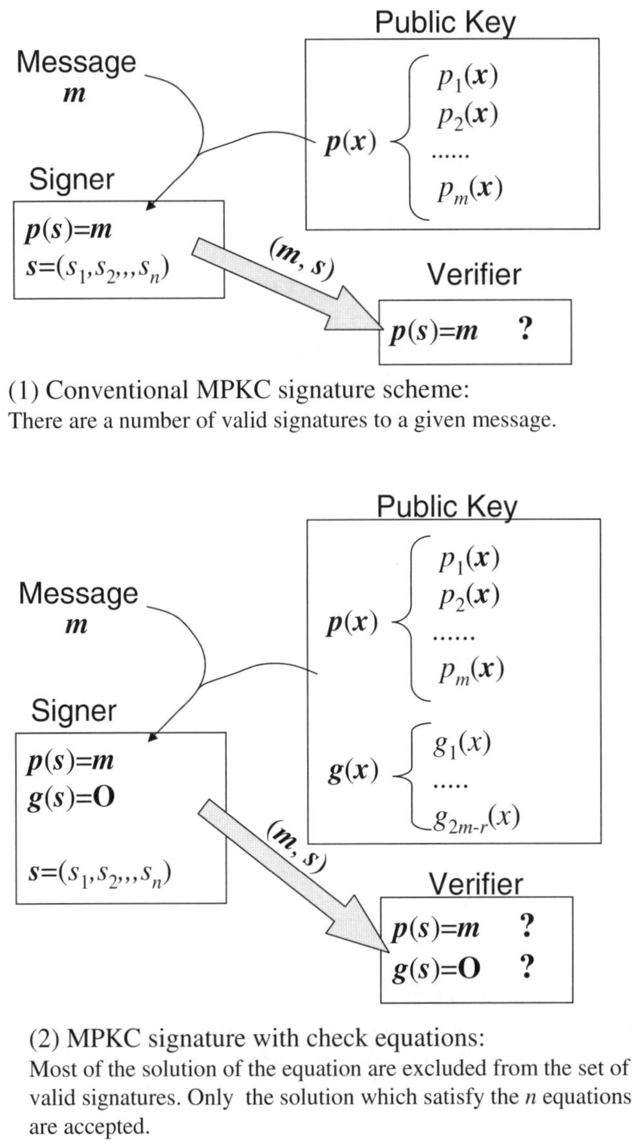

Fig. 8. Comparison between conventional Signature and the Signature with Check Equation System

System of Check Equations
In case even either one of the two linear spaces spanned by the set of vectors $\boldsymbol{u}$ and the one spanned by $\boldsymbol{v}$ should be found by any remote chance, the signatures would be forged by solving the equation. Although, it is possible to further improve its security by limiting the acceptable value of the variables in $\boldsymbol{v}$. Together with the public key $\boldsymbol{p}(\boldsymbol{x})$, the system of check equations $\boldsymbol{g}(\boldsymbol{x})$ is published. It is specified as a rule that the valid signature must satisfy both the system of equation $\boldsymbol{p}(\boldsymbol{x}) = \boldsymbol{m}$ and $\boldsymbol{g}(\boldsymbol{x}) = \boldsymbol{o}$. The difference of the signing and verifying procedure between the conventional MPKC signature and the one using the check polynomials is illustrated in Figure 8.

Generation of the System of Check Equation
It is possible to create a polynomial set $\boldsymbol{g}(\boldsymbol{x})$, all elements of which become 0 when $\boldsymbol{v}$ is equal to the pre-defined vector $\boldsymbol{\alpha} \in \boldsymbol{F}_2^{m-r}$. Let $\boldsymbol{f}(\boldsymbol{u}, \boldsymbol{v}) \in \boldsymbol{F}_2[\boldsymbol{u}, \boldsymbol{v}]^{m-r}$ be a set of random polynomials of $\boldsymbol{x}$. Then the polynomial set $\boldsymbol{g}(\boldsymbol{x}) = \boldsymbol{f}(\boldsymbol{u}, \boldsymbol{v}) - \boldsymbol{f}(\boldsymbol{\alpha}, \boldsymbol{v})$ satisfies the condition. The system of check equations is one-time use. The system is renewed every time a message is signed.
Then messages are signed in the following way:

Signing a Message

(i) Invert the Affine transformation T^{-1} to the message $\boldsymbol{m}$
(ii) Assign the value $\boldsymbol{\alpha}$ to the variables $\boldsymbol{u}$
(iii) The consequent STS polynomials are solved. The solution is $\boldsymbol{s}' \in \boldsymbol{F}_2^n$
(iv) The Affine transformation is inverted to the solution. $\boldsymbol{s} := S^{-1}\boldsymbol{s}'$.

Verification

(i) It is checked whether $\boldsymbol{p}(\boldsymbol{s})$ is equal to $\boldsymbol{m}$
(ii) It is checked whether $\boldsymbol{g}(\boldsymbol{s})$ is zero vector.

7 Conclusion

We proposed a new basic trapdoor for signature scheme based on STS, with two different STS polynomial systems combined together —a system to be called "Enhanced STS." This signature scheme is secure against various existing attacks and more efficient than existing schemes such as UOV, in itself.

Based on the above concept, we proposed a signature system where the signature is still shorter. Consequently this system has a compact public key.

We are going to study further to evaluate and improve the proposed system.

Acknowledgment

This work is supported by the Strategic Information and Communications R & D Promotion Programme (SCOPE) from the Ministry of Internal Affairs and Communications of Japan.

References

1. Baena, J., Clough, C., Ding, J.: Square-Vinegar signature scheme. In: Buchmann, J., Ding, J. (eds.) PQCrypto 2008. LNCS, vol. 5299, pp. 17–30. Springer, Heidelberg (2008)
2. Braeken, A., Wolf, C., Preneel, B.: A study of the security of unbalanced oil and vinegar signature schemes. In: Menezes, A. (ed.) CT-RSA 2005. LNCS, vol. 3376, pp. 29–43. Springer, Heidelberg (2005)
3. Chen, J.M., Yang, B.Y.: A more secure and efficacious TTS signature scheme. In: Lim, J.-I., Lee, D.-H. (eds.) ICISC 2003. LNCS, vol. 2971, pp. 320–338. Springer, Heidelberg (2004)
4. Clough, C., Baena, J., Ding, J., Yang, B.Y., Chen, M.S.: Square, a new multivariate encryption scheme. In: Fischlin, M. (ed.) CT-RSA 2009. LNCS, vol. 5473, pp. 252–264. Springer, Heidelberg (2009)
5. Coppersmith, D., Stern, J., Vaudenay, S.: Attacks on the birational permutation signature schemes. In: Stinson, D.R. (ed.) CRYPTO 1993. LNCS, vol. 773, pp. 435–443. Springer, Heidelberg (1994)
6. Courtois, N., Daum, M., Felke, P.: On the security of HFE, HFEv- and Quartz. In: Desmedt, Y.G. (ed.) PKC 2003. LNCS, vol. 2567, pp. 337–350. Springer, Heidelberg (2003)
7. Courtois, N., Goubin, L., Patarin, J.: SFLASHv3, a fast asymmetric signature scheme. Cryptology ePrint Archive, Report 2003/211 (October 2003), `http://eprint.iacr.org/2003/211`
8. Ding, J.: A new variant of the Matsumoto-Imai cryptosystem through perturbation. In: Bao, F., Deng, R., Zhou, J. (eds.) PKC 2004. LNCS, vol. 2947, pp. 305–318. Springer, Heidelberg (2004)
9. Ding, J., Schmidt, D.: Cryptanalysis of HFEv and internal perturbation of HFE. In: Vaudenay, S. (ed.) PKC 2005. LNCS, vol. 3386, pp. 288–301. Springer, Heidelberg (2005)
10. Ding, J., Schmidt, D.: Rainbow, a new multivariable polynomial signature scheme. In: Ioannidis, J., Keromytis, A.D., Yung, M. (eds.) ACNS 2005. LNCS, vol. 3531, pp. 164–175. Springer, Heidelberg (2005)
11. Ding, J., Wolf, C., Yang, B.Y.: ℓ-Invertible Cycles for $\mathcal{M}$ultivariate $\mathcal{Q}$uadratic ($\mathcal{MQ}$) public key cryptography. In: Okamoto, T., Wang, X. (eds.) PKC 2007. LNCS, vol. 4450, pp. 266–281. Springer, Heidelberg (2007)
12. Ding, J., Wagner, J.: Cryptanalysis of rational multivariate public key cryptosystems. In: Buchmann, J., Ding, J. (eds.) PQCrypto 2008. LNCS, vol. 5299, pp. 124–136. Springer, Heidelberg (2008)
13. Dubois, V., Granboulan, L., Stern, J.: Cryptanalysis of HFE with internal perturbation. In: Okamoto, T., Wang, X. (eds.) PKC 2007. LNCS, vol. 4450, pp. 249–265. Springer, Heidelberg (2007)
14. Dubois, V., Fouque, P.A., Shamir, A., Stern, J.: Practical cryptanalysis of SFLASH. In: Menezes, A. (ed.) CRYPTO 2007. LNCS, vol. 4622, pp. 1–12. Springer, Heidelberg (2007)
15. Faugère, J.C., Joux, A.: Algebraic cryptanalysis of hidden field equation (HFE) cryptosystems using Gröbner bases. In: Boneh, D. (ed.) CRYPTO 2003. LNCS, vol. 2729, pp. 44–60. Springer, Heidelberg (2003)
16. Fouque, P.A., Granboulan, L., Stern, J.: Differential cryptanalysis for multivariate schemes. In: Cramer, R. (ed.) EUROCRYPT 2005. LNCS, vol. 3494, pp. 341–353. Springer, Heidelberg (2005)

17. Goubin, L., Courtois, N.: Cryptanalysis of the TTM cryptosystem. In: Okamoto, T. (ed.) ASIACRYPT 2000. LNCS, vol. 1976, pp. 44–57. Springer, Heidelberg (2000)
18. Hasegawa, S., Kaneko, T.: An attacking method for a public-key cryptosystem based on the difficulty of solving a system of non-linear equations. In: Proc. 10th SITA, JA5-3 (November 1987) (in Japanese)
19. Hashimoto, Y., Sakurai, K.: On construction of signature schemes based on birational permutations over noncommutative rings. In: Proceedings of the First International Conference on Symbolic Computation and Cryptography (SCC 2008), pp. 218–227 (2008)
20. Kasahara, M., Sakai, R.: A construction of public key cryptosystem for realizing ciphertext of size 100 bit and digital signature scheme. IEICE Transactions on Fundamentals E87-A(1) , 102–109 (2004)
21. Kasahara, M., Sakai, R.: A construction of public-key cryptosystem based on singular simultaneous equations. IEICE Transactions on Fundamentals E88-A(1), 74–80 (2005)
22. Kipnis, A., Shamir, A.: Cryptanalysis of the oil and vinegar signature scheme. In: Krawczyk, H. (ed.) CRYPTO 1998. LNCS, vol. 1462, pp. 257–266. Springer, Heidelberg (1998)
23. Kipnis, A., Patarin, J., Goubin, L.: Unbalanced Oil and Vinegar signature schemes. In: Stern, J. (ed.) EUROCRYPT 1999. LNCS, vol. 1592, pp. 206–222. Springer, Heidelberg (1999)
24. Matsumoto, T., Imai, H., Harashima, H., Miyakawa, H.: A class of asymmetric cryptosystems using obscure representations of enciphering functions. In: 1983 National Convention Record on Information Systems, IECE Japan, S8-5 (1983) (in Japanese)
25. Matsumoto, T., Imai, H.: Public quadratic polynomial-tuples for efficient signature-verification and message-encryption. In: Günther, C.G. (ed.) EUROCRYPT 1988. LNCS, vol. 330, pp. 419–453. Springer, Heidelberg (1988)
26. Moh, T.T.: A public key system with signature and master key functions. Communications in Algebra 27(5), 2207–2222 (1999)
27. Patarin, J.: Cryptanalysis of the Matsumoto and Imai public key scheme of Eurocrypt'88. In: Coppersmith, D. (ed.) CRYPTO 1995. LNCS, vol. 963, pp. 248–261. Springer, Heidelberg (1995)
28. Patarin, J.: Hidden fields equations (HFE) and isomorphisms of polynomials (IP): two new families of asymmetric algorithms. In: Maurer, U.M. (ed.) EUROCRYPT 1996. LNCS, vol. 1070, pp. 33–48. Springer, Heidelberg (1996)
29. Patarin, J.: The oil and vinegar signature scheme. Presented at the Dagstuhl Workshop on Cryptography (September 1997) (transparencies)
30. Patarin, J., Goubin, L., Courtois, N.: C^*_{-+} and HM: Variations around two schemes of T. Matsumoto and H. Imai. In: Ohta, K., Pei, D. (eds.) ASIACRYPT 1998. LNCS, vol. 1514, pp. 35–50. Springer, Heidelberg (1998)
31. Patarin, J., Courtois, N., Goubin, L.: QUARTZ, 128-bit long digital signatures. In: Naccache, D. (ed.) CT-RSA 2001. LNCS, vol. 2020, pp. 282–297. Springer, Heidelberg (2001)
32. Shamir, A.: Efficient signature schemes based on birational permutations. In: Stinson, D.R. (ed.) CRYPTO 1993. LNCS, vol. 773, pp. 1–12. Springer, Heidelberg (1994)
33. Tsujii, S.: Public key cryptosystem using nonlinear equations. In: Proc. 8th SITA, December 1985, pp. 156–157 (1985) (in Japanese)

34. Tsujii, S., Kurosawa, K., Itoh, T., Fujioka, A., Matsumoto, T.: A public-key cryptosystem based on the difficulty of solving a system of non-linear equations. IEICE Transactions (D), J69-D(12) (1986) (1963–1970) (in Japanese)
35. Tsujii, S., Fujioka, A., Hirayama, Y.: Generalization of the public-key cryptosystem based on the difficulty of solving a system of non-linear equations. IEICE Transactions (A), J72-A(2), 390–397 (1989) (in Japanese); An English translation of [35] is included in [36] as an appendix
36. Tsujii, S., Tadaki, K., Fujita, R.: Piece in hand concept for enhancing the security of multivariate type public key cryptosystems: public key without containing all the information of secret key. Cryptology ePrint Archive, Report 2004/366 (December 2004), `http://eprint.iacr.org/2004/366`
37. Tsujii, S., Tadaki, K., Gotaishi, M., Fujita, R., Kasahara, M.: Proposal of PPS multivariate public key cryptosystems. Cryptology ePrint Archive, Report 2009/264 (June 2009), `http://eprint.iacr.org/2009/264`
38. Tsujii, S., Tadaki, K., Gotaishi, M., Fujita, R., Kasahara, M.: Proposal of integrated MPKC: PPS — STS enhanced by perturbed piece in hand method —. Technical Report of IEICE, ISEC2009-27, SITE2009-19, ICSS2009-41 (2009-2007) (July 2009) (in Japanese)
39. Wang, L.C., Chang, F.H.: Revision of tractable rational map cryptosystem. Cryptology ePrint Archive, Report 2004/046 (2006), `http://eprint.iacr.org/2004/046`
40. Wang, L.C., Hu, Y.H., Lai, F., Chou, C.Y., Yang, B.Y.: Tractable rational map signature. In: Vaudenay, S. (ed.) PKC 2005. LNCS, vol. 3386, pp. 244–257. Springer, Heidelberg (2005)
41. Wang, L.C., Yang, B.Y., Hu, Y.H., Lai, F.: A "medium-field" multivariate public-key encryption scheme. In: Pointcheval, D. (ed.) CT-RSA 2006. LNCS, vol. 3860, pp. 132–149. Springer, Heidelberg (2006)
42. Wolf, C., Braeken, A., Preneel, B.: Efficient cryptanalysis of RSE(2)PKC and RSSE(2)PKC. In: Blundo, C., Cimato, S. (eds.) SCN 2004. LNCS, vol. 3352, pp. 294–309. Springer, Heidelberg (2005)
43. Yang, B.Y., Chen, J.M.: Building secure tame-like multivariate public-key cryptosystems: the new TTS. In: Boyd, C., González Nieto, J.M. (eds.) ACISP 2005. LNCS, vol. 3574, pp. 518–531. Springer, Heidelberg (2005)

Selecting Parameters for the Rainbow Signature Scheme

Albrecht Petzoldt[1], Stanislav Bulygin[2], and Johannes Buchmann[1,2]

[1] Technische Universität Darmstadt, Department of Computer Science
Hochschulstraße 10, 64289 Darmstadt, Germany
{apetzoldt,buchmann}@cdc.informatik.tu-darmstadt.de
[2] Center for Advanced Security Research Darmstadt - CASED
Mornewegstraße 32, 64293 Darmstadt, Germany
{johannes.buchmann,Stanislav.Bulygin}@cased.de

Abstract. Multivariate public key cryptography is one of the main approaches to guarantee the security of communication in a post-quantum world. One of the most promising candidates in this area is the Rainbow signature scheme, which was first proposed by J. Ding and D. Schmidt in 2005. In this paper we develop a model of security for the Rainbow signature scheme. We use this model to find parameters which, under certain assumptions, guarantee the security of the scheme for now and the near future.

Keywords: Multivariate cryptography, Rainbow signature scheme, parameters.

1 Introduction

To guarantee the security of communication it is important to have fast and secure signature schemes. One major field of application for them is the authenticity of data and information, for example software updates.

One of the most promising candidates in this area is the Rainbow signature scheme, which was presented by J. Ding and D. Schmidt in [DS05]. Similarly to other multivariate schemes like $3iC^{-}p$ [DW07] and Projected Flash [PC01], [DY07] it is very efficient and provides fast signature generation and verification. In opposite to classical schemes, e.g. RSA or ECDSA, Rainbow is believed to be secure against attacks with quantum computers [BB08].

In the last years a lot of work has been done to study the security of multivariate schemes and many attacks were proposed. Among these are direct attacks on which a lot of work was done [YC07], [Fa99] as well as rank attacks which were introduced in [CS94] by Coppersmith and Stern to attack the Birational Permutation Scheme and later improved by a number of other researchers [YC05], [BG06]. A good overview of these attacks can be found in [GC00]. Special attacks on Rainbow-like schemes were proposed by Ding and Yang in [DY08]. There have also been some attempts to derive appropriate parameters from the complexities of these attacks [CC08]. However, it is still an open problem how

N. Sendrier (Ed.): PQCrypto 2010, LNCS 6061, pp. 218–240, 2010.

we have to adapt the parameters of multivariate schemes to future developments in cryptanalysis and computing power.

In this paper we try to answer this question for the Rainbow signature scheme. We start with the security model of Lenstra and Verheul [LV00] to compute necessary security levels for the years 2010 to 2050. After that we look at the known attacks against the Rainbow signature scheme and observe that the security of the scheme is mainly determined by two of them, namely the direct attack and the Rainbow-Band-Separation attack. We study the complexity of these two attacks, both with data from the literature and with own experiments, for which we use two of the most efficient available software packages, namely MAGMA and Singular. Finally, we use the results of these experiments to find appropriate parameters for Rainbow such that it fulfills the given security levels, as well as Rainbow schemes for limited hash sizes. One of our main results here is, that we need at least 26 equations to achieve the necessary security level for 2010. So, the often proposed scheme Rainbow(18,12,12) does not provide adequate security.

The structure of the paper is as follows: In Section 2 we describe the Rainbow signature scheme. Section 3 describes our model of security for the Rainbow scheme. In Section 4 we take a closer look at the complexities of the direct and the Rainbow-Band-Separation attack and present the results of our experiments. Section 5 gives secure parameter sets optimized for small public key sizes as well as Rainbow schemes for limited hash sizes. Finally, Section 6 concludes the paper.

2 Multivariate Public Key Cryptography

Multivariate Public Key Cryptography is one of the main approaches for secure communication in a post-quantum world. The principle idea is to choose a multivariate system F of quadratic polynomials which can be easily inverted (central map). After that one chooses two affine linear invertible maps S and T to hide the structure of the central map. The public key of the cryptosystem is the composed map $P = S \circ F \circ T$ which is difficult to invert. The private key consists of S, F and T and therefore allows to invert P.

There are several ways to build the central map F. One approach are the so called BigField-Schemes like Matsumoto-Imai [MI88] and HFE [Pa96] with many variations and improvements [BB08], [Di04], [PC01]. On the other hand, we have the so called SingleField family with schemes like UOV [KP99] and Rainbow [DS05]. Recently, a third family called MediumField has been proposed which contains schemes like ℓ-iC [DW07].

2.1 The Principle of Oil and Vinegar (OV)

One way to create easily invertible multivariate quadratic systems is the principle of Oil and Vinegar, which was first proposed by J. Patarin in [Pa97].

Let K be a finite field (e.g. $K = GF(2^8)$). Let o and v be two integers and set $n = o + v$. Patarin suggested to choose $o = v$. After this original scheme was broken by Kipnis and Shamir in [KS98], it was recommended in [KP99] to choose $v > o$ (Unbalanced Oil and Vinegar (UOV)). In this Section we describe the more general approach UOV.

We set $V = \{1, \ldots, v\}$ and $O = \{v+1, \ldots, n\}$. Of the n variables $x_1, \ldots, x_n$ we call $x_1, \ldots, x_v$ the Vinegar variables and $x_{v+1}, \ldots, x_n$ Oil variables. We define o quadratic polynomials
$f_k(\mathbf{x}) = f_k(x_1, \ldots, x_n)$ by

$$f_k(\mathbf{x}) = \sum_{i \in V,\ j \in O} \alpha_{ij}^{(k)} x_i x_j + \sum_{i,j \in V,\ i \leq j} \beta_{ij}^{(k)} x_i x_j + \sum_{i \in V \cup O} \gamma_i^{(k)} x_i + \eta^{(k)} \ (k \in O)$$

Note that Oil and Vinegar variables are not fully mixed, just like oil and vinegar in a salad dressing.

The map $F = (f_{v+1}(\mathbf{x}), \ldots, f_n(\mathbf{x}))$ can be easily inverted. First, we choose the values of the v Vinegar variables $x_1, \ldots, x_v$ at random. Such we get a system of o linear equations in the o variables $x_{v+1}, \ldots, x_n$ which can be solved by Gaussian Elimination. (If the system doesn't have a solution, choose other values of $x_1, \ldots, x_v$ and try again).

2.2 The Rainbow Signature Scheme

In [DS05] J. Ding and D. Schmidt proposed a new signature scheme called Rainbow, which is based on the idea of Oil and Vinegar.

Let K be a finite field (e.g. $K = GF(2^8)$) and S be the set $\{1, \ldots, n\}$. Let $v_1, \ldots, v_{u+1}, u \geq 1$ be integers such that $0 < v_1 < v_2 < \cdots < v_u < v_{u+1} = n$ and define the sets of integers $S_i = \{1, \ldots, v_i\}$ for $i = 1, \ldots, u$. We set $o_i = v_{i+1} - v_i$ and $O_i = \{v_i + 1, \ldots, v_{i+1}\}$ $(i = 1, \ldots, u)$. The number of elements in S_i is v_i and we have $|O_i| = o_i$. For $k = v_1 + 1, \ldots, n$ we define multivariate quadratic polynomials in the n variables $x_1, \ldots, x_n$ by

$$f_k(\mathbf{x}) = \sum_{i \in O_l,\ j \in S_l} \alpha_{i,j}^{(k)} x_i x_j + \sum_{i,j \in S_l,\ i \leq j} \beta_{i,j}^{(k)} x_i x_j + \sum_{i \in S_l \cup O_l} \gamma_i^{(k)} x_i + \eta^{(k)},$$

where l is the only integer such that $k \in O_l$. Note that these are Oil and Vinegar polynomials with $x_i,\ i \in S_l$ being the Vinegar variables and $x_j,\ j \in O_l$ being the Oil variables.

The map $F(\mathbf{x}) = (f_{v_1+1}(\mathbf{x}), \ldots, f_n(\mathbf{x}))$ can be inverted as follows: First, we choose $x_1, \ldots, x_{v_1}$ at random. Hence we get a system of o_1 linear equations (given by the polynomials f_k $(k \in O_1)$) in the o_1 unknowns $x_{v_1+1}, \ldots, x_{v_2}$, which can be solved by Gaussian Elimination. The so computed values of x_i $(i \in O_1)$ are put into the polynomials $f_k(\mathbf{x})$ $(k > v_2)$ and a system of o_2 linear equations (given by the polynomials f_k $(k \in O_2)$) in the o_2 unknowns x_i $(i \in O_2)$ is obtained. By repeating this process we can get values for all the variables x_i $(i = 1, \ldots, n)$ [1].

[1] It may happen, that one of the linear systems does not have a solution. If so, one has to choose other values of $x_1, \ldots x_{v_1}$ and try again.

The Rainbow signature scheme is defined as follows:

Key Generation. The private key consists of two invertible affine maps $L_1 : K^m \to K^m$ and $L_2 : K^n \to K^n$ and the map $F = (f_{v_1+1}(\mathbf{x}), \dots, f_n(\mathbf{x}))$. Here, $m = n - v_1$ is the number of components of F.

The public key consists of the field K and the composed map $P(\mathbf{x}) = L_1 \circ F \circ L_2(\mathbf{x}) : K^n \to K^m$.

Signature Generation. To sign a document d, we use a hash function $\mathbf{h} : K^* \to K^m$ to compute the value $\mathbf{h} = \mathbf{h}(d) \in K^m$. Then we compute recursively $\mathbf{x} = L_1^{-1}(\mathbf{h})$, $\mathbf{y} = F^{-1}(\mathbf{x})$ and $\mathbf{z} = L_2^{-1}(\mathbf{y})$. The signature of the document is $\mathbf{z} \in K^n$. Here, $F^{-1}(\mathbf{x})$ means finding one (of the possibly many) pre-image of $\mathbf{x}$.

Verification. To verify the authenticity of a signature, one simply computes $\mathbf{h}' = P(\mathbf{z})$ and the hashvalue $\mathbf{h} = \mathbf{h}(d)$ of the document. If $\mathbf{h}' = \mathbf{h}$ holds, the signature is accepted, otherwise rejected.

The size of the public key is (for $K = GF(2^8)$)

$$\text{size(public key)} = m \cdot \left(\frac{n \cdot (n+1)}{2} + n + 1 \right) = m \cdot \frac{(n+1) \cdot (n+2)}{2} \text{ bytes}, \quad (1)$$

the size of the private key

$$\begin{aligned} \text{size(private key)} = \; & m \cdot (m+1) + n \cdot (n+1) \\ & + \sum_{l=1}^{u} o_l \cdot \left(v_l \cdot o_l + \frac{v_l \cdot (v_l+1)}{2} + v_{l+1} + 1 \right) \text{ bytes}. \quad (2) \end{aligned}$$

The length of the needed hash value is m bytes, the length of the signature is n bytes.

The scheme is denoted by Rainbow$(v_1, o_1, \dots, o_u)$. For $u = 1$ we get the original UOV scheme.

3 Our Model of Security

In this Section we describe the model underlying our parameter choices below. We base on the approach of Lenstra and Verheul [LV00].

3.1 The Model

In [LV00] Lenstra and Verheul developed a security model, which they used to find appropriate parameters for symmetric cryptography and some asymmetric schemes. The main points of their model are:

1. Security margin: a definition of the term "adequate security".
2. Computing environment: the expected change in computational resources available to attackers.
3. Cryptanalytic development: the expected development in cryptanalysis.

In the following we take a closer look at these items.

Security margin. To decide, whether a given scheme offers adequate security, one has to define the term "adequate security". [LV00] defines it by the security offered by DES in 1982. That is, in 1982 a computational effort of $5 \cdot 10^5$ MIPS years provided an adequate security. We follow this definition.

Computing environment. Here [LV00] use a slightly modified version of Moore's law, which states that the amount of computing power and random access memory one gets for 1 dollar doubles every t months. Our default setting of t is 18, see [LV00].

Another thing we have to take into account, is the budget of an attacker, which might increase over time. The variable $b > 0$ is defined as the number of years it takes on average for an expected two-fold increase of a budget. Statistical data says, that the US Gross National product (in today's prices) doubles about every ten years. So our default setting for b is 10.

Cryptanalytic Development. The number $r > 0$ is defined to be the number of months it is expected to take on average for cryptanalytic developments affecting Multivariate Public Key Cryptosystems to become twice as effective.

Under the assumption, that the pace of cryptanalytic findings in the area of multivariate cryptography will not vary dramatically from those in the field of classical cryptosystems, our default setting for r is $r = 18$.

After having developed concrete security levels based on these three items, Lenstra and Verheul analyzed known attacks against several schemes to get concrete parameter sets.

Analogous to [LV00], we will use "Infeasible number of MIPS years" (IMY) to define security requirements for the Rainbow signature scheme. Given that breaking DES takes $5 \cdot 10^5$ MIPS years, which was infeasible to do in year 1982, we get the number of MIPS years that are infeasible to break in the year y by the formula

$$IMY(y) = 5 \cdot 10^5 \cdot 2^{12(y-1982)/t} \cdot 2^{(y-1982)/b} \quad \text{MIPS years.} \tag{3}$$

With our default settings we get

$$IMY(y) = 2^{\frac{23}{30} \cdot y - 1500.6} \text{ MIPS years} \tag{4}$$

So far, we have not considered the possible advances in cryptanalysis. To cover these, we have to adapt the upper formula slightly. So, a cryptosystem, which shall be secure in the year y, must reach the security level

$$\text{Security level}(y) \geq IMY(y) \cdot 2^{12(y-2009)/r} \text{ MIPS years} \overset{r=18}{=} 2^{\frac{43}{30} \cdot y - 2839.9} \text{ MIPS years} \tag{5}$$

3.2 Security Level of Rainbow

In this subsection we look at the known attacks against the Rainbow signature scheme. We will find, that the security of the scheme is mainly given by the complexities of two attacks, namely the direct and the Rainbow-Band-Separation attack and therefore can be said to be the minimum of those two complexities.

The known attacks against the Rainbow Signature Scheme are:

1. direct attacks [BB08], [Ya07]: Direct attacks use equation solvers like XL and its derivatives as well as Gröbner Basis algorithms: Buchberger, F_4, and F_5. The complexity is approximately given as

$$C_{\text{direct}}(q, m, n) = C_{MQ(q,m,n)}, \tag{6}$$

where $C_{MQ(q,m,n)}$ denotes the complexity of solving a "generic" system of m quadratic equations in n variables over a field with q elements.
2. MinRank attack [GC00], [YC05]

$$C_{\text{MR}}(q, m, n, v_1) = [q^{v_1+1} \cdot m \cdot (n^2/2 - m^2/6)] \text{ m} \tag{7}$$

3. HighRank attack [GC00], [DY08]

$$C_{\text{HR}}(q, n, o_u) = [q^{o_u} \cdot n^3/6] \text{ m} \tag{8}$$

4. UOV attack [KP99]

$$C_{\text{UOV}}(q, n, o_u) = [q^{n-2\cdot o_u-1} \cdot o_u^4] \text{ m} \tag{9}$$

5. UOV-Reconciliation attack [BB08], [DY08]

$$C_{\text{UOVR}}(q, m, n, o_u) = C_{MQ(q,m,n-o_u)} \tag{10}$$

6. Rainbow-Band-Separation attack [DY08]

$$C_{\text{RBS}}(q, m, n) = C_{MQ(q,m+n-1,n)} \tag{11}$$

Here, m stands for the number of field multiplications needed during the attack. Defending a Rainbow scheme against the attacks from the items 2 to 4 is relatively easy:

Proposition 1: A Rainbow instance over $GF(2^a)$ with parameters $v_1, o_1, \ldots, o_u$ (see Section 2.2) and $n \geq m \geq 10$, for which the items

1. $v_1 \geq \frac{\ell}{a} - 1$
2. $o_u \geq \frac{\ell}{a}$
3. $n - 2 \cdot o_u \geq \frac{\ell}{a} + 1$

hold, has a security level of ℓ bits against the MinRank, the HighRank and the UOV attack.

Proof. The proof of Proposition 1 can be found in the appendix of this paper.

Table 1 shows how we have to adapt the parameters of Rainbow over time according to Proposition 1.

Table 1. Parameter restrictions according to Proposition 1

years	MinRank $v_1 \geq$	HighRank $o_u \geq$	UOV-Attack $n - 2o_u \geq$
2010	9	10	11
2011-2015	10	11	12
2016-2021	11	12	13
2022-2027	12	13	14
2028-2032	13	14	15
2033-2038	14	15	16
2039-2043	15	16	17
2044-2049	16	17	18
2050-2055	17	18	19

To defend the scheme against the UOV-Reconciliation attack, we need $v_1 \geq o_u$. Then, the algebraic part of the attack leads to an underdetermined system of quadratic equations which is as difficult to solve as a direct attack against the original scheme.

In the following, we look at Rainbow instances which are secure against these four attacks. So, the security of a Rainbow scheme depends only on the complexities of the direct and the Rainbow-Band-Separation (RBS) attack and therefore can be said to be the minimum of those two complexities. Hence, it depends only on the number of equations m and the number of variables n. The security of a scheme is therefore given by

$$\mathrm{Sec}(m,n) = \min\{C_{\mathrm{direct}}(q,m,n), C_{\mathrm{RBS}}(q,m,n)\} \tag{12}$$

In the next Section, we will take a closer look at these two complexities.

4 Complexity Estimations for the Direct and RBS Attacks

In this Section we look at the complexities of the direct and the RBS attack against Rainbow schemes. For both of these two attacks we have to solve systems of quadratic equations. We look at several ways to do this step, namely XL-Wiedemann, the implementation of Faugere's F4 algorithm contained in MAGMA and Singular's implementation of Buchberger's algorithm. Unfortunately, our analysis does not contain the F5 algorithm, because no implementation of it is publicly available. Throughout this section, we look at Rainbow Schemes defined over a field of 256 elements.

4.1 XL-Wiedemann

In this subsection we look at XL-Wiedemann, which it is the best analyzed general method for solving systems of quadratic equations. The complexity of

XL-Wiedemann for an overdetermined system of m quadratic equations in n variables ($m \geq n$) over a field with q elements is given by the formula [BB08]

$$\mathrm{C}_{\mathrm{XL-Wiedemann}} = [3 \cdot T^2 \cdot \tau] \text{ m}, \tag{13}$$

where T is the number of monomials up to a certain degree D reduced mod $x^q - x$ ($T = \binom{n+D}{D}$ for larger fields), and τ stands for the average number of terms per equation, which in our case is given by $\tau = \frac{(n+1)\cdot(n+2)}{2}$. The minimal degree D_0, for which XL works is given by

$D_0 = \min\{D : [t^D]((1-t)^{m-n-1}(1+t)^m) \leq D\}$, where $[t^D](p)$ denotes the coefficient of t^D in p.

By guessing some of the variables before applying the algorithm it might be possible to decrease the necessary degree D. This can speed up the time needed to solve the system even if one has to run the algorithm several times with different guesses (see also the discussion of FXL in [Ya07]).

Direct attacks on Rainbow Schemes. When attacking a Rainbow instance directly we have to solve an underdetermined system of quadratic equations. Since XL-Wiedemann doesn't work for underdetermined systems, we have to guess at $n - m$ variables to create a determined system before applying the algorithm[2]. We computed the complexity of solving determined systems for $10 \leq m \leq 50$ equations by formula (13) with guessing at 1, 2, 3 or 4 variables[3]. We found, that for $m \leq 30$ we get the best results when guessing at 2 variables and then try to solve the 256^2 overdetermined systems with m equations in $m - 2$ variables. For $m \geq 31$ it seems to be even better to guess at 3 variables before applying the algorithm to all of the 256^3 overdetermined systems (see figure 1 in the appendix of this paper).

When guessing at more variables, the slope of the corresponding graphs is even less, but due to the guessing part we have to run the algorithm so often, that this does not help much. By guessing at 2 resp. 3 variables, we get the following approximation for the complexity of solving an (under-)determined system by XL-Wiedemann

$$\begin{aligned} C_{\mathrm{XL-Wiedemann}}(m) &= \left[2^{2.84 \cdot m + 17.6}\right] \text{m} \quad (10 \leq m \leq 30) \\ C_{\mathrm{XL-Wiedemann}}(m) &= \left[2^{2.62 \cdot m + 24.3}\right] \text{m} \quad (31 \leq m \leq 50) \end{aligned} \tag{14}$$

Complexity of the RBS attack. The algebraic part of the RBS attack leads to a system of $m + n - 1$ quadratic equations in n variables. So we have to solve an overdetermined system of equations. We can use XL-Wiedemann on this system without guessing at any variables. Figure 2 (in the appendix) shows the complexity of this attack for some fixed values of m.

---

2 It might occur that the determined system one gets after the guessing part does not have a solution. If this happens, one has to choose other values for the variables to be guessed and try again. However, this occurs very rarely, so that we do not take this case into further consideration.

3 Without guessing, XL runs at degree q, which is impractical for $q = 256$ [Ya07].

While the number of equations we need for the security of the scheme is given by the complexity of the direct attack, the necessary number of variables is determined by the complexity of the RBS attack.

We define $\bar{n}(m)$ to be the minimum number of variables, such that the RBS attack on the Rainbow instance with m equations and n variables has at least the complexity of the direct attack, i.e.

$$\bar{n}(m) = \min\{n|\ C_{\mathrm{RBS}}(q,m,n) \geq C_{\mathrm{direct}}(q,m,n)\} \tag{15}$$

This number $\bar{n}$ is optimal in the following sense: (1) for less than $\bar{n}$ variables the security of the Rainbow scheme is not as high as it would be possible for a Rainbow scheme with m equations and (2) more than $\bar{n}$ variables will not provide higher security, but increase the size of the public (and the private) key.

The optimal ratio between m and n depends on the algorithm one uses for solving the systems of quadratic equations.

To get $\bar{n}$ for XL-Wiedemann, we computed the complexity of the direct attack on Rainbow schemes with m equations ($10 \leq m \leq 50$). After that, we computed the complexity of the RBS attack on a Rainbow scheme with m equations and $n = m+1$ variables. Then we increased n until this complexity was at least the same as that of the direct attack against a scheme with m equations. We found

$$\bar{n}_{\mathrm{XL-Wiedemann}} = 2 \cdot (m-1). \tag{16}$$

To translate the complexity estimations of formula (14), which are given in $GF(2^8)$-field multiplications, into MIPS years, we use a data-point computed by J. Ding et al. in [DY08]. There the authors solve a system of 37 quadratic equations in 22 variables over $GF(2^8)$ in about $1.06 \cdot 10^6$ seconds on a single 2.2 GHz Opteron machine by XL-Wiedemann. This corresponds to approximately 329.7 MIPS years [4]. Since the complexity of the system is about $2^{46.7}$ m, we get

$$1 \text{ MIPS year} = 3.49 \cdot 10^{11} \text{ m} \tag{17}$$

4.2 MAGMA's Implementation of the F4 Algorithm

We carried out a number of experiments with MAGMA, which contains an implementation of Faugere's F4 algorithm for computing Gröbner bases. We used MAGMA version 2.13-10 and solved the quadratic systems (given as sequences of polynomials in reversed graded lexicographical order) by the function `GroebnerBasis`. The experiments were carried out on a single core Opteron 2.3 GHz CPU, which achieves about 10200 MIPS. So a MIPS year corresponds to 3094 seconds or roughly 52 minutes of computation.

Running time of direct attacks. For a direct attack on a Rainbow scheme one has to solve an underdetermined system of m quadratic equations in $n > m$ variables. Since the Gröbner bases MAGMA creates for underdetermined systems are not convenient for our purposes (because of the high complexity of the

[4] The given processor achieves about 9800 MIPS (SiSoft Sandra).

Table 2. Solving determined systems with F4 with guessing

# equations	11	12	13	14	15	16
no guessing	6.4 m 342 MB	0.8 h 1236 MB	6.6 h 7426 MB	47.2 h 35182 MB	- ooM	-
guessing 1 variable	29 m 11 MB	2.8 h 23 MB	23 h 76 MB	134 h 285 MB	48 d 997 MB	257 d 3953 MB
guessing 2 variables	264 m 8.6 MB	30 h 10.7 MB	170 h 14.5 MB	1214 h 42 MB	230 d 118 MB	1259 d 335 MB
guessing 3 variables	5880 m 8.3 MB	715 h 9.0 MB	3830 h 11.2 MB	23597 h 14.8 MB	4449 d 24.8 MB	18443 d 51.7 MB
guessing 4 variables	93807 m 7.9 MB	8126 h 8.6 MB	43465 h 10.6 MB	22652 h 11.8 MB	67129 d 12.9 MB	382986 d 18.0 MB

corresponding variety), we had to guess at at least $n - m$ variables before applying the algorithm. Table 2 shows the results of our experiments when solving determined systems and guessing at $a = 0, 1, 2, 3$ or 4 variables. When doing so, we had to multiply the running time of MAGMA by a factor 256^a.

So, in our examples, we get the best results without guessing. But, as our extrapolation shows, for $m \geq 22$ equations it will be better to guess at one variable, and for $m \geq 29$ to guess at two variables before applying F4 (see figure 3 in the appendix).

The time MAGMA needs for solving a determined system with m equations can then be estimated by the formula

$$\begin{aligned} \mathrm{RT_{F4}}(2^8, \mathrm{m}) &= 2^{2.74 \cdot m - 19.4} \text{ sec} \quad (22 \leq m \leq 28) \\ \mathrm{RT_{F4}}(2^8, m) &= 2^{2.55 \cdot m - 13.9} \text{ sec} \quad (29 \leq m \leq 50) \end{aligned} \tag{18}$$

Running time of the RBS attack. In this paragraph we try to find out the optimal number of variables $\bar{n}(m)$ we should use in our Rainbow scheme (as defined by formula (15)). To get this number, we carried out some experiments where the number m of equations is a small multiple of the number n of variables. Table 3 shows the results.

Systems like these are created during the first part of the RBS attack, where an underdetermined system of m equations in n variables leads to an overdetermined system with $m + n - 1$ equations in n variables. So, a system of n variables and $a \cdot n$ equations is created from a Rainbow scheme with n variables and $(a - 1) \cdot n + 1$ equations. The other way round, a Rainbow scheme with m equations and $n = a \cdot (m - 1)$ variables leads via the first part of the RBS attack to an overdetermined system of $\frac{a+1}{a} \cdot n$ equations in n variables. For example, a Rainbow scheme with $m = 16$ equations in $n = \frac{5}{3} \cdot (m - 1) = 25$ variables leads to an overdetermined system of $\frac{8}{5} \cdot n = 40$ equations in $n = 25$ variables. Figure 4 shows the data-points from the table in terms of the number of equations of the original scheme.

Table 3. Solving overdetermined systems with F4

$m = \frac{3}{2} \cdot n$	# equations	21	24	27	30
	# variables	14	16	18	20
		36 s 30 MB	804 s 214 MB	7293 s 765 MB	120831 s 2890 MB
$m = \frac{8}{5} \cdot n$	# equations	16	24	32	
	# variables	10	15	20	
		0.15 s 0.7 MB	52.5 s 37 MB	18263 s 2081 MB	
$m = \frac{5}{3} \cdot n$	# equations	20	25	30	35
	# variables	12	15	18	21
		0.8 s 1.2 MB	42,7 s 36 MB	985 s 231 MB	40298 s 3291 MB

As can be seen from the graph, for a Rainbow scheme with m and $n = \frac{5}{3} \cdot (m-1)$ variables the running time of the RBS attack is nearly the same as that of a direct attack on the same scheme (when solving the quadratic systems with MAGMA). So, for MAGMA, the number $\bar{n}$ of variables we should use in our Rainbow scheme is given by

$$\bar{n}_{\mathrm{F4}}(m) = \lceil \tfrac{5}{3} \cdot (m-1) \rceil \tag{19}$$

4.3 Singular's Implementation of Buchbergers Algorithm

For better comparison, we also carried out some experiments with Singular [GP09], which contains an efficient implementation of Buchberger's algorithm. We used Singular version 3-1-0 and the command `std` to find Groebner bases for ideals of polynomials in reversed graded lexicographical order. The experiments with Singular were carried out in the same environment as those with MAGMA, namely on a single core Opteron 2.3 GHz CPU, which achieves about 10200 MIPS.

Running time of direct attacks. When attacking a Rainbow scheme directly, one has to solve an underdetermined system of m quadratic equations in $n > m$ variables. Since Buchberger's algorithm does not lead to a "nice" Gröbner basis for such a system, one has to guess at at least $n - m$ variables. We carried out experiments on determined systems by guessing at $a = 0, 1, 2, 3$ or 4 variables before applying Buchberger's algorithm. Again we had to run the algorithm 256^a times. Table 4 shows the results of these experiments.

So, in our experiments, we get the best results without guessing. But, as it seems, for $m \geq 23$ it should be better to guess at one variable and then to find Gröbner bases for all the 256 overdetermined systems with m equations and $m-1$ variables. And for $m \geq 30$, it might be even better to guess at 2 variables before applying Buchbergers algorithm (see figure 5 in the appendix). Note, that these results are very similar to those with MAGMA.

Table 4. Solving determined systems with Buchberger's algorithm with guessing

# equations	11	12	13	14	15	16
no guessing	12.3 m 137 MB	1.7 h 264 MB	15 h 1167 MB	146 h 4268 MB	-	-
guessing 1 variable	96.5 m 8.4 MB	11.9 h 29 MB	62.4 h 99 MB	548 h 354 MB	137 d 1280 MB	957.2 d 4631 MB
guessing 2 variables	1442 m 1.7 MB	142 h 4.8 MB	975 h 14 MB	4174 h 40 MB	1041 d 145 MB	8134 d 467 MB
guessing 3 variables	19712 m 0.7 MB	1590 h 1.2 MB	12175 h 3.3 MB	63847 h 8.0 MB	10892 d 23 MB	95313 d 69 MB
guessing 4 variables	456167 m 0.6 MB	45661 h 0.8 MB	267564 h 1.2 MB	1593056 h 2.3 MB	382769 d 5.4 MB	2250127 d 14 MB

Hence, we can estimate the time needed for solving a determined system with m equations with Buchberger's algorithm by the formula

$$\begin{aligned} \mathrm{RT}_{\mathrm{Buchberger}}(2^8, m) &= 2^{2.76 \cdot m - 17.9} \text{ s} \quad (23 \leq m \leq 29) \\ \mathrm{RT}_{\mathrm{Buchberger}}(2^8, m) &= 2^{2.55 \cdot m - 11.7} \text{ s} \quad (30 \leq m \leq 50) \end{aligned} \tag{20}$$

As a comparison of formulas (18) and (20) shows, for large m MAGMA solves the systems about 4.5 times faster.

Running time of the RBS attack. In this paragraph we try to find out the optimal number of variables $\bar{n}$ we should use in our Rainbow scheme (as defined by formula (15)). To get this number, we carried out the same experiments as presented for MAGMA in the previous subsection with Singular, too (see Table 5).

Table 5. Solving overdetermined systems with Buchberger's algorithm

$m = \frac{3}{2} \cdot n$	# equations	21	24	27	30
	# variables	14	16	18	20
		219 s 35 MB	1871 s 178 MB	16500 s 960 MB	179473 s 4953 MB
$m = \frac{8}{5} \cdot n$	# equations	16	24	32	
	# variables	10	15	20	
		0.7 s 2.3 MB	250 s 50 MB	109468 s 2130 MB	
$m = \frac{5}{3} \cdot n$	# equations	20	25	30	35
	# variables	12	15	18	21
		4.1 s 5.9 MB	113.5 s 37 MB	4723 s 335 MB	172863 s 2520 MB

Again we looked at the Rainbow schemes from which these systems were created during the first part of the RBS attack (see figure 6 in the appendix).

As the figure shows, the running time of the RBS attack against a Rainbow scheme with m equations in $n = \frac{5}{3} \cdot (m-1)$ variables is nearly the same as the running time of a direct attack against a scheme with m equations. The results are very similar to those with MAGMA, and so we get

$$\bar{n}_{\text{Buchberger}}(m) = \lceil \tfrac{5}{3} \cdot (m-1) \rceil \tag{21}$$

4.4 Storage

As you can see from tables 2 and 4, the storage both MAGMA and Singular need for solving determined systems is generally large (for example, we can't solve a determined system of 15 equations on our server with 128 GB main memory using MAGMA's F_4 algorithm). However, when guessing at some of the variables, the storage needed for solving the systems reduces by a large factor. To this, we want to remark the following:

When fixing a variables before applying F_4 or Buchbergers algorithm, one has to run the algorithm q^a times to find a solution (where q is the number of elements in the underlying field). So the time needed to solve the original system is $q^a \cdot t_a$, where t_a is the time one needs to solve the overdetermined system. But, the storage needed to solve the system is not influenced by the repeated execution of the algorithm. If one overdetermined system does not have a solution, one discards it and tries again with a different choice of the fixed variables. That is why fixing some variables reduces the storage needed to solve the systems by a large amount.

Since we found out in the previous subsections, that guessing 2 or 3 variables is also a good strategy to reduce the time you need to solve the system, we do not think that storage is a bigger problem when attacking Rainbow. That's why we don't take storage into account when proposing the parameters.

One interesting thing concerning the storage is, that the values for Singular (see tables 4 and 5) are not much better (and in some cases even worse) as those for MAGMA, especially for large numbers of equations. This is against our expectations, according to which Buchbergers algorithm should require less memory than F_4.

5 Parameter Choice

In this Section we give actual parameters which guarantee the security of the Rainbow signature scheme for now and the near future under the model assumptions presented in Section 3. The parameters are chosen for an underlying field of 256 elements.

5.1 Parameters for Rainbow Optimized for Small Public Key Size

The following table shows the number of equations m and variables n we propose to use for Rainbow in the year y. The numbers are chosen to be the smallest ones, such that a Rainbow scheme with m equations in n variables fulfills the necessary security levels for each of the three algorithms we looked at.

In each case there are various possibilities for the actual layout of the Rainbow layers. As long as one takes into account the limitations given in Table 1, the details of the layout will not affect the security of the scheme. For each pair of m and n we give one example scheme.

To get the numbers in the table, we first computed for each year y the minimal number m_0 of equations such that the complexity of a direct attack against the scheme is as least as high as the security level for the year y , i.e.

$$m_0(y) = \min\{m| \; C_{\text{direct}}(q, m) \geq \text{ Security level}(y)\} \tag{22}$$

For this step we used our results with MAGMA (as presented in Section 4.2), because they lead to the most conservative parameter choices.
Such we get (with formulas (5) and (18))

$$\begin{aligned} m_0(y) &= \lceil 0.523 \cdot y - 1025.3 \rceil \; (y \leq 2014) \\ m_0(y) &= \lceil 0.562 \cdot y - 1103.7 \rceil \; (2015 \leq y \leq 2050) \end{aligned} \tag{23}$$

We define $n_0(y)$ to be the minimal number of variables such that the complexity of the RBS attack against a Rainbow Scheme with m_0 equations and n_0 variables lies above our security margin, i. e.

$$n_0(y) = \min\{n| \; C_{\text{RBS}}(q, m_0(y), n) \geq \text{ Security level}(y)\}, \tag{24}$$

where $m_0(y)$ is defined by formula (22).

One can easily see that $\bar{n}(m_0)$ (as defined by formula (15)) fulfills this condition. Thus we have $n_0(y) \leq \bar{n}(m_0)$.

To find $n_0(y)$ for XL-Wiedemann, we use a similar technique as we used in Section 4.1 to find $\bar{n}$.

For each year y ($2010 \leq y \leq 2050$) we first computed the neccessary number $m_0(y)$ of equations and the complexity of an RBS attack against a scheme with m_0 equations in $n = m_0 + 1$ variables. Then we increased n until the complexity of the RBS attack reached our Security level. Note that the numbers $n_0(y)$ we get by doing so fulfill the conditions

$$\begin{aligned} n_0(y) &\geq \bar{n}_{\text{MAGMA}}(m_0) \;\; \text{and} \\ n_0(y) &\geq \bar{n}_{\text{Singular}}(m_0) \end{aligned} \tag{25}$$

(see formulas (19) and (21)).

Therefore we have

$$C_{\text{RBS}_{\text{MAGMA}}}(q, m_0, n_0) \geq C_{\text{direct}_{\text{MAGMA}}}(q, m_0, n_0) \geq \text{Security level}(y) \text{ and} \tag{26}$$

$$C_{\text{RBS}_{\text{Singular}}}(q, m_0, n_0) \geq C_{\text{direct}_{\text{Singular}}}(q, m_0, n_0) \geq \text{Security level}(y) \tag{27}$$

So, the proposed schemes will be secure for MAGMA and Singular, too.

Table 6. Proposed parameters for the Rainbow Signature Scheme

Year	(m, n)	public key size (kB)	hash size (bit)	signature size (bit)	example scheme (v_1, o_1, o_2)	example scheme private key size (kB)
2010	(26,43)	25.7	208	344	(17,13,13)	19.1
2020	(32,53)	47.5	256	424	(21,16,16)	34.3
2030	(38,65)	84.0	304	520	(27,19,19)	60.5
2040	(43,74)	122.6	344	592	(31,21,22)	87.7
2050	(49,85)	183.3	392	680	(36,24,25)	130.2

Proposition 2: By following the above strategy we get not only the minimal m but also the minimal n required for the security of Rainbow in the year y. Hence, the schemes proposed in the table below also minimize the size of the public key.

Proof: The proof of Proposition 2 can be found in the appendix of this paper.

The complete table of the proposed parameters can be found in the appendix of this paper.

5.2 Rainbow Schemes for Limited Hash Size

In this subsection we look at the question what security level we can achieve with restricted hash sizes. We want to examine until what year it is safe to use Rainbow along with a hash function of a given size and look for the optimal Rainbow parameters in this scenario.

A given size s of the hash value determines the number of equations in our system by $m = \frac{s}{8}$. So the maximal security we can obtain is upper bounded by the complexity of solving an underdetermined system of m quadratic equations. In the following, we use the results we got from our experiments with MAGMA, because they lead to the most conservative parameter choices.

To compute the year until which it is secure to use Rainbow along with a hash function of a given size s ($s \equiv 0 \bmod 8$ bit) we have to invert formula (23) and come up with

$$y = \lfloor 0.239 \cdot s + 1960.1 \rfloor \ (s \leq 224)$$
$$y = \lfloor 0.223 \cdot s + 1963.9 \rfloor (232 \leq s \leq 400) \tag{28}$$

Table 7 shows for several hash sizes the year until which it is safe to use Rainbow along with a hash function of the given size as well as one example scheme.

As the table shows, using Rainbow along with a hash function which provides a hash length of 160 bit (like SHA-1), is no longer secure.

Table 7. Rainbow Schemes for limited hash size

hash size (bit)	m	secure until (formula (27))	proposed scheme (m,n)	public key size (kB)	(v_1, o_1, o_2)	private key size (kB)
208	26	2010	(26,43)	25.7	(17,13,13)	19.1
224	28	2013	(28,46)	31.6	(18,14,14)	23.1
240	30	2017	(30,51)	41.3	(21,15,15)	30.5
256	32	2020	(32,53)	47.3	(21,16,16)	34.4
288	36	2027	(36,60)	68.1	(24,18,18)	48.7
320	40	2035	(40,69)	99.4	(29,20,20)	71.6
352	44	2042	(44,78)	139.0	(32,22,22)	94.4
384	48	2049	(48,85)	179.6	(37,24,24)	128.8

6 Conclusion

Although nobody can say, which cryptanalytic developments and developments in computing devices will take place in the next years, we hope that this paper will help people to choose appropriate parameters for the Rainbow signature scheme. The proposed parameter sets should give the reader an impression, what public key sizes are needed to achieve given levels of security.

Acknowledgements

The first author wants to thank Jintai Ding, Bo-Yin Yang and Erik Dahmen for many helpful comments.

References

[BB08] Bernstein, D.J., Buchmann, J., Dahmen, E. (eds.): Post Quantum Cryptography. Springer, Heidelberg (2009)

[BG06] Billet, O., Gilbert, H.: Cryptanalysis of Rainbow. In: De Prisco, R., Yung, M. (eds.) SCN 2006. LNCS, vol. 4116, pp. 336–347. Springer, Heidelberg (2006)

[CC08] Chen, A.I.-T., Chen, C.-H.O., Chen, M.-S., Cheng, C.M., Yang, B.-Y.: Practical-Sized Instances for Multivariate PKCs: Rainbow, TTS and ℓIC-Derivatives. In: Buchmann, J., Ding, J. (eds.) PQCrypto 2008. LNCS, vol. 5299, pp. 95–108. Springer, Heidelberg (2008)

[CS94] Coppersmith, D., Stern, J., Vaudenay, S.: Attacks on the Birational Signature Scheme. In: Stinson, D.R. (ed.) CRYPTO 1993. LNCS, vol. 773, pp. 435–443. Springer, Heidelberg (1994)

[DS05] Ding, J., Schmidt, D.: Rainbow, a new multivariate polynomial signature scheme. In: Ioannidis, J., Keromytis, A.D., Yung, M. (eds.) ACNS 2005. LNCS, vol. 3531, pp. 164–175. Springer, Heidelberg (2005)

[Di04] Ding, J.: A new variant of the Matsumoto-Imai cryptosystem through perturbation. In: Bao, F., Deng, R., Zhou, J. (eds.) PKC 2004. LNCS, vol. 2947, pp. 305–318. Springer, Heidelberg (2004)

[DY08] Ding, J., Yang, B.-Y., Chen, C.-H.O., Chen, M.-S., Cheng, C.M.: New Differential-Algebraic Attacks and Reparametrization of Rainbow. In: Bellovin, S.M., Gennaro, R., Keromytis, A.D., Yung, M. (eds.) ACNS 2008. LNCS, vol. 5037, pp. 242–257. Springer, Heidelberg (2008)

[DW07] Ding, J., Wolf, C., Yang, B.-Y.: ℓ-invertible Cycles for Multivariate Quadratic Public Key Cryptography. In: Okamoto, T., Wang, X. (eds.) PKC 2007. LNCS, vol. 4450, pp. 266–281. Springer, Heidelberg (2007)

[DY07] Ding, J., Yang, B.-Y., Cheng, C.-M., Chen, O., Dubois, V.: Breaking the symmetry: A way to resist the new Differential attacks, `http://www.eprint.iacr.org/2007/366.pdf`

[Fa99] Faugere, J.C.: A new efficient algorithm for computing Groebner bases (F4). Journal of Pure and Applied Algebra 139, 61–88 (1999)

[Fa02] Faugere, J.C.: A new efficient algorithm for computing Groebner bases without reduction to zero (F5). In: International Symposium on Symbolic and Algebraic Computation — ISSAC 2002, pp. 75–83. ACM Press, New York (2002)

[FP08] Faugere, J.-C., Perret, L.: On the security of UOV. In: Proceedings of the First International Conference on Symbolic Computation and Cryptology, Beijing (2008)

[GC00] Goubin, L., Courtois, N.T.: Cryptanalysis of the TTM cryptosystem. In: Okamoto, T. (ed.) ASIACRYPT 2000. LNCS, vol. 1976, pp. 44–57. Springer, Heidelberg (2000)

[GP09] Greuel, G.-M., Pfister, G., Schönemann, H.: Singular 3.1.0 — A computer algebra system for polynomial computations (2009), `http://www.singular.uni-kl.de`

[KP99] Kipnis, A., Patarin, L., Goubin, L.: Unbalanced Oil and Vinegar Schemes. In: Stern, J. (ed.) EUROCRYPT 1999. LNCS, vol. 1592, pp. 206–222. Springer, Heidelberg (1999)

[KS98] Kipnis, A., Shamir, A.: Cryptanalysis of the Oil and Vinegar Signature scheme. In: Krawczyk, H. (ed.) CRYPTO 1998. LNCS, vol. 1462, pp. 257–266. Springer, Heidelberg (1998)

[LV00] Lenstra, A.K., Verheul, E.R.: Selecting Cryptographic Key Sizes. In: Imai, H., Zheng, Y. (eds.) PKC 2000. LNCS, vol. 1751, pp. 446–465. Springer, Heidelberg (2000), `www.keylength.com`

[MI88] Matsumoto, T., Imai, H.: Public Quadratic Polynomial-Tuples for efficient Signature-Verification and Message-Encryption. In: Günther, C.G. (ed.) EUROCRYPT 1988. LNCS, vol. 330, pp. 419–453. Springer, Heidelberg (1988)

[Pa96] Patarin, J.: Hidden Field equations (HFE) and Isomorphisms of Polynomials (IP). In: Maurer, U.M. (ed.) EUROCRYPT 1996. LNCS, vol. 1070, pp. 33–48. Springer, Heidelberg (1996)

[Pa97] Patarin, J.: The oil and vinegar signature scheme. Presented at the Dagstuhl Workshop on Cryptography (September 1997)

[PG98] Patarin, J., Goubin, L., Courtois, N.: C_+^* and HM: Variations about two schemes of H. Matsumoto and T. Imai. In: Ohta, K., Pei, D. (eds.) ASIACRYPT 1998. LNCS, vol. 1514, pp. 35–50. Springer, Heidelberg (1998)

[PC01] Patarin, J., Courtois, N., Goubin, L.: Flash, a fast multivariate signature algorithm. In: Naccache, D. (ed.) CT-RSA 2001. LNCS, vol. 2020, pp. 298–307. Springer, Heidelberg (2001)

[YC05] Yang, B.-Y., Chen, J.-M.: Building secure tame like multivariate public-key cryptosystems: The new TTS. In: Boyd, C., González Nieto, J.M. (eds.) ACISP 2005. LNCS, vol. 3574, pp. 518–531. Springer, Heidelberg (2005)

[YC07] Yang, B.-Y., Chen, J.-M.: All in the XL family: Theory and practice. In: Park, C.-s., Chee, S. (eds.) ICISC 2004. LNCS, vol. 3506, pp. 67–86. Springer, Heidelberg (2005)

[Ya07] Yang, B.-Y., Chen, C.-H.O., Bernstein, D.J., Chen, J.-M.: Analysis of QUAD. In: Biryukov, A. (ed.) FSE 2007. LNCS, vol. 4593, pp. 290–308. Springer, Heidelberg (2007)

Appendix

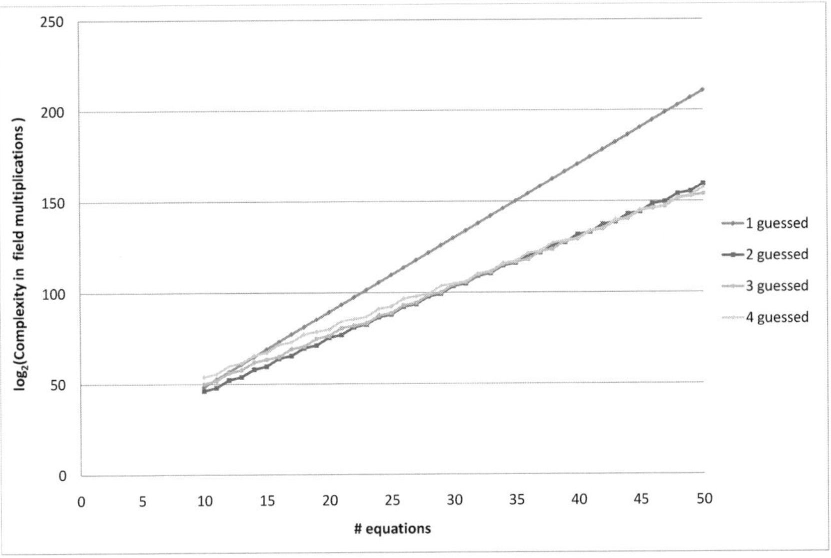

Fig. 1. Solving determined systemes with XL-Wiedemann with guessing additional variables

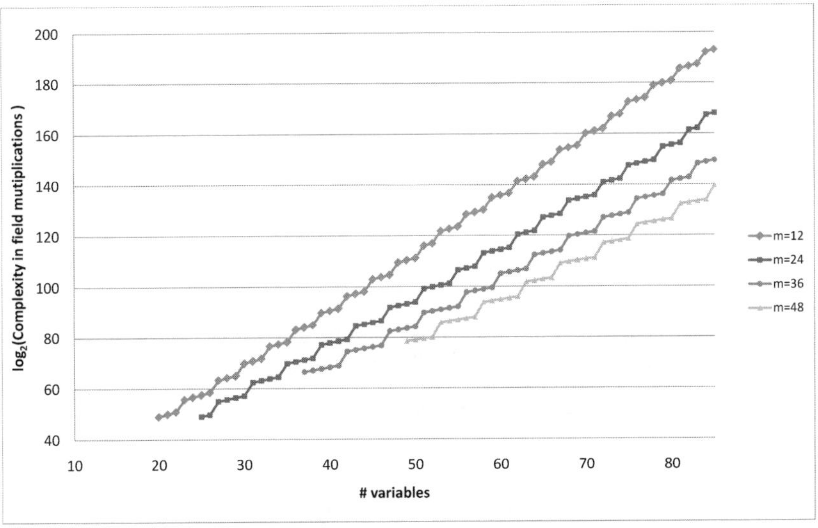

Fig. 2. Complexity of the RBS attack with XL-Wiedemann for different numbers of equations

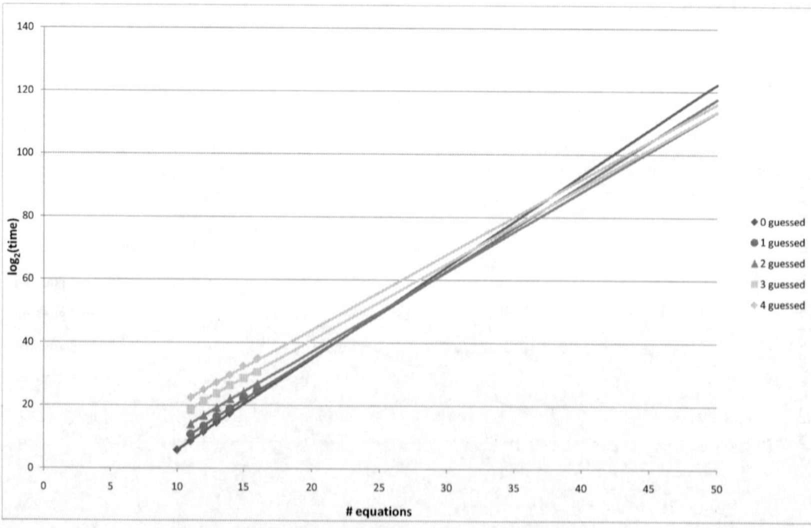

Fig. 3. Solving determined systems with F4 with guessing (datapoints and extrapolation)

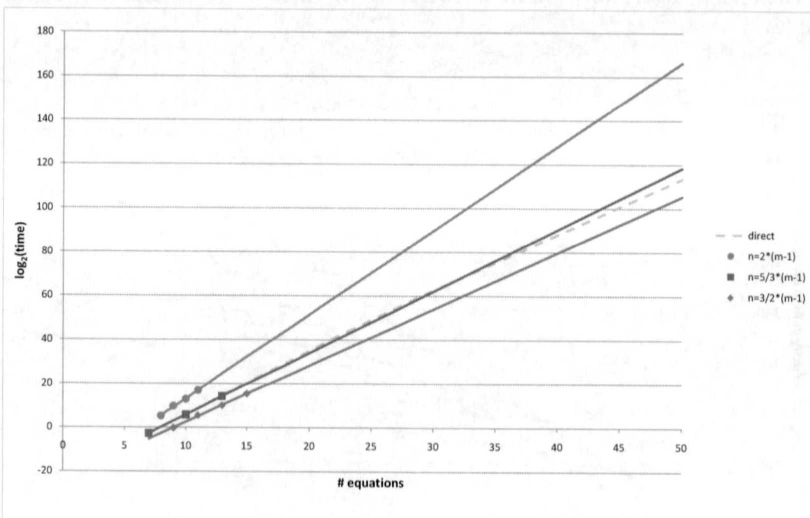

Fig. 4. Running time of the RBS attack with F4 for different ratios of m and n The dotted line marks the running time of a direct attack against a scheme with m equations

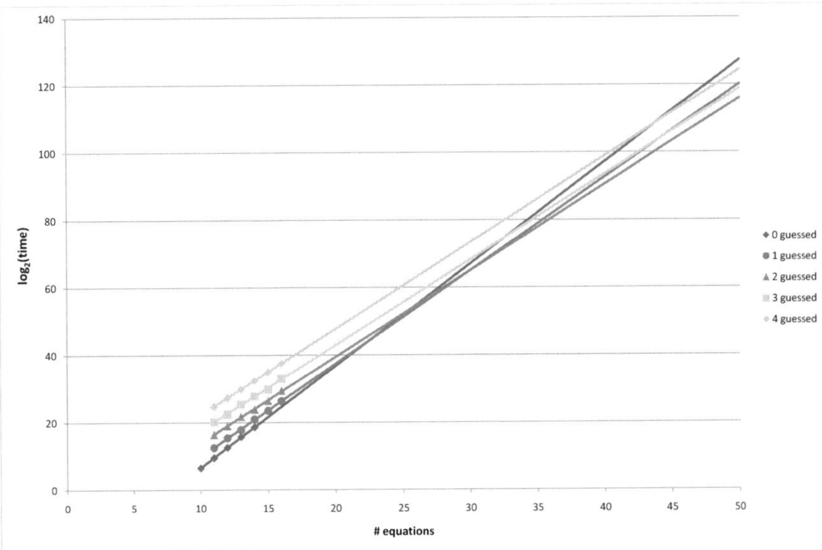

Fig. 5. Running time of the direct attack with Buchberger's algorithm (datapoints and extrapolation)

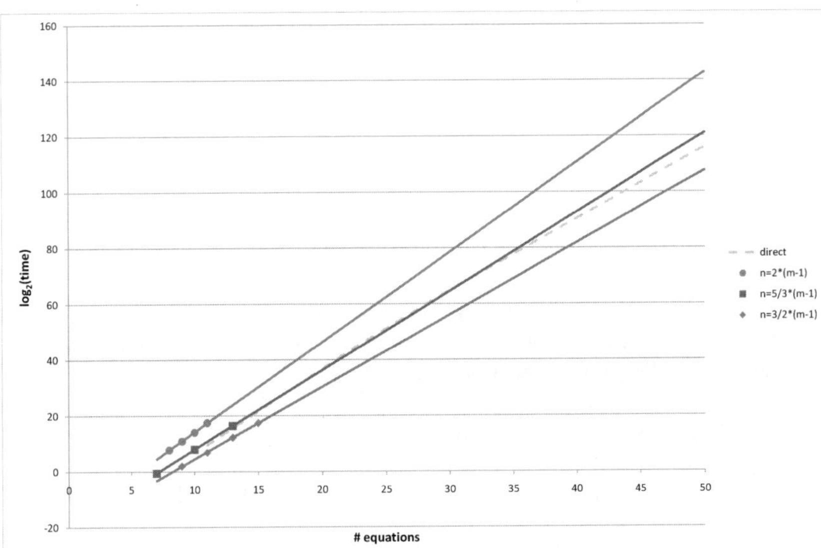

Fig. 6. Running time of the RBS attack with Buchberger's algorithm for different ratios of m and n The dotted line marks the running time of a direct attack against a scheme with m equations

Proof of Proposition 1

Proposition 1: A Rainbow instance over $GF(2^a)$ with parameters $v_1, o_1, \ldots, o_u$ and $n \geq m \geq 10$, for which the items

1. $v_1 \geq \frac{\ell}{a} - 1$
2. $o_u \geq \frac{\ell}{a}$
3. $n - 2 \cdot o_u \geq \frac{\ell}{a} + 1$

hold, has a security level of ℓ bits against the MinRank, the HighRank and the UOV attack.

Proof:

$$C_{\mathrm{MR}}(q,m,n,v_1) = [q^{v_1+1} \cdot m \cdot (n^2/2 - m^2/6)]\,\mathrm{m} \overset{1.}{\geq} [2^{a \cdot \ell/a} \cdot m \cdot (n^2/2 - m^2/6)]\,\mathrm{m} > 2^\ell\,\mathrm{m}$$

$$C_{\mathrm{HR}}(q,n,o_u) = [q^{o_u} n^3/6]\,\mathrm{m} \overset{2.}{\geq} [2^{a \cdot \ell/a} \cdot n^3/6]\,\mathrm{m} > 2^\ell\,\mathrm{m}$$

$$C_{\mathrm{UOV}}(q,n,o_u) = [q^{n-2o_u-1} \cdot o_u^4]\,\mathrm{m} \overset{3.}{\geq} [2^{a \cdot \ell/a} \cdot o_u^4]\,\mathrm{m} > 2^\ell\,\mathrm{m} \qquad \square$$

Proof of Proposition 2

Proposition 2: By following the above strategy we get not only the minimal m but also the minimal n required for the security of Rainbow in the year y. Hence, the schemes proposed in the table below also minimize the size of the public key.

Proof: It is clear, that m_0 is the minimal number of equations we need for the security of Rainbow in the year y. So, it remains to show that we get with n_0 the minimal required number of variables, too. To show this, we assume that we had another Rainbow instance with m' equations and $n' < n_0$ variables which also fulfills our security level.
Since m_0 was defined to be the minimal number of equations such that the complexity of the direct attack lies above our security level, we have $m' \geq m_0$. In the following, we distinguish between two cases:

Case 1: $m' = m_0$: Since n_0 was defined by

$$n_0 = \min\{n | C_{\mathrm{RBS}}(q, m_0, n) \geq \text{Security level}\}$$

we have $n' \geq n_0$ which contradicts our assumption.

Case 2: $m' > m_0$: Here we assume that we had a Rainbow instance with $m' > m_0$ equations and $n' < n_0$ variables which fulfills our security level. Such a Rainbow Scheme leads via the first part of the RBS attack to an overdetermined system of $m' + n' - 1$ equations in n' variables, which has a complexity to solve of about $C_{MQ(q,m'+n'-1,n')}$, which lies (as we assume) above the security margin. Thus we have

$$\text{Security margin} \leq C_{MQ(q,m'+n'-1,n')} \overset{m'>m_0}{\leq} C_{MQ(q,m_0+n'-1,n')}$$

So we have found a Rainbow instance with m_0 equations and $n' < n_0$ variables which fulfills our security level. This is a contradiction to Case 1.

As a consequence, the strategy described in Section 5 minimizes both the number m of equations and the number n of variables.
Since the public key size of Rainbow is given as (see formula (1))

$$\text{size(public key)} = m \cdot \frac{(n+1)\cdot(n+2)}{2} \text{ byte},$$

the strategy also minimizes the public key size. $\square$

Table 8. Proposed parameters (for $K = GF(2^8)$, $t = 18$, $b = 10$ and $r = 18$), optimized for small public key size

Year	Rainbow $(m,\ n)$	public key size (kB)	example scheme (v_1, o_1, o_2)	private key size (kB)	Symmetric Key Size	RSA Key Size and SDL Field Size		Elliptic Curve Key Size $c = 0$	Elliptic Curve Key Size $c = 18$	Infeasible number of MIPS years
1982					56	417	288	105	85	$5.00 \cdot 10^5$
2010	(26,43)	25.7	(17,13,13)	19.1	78	1369	1056	146	160	$1.45 \cdot 10^{12}$
2011	(27,45)	29.2	(18,13,14)	21.7	79	1416	1088	148	163	$2.47 \cdot 10^{12}$
2012	(27,45)	29.2	(18,13,14)	21.7	80	1464	1120	149	165	$4.19 \cdot 10^{12}$
2013	(28,46)	31.6	(18,14,14)	23.1	80	1513	1184	151	168	$7.14 \cdot 10^{12}$
2014	(29,47)	34.1	(18,14,15)	24.8	81	1562	1216	152	172	$1.21 \cdot 10^{13}$
2015	(29,47)	34.1	(18,14,15)	24.8	82	1613	1248	154	173	$2.07 \cdot 10^{13}$
2016	(30,49)	38.3	(19,15,15)	27.7	83	1664	1312	155	177	$3.51 \cdot 10^{13}$
2017	(30,51)	41.3	(21,15,15)	30.5	83	1717	1344	157	180	$5.98 \cdot 10^{13}$
2018	(31,52)	44.4	(21,15,16)	32.4	84	1771	1376	158	181	$1.02 \cdot 10^{14}$
2019	(31,52)	44.4	(21,15,16)	32.4	85	1825	1440	160	185	$1.73 \cdot 10^{14}$
2020	(32,53)	47.3	(21,16,16)	34.4	86	1881	1472	161	188	$2.94 \cdot 10^{14}$
2021	(33,54)	50.8	(21,16,17)	36.5	86	1937	1536	163	190	$5.01 \cdot 10^{14}$
2022	(33,55)	52.7	(22,16,17)	38.1	87	1995	1568	164	193	$8.52 \cdot 10^{14}$
2023	(34,57)	58.2	(23,17,17)	42.0	88	2054	1632	166	197	$1.45 \cdot 10^{15}$
2024	(34,58)	60.2	(24,17,17)	43.8	89	2113	1696	167	198	$2.47 \cdot 10^{15}$
2025	(35,59)	64.1	(24,17,18)	46.3	89	2174	1728	169	202	$4.20 \cdot 10^{15}$
2026	(35,59)	64.1	(24,17,18)	46.3	90	2236	1792	170	205	$7.14 \cdot 10^{15}$
2027	(36,60)	68.1	(24,18,18)	48.7	91	2299	1856	172	207	$1.21 \cdot 10^{16}$
2028	(37,61)	72.3	(24,18,19)	51.4	92	2362	1888	173	210	$2.07 \cdot 10^{16}$
2029	(37,63)	77.0	(26,18,19)	55.6	93	2427	1952	175	213	$3.52 \cdot 10^{16}$
2030	(38,65)	84.0	(27,19,19)	60.5	93	2493	2016	176	215	$5.98 \cdot 10^{16}$
2031	(38,65)	84.0	(27,19,19)	60.5	94	2560	2080	178	219	$1.02 \cdot 10^{17}$
2032	(39,66)	88.8	(27,19,20)	63.6	95	2629	2144	179	222	$1.73 \cdot 10^{17}$
2033	(39,66)	88.8	(27,19,20)	63.6	96	2698	2208	181	224	$2.95 \cdot 10^{17}$
2034	(40,68)	96.7	(28,20,20)	69.1	96	2768	2272	182	227	$5.01 \cdot 10^{17}$
2035	(40,69)	99.4	(29,20,20)	71.6	97	2839	2336	184	229	$8.53 \cdot 10^{17}$
2036	(41,72)	110.7	(31,20,21)	80.3	98	2912	2400	185	232	$1.45 \cdot 10^{18}$
2037	(42,73)	116.6	(31,21,21)	83.8	99	2986	2464	187	236	$2.47 \cdot 10^{18}$
2038	(42,73)	116.6	(31,21,21)	83.8	99	3061	2528	188	239	$4.20 \cdot 10^{18}$
2039	(43,74)	122.6	(31,21,22)	87.7	100	3137	2592	190	241	$7.14 \cdot 10^{18}$
2040	(43,74)	122.6	(31,21,22)	87.7	101	3214	2656	191	244	$1.22 \cdot 10^{19}$
2041	(44,76)	132.1	(32,22,22)	94.4	102	3292	2720	193	246	$2.07 \cdot 10^{19}$
2042	(44,78)	139.0	(32,22,22)	94.4	103	3371	2784	194	248	$3.52 \cdot 10^{19}$
2043	(45,79)	145.8	(34,22,23)	104.8	103	3451	2880	196	251	$5.99 \cdot 10^{19}$
2044	(46,80)	152.8	(34,23,23)	109.1	104	3533	2944	197	255	$1.02 \cdot 10^{20}$
2045	(46,80)	152.8	(34,23,23)	109.1	105	3616	3008	199	258	$1.73 \cdot 10^{20}$
2046	(47,81)	159.9	(34,23,24)	113.6	106	3700	3072	200	260	$2.95 \cdot 10^{20}$
2047	(47,82)	163.8	(35,23,24)	117.1	106	3785	3168	102	262	$5.02 \cdot 10^{20}$
2048	(48,84)	175.4	(36,24,24)	125.2	107	3871	3232	203	265	$8.53 \cdot 10^{20}$
2049	(48,85)	179.6	(37,24,24)	128.8	108	3958	3296	105	269	$1.45 \cdot 10^{21}$
2050	(49,85)	183.3	(36,24,25)	130.2	109	4047	3392	206	272	$2.47 \cdot 10^{21}$

Author Index

Bernstein, Daniel J. 73
Boucher, Delphine 126
Buchmann, Johannes 218
Bulygin, Stanislav 218

Cao, Weiwei 41
Clough, Crystal Lee 153

Ding, Jintai 13, 28, 41, 153

Fujita, Ryo 201

Gaborit, Philippe 126
Geiselmann, Willi 126
Gotaishi, Masahito 201

Heyse, Stefan 108, 165
Hodges, Timothy J. 13
Hu, Lei 41

Kruglov, Victoria 13

Loidreau, Pierre 142

Moradi, Amir 108

Nie, Xiuyun 41

Paar, Christof 108
Peters, Christiane 81
Petzoldt, Albrecht 218

Ruatta, Olivier 126
Rückert, Markus 182

Schmidt, Dieter S. 28
Smith-Tone, Daniel 1
Strenzke, Falko 95

Tadaki, Kohtaro 201
Tang, Xiling 41
Tsujii, Shigeo 201

Ulmer, Felix 126

Wieschebrink, Christian 61

Printing: Mercedes-Druck, Berlin
Binding: Stein+Lehmann, Berlin